The Metaphysics of Action

David-Hillel Ruben

The Metaphysics of Action

Trying, Doing, Causing

palgrave
macmillan

David-Hillel Ruben
Department of Philosophy
University of London
London, UK

ISBN 978-3-030-07996-3   ISBN 978-3-319-90347-7 (eBook)
https://doi.org/10.1007/978-3-319-90347-7

© The Editor(s) (if applicable) and The Author(s) 2018
Softcover re-print of the Hardcover 1st edition 2018
This work is subject to copyright. All rights are solely and exclusively licensed by the Publisher, whether the whole or part of the material is concerned, specifically the rights of translation, reprinting, reuse of illustrations, recitation, broadcasting, reproduction on microfilms or in any other physical way, and transmission or information storage and retrieval, electronic adaptation, computer software, or by similar or dissimilar methodology now known or hereafter developed.
The use of general descriptive names, registered names, trademarks, service marks, etc. in this publication does not imply, even in the absence of a specific statement, that such names are exempt from the relevant protective laws and regulations and therefore free for general use.
The publisher, the authors and the editors are safe to assume that the advice and information in this book are believed to be true and accurate at the date of publication. Neither the publisher nor the authors or the editors give a warranty, express or implied, with respect to the material contained herein or for any errors or omissions that may have been made. The publisher remains neutral with regard to jurisdictional claims in published maps and institutional affiliations.

Cover illustration: redmal

Printed on acid-free paper

This Palgrave Macmillan imprint is published by the registered company Springer International Publishing AG part of Springer Nature.
The registered company address is: Gewerbestrasse 11, 6330 Cham, Switzerland

עֲטֶרֶת זְקֵנִים, בְּנֵי בָנִים. Children's children are the crown of old men.

PROVERBS 17.6

For Arielle, Ella, Zara, Theo, Asher, Gabriella, and Amalia.

Preface

It is a pleasure to offer thanks where they are due. David Enoch helped me with many of the issues in Chap. 4. He invariably responded to my questions with care and in detail. Florian Schäfer was always there to sort me out in matters linguistic; R. M. Sainsbury similarly was always available to discuss with me any matters philosophical. Thanks to John Hyman for reading and commenting on a terrible first draft of Chap. 5, which saved me from untold errors, and for (what I hope was) a somewhat more pleasurable reading for him and discussion of Chap. 6. Erasmus Mayr read my account of his unpublished comments to some of Maria Alvarez' ideas, and I thank him for reading it and for letting me use in Chap. 7 what he wrote. I have also talked to Maria Alvarez about her 'ingenious solution' to Mayr's challenge and I can no longer be sure of what I said, what she said, what I said she said, what she said I said that she said, and so on. She also read a full version of Chap. 7 and discussed it with me. I have profited from an exchange with Gillman Payette, about certain problems with my analysis in Chap. 4. An anonymous referee at the *Canadian Journal of Philosophy* helped me with Chap. 5. Since it is I, and no one else, who has written this book, it seems quite unnecessary to say that I alone am responsible for its contents. How could anyone else be responsible, since I was neither coerced nor compelled into writing what I did?

I also want to thank Birkbeck, University of London, and Kings College, University of London, for providing me with agreeable homes, and colleagues, post retirement. I have read parts of the book at staff seminars at both institutions and have benefited from the comments of many colleagues in both. Over the course of a number of years, I have been lucky to have truly exceptional students in my University of London Postgraduate Students' Seminar in Metaphysics. I wish to thank them all, and to offer special thanks to Andrea White and Hsuan-Chih Lin for their contributions to the seminar.

Throughout the book, I have used 'he' when I wanted to refer back to the anonymous person/agent P. I trust that the reader will understand this as a grammatical decision, with no further implications or overtones related to gender inequality intended. Must 'P' even refer to an individual person? I think that institutions, organisations, firms, and many other social groups are capable of action, so 'P' might even refer to an agent of one of those kinds as well.

Some of the material in this book is reworked from the following articles. Acknowledgement to the relevant journals is hereby gratefully given: 'The Physical Action Theory of Trying', *Methode: Analytic Perspectives*, Vol. 4, No. 6, 2015, 1–19; 'A Conditional Theory of Trying', *Philosophical Studies*, Vol. 173, No. 1, 2016, 271–287; 'One-Particularism in the Theory of Action', *Philosophical Studies*, 2018, Vol. 175.

Although the original texts differ markedly from that in the book, by way of additions, deletions, and substantive alternations in the arguments, there is sufficient overlap in some of them to make quotation within the latter, of passages from the former, inappropriate as a way of guarding against self-plagiarism. I trust that the admission of overlap will suffice.

London, UK										David-Hillel Ruben

Contents

1 Introduction — 1

2 The Physical Action Theory of Trying — 13

3 Trying in Some Way — 53

4 A Conditional Theory of Trying — 103

5 Causing and Doing — 165

6 Doing and Causing — 223

7 Causing in Some Way — 269

8 Regress Issues and Action Scepticism — 303

Bibliography 333

Index 345

1

Introduction

I intend to use this introduction as a vehicle for situating the topics discussed in this book within a wider philosophical context, and to describe the main ideas in each chapter. This introduction contains no arguments defending or justifying that context or the presuppositions of my discussion (there will be arguments aplenty about other matters in the following chapters). In theology, a distinction is sometimes drawn between apologetic and confessional theological literature. Apologetic literature seeks to defend a point of view to an audience that is outside the circle of believers; it attempts to convince them of something. Confessional theological literature accepts a point of view as given, but then explains and develops it for those inside the tradition, those who have already 'bought in' to the basic assumptions. This Introduction might be thought of as a piece of confessional philosophy, making explicit some of the doxological presuppositions of the book to the already-believers.

Here is that to which I confess: there is something called analytic metaphysics, a philosophical project of establishing both what exists and what it is like. Further, my confession includes the belief that there is a significant role for analytic metaphysics to play in its application to the theory of action (and to the philosophy of social science more generally). I have long held this belief about analytic metaphysics and its applications to other areas of philosophy, a belief evidenced by my first book, *Marxism and Materialism* (1977, 1979), by *The Metaphysics of the Social World* (1985) and finally by an earlier book in action theory, *Action and Its Explanation* (2003). Not all philosophers think that there is such a project. I think that there is such a philosophical project and that it is, in the main, an a priori exercise. I'm hardly alone in the belief that it can be applied in action theory. There are many examples of other philosophers who have worked similarly in a more metaphysical tradition in the philosophy of action.[1] Whether I agree with their views or not, I recognise that they are doing, in whole or in part, what I am also trying to do in this book. I admire much of their work.

I can identify at least two stands to the project of analytic metaphysics; the dividing line between them is not sharp. (I'm a big fan of both strands.) The first strand is 'ontological': are there objects independent of minds, simples, complex objects, mereological sums, tropes, universals, sense data, abstract objects, or four-dimensional objects? The main tool of this strand is what we might call 'ratiocination'. Typically, such items are shown to exist or not to exist by a priori argument. It makes no difference that The Man on the Clapham Omnibus has never heard of such things, and so doesn't talk or think thoughts about them. That bus-rider will have heard of tables, chairs, and the like, but a trope, or the mereological sum of two arbitrary objects, will come as news. By that, it might be meant that they do not accord with pre-analytic ontology. If so, the criticism does not move me much. I suppose that other things being equal, such accord would be desirable. But things are never equal, or anyway hardly ever. I believe that philosophy often comes to truths about what exists that are strange to the ears of the uninitiated.

A second strand (call it 'metaphysics proper') attempts to uncover what the entities that we admit into our ontology are like. The aforementioned bus-rider will certainly have heard of action, but he won't necessarily have a view about what an action *is*. He will also have heard that people try to do various things, and that agents cause things to happen, but he won't necessarily have a view about what is involved by what he hears. One reaction that I have encountered to the three main theses of the book, one on trying, one on the nature of action, and one on causing, is that they are 'implausible'. Again, the criticism does not move me much, unless that charge can be supported by arguments that show that the views are either internally inconsistent or have consequences that are patently false. I can't help but think of Hamlet to Horatio: 'There are more things in heaven and earth, Horatio, than are dreamt of in your philosophy' (Hamlet, 1.5.167–168). That may be true of poor Horatio's philosophy, but evidently not of Hamlet's, nor of mine.

I also intend my discussion in the book to be metaphysical in the following sense. I want to know about actions, causing, and trying, not about the concepts of action, causing, and trying, or about action-, causing-, and trying- sentences, although of course access to knowledge about them must commence with language, commence with thinking about those sentences and concepts, knowing what we say, when and why. I want to explain what I am doing in a somewhat minimalist way in this Introduction, since this question raises profound questions about philosophical method, analysis, logical form, and how analysis and logical form relate. That would be the subject of another book, one that I am not capable of writing.

If one looks at earlier examples of metaphysical analysis-say, what a physical object is or what a social whole is-it is true that philosophers, especially those writing in the middle of the last century, often wrote as if the object of interest is language or concepts. Two striking examples of this are the Appendix to Roderick Chisholm's 1957 *Perceiving*, in which he undertakes to refute phenomenalism, and a well-known article on the relation between the social and the individual by Maurice Mandelbaum (1955). Chisholm's discussion is framed in terms of the logical relations between appearance statements on the one hand and our 'ordinary statements about physical things' on the other (190). Mandelbaum's discussion is framed as being about the reducibility of societal concepts to individual concepts 'without remainder' (223). Mandelbaum speaks interchangeably about concepts and facts. It may be that such writers were influenced by the doctrine of semantic ascent, and that this is reflected by their choice of method and the terms in which they set their metaphysical discussion, but it certainly should not have changed their objectives. After all, there could be two sets of statements, S1 and S2, such that, although there were no 'translations' of any statement from one set into statements solely from the other set, S1 and S2 were still about the same things. And there can surely be two distinct concepts, C1 and C2, with the same extension or even necessarily with the same extension (the concepts of trilaterality and triangularity are such an example). So irreducibility of concepts and untranslatability of discourses do not tell us all that we want to know about the metaphysical nature of the world.

But what was really of interest to these and other philosophers who discussed ontological issues, rightly or wrongly, in terms of statements or sentences or concepts, was the question of whether there are such things as, e.g., mind-independent physical objects or social wholes, in addition to appearances or individual entities, and their choice of terminology, in terms of statements and concepts, was only the vehicle with which they thought best to get at those ontological issues. It was perhaps part of the philosophical method of that era to pose such questions in the formal rather than in the material mode, as an accompaniment to the idea of semantic ascent. That is speculation on my part. But whether my speculation is sound or not, I have posed the questions as far as I could in the material mode.

So, since this book is about the METAPHYSICS of action (and NOT about the SEMANTICS of action sentences or the CONCEPT of action), I intend that what I am doing to be about trying, acting, and causing, not about the concepts of trying, acting, and causing, nor about any discourse about them. My goal is to reach results about trying and causing (the phenomena) and about acting (the real-life occurrences), about what these 'things' really are.

It is important to stress this, because the extent to which I do discuss issues about sentences, language, grammar, and so on might strike the reader as somehow at odds with what I have just said. It is part of the tradition in which I work to approach metaphysical and ontological questions often by looking at language, but the goal is not the analysis of the assertions or sentences or concepts, but an understanding of the metaphysics and ontology of the human world to which such discourse commits us. In spite of his talking about 'definitions' of knowledge, Gettier (1963) wasn't interested in knowledge-talk or even the concept of knowledge; he wanted to describe what has to be the case in order for someone to know some proposition p. The objective of the analyses in the book (in Chaps. 4, 5 and 6, for example) are not sentences or statements or discourse or concepts, but what these things are about or true of, even though such discovery typically comes through a careful consideration of the ontic commitments embedded in the sentence. For instance, in Chap. 4, I argue that P tries to F iff (if a certain set of conditions are fulfilled, P acts). (Note that one can say this without switching away from the material to the formal mode.) I have certainly adopted the method of looking at language as a way to uncovering metaphysical truths; two good examples are the attention I have paid to questions about imperfective aspect and to the topic of causative alternation. But method is one thing, but goal is another. I spend a fair amount of space and energy thinking about imperfectivity, but my interests are not narrowly linguistic insofar as I do this. Behind the contrast of perfective and imperfective verb aspect lies a distinction between actions-in-progress and actions-as-completed, and that latter contrast is a metaphysical one.

The metaphysics or ontology of action (including trying and agent causing) is a very large area. There are many issues with which I do not deal, so I make no claim about the book's completeness and comprehensiveness. For example, I have only a little to say about intentions, and nothing to say about beliefs, desires, and reasons, topics that are mainstays in theories of action. Instead I have selected three ideas on which to focus: trying, doing, and causing, and the metaphysics needed to explain them. Why these three? The three ideas seem to me to form a natural trinity. One might think: first, one tries to do something, then, if lucky, one does that thing, and finally as a result of what one did, the doer causes some things to happen.

In the main, Chaps. 2, 3 and 4 (on trying) are well integrated as a unit, and Chaps. 5, 6 and 7 (on acting and causing) are well integrated as another unit, with Chap. 8 serving as a further bridge by dealing with themes that are treated in both sections. All of the chapters state the main ideas of that chapter and how those ideas relate within one or the other of the two units. But what of the integration between these two units?

Many philosophers think that one of these ideas can be explained in terms of the other. The most salient example is the explanation of the second member of the trinity, doing, in terms of the third, agent causing; it has been argued that to act is for the agent to cause something to happen. Even the first member, trying, has not escaped the same type of explanation, but this time in terms of the second member, doing. No one of course disputes that you can try to do something and fail, so the explanation of the one in terms of the other must be qualified: '…an action (very nearly always) *is* [H's italics] an event of the agent's trying to do something…' (Hornsby 1997, 85). One of the central features of my own account of trying is the way in which I explain trying by a subjunctive conditional whose consequence is about acting.

One of the threads that unite the book's two units is an anti-clutter message: 'don't clutter one's ontology with a kind of thing unless it is really necessary to do so'. Causings and tryings as particulars are clutter. The one-particular view of action, developed in Chaps. 5, 6 and 8, in its own way, also has an anti-clutter message ('one is better than two'). I count myself a great friend of the mind. I think there are such things as token sensations, pains, tickles, itches, afterimages, dreams, and hallucinations. These may or may not be identical to physical particulars (for the record, I do not think that they are but I do not rely on that view anywhere in this book). Still, whatever the metaphysical category into which one places those things, there are such things. However, I have argued elsewhere that even friends of the mind should practice some form of limited birth control (Ruben 1995). Being a friend of the mind does not require complicity in population explosion. In this way, I am a semi-Rylean of sorts. A Rylean approach is justified in some cases but most certainly not in others, not for example in the ones listed in the fifth sentence of this paragraph. But I do doubt whether there are such things as tryings or volitions or causings, for example. Of course I think that it is true that agents want certain things and try to do certain things and cause certain things to happen. So the trick is to give an account of sentences with those verbs that do not require quantifying over tryings or acts of the will or events of causing something to occur. I offer such an account for trying-sentences in Chap. 4, and for causing-sentences in

Chap. 7. (I leave volitions, if they differ from trying, as another project, not to be dealt with here.) But in the end of the day, the book does have these two different foci: trying to act and acting. I think it is fair to say that the two topics are visibly and clearly related.

I have in all cases let the argument take me wherever it seemed to me to go. I feel somewhat diffident, because both the theory of trying and the theory of action that I develop are so non-standard and question so many orthodoxies all at once. I confess to finding this a little strange. But there it is: I believe they are in the main correct (after all, otherwise I would not publish the book). The truth is, as I explained above, sometimes strange, especially in philosophy. But for those readers who cannot quite swallow it whole, perhaps the arguments will at least get them to see things in a different light, and will raise legitimate issues that were not salient on other theories.

One reader of the draft manuscript commented that the text seems to meander. That may be true, but if it does, it arises, I think, from the way in which philosophy of action, on my conception, is so closely intertwined with metaphysics and epistemology (epistemology comes into play in the final chapter). In many cases, I felt I had to say something about the metaphysical and epistemological issues that my views presuppose or entail: supervenience, multiple realisability, existential dependence, and certain issues that arise on Davidson's analysis of action sentences, are cases of this. I can only defend myself by saying that the meandering could have been worse; there are times when I felt that I should have had more to say about something but managed to restrain myself. Examples of this would include my use of Moore's open question argument, the distinction between mass nouns and count nouns, the issue of whether properties are abundant, and the nature of observability, about all of which there is more that I could have said but have not said.

No book in philosophy can do everything. I use, in an absolutely essential way, the idea of a particular, without elaborating on it further. I set out some 'marks' of particularity: countability, pluralisation, individuation, identity, and quantification. Other than that, I rely on the idea of a particular that I think is fairly standard in contemporary philosophy. (Does it help if I say that I was trained at Harvard when Quine was there?) Of course, everything in philosophy is controversial, including the claim that everything in philosophy is controversial. There are unclear cases of particularity: states of affairs and facts, to name but two. Alvarez has spoken (to me, anyway) of semi-particulars, and the idea is certainly an intriguing one. But, all things considered, I guess that the otherwise unexamined idea of a particular offers as a good place as any at which to start this book.

In Chap. 2, I examine what one might consider the most plausible account of trying, at least most plausible from a naturalistic perspective. That account is the Physical Action Theory of Trying, according to which trying is to be identified with a physical action. In Chap. 2 I argue against that account of trying. I put a lot of weight on the cases of so-called naked trying, cases in which an agent tries but there is no physical action as a result. I stress that I think that the existence of naked trying is an empirically established fact, not based on 'intuitions' about such cases that philosophers might dispute.

I identify an assumption that I think underlies not only the Physical Action Theory of Trying but also its main competitors: that the expression 'person P's trying to do such-and-such' refers to some particular, viz., an act of trying or to *a* trying (I don't distinguish these last two), something that can be quantified over, pluralised, and that can be preceded by a definite or indefinite article. I call any account that makes this assumption 'a particularist theory of trying'. In Chap. 3 as a preliminary to offering my own account, I examine the way in which adverbial modification works in sentences about trying, as a way of undercutting that assumption.

In Chap. 4 I present a general argument against any particularist account of trying, and most importantly, I offer my own account of trying, a conditional theory of trying, which does not make that same particularist assumption. I think a novel account of trying is needed, that describes in a new way the relation between trying and doing. In sum, I motivate my account of trying: (1) by arguing that its most promising competitor account is faulty (Chap. 2); (2) by arguing that one argument that might be thought to offer support for a particularist account of trying fails (Chap. 3); (3) by producing a general argument against any particularist account of trying (the first part of Chap. 4); and (4) by offering and developing an alternative, which I defend from various objections (the second and longer part of Chap. 4).

The identification of doing with causing is widespread and I describe in some detail and argue against that misidentification in Chaps. 5 and 6. I discuss two views: first, in Chap. 5, whether if one causes something to happen, it follows that one acts, and second, in Chap. 6, whether, if one acts, it follows that the agent has caused something to happen. Chapter 6 develops what I think is a novel account of action, which builds on, but substantially changes, one I have previously defended (Ruben 2003). I call the view of action that I develop 'one-particularism'. Another name for the view could be 'the actions-in-the-world view'. But that is rather a mouthful. Chapter 5 has an appendix, in which I describe the 'derivation thesis' (DT). The DT is not a philosophical thesis at all and it is easy (it was for me, at any rate) to confuse it with the substantive philosophical analysis that is the subject matter of Chaps. 5 and 6; hence, my justification for including something about it.

In Chap. 7, I ask the question: are there any causing particulars? I am sceptical of there being any, and some of my arguments I use in Chap. 7 parallel the ones I made in Chap. 3 about trying particulars. In the course of Chap. 7, I examine a view of Maria Alvarez'. I describe and amplify some criticisms of her view made by Erasmus Mayr. I claim little originality in this section of Chap. 7.

Chapter 8 is composed of two, only loosely connected, sections. Each section spells out a further consequence of one-particularism. In the first section, I raise the question of whether the conjunction of one-particularism and the thought that if an agent act, he causes an event intrinsic to his action, generates a regress. One might think that some regress is brought about by that conjunction. I show why that is not so, in light of my argument in Chap. 7. In the second section, I discuss some epistemological issues about one's knowledge of the actions of others. I ask whether one can raise a sceptical question about one's knowledge of the actions of others, in the sense of Cartesian hyperbolic doubt. I think one can. I also suggest, very briefly, two philosophical moves that might be made, in order to reply to that sceptical position, and (regrettably) conclude that no compelling reply is forthcoming. But I think we will have learned something about the epistemology of action along the way.

Many philosophers have rejected the austere theory of act individuation as I do in Chap. 6; I am not very original in that regard. I think a natural progression of thought runs like this (I am not claiming that these are entailments): if non-basic actions are not just basic actions under non-basic descriptions, but actions in their own right, then where and when do they occur? If they do not occur when and where the basic actions on which they depend occur (a view for which I argue at some length), then there are reasons to place them where and when the events intrinsic to them occur (a lot more on intrinsic events in the book). For example, a person's opening a door occurs where and when the door opens. So let readers be forewarned: my view is that many actions are out in the world, far removed from an agent's body. I think that the idea that all actions occur at or within the surface of the agent's body is a presumption that does not sustain close scrutiny.

Now, it is possible to hold that, in this case for instance, even though both the person's opening of the door and the door's opening occur at the same time and same place, perhaps far removed from the agent's body and long after his body has moved, the person's opening of the door$\neq$the door's opening. However, such a view does seem rather ontologically extravagant even by my liberal standards. Better to identify them, letting actions be identical to their so-called intrinsic events. This identification will have many implications, and so, in order not to spoil your fun, I won't spell them out here. But what I think unites Chaps. 5, 6, 7, and 8 is just that: drawing the conclusions, both logical ones and plausible ones, from that identification.

I use throughout the book the subscripts 't' and 'i' to mark the transitive and intransitive use of the same verb respectively. I am not wholly consistent in this. The subscripts are ugly and clutter the text, so I have used them only when I thought that they were necessary to achieve clarity (perhaps my own clarity). When that wasn't the case, I omitted them, although I suspect I have erred on the side of overuse. Unless I am using another author's formulations, I often use 'b' as the direct object of the transitive verb and the subject of the corresponding intransitive verb. 'P' is, as I said in the Preface, my nameless and genderless agent. Throughout the book, I use 'LHS' and 'RHS' to refer to the left hand side and the right hand side respectively of an entailment or biconditional.

A caveat: often, when I produce a sentence on which to reflect, I refer to P as an agent. I mean by that 'at least a potential or alleged actor with regard to some specific action'. Perhaps 'participant in an action' would have been a better choice, but since I hold that there are more ways in which to participate in an action than by being the actor who is the agent of that action, that choice was not really available to me. On some occasions, 'P' is the subject of a sentence that might not show him expressing or demonstrating any activity or agency relative to that particular action at all. ('The agent P tried to F but was so constrained that he did nothing', might count as an extreme example of this usage.) So designating P as an agent in a discussion of some action of type F is not intended to beg any questions about whether P is actually expressing his agency with regard to any token action of that type.

Finally, many who have read the manuscript of the book, or various portions thereof, have commented on my neglect of the neo-Anscombian, neo-Aristotelian, and other similar, contributions to action theory in the past decade or so. Names like Michael Thompson, Doug Lavin, Eric Marcus, Rowland Stout, Sebastian Roedl, and, of course, John McDowell, come to mind. I have no particular criticisms to make of these authors, but I simply don't find the traditions within which they are working sufficiently illuminating. That's how it is with philosophy: one has a methodology and chooses philosophical interlocutors as important reference points in order to enter into the dialect of argumentation. I have chosen what I think is most worthwhile and interesting. Even if you don't think that my approach in the theory of action is the *most* worthwhile, I hope you will think it worthwhile enough to justify my having written this book and your having read at least some part of it.

I was trained in philosophy to strive for the highest degree of precision, rigour, and clarity. That is always my aim; it is not for me to say, of course, to what I extent I have been able to achieve that standard. I don't think that precision, rigour, and clarity are by themselves sufficient for success in philosophy; they are, after all, only method, not content. There is also a need for imagination, insight, and creative thought. But those first three goals are certainly a necessary way to begin doing any philosophy that is worthwhile and that is able to make any real progress. They are certainly three goals at which I have aimed throughout.

Notes

1. Much of Donald Davidson's work, and the extensive comment on it, are in this tradition. John Bishop's *Natural Agency* (1989), Helen Steward's *The Ontology of Mind* (1997), Anton Ford's splendid 'Action and Generality' (2011) and 'Action and Passion' (2014), Maria Alvarez' 'Actions and Events: Some Semantical Considerations' (1999), and E.J. Lowe's *Personal Agency: The Metaphysics of Mind and Action* (2010), are six further excellent examples that spring to mind. There are, of course, many, many others.

Bibliography

Alvarez, Maria. 1999. Actions and Events: Some Semantical Considerations. *Ratio*, new series XII (3): 213–239.

Bishop, J. 1989. *Natural Agency*, 117–120. Cambridge: Cambridge University Press.

Ford, Anton. 2011. Action and Generality. In *Essays on Anscombe's Intention*, ed. Anton Ford, Jennifer Hornsby, and Frederick Stoutland. Cambridge, MA: Harvard University Press.

———. 2014. Action and Passion. *Philosophical Topics* 42 (1): 13–42.

Gettier, Edmund. 1963. Is Justified True Belief Knowledge? *Analysis* 23 (6): 121–123.

Hornsby, Jennifer. 1997. *Simple Mindedness*. Cambridge: Harvard University Press.

Lowe, E.J. 2010. *Personal Agency: The Metaphysics of Mind and Action*. Oxford: Oxford University Press.

Mandelbaum, Maurice. 1955. Societal Facts. In *Modes of Individualism and Collectivism*, ed. John O'Neill, 221–234. London: Heinemann Educational Books.

Ruben, David-Hillel. 1977, second edition 1979. *Marxism and Materialism*. Hassocks, Sussex: Harvester Press.

———. 1985. *The Metaphysics of the Social World*. London: Routledge & Kegan Paul.

———. 1995. Mental Overpopulation and the Problem of Action. *Journal of Philosophical Research* 20: 511–524.

———. 2003. *Action & Its Explanation*. Oxford: Oxford University Press.

Steward, Helen. 1997. *The Ontology of Mind*. Oxford: Oxford University Press.

2

The Physical Action Theory of Trying

What's in the Chapter

After making some preliminary remarks that help me to introduce the idea that an act of trying is identical to some physical action, an idea that I reject, I discuss multiple-realisability in order to get clear exactly what claim I am discussing, a claim of identity between two particulars or tokens. Identity requires (at least) one-one correspondence: for each token trying act, there would have be one and only one token physical act (of course, namely itself) with which it is identical. There are two obstacles that I describe to the physical action theory of trying that are the opposite of one another: first, the availability of too many particular physical action tokens, and second, the lack of any. My discussion of the too-many-tokens problem leads me into a consideration of what I call the 'mereological strategy'. I argue that that strategy fails but I leave it open whether or not some non-mereological parallel strategy might succeed. Finally, I look at the lack-of-any-physical-tokens problem, sometimes called 'naked trying'. I sharpen the argument from the premiss that there are naked tryings to the conclusion that the physical identity theory fails. I believe that it is a scientifically established fact that there are such cases (it's not just a matter about one's 'philosophical intuitions' about such cases) and I examine two attempts to circumvent the naked trying argument and I conclude that they are unsuccessful.

Introduction

Before I begin the discussion of this chapter, I want to repeat and amplify what I said in the Introduction to the book about my overall strategy in developing an account of trying that requires no particular events as tryings. (An account of trying is particularist if it identifies trying with some particular; it is non-particularist if it does not.) I work with the idea of a particular without further explaining that idea, but it is a familiar idea in philosophy, and I rely on that familiarity. I take it that it can be true that someone tries to do something, without it being true that there is some particular, an act of trying, or a trying. (I make no distinction between a trying and an act of trying.) I amplify and explain the distinction in what follows, mostly though in Chap. 3 (and make a similar point about causing, in Chap. 7).

To repeat what I said in the Introduction: I motivate my non-particularist account of trying: (1) by arguing that its most promising particularist competitor account, the physical action theory, is faulty (Chap. 2, below); (2) by arguing that one possible argument for a particularist account of trying fails (Chap. 3); (3) by producing a general argument against any particularist theory of trying (the beginning of Chap. 4); and, (4) most importantly, by offering and developing a non-particularist alternative, which I defend from various objections (the remainder of Chap. 4). The three chapters should, then, be taken as a unit, in order to establish the conclusion I want, that there are no particular events that are tryings (or acts of trying) and that there is a better construal of trying-sentences that does not assume that there are.

In this chapter, I discuss only one specific form of the particularist view: the physical action theory of trying, the view that identifies each trying with a particular physical action occurring at or beyond the body's surface, although at the end of the chapter I discuss the 'last refuge' for those with a physicalist perspective, in their response to what is called 'naked trying', when they locate the trying as a physical event internal to or inside the agent's body.

If trying is a particular, there appear to be two options: to place it on the inside of the agent (hereafter, 'the inside view' or 'inside-agent view') or on the side of the world (where the latter includes the surface of the agent's body and beyond). Volitionists, who think that to try is to engage in a mental act, perhaps identical to willing and perhaps not, take the inside option.[1] Such an inside-agent view might be compatible with physicalism, if the mental act is then identified with a brain state. Hobbes took this view: 'These small beginnings of Motion, within the body of Man, before they appear in walking, speaking, striking, and other visible actions, are commonly called ENDEAVOUR' (*Leviathan*, Chapter VI). The contrast I want is not between the mental and the physical per se, but between what is inside the body or in the mind of the agent on the one hand, and what is at the body's surface or beyond it, on the other hand.

The second, or world-side option *identifies* trying to do something with one of the relatively more basic actions by which one tries to do that thing. Richard Taylor (1973, 79) is an example of a philosopher who takes this option: he says, '[T]rying to do something is always…actually doing something with a view to accomplishing a certain result'. George Wilson and Timothy Cleveland hold roughly that same view: 'to try to A is to perform an action that is directed by the agent at (in an appropriate way) promoting his F–ing' (Wilson 1989, 155–156); when the agent tried, he 'performed a movement, and intended of that movement that it be a raising of his arm' (Cleveland 1997, 142). Wilson calls his view 'the omnipresence of physical action in all trying (i.e., in all cases of trying to perform a physical action.)' (159).

Perhaps there are other ways in which to construe the remarks by Taylor, Cleveland, and Wilson, ways that do not involve commitment to particular acts of trying. One possibility is this: make the trying sentence equivalent to a sentence or set of sentences about physical actions, so that any apparent commitment to a trying particular does not re-appear in the sentences to which the tying sentence is equivalent. This strategy may have no need to think of trying as a particular at all. The non-particularist view I advance and defend in Chap. 4 is one possible view of this type, but for now I will construe the physical action theorists of trying whom

I have identified as making identity claims about tryings of the sort I have claimed. This is the way in which the philosophers named above understand their own views as well. Each act of trying on this construal is a particular and is said to be identical with some physical action, or at least some other action-rich particular, for example, a set or a sum of actions, or an action plus an appropriate mental state.[2]

The purpose of this chapter is to argue against the second, world-side option (although, as I indicated above, at the very end of this chapter the 'last refuge' physicalist version of the particularist view of trying that I discuss is inside the agent). I won't query whether these two options really exhaust the alternatives until Chaps. 3 and 4. In Chap. 4, I offer what I take to be a novel alternative to the inside and world-side choice. But if I succeed in dismissing the most plausible form of the world-side option (and also the one inside-the-agent view I look at the end of the chapter) in its particularist form, we will have made considerable progress in coming to a view of what trying is, because we will have learned something important about what it is not. This dismissal will, I hope, help to motivate the desirability of my non-particularist alternative that I sketch in the later chapters.

There are to be sure, hybrid views that incorporate both inside and world-side options. For example, there is a view that claims that the trying is a composite of an intention and a physical action or a bodily movement (Buckareff 2007, 52): '…I suggest that we take mental trying to be a composite event that consists of some relevant mental state or event [an intention]… M1 causing some relevant state or event M2 for a reason'. Buckareff does not say to what 'M2' refers in the case of unsuccessful trying. In the case of a successful trying, M2 is an action or a piece of bodily behaviour. Olivier Massin's view, mentioned in note 2, is best construed as a hybrid theory. I won't examine these hybrid views separately. The difficulties I discuss with regard to the simpler view carry over to hybrid views.

So I construe the rather unspecific thought, 'to try is to perform a physical action' as an identity claim: 'P's trying to F=X', where our task in this chapter will be to see what particular the world-side theorist can plausibly substitute for 'X' on the right hand side (the RHS) of the identity. It is essential, for the physical action theory of trying, as I understand it, to locate a single particular with which to identify each token trying. That's the form that all identity claims must take. It is not sufficient if an identity claim is in the offing just to say: 'Trying to do something is always...actually doing some thing [a physical action]'. A single, numerically identical, trying can last over a period of time, say from t to t*. So the physical action identity theory must find some single action, or some single set or aggregate of actions, to which the trying is identical and which therefore must have the same temporal expanse.

One thing that a physical action theory of trying does not do, by self-definition, is to give an account of mental action, if such there be. I don't discuss this problem in the book, since I restrict my discussion throughout to trying to do a physical act. I will remind the reader of this exclusion from time to time in the book. But for those of us who believe that there is such a thing as mental action, e.g., searching one's memory, forming an intention, deciding what to do, concentrating on the matter at hand, the inability of the physical action theory of trying to give a uniform account to both sorts of action, mental and physical, is a strike against it.

The Physical Action Theory of Trying: The Multiple-Realisability Claim

The initial world-side thought is that if agent P wants to G, and so he tries to G by doing some physical action, say, by F–ing, then his trying to G=his F–ing. But the world-side view is rarely described in any significant detail. I think the world-side view is best expressed as the conjunction of (1) and (2) and I shall explain why below:

(1) If one can try to do something, G, by doing some action, there may be indefinitely many physical action types by whose tokens one can try to G, i.e., whose instances can realise that same type of trying on different occasions. There are many different ways in which to try and skin a cat. So for example, a person might on one occasion try to G by F-ing and on a different occasion try to G by E-ing. So on the first occasion, the person tries to G by a token action, his F-ing, and on the second occasion he tries to G by a token action, his E-ing.

(2) Every token trying is identical to some token physical action of one of those physical action types, by the tokens of which the person can try. It might be that the earlier token trying to G=his token action, his F-ing and the later token trying to G=his token action, his E-ing.

Whether there is more than one action by which one can try to do something is a contingent matter. Even if there were really only one way in which to skin a cat, there are as many ways in which to try to skin it, as there are beliefs, false or true, about how to skin it. Even if doing F is really no way at all in which to get the cat skinned, if a person believes that it is, then he can try to skin the cat by F–ing (my goodness, he tried to skin the cat by F–ing. Just imagine! How silly. He was bound to fail). (1) allows for the multiplicity of ways by which one can try, but it does not require such a multiplicity.

The view of trying expressed by the conjunction of (1) and (2) is tailor-made for the case of non-basic action, so that one tries to do a non-basic action by doing a relatively more basic one. There are many views about what it is in virtue of which an action counts as basic. I use this account, about which I will say more later in the book: a token action a (of type A) is basic for agent P at time t iff there is no other token action a* (of any type) such that P a's at t by a*-ing.

But what of basic action itself, action one does but not by doing anything else? I agree with Hornsby (1995, 532) that it makes perfect sense to speak of trying to do a basic action. The thought might be that trying to do a basic action is identical to the basic action itself, there being no other obvious physical action alternative. If one tries to G, where G-ing is an action type whose token at t is a basic action, then the token trying to G at t=the token G-ing at t. Either the case of basic action needs to be added as an explicit (3) to (1)–(2) above, or alternatively we could accept that one tries to G by G-ing, odd as that might sound.

Consider a type like 'trying to stop the flood'. On different occasions of flood stopping, doing different things might stop the flood. Agent P on one occasion might try to stop the flood by his starting of the pump (hereafter, his starting), agent P* might on a different occasion try to stop it by his lowering of the flood barrier (hereafter, his lowering), and on a third occasion agent P** might try to stop the flood by his closing of the sluice on a dam (hereafter, his closing).

No *type* of trying, like trying to stop the flood, can be identical to any one of the physical action types, by whose tokens one can try. The relationship here is well known from the philosophy of mind more generally: the multiple-realisation relation.[3] (Type G is multiply-realised by types A, B, and C iff tokens of G are sometimes identical with tokens of A, other tokens of G identical with tokens of B, and still other tokens of G identical with tokens of C.)

The use of multiple-realisation in this context it is much less problematic than its use in the brain-mind identity theory. Some critics of the multiple-realisation argument, as it occurs in the brain-mind identity theory literature, have suggested that it arises only as an artificial creation of describing the mental type at one level of abstraction or generality and describing the brain state at a different, more specific level of generality. The suggestion is that, were we to insure that the levels of generality in description match, we might find that we had a type-type identity theory of mind and brain after all. Another reply in favour of retaining type-type identity for the expression of the brain-mind identity theory is to restrict the type identity to individual species, thereby making a species-specific type-type identification more plausible.

These issues do not appear to affect the use of multiple-realisability in the case of trying. The level of generality required both for the content of the trying and for the action by which one tries is set by the intentions or plans of the agent and hence both are taken from the personal level. The agent will have a plan to try to obtain some end, and that plan will include the salient steps he needs to take in order to try and obtain that goal or end. In the more general mind-brain use of multiple-realisability, there is a question of the right level of generality needed for the scientific description of the brain state, and the consequent need to match up the right personal and impersonal levels. But no such problem arises in the case of trying-both the action and the trying are located at the personal level and have the same level of generality.

The comparison between uses of multiple-realisability in mind-brain theories and trying theories is instructive. There appear to be two different uses of multiple-realisability, a horizontal use and a vertical use. Its use in mind-brain identity theory is a vertical use: something from one level ('the personal') is said to be multiply realised by many things at a different level, the impersonal level of neuroscience. Since each level has its own discourse, a question can arise as to how to match types from the two discourses in terms of level of generality.

The use of multiple-realisability in the physical action theory of trying is a horizontal use: different levels are not involved in the sense that both the action descriptions and trying descriptions are part of our ordinary or psychological discourse about mind and action. As far as species specificity is concerned, to whatever extent some specific species of animal can try and act, it might be true that for at least some cases of that animal's trying, there may be more than one way in which the same animal can try to do that thing. Multiple-realisability won't disappear, but the application of multiple-realisability in a horizontal use is much less problematic than in a vertical use.

So, yesterday, trying to stop the flood was realised by a token starting of the pump, realised today by a token lowering of the flood barrier, to be realised tomorrow by a token opening of the sluice. Indeed, as I indicated above, given oddball enough beliefs about what causes what, a token of almost any type of physical action could on some occasion realise a type like trying to G. The three token physical actions can either be the actions of three different persons or the actions of one person done at three different times. Hence, the point of (1).

The Physical Action Theory of Trying: The Token-Token Identity Claim

What is the relation between a token trying and the token actions that realise that trying? Consider now only a single occasion of flood stopping by a single agent. In a simple case, the agent might try to G by doing a single token action, F-ing (say, starting the pump). So the physical action identification theory would have it that his token trying to G=his token F-ing. Hence, the point of (2). (For the sake of simplicity, I omit time indexing.)

But many cases are not like that. There are many cases in which an agent, P, tries to do something by doing numerous things. Unlike a simple case like trying to open the door by turning the handle, many action plans will typically have many nodes on them. Two different sorts of cases need distinguishing.

- *Case 1: Consider building a ship*: construct the hull outline, fix the planks, put pitch in the joins, paint the result, fix a mast, run up a sail, and so on, and finally-voila!- a ship. Each node is a separate, distinct action on its own. In some sense, the 'overall' building of the ship is composed or made up of the series of the other actions. Plans might not be of course just the plans of a single individual. In the case of the ship construction, there may be a single Ibsenian Master Builder who organises others to carry out each individual task, and it may be only he who has a grasp of the whole plan.
- *Case 2: The action plans most loved by philosophers of action are ones where each action is accomplished by its prior by-action*: An agent, P, bends his finger, turns the valve, closes the sluice on a dam, stops the flood, and thereby improves the lives of the inhabitants living downstream. Such a plan generates a series of non-basic actions, grounded finally in some basic action, such that each action is done by doing its predecessor, if it has one. I call these chains of action 'action chains'. The other more basic actions don't make up or compose the stopping of the flood or the improving of the inhabitants' lives. Or, if you hold what I call an austere theory, like Davidson's or Anscombe's, the action plan generates a series of non-basic descriptions grounded in a basic description.[4] There will be much more to come about action chains in Chap. 6.

The action plans under discussion in this chapter are like case 1, and not like case 2. In building the ship, no one fixes the mast by painting the result, etc. The agent must take a series of (usually but not necessarily) successive and independent actions in order to achieve some end. Each action on the plan is not related to its predecessor by the by-relation (except insofar as the agent may achieve completion of the overall plan by doing all of the distinct actions equally).

In our example, Agent P might try to stop the flood (a) by his starting of the pump from t to t*, and (b) by his lowering of the flood barrier from t* to t**, and (c) by his closing of the sluice on a dam from t** to t***. In this case, let us suppose that the same agent must do three separate actions, each of which is individually necessary but insufficient to stop the flood (and he knows this). Imagine that none of the actions on its own can even partially stop the flood. Suppose a threshold effect so that all three actions must be undertaken, in order for any bit of flood stopping at all to occur. No single token action can even do a little stopping. In this case, there is one token trying to stop the flood (that lasts from t to t***) and three token actions taken seriatim in order to try and stop it.

On whatever theory of act individuation one might chose to adopt, austere or prolific or otherwise, these are three distinct actions and not three descriptions of one action. The agent simply does each particular action seriatim, and the order in which he does them may or may not matter. He tries only once to stop the flood, but he must do three quite different things (let us suppose) in order to try even that one time. So he tries to stop the flood once by doing three distinct actions. In this sort of case, what would be the relationship between the token trying to stop the flood (if that is what it is) and the three token actions the agent must take?

On the version of the physical action theory of trying that we are discussing, we need to find the particular X, so that 'P's trying to G=X' is true. With what physical token action would the token trying be identical? As we have understood the physical action theory, there must be some single particular with which to identify each token trying. What is the one single particular with which to identify his trying to stop the flood in the case in which the agent has three actions to perform when he tries to stop the flood?

Choice of one rather than the others of the three token actions with which to identify the token trying would be unmotivated. The apparently equal claim of all three of the physical actions is an indication that the relationship between the token trying and each of the several distinct token actions, whatever it might be, is not identity. The trying$\neq$the lowering; the trying$\neq$the closing; and the trying$\neq$the starting. What other relationship might we substitute in place of identity, as a relation between the token trying and the multiple token physical actions?

An alternative suggests itself. Tryings can go on for a period of time-'he tried for several days'. On the physical action theory's assumption that tryings are some sort of particular, tryings would be, or would be metaphysically very much like, events, since both are ocurrents rather than continuants: they are not fully present at any subportion of the time during which they exist. They would have proper temporal parts; they are the temporally restricted parts of the whole trying. If an agent tries, for instance, from t-t***, then amongst the temporal parts of the trying, there would be these segments of it: the trying from t to t*, from t* to t**, and so on.

A natural suggestion then, for the physical identification theory of trying, would be to identify each of the temporal parts of the token trying with a different physical action token on the action plan to stop the flood. (This is consistent with the assumption of the threshold effect described above. Even if no portion of the flood gets stopped until all three actions are done, the trying to stop the flood could still have temporal segments or parts.) So the temporal trying part from t*-t** might be identical to (say) the token lowering of the flood barrier. Each of the different token actions on the action plan could be identical to a different trying temporal part.

Most of us can walk and chew gum at the same time. The temporal parts strategy as described above won't work if the agent engages in two or more of the independent actions at the same time rather than seriatim. With one hand, the agent lowers the flood barrier; with the other, he closes the sluice. The same argument for non-identity applies as before. The two actions, the lowering and the closing, are not identical, so the temporal part of the trying from t*-t** can't be identical to both, and neither has a better claim than the other to the identification. What option is left to the physical action theorist of trying? Perhaps this: the appropriate temporal part of the trying would need to be identical to the mereological sum (or fusion or conjunction) of the two actions (the actions being the parts of the sum). (I don't even consider the set whose members are the two actions, since the idea that a trying could be identical to a set, which is an abstract object, seems quite preposterous.)

So the suggestion is this: (1) the whole trying has temporal parts, and (2) each temporal part of the trying has its own parts (the actions), such that each temporal part of the trying is identical to the sum of its parts. My argument assumes that the physical action theorist of trying has adopted (1) as a part of his response to the walk-and-chew gum problem, so I won't be disputing or examining the plausibility of (1). It is in any case generally accepted that events are not continuants but ocurrents; they do not exist in their entirety at all the times at which they exist. Whatever your view may be about substances having temporal parts, it seems clear that events have temporal parts. So my argument that follows only addresses (2). I'm going to argue that events and tryings (if one assumes that they are event-like particulars) are not identical to the sums of their parts. If tryings are not identical to the sums of their parts, temporal parts of tryings are not identical to the sums of their parts either.

In the paragraph above, 'parts' is being used in two different ways: the more controversial idea of a temporal part and the uncontroversial mereological idea of a part of a sum. I would have preferred to use the expression 'a temporal segment' instead of 'a temporal part' in order to keep the two views clearly separated, but the idea of a temporal part is so well established in the literature that such a switch could engender confusions of its own.

If tryings are particulars, with temporal parts, then it is fair to ask about their mereological characteristics. (Of course, trying particulars, if such there were, could also be partless mereological simples, but the strategy of the physical action theory of trying that we are now considering gives them parts.) An exposition of classical or extensional mereological theory would take us far beyond the limits of this chapter (and beyond my ability as well), but the essential point for us is this: on classical mereological theory, two sums (or synonymously, fusions) are identical iff they have all the same parts. (Classical mereology says that if two sums have the same parts, they are identical. The claim that if they are identical, they have the same parts is just an application of Leibniz' Law, the Indiscernibility of Identicals).

The Mereological Sum Strategy

In some object o, which has (let us say) 100 parts, one can sometimes replace at least one of those parts with a different part and yet o retains its numerical identity. I'm assuming that mereological essentialism is false for objects or substances. Massive part replacement, particularly if it occurs at a fell swoop, may be inconsistent with the numerical identity of o before and after replacement. It may even be that there is some particular part, because of its size or its function, which cannot be replaced consistent with numerical identity of the object before and after replacement. But at least some parts of some objects or substances are not essential to them. Objects or substances can change and sometimes at least remain numerically the same object or substance across the change.

Sums or fusions, on the other hand, are like sets in at least one way; all of their parts are essential to them. No sum can gain or lose parts. If sum a=sum b, then a and b have exactly the same parts. Contrapositively, if a has a part that b lacks or b has a part that a lacks, then a≠b. That this is so follows from the Indiscernibility of Identicals: if a and b are discernible, then they are not identical.[5] In terms of transworld identity claims, no sum could gain a part that it does not have and could not lose a part that it does have.

Like substances or objects, events (and their temporal parts) can change; they can gain or lose their own parts. They might not be as mereologically robust as physically objects, but on the other hand they do not seem to be as mereologically fragile as sums.[6] Imagine that two disputants are disputing whether or not the Great War, or its 1916 temporal part, included some battle, the Battle of the X. If the Great War were a mereological sum (of battles, say), the two disputants would not even be disputing about the same world war; they would have two numerically different although very similar world wars in mind. On the contrary, it certainly seems that The Great War could have had one less or more battle than it did have, and still it would have been the numerically same Great War.

Sir Edmund Hilary tried to climb Mt. Everest (and succeeded on 29 May 1953). Suppose two disputants are arguing whether Hilary, during this attempt, forged a route through the treacherous Khumbu Icefall (the forging). If the mereological sum view were correct, they can't be disputing about the same attempt by Sir Hilary. On the mereological sum view, one is probably speaking about the actual attempt; the other, about a similar possible but non-actual attempt that he thinks was the actual attempt. That doesn't seem correct. They are arguing about one and the same attempt and disagreeing about whether it included the forging. Of course, there are some changes that attempts could not survive without losing their numerical identity, but then there are some changes physical objects and battles or other events cannot survive either without losing their numerical identity. Attempts, or acts of trying, or their temporal parts, if there were any, couldn't be mereological sums of actions.

What's the argument for events being able to loose or gain parts? Here is one, taken from David Lewis: 'So, while it is clear enough what it would mean to specify events essentially, often that does not seem to be what we really do. At any rate, it is not what we do when we specify events by means of our standard nominalisations' (Lewis 1986, 250–251). Consider for instance the example of the time of an event. As Lewis observes, it is one thing to postpone an event, another to cancel it. One and the same death for instance could have occurred somewhat earlier or somewhat later (see also Evnine 2016, 247–249, on the alleged essentiality of time for actions).

Suppose a doctor delays someone's death from t to t*. If the actual death at the later time≠the death that there would have been at the earlier time, then the doctor, praiseworthy as he may be for preventing the earlier death, is blameworthy for causing the later one and that is surely absurd. True, the variations in time and in other of an event's properties are not limitless, so that a death at t, and an otherwise qualitatively similar one 50 years later may not be one and the same death.[7] But in general, even discounting the case of temporal location, not all of an event's properties (including its property of having such-and-such part) are essential to it (see Ehring 1997, 46–47).

The same is true, I think, for actions and their temporal parts, like the building of the ship (also see for example Evnine 2016, 209, on the 'modal flexibility of events and actions'). In the same vein, if two disputants are arguing whether a third person, P, did remember to put pitch in the joints of the planks yesterday, they are disputing about the same token ship-building, or the yesterday temporal part of it, and disagreeing over whether it did or did not contain some important part, P's pitching of the joints.

Another argument for the conclusion that, like objects and unlike sums, not all the parts of events are essential to them is loosely based on an argument given by Lombard (1986, 200–206). Grant that objects or substances could have different parts, as I assumed above. Grant also that at least some events have substances as their subjects (this is hardly controversial): the eruption of Vesuvius, the birth of Napoleon, and the collapse of the Tay Bridge. Perhaps some events are not substance-involving (a flash of light, a clap of thunder) but it is surely obvious that some, even most, are substance-involving.

Now consider a substance o in the actual world w with 100 parts, numbered 1…100. (In Lombard's presentation of the argument, o is the Ship of Theseus.) That same substance could have had part 56 replaced by a different part, 56*, and still be the same substance; so there is a possible world w* in which o (or o's counterpart, but I shan't keep repeating that qualification) has parts 1…0.55, 56*, 57…100. That much is agreed by accepting that some substances are susceptible at least to some part replacement.

As in the Lombard story, o is a ship. There are two possible worlds we want to consider, w and w*. (w can be the actual world, but it does not need to be in this story.) Suppose o sinks in world w at t, so there is an event, the sinking of o in w at t. The same thing happens to o in w*. o sinks in w* at the same time t, so there is a sinking of o in w* at t. Events and actions, and their temporal parts, like substances, can have parts. The event, sinking of o-in-w's parts, includes at least the following 100 (sub) events as its parts: the sinking of part 1…the sinking of part 56…the sinking of part 100.

Consider further the sinking of o in w*, which has one (sub)event part different (e.g., the sinking of part 56*) from the ones the sinking in w has. Is the sinking of o in w=the sinking of o in w*? It does not follow that the sinkings are identical just because they are both sinkings, both of the same ship, and both at the same time; one might try to deny that they are. However, it is plausible that the sinking of o in w and the sinking of o in w* are numerically identical; there is no reason whatever to hold that they are non-identical, given that their subjects, the ships, their times of occurrence, and their constituent property types (a ship sinking) in w and w* are identical. On the Kim-Goldman account of action or event identity for example, two act-tokens or event tokens 'are identical if and only if they involve the same agent [or subject], the same property, and the same time' (Goldman 1970, 10). (In a footnote, Goldman lists other philosophers who share this criterion.) My claim of plausibility uses that same criterion but applies it across worlds rather than only within a world. In Chap. 6, I will loosen this 'prolific' criterion for an intermediate theory, but that will not affect the point being made here.

Of course, it is true that the sinking in w and the sinking in w* have a different part. That's part of the assumption about the case. But there must be some way in which to make the fact of change and the Indiscernibility of Identicals consistent, so in whatever way we make a difference in the parts of some substance o at t and o in t* compatible with o's identity at the two different times, we can use that same way in the case of the sinkings.

If this is right, then it follows that if mereological essentialism is false of substances, then it is also false of events, whose subjects are those substances. The sinking in w* has a different event as a part than *it* had in w. Acts, events, or their temporal parts, could have parts other than the parts they do have; they can't be identical to the mereological sums of their subparts.

In Lombard's example, the argument is simplified by having (a) events with easily identified parts, (b) events with an easily identified subject, and (c) whatever it is that happens to the subject of the whole event being the same as what happens to each part of the event: a sinking. o sinks and each part sinks. But other examples will make the same point, even if their subjects and parts are not so easy to identify and if what happens to the parts of the subject (their sinking, in the case we used) is not the same as what happens to the subject of the whole act or event (its sinking). Relaxing those simplifying assumptions would make the examples much messier, but it would not alter the result: events and actions can gain or lose parts, so they can't be identical to any sum of those parts. If tryings (and temporal slices thereof) are particulars, they too could lose or gain parts; sums or fusions can't, so if tryings (and temporal slices of tryings) are particulars, they can't be identical to the sum of their parts.

Might there be conjunctive actions, for example, the action of lowering-and-closing-and-starting? I'm not sure what a conjunctive action is, if not the same as a mereological sum. Is the following meant to be true: 'P (F-ed & G-ed & H-ed) iff P F-ed & P G-ed & P H-ed' (F, G, and H are action types, so these are to be read, e.g., as: P did some token action of type F)? Assuming that the left hand side of the biconditional is about a conjunctive action, the biconditional, if true, would show that to do a conjunctive action is just to do a conjunction of actions (the right hand side). If a conjunction of actions is merely a sum of actions, then the conjunctive action view would be susceptible to the same objections as the mereological view. A proponent of the conjunctive action alternative would at least have to show why the biconditional fails (but see Enrico Pattaro 2005).

To be sure, classical extensional mereology does not exhaust the options for understanding the ideas of part and whole. There are accounts alternative to the extensional mereological one for the relation between an event or an action and its 'parts': (a) constitution and (b) composition are good candidates. The relation between composition and constitution is a matter of some controversy (Evnine 2011). There is a vast literature here and I will by necessity be brief. There is little agreement on terminology in these matters; mine may well be idiosyncratic but I think it is plausible.

(a) Objects are composed of matter of different types (wood, plastic, mud, and glass). These are mass nouns, not count nouns. It could be held that Goliath=the lump of clay, but Goliath is composed, not by the lump of clay (a dummy count noun), but from clay (a mass noun). The table is composed of wood. There is no identity associated with composition so understood, and hence this idea of composition provides no model for grasping the alleged identity between a trying temporal part and its parts. There are of course portions of wood, plastic, mud, and glass, but a portion is also an extensional entity, like a sum or fusion or a set. Similarly for the idea of an aggregate. Aggregate a=aggregate b iff a and b have exactly the same parts or components.

(b) However, there clearly is a sense of constitution that is not captured by extensional mereology. Physical objects can surely have parts in that sense, even though such parthood cannot be understood as extensional mereological parthood. Our bodies are constituted by or made up from parts for example (heads, torsos, limbs), as are countries and continents. Our ordinary non-technical discourse licenses this non-extensional way of thinking about the constitution of objects and their parts. But the thought that tryings have parts, and these parts are the physical actions by which one tries, is hardly a non-technical, ordinary idea. It would be to use 'part' as a specialised term of art, introduced for theoretical purposes. But that idea, that physical objects are constituted by or have parts in a non-extensional sense, provides no plausibility for the thought that tryings are identical to the sum of their parts.

I won't pursue here the counterarguments to this critique of the constitution alternative or to the parts strategy (I acknowledge that there are possible replies). However, there is another problem that affects equally the case when there is only one and when there is more than one action associated with a single temporal part of the trying. Suppose that the only action the agent undertakes between t-t* in order to try and stop the flood is to lower the flood barrier. In this simple case, the physical action theorist might say that the temporal part from t to t* of his trying to stop the flood=his lowering of the flood barrier from t to t*. So what's wrong with that?

The Physical Action Theory and Problems of Action Failure

The agent may try to stop the flood by lowering the barrier. But he might fail to lower the barrier (it was so much harder to do than he imagined), even though he tried to lower the barrier and of course still tried to stop the flood. So what, in such a circumstance of failure, could the t-t* temporal part of his trying to stop the flood be identified?

A candidate with which the t-t* temporal part of trying to stop to flood could be identified might to be with his trying to lower the barrier from t to t*, for that surely did occur even in the case of failure in lowering the barrier. But the problem here is obvious. Far from identifying trying with any physical action, we have only another trying, (say) trying to lower the barrier, with which to identify the temporal part of trying to stop the flood. That isn't an illuminating identification theory of trying with a physical action at all. It might be true but it doesn't permit us to go beyond trying, to a physical action, in the way in which the physical action theorist of trying had hoped.

Why not say that the temporal part of his trying to stop the flood is identical to the lowering of the barrier when the agent successfully lowers the barrier, but not otherwise? This is a perfectly possible theory but it creates a partition among tokens of trying in an unexpected way that otherwise has no motivation. It commits us to two kinds of trying when from all appearances they seemed to be a homogenous class, and it still leaves us with the identification question for the tryings to lower the barrier in the case of failure.

But the physical action theorist of trying has a better reply than identifying the t-t* temporal part of trying to stop the flood with his trying to lower the barrier from t-t*. True, trying to stop the flood, or rather the appropriate temporal part of that trying, might be only identical to trying to lower the barrier. So far, no break out from the trying circle. But trying to lower the barrier, in its turn, might be identical to the physical action by which one tries to do that. Perhaps trying to lower the barrier=turning the handle of the gizmo. So the t-t* temporal part of his trying to stop the flood=his trying to lower the barrier=his (actually) turning of the handle of the gizmo. But what then happens if the agent fails to turn the handle although he tried to do that? Well, he moved his hand, and perhaps that is a basic physical action, done by means of no other physical action of his. If so, we could anchor the tryings all the way down if needs be, until we hit a rock-bottom basic physical action. Somewhere along the line, one might suppose, a physical action must come into the story. Surely it can't just be turtles all the way down. Or can it?

This reply only works if the possibility of failure is not recursive, if it is not turtles all the way down. But failure all the way down can occur in the following kind of well-known case. An agent could try, without any action whatever happening, not even a basic action, as in the case of Dr. Landry's or Professor Strümpell's patients ('his wonderful anaesthetic boy', as Strümpell calls him).[8] In William James' description of these cases (let's call them 'pathological cases'), somewhat enhanced in my retelling, the patient lacks any 'kinaesthetic impressions' or any proprioception in some limb, so is unable to sense any movement of that limb or its location. The patient is blindfolded, so that he cannot see where his limb is. Finally, another person, unseen, forcibly holds down the patient's hand, so that the patient, being anaesthetised, is unable to feel this pressure on his hand either.

After being asked to move the limb, the patient is surprised to discover, when the blindfold is removed, that he has failed to do so. He believed that he had moved it. In the cases reported by James, it may be that some muscular contractions occur even in the absence of bodily movement. In cases of total paralysis not reported by James, but reported in the more recent literature,[9] not even muscle contractions occur; there is only some brain activity on the part of the patient, which fails to result in either bodily movement or muscle contractions.

Some philosophers distinguish between 'action' as a count noun ('there are n actions', 'action a=action b', 'the action', and so on) and 'action' as a mass noun, like 'mud' and 'blood' ('Man, there sure is a lot of action going on around here') (Bennett 1998, 29–30, 35). Bennett also says that we sometimes use the mass noun to refer to the universal: 'Philosophers often discuss action'. My arguments are directed at the count noun, 'actions'. I have no view in the book about action as a mass noun or about the universal, although in the case of naked trying, if there is no action (count noun), I can't see how or why anyone would hold that there was still action (mass noun) (certainly Bennett does not claim that.).

But is this right? Action as a mass noun seems to align with the exercise of agency. Is there exercise of agency in a case of naked trying? When a person tries but fails to do anything whatever, is he *exercising* his agency? The person may still be an agent: that is the way in which I use 'agent' in the book, so that it does not imply actual action, only the potentiality for acting. But the exercise of agency without action (mass noun or count noun) would need some explaining. On my view, an agent is not exercising his agency in a case of naked trying. He is trying to exercise his agency insofar as he is trying to act, but if he fails to act in a naked try, it follows that he fails to exercise any agency. I hope that my account of trying in Chap. 4 will be able to substantiate that claim.

For the purposes of my argument, do we need to show that there are actual cases of naked trying or only that there could be such cases? The discussion of naked trying assumes that there are such cases, and describes them, namely the cases of Dr. Landry's or Professor Strümpell's patients, as reported by William James, but also confirmed repeatedly in other investigations in more recent psychological literature. In cases of failed action, James is clear that in paralysis, '[T]he volition occurs, but the hand remains as still as the table…He tries harder, i.e., he mentally frames the sensation of muscular effort…but the palsied arm lies passive as before' (561). In their discussions of effort, psychologists assume that trying has also taken place, whether or not there has been any effort of which the wanna-be actor is aware.[10]

One might also argue that the fact that cases of naked trying are conceptually possible would by itself show us something important about the nature of trying, whether or not there are any such actual cases. I think there is much to be said for this view. But I shan't pursue that thought further. It might not occur to us that such cases are even possible unless or until we confronted actual cases. I will discuss Landry-like cases as actual and not as merely possible.

The conclusion that there are naked trying requires that the cases used as evidence actually be ones of trying, and not of something else. But might it be disputed whether these are really cases of trying at all? I do think that the scientific literature about these examples is often confused, especially on the question of effort, exertion, and their relation to trying. Whatever confusion there may be in the literature, James, and subsequent writers, do claim that in the Landry and similar cases, the patient tries. But we don't need to take James' word for this. We can argue for this as a conclusion, based on his experiment but not necessarily on his description of it.

We might attempt to construe James's report, and the ample empirical evidence in the current scientific literature, about total action failure, as showing something less than that these agents try. Action failure in these cases is an undisputed fact. True, James, and the scientists I quote in fn. 10, all assume that these cases of total action failure are cases of trying. But all I need to take from James', and others', reports is the experimental description of the case: 'If, having the intention of executing a certain movement, I prevent him, he does not perceive it, and supposes the limb to have taken the position he intended to give it' (James 1950, 490). We do not need to rely on James' judgment that this is a case of trying. So, on this reading, (a) the undisputed scientific fact is action failure. That is a premiss. Further premisses are these: (b) Landry does also ascribe the intention to move his hand to his patient, and this is something I accept from James' own account of the case. I also accept from the description of the case that (c) the patient is surprised at the position of his limb. The existence of trying is then the *conclusion* of an argument that uses as premisses (a)–(c). The existence of trying in these pathological cases is not an *assumption*.

So, we can argue from the fact of total action failure (plus intention and surprise) to the conclusion that the wanna-be agent tried. The patient finds that he has a false belief about the position of his arm. (This is what I mean by saying that he is surprised: he finds that he is holding a false belief about the position of his arm.) The claim that the patient has tried but failed to do anything at all is a conclusion that *we* can draw about the case as described.

Does Dr. Landry's patient try to move his arm, as well as intend to do so, in a case of surprising total action failure? The claim is that it is plausible to say, about cases like this, that the patient has tried but utterly failed to do anything whatever. The argument runs like this: how can one explain the patient's surprise, (c)? James reports that Landry's patient had the 'intention' to execute the movement. Certainly the occurrence of ordinary intentions to F, even proximate intentions to F right now, would not necessarily occasion any surprise at failure to F. There are very many things that a person intends to do but which he never does; the road to Hell is paved with good intentions, even good proximate ones.

So suppose Landry's patient had proximally intended to execute the movement; he had a proximal intention to make the movement immediately, 'at once'. Remember, the patient does not know or have any beliefs about any of the various constraining conditions that made for his failure, and yet he is surprised at his failure. How could that be?

Would Landry's patient be surprised just because he does not do what he had proximally intended to do, had not altered his intention, and, believed, falsely as it happens, that nothing prevented him from acting? *Must* an agent, in those circumstances, be surprised that he had not managed to do what he proximately intended to do? Not necessarily. Failure to execute intentions to do something might not explain surprise in one's not having done it. To explain the agent's surprise in Landry's experiment, it must also be true that the agent tried to act, in addition to having had these unchanged proximal intentions and beliefs.

In cases in which an agent tries to do something, the agent typically (although perhaps not invariably) is in various mental states: specific beliefs, desires, and intentions, including proximal intentions. It is widely accepted in the literature that to intend to do something is to be settled on doing it. Intentions are closely related to plans. That makes intentions much like decisions. But it is a widespread misnomer to call intentions (or indeed decisions) 'executive states'. Legislatures make decisions and settle upon courses of action. Executives execute the plans or proposals. It is one thing to be settled on doing something, or to have decided to do it, as that is a legislative function, but it is quite another to execute, or to commence the execution of, what has been settled or decided upon, which is an executive function.

There are about as many views about the nature of intentions, as there are Carter's Little Liver Pills.[11] I can't do justice to them all. I will return to the issue of intentions in Chap. 4. The only point I need to insist on here is that Landry's patient had the intention, even the proximal intention, and still did nothing. Intending to raise his arm was not enough on its own to lead him to raise his arm. It was not enough to lead to action and it would also not be enough to lead to his surprise at his action failure.

The thought is this: someone could be in all those mental states and still not act, even in the case in which the intention to act is a proximal intention to do something now and nothing internal or external to the agent prevents or blocks the agent's acting. Inertia, forgetfulness, lack of know how, weakness of will, procrastination, distraction, or inattention might intervene, so that the agent does not do what he has settled on doing at once, although he has not changed his intention, and nothing prevents him for acting. Sarah Paul sums up the point: '…while we might assume that God never procrastinates or forgets to do what he intends, we sublunary creatures cannot say the same. Quite simply, for us, merely having an intention falls far short of ensuring that we will get it done'; 'We are not divine agents; there is a gap for us between intending and doing' (Sarah Paul, 1 and 19, 2009).

This argument seems to me sound in cases in which the intention is an event or state whose occurrence predates the initiation of the action. I think of a proximate intention to do something now as an intention that leaves at least a tiny gap in time between intention and action: first, the agent intends to do something now, and then commences doing it. If a proximate intention were simultaneous with the action for which it is the intention, then of course there could be no such intentions in Landry-style cases, since there are no actions. In those cases, since there are no actions, a fortiori there could be no proximate intentions in that sense. So I do not think my argument applies to what has been called 'intention-in-action'. (Of course if no action, no intention-in-action either.) If a finite amount of time, however small, elapses between the time of coming to hold the proximate intention to F and time of the intended action, to F (I do not claim that all actions and intentions conform to what has been called this simple model), there is always space for Descartes' Evil Genius to do his dirty work. He could make us forget what we intended to do. Alternatively, imagine a super-scatter-brained agent, easily distracted by all manner of things, who, after deciding to F, and forming the proximal intention to do so, finds his mind just wanders elsewhere in that brief interlude. I will return to the question of intentions and their relation to trying in Chap. 4.

On my view, the desires, beliefs, and intentions, even proximal ones, by themselves do not get us close enough to the action, as it were. There must be, it might be thought, some missing link to bridge the gap between the aforementioned mental states and the action (when of course the agent is successful). (More on bridging the gap in Chap. 4.) Something more than the beliefs, desires, and intentions must provide a bridge, from the agent's having these mental states, leading all the way up to the action. The agent must have tried, in addition to have intended, wanted, and so on. So if Landry's patient is surprised, while not knowing about the internal and external physical conditions that prevented his action, it must be because he tried but failed. If the agent is surprised, some sort of endeavouring must have gone on. So he must have tried if surprised, but since no action whatever results from his trying, this type of trying is 'naked trying' (cf. Hornsby 1980, 40–42).

A possible rejoinder to my argument might go like this. In order to explain his surprise, do we really need to assume that he really did try? Would it not be enough to assume that he falsely believed that he had tried? If he believes that he tried, but unbeknownst to him his belief is false, then he would be surprised in the same way as he would have been had his belief about his trying been true. So the idea would be that he might falsely believe that he has moved his limb, and hence be surprised, not because he did try to move it, but because he falsely believed that he has tried to move it.

The argument against this suggestion runs as follows. We assume that the person who falsely believes that he has tried to F is rational. Perhaps there are some beliefs of an agent, for which there is no possible evidence, neither other beliefs that entail or support them nor experiences that non-propositionally justify them. But when that is not the case, a rational person only believes what his evidence supports or justifies. If there is or can be evidence for a person's belief that he has tried, then a rational agent believes that he has tried to F only if his evidence, whatever it might be, supports or justifies his belief that he has tried to F.

What evidence might he have that encourages him to falsely believe that he has tried to move his limb? Well, he does believe that he has moved his limb (falsely, it transpires), and let us suppose that he also believes (in my view, truly) that if a person Fs intentionally, it follows that he has tried to F (that presupposes the Thesis of the Ubiquity of Trying (TUT)). But that is hardly going to help in this case, since we started by looking for an explanation of why he falsely believes that he has moved his limb and is surprised to find that he has not done so, in the absence of his believing anything about the constraints he faced (the explanandum), and the explanans being proposed is that it is because he falsely believes that he has tried to move his limb. We cannot then use the same explanandum, namely that he falsely believes that he has moved his limb, as the explanans for why he falsely believes he has tried to move it, on pain of circularity.

In fact, the only plausible evidence he could have for falsely believing that he has moved his limb is that he has in fact tried to move it, and not just that he falsely believes that he has tried to move it. We require some error theory for Landry's patient's false belief that he has moved his limb and I do not think there are any other plausible candidates for explaining this other than that he has tried to move it. So it is perfectly plausible to ascribe to Landry's patient his trying to move his limb, and since no action ensured, the trying is naked.

The Denial of Naked Trying

Some philosophers agree that there is such a phenomenon as naked trying. Hornsby defended the idea: 'even if all actions are tryings, not all tryings are actions' (Hornsby, 42; McCann 1975; Annas 1977–78; Davis 1979, 16). More recently, Gideon Yaffe has also taken this view: '…trying need not be, itself, an action' (Yaffe, 91). Yaffe doesn't mention the Landry case explicitly, but he has something like this in mind: in the case of a paralysed patient, all that may happen is that acetylcholine might be released by the postsynaptic nerve that normally activates the muscles but which may in the case of the paralysed patient be blocked (Yaffe, 91). Other philosophers have denied the possibility of naked trying.[12] Wittgenstein might have denied the possibility (if we equate willing and trying) but it is not easy to decipher what exactly he means by his aphorisms on this topic (Wittgenstein 1984, 86).

On the other hand, Thor Grünbaum, George Wilson, and Timothy Cleveland have offered several arguments against the possibility of total action failure, and these are the only sustained philosophical discussions of the Landry phenomenon post-William James of which I am aware (in contrast to the Landry case merely being rather frequently mentioned or cited en passant). In dealing with Landry cases, there appear to be two options: deny that there are any Landry-like cases and hence save the Physical Action Identity Theory in its initial form; accept that there are Landry-like cases and modify the Physical Action Theory to include options for physical action which are inside-the-agent rather than world-side.

Thor Grünbaum takes the first option; he denies that there are any such cases. My disagreement with Grünbaum is actually more limited than might at first appear. Here is what we disagree about:

(A) There are cases of naked trying, i.e., cases in which, for some F, it is true that the agent tries to F but in which there is no action whatever that the agent succeeds in doing.

I think (A) is true; Grünbaum thinks that (A) is false. But Grunbäum's target is what he calls New Volitionalism (it doesn't matter what that is, it is just important to note that it is not the view I hold). As a consequence, he takes the naked trying assumed by (A), and whose existence he denies, to be a mental particular: '2.2 An agent's trying to F is an independent mental particular-a mental event capable of existing independently of any bodily or otherwise worldly effects' (Grünbaum 2008, 68). He also assumes that his opponent holds that if cases of naked trying show that there is such a mental particular in Landry-like cases, then the same mental particular would occur in all cases of trying, normal as well as pathological cases.

Both he and I agree that there are no mental particulars that might be called 'tryings'. The theory of trying I develop in Chap. 4 shows how and why this is so. I do not think that the truth of (A) requires trying mental particulars. Grünbaum raises some interesting and compelling points about what the phenomenology of these naked trying particulars could be like, if there were any. Compatibly with my view that there are no trying particulars, I think that there is no phenomenology associated with an agent trying to do something, just as there is no phenomenology associated, for example, with an agent being free to do something, or believing some proposition.[13] Grunbäum's scepticism about the phenomenology that could be associated with naked trying particulars is consistent with what I want to hold. I therefore don't face the sorts of issues William James faced in his dispute with Mach on the existence of a sense of enervation, to which Grünbaum refers.

Since I hold the Thesis of the Ubiquity of Trying (TUT),[14] that, for all physical action types F, whenever an agent Fs intentionally, it follows that he has tried to F, it would be extraordinary if trying per se did have a phenomenology. In most cases of action, we are not aware of trying; awareness of trying occurs, when it does, only in cases that are hard, or about whose success we harbour doubts. If trying always had a phenomenology, it would be more difficult to account for the fact that in most normal cases of action, we are unaware that we try, even though we do try.

Moreover, my opponent, but not his, is the physical action theory of trying. I assume that that theory can be shown to be false if there is even a single case of an agent trying and yet there is no action that agent succeeds in doing. So I do not necessarily assume that all the features of Landry-like cases can be generalised in any interesting way to all cases of trying, including normal action cases. I only assume that Landry-like cases show us that the Physical Action Theory of trying is false.

There are some points that Grünbaum makes that are independent of the any view of trying as a mental particular and that therefore do need a reply. One is this: Grünbaum challenges his opponent to show what distinction could be drawn between idly wishing to move one's body and nakedly trying to move one's body (Grünbaum 72–75). Since the agent allegedly does nothing in a case of naked trying, how can we justify the thought that what the agent is doing is a bona fide trying rather than just idly wishing? Both idly wishing and trying have the same world-to-mind direction of fit. What is the difference between them if we are not allowed to include the idea that in trying the agent must succeed in doing something?

There is an answer to Grünbaum's challenge. Idly wishing is not an executive state in the sense that I give to that term. To idly wish that p (and similarly, to merely hope that p) is not necessarily to have any plan for bringing about that p. Idle wishing may have, unlike trying, no connection with practical thought and action. 'What distinguishes…[trying to move my arm] from other mental acts such as idly wishing that it moves? The answer appears to be that…[the former] is practical though' (Duff 1996, 275). Someone who tries will have some idea, however rough and ready, about how to achieve what he wants.

There is also an epistemic difference: the person who tries will believe that he has some chance of success, however small. He can't think that it is utterly impossible that he will succeed. If the agent is absolutely certain that he can't F, whatever he does can't be construed as his trying to F, but at most his trying to show others, or perhaps himself, that he can't F after all.[15] The idle wisher might be certain that he could never obtain that for which he merely wishes.

Wishes have propositions as their objects; tryings do not. Wishing and trying, including naked trying, relate to action in different ways. I will only be able to explain this contrast more fully after I have developed my own account of trying in Chap. 4. The account that I there offer for trying is inapplicable to wishing, or idly wishing, and this is another crucial way in which the two differ.

The second option I mentioned above is to accept that there are Landry-like cases and modify the Physical Action theory from the initial way I presented it, as a world-side theory, to include options for physical action that are inside the agent rather than world-side. (Remember, I mean by 'inside' only 'not at the surface of the agent's body or beyond'.) What sense can we give to the thought that there may be such inside-the-agent physical actions? What might they be? Perhaps such actions are events of muscular contraction or flexing. But in cases of naked trying that arise from complete paralysis, there may even be none of those.

Some philosophers hold that there are mental actions; everyone holds that there are brain (and hence physical) events. When neither any world-side action nor the contracting of muscles occurs, some sort of brain or other neurological activity must go on at the same time as the agent tries to move his hand. We are not like the Straw Man in the Wizard of Oz, who can act in the absence of a brain. Perhaps the persistent physical action theorist will give up on the physical action being world-side and could argue that the agent's token trying=his token brain activity.

This is the line of argument taken by George Wilson and Timothy Cleveland. Looking back to the presentation of the theories at the beginning of the chapter, it is apparent that their concern is to connect trying with physical action, not necessarily to world-side physical action, as we first construed their theories. If there can be physical action that is internal to the agent, in some sense, that option would be available to them in dealing with cases of naked trying.

Using the idea of a de re intention, Wilson says that in a pathological case, '…to put it bluntly, electro-chemical activity … [occurs] in the brain … Why can we not say that it is this activity of the paralyzed man that was intended, by him, to make his arm rise?' (161). 'Activity' can refer either to an action or to a non-actional process, as in 'there was a great deal of sun spot activity recently.' By activity, both Wilson and Cleveland mean action. Wilson and Cleveland say repeatedly that the brain activity (or movement) is something the agent performs.[16]

'Movement' can refer either to an action, using 'to move' in the transitive sense, or to a passive event, using 'to move' in an intransitive sense. (I deal with this distinction fully in Chaps. 5, 6 and 7.) But I will ignore marking the distinction here in those terms, using instead the terms they have chosen for the discussion. ('Performing an action' is something of a neologism, but let's let that pass. In later chapters, I often speak of 'doing an action', and that is really no better. I think one could avoid these expressions but so doing would involve more cumbersome circumlocution.)

In the case of the paralysed man, their idea would be this: 'The agent performed a movement and intended of that movement that it cause his arm to rise'. In such a case, the brain activity is the action the agent performs, but his intentions about it are claimed to be de re, so the agent may have no real knowledge about the nature of the brain movement or even that it is brain movement. This allows Wilson (and Cleveland) to dodge the objection that the agent 'must have some intrinsic awareness of' the brain activity. The agent 'can intend of activity that it do so-and-so, even if [he has] no awareness of what that activity consists in' (162). An agent who believes that he has no brain could still have such a de re intention. (One of Cervantes' characters is a madman who believes that his body is made entirely of glass.)

Wilson says that the agent might only be aware that he is doing something or other intended to lead to a certain result, he may have no other knowledge about what that something is. So, for Wilson and Cleveland, the agent's trying at time t=his brain activity at t. The brain activity is the agent's action. If so, there would be no naked trying after all. Even naked trying is accompanied by physical action, on this account, but physical action that is inside the agent rather than world-side. Such a physical action theorist could then identify the trying with that physical action, viz., with the brain activity.

They are committed to the view that in the paralysed arm case, the agent not only has a general intention to F (which is what he is trying to do) but also that he has a de re intention about something else, such that he intends, concerning whatever it is, that it cause his F-ing. He is, however, in the dark about exactly what that latter intention is about, what its content is. So he has no general intention regarding that activity for whose performance he has the de re intention.

There are a number of things wrong with their suggested way of dealing with naked trying. First, why attribute two intentions to the person (the general intention to F, and the de re intention to do whatever causes him to F) only in the case of naked trying? If a person has a de re intention in the naked trying case, and since no one can be certain before they try to act, even in the case of basic action, whether they will succeed, if there is a de re intention in the pathological case, there ought with equal reason be such a de re intention in all cases of trying, including non-pathological cases. There is, after all, brain activity in all cases of action, both pathological and non-pathological. So all cases of trying to act should be accompanied by an extra de re intention. But that really is extravagant.

Moreover, even if one wants to add an extra intention to pathological cases, or even to both pathological and non-pathological cases, why must it be a de re intention? Perhaps we should simply accept that in a pathological case, the agent fails to have any de re intentions at all in Wilson's sense and has only an additional general intention. The agent might only have a general intention in such a case; he intends that he perform some action that will cause his raising of his arm (but of course he fails to perform any such action). Such a general intention would not be 'directed' at any particular action or activity or movement.

Second, what exactly is the content of this alleged de re intention? Wilson says: 'The agent performed a movement and intended of that movement that it cause his arm to rise'. But intending, of a movement, that it cause his arm to rise is not necessarily to intend to act, even de re, and so 'the agent performed a movement (acted)' does not follow from 'the agent intended, of some movement, that it cause his arm to rise'.

Why is this so? I can discover a device to which I am hooked up, and that will lead, via some complicated wiring, to my arm's rising. Part of that device is the movement of clock hands. If I don't disconnect the device from myself, I can intend, concerning that clock's movement, that it causes my arm to rise, but intending something of that movement does not make its movement, or anything else, into an action of mine. Putting the clock with its hand inside me should not make a difference to its status. Isn't the internalised clock like my brain? I can intend de re, of some of my brain movements-whatever they may be-that they cause my arm to rise, but that might yield by itself no action of mine.

Third, what would it take to make the movement in the brain an action, even suppose an unintentional action, if having a de re intention about the movements alone were insufficient? Wilson poses what I take to be the major objection to his own view: '...there may be some residual worry about whether electro-chemical activity in the brain...can be activity that the agent performs' (164). He says that he cannot see that this is a substantive issue, because he sees the issue as one about the ordinary use of 'performs', which he suggests can simply be extended to cover brain activity if it doesn't cover it already. I agree with Wilson thus far: given certain limitations to be described below, I concur that in principle 'electro-chemical activity in the brain...can be activity that the agent performs.'

It is easy to state a contrary case to Wilson and Cleveland (which neither they nor I would accept): brain activity is not an action; it is nothing the agent does (or performs, as they say). Not everything internal to an agent that is a necessary condition for (or a cause of) his action is itself an action.

But here is a possible further reply to that too easy contrary case, a reply in defence of Wilson and Cleveland. Joel Feinberg spoke of the accordion effect of action: 'We can if we wish, inflate our conception of an action to include one of its effects...Instead of saying that Peter did A...and thereby caused X in Y, we might say something of the form, "Peter X-ed Y"....' (Joel Feinberg 1970, 134).[17] (I will return to the accordion effect in Chap. 5. It is not something I accept in its unrestricted form, but more on that much later.)

By puffing out the action, many of the things that Smith does, like X-ing, will be unintended, or anyway unintended under the description 'X-ing'. For example, in a well-known example, the agent turned on the light and as a causal consequence the prowler was unintentionally alerted. It is true that the agent alerted the prowler, although his action of alerting him was unintentional (or unintentional under that description).

But instead of only puffing out action forward or outwards into the world, why not also deflate action backwards or inwards into the agent? Don't think of the accordion as fully deflated at the surface of the agent's body. At the surface of the agent's body, the accordion is only half 'puffed out'. It can then be either more fully inflated outwards or more fully deflated inwards.

So where a token event f's (of type F) occurrence at t is a cause internal to Smith of his G-ing at t*, can we not also say, at least in some cases, that Smith F-ed, perhaps unintentionally? Smith's neurones fired at t. So since the accordion can extend backwards as well as forwards, we might say that Smith fired his neurones, and he fired them by (say) moving his arm at t*. (I leave open until Chap. 6 the question of what the time would be at which he fired his neurones, t or t*?) The 'by' here is of course teleological and not temporal. His neurones' firing at t occurs before his moving of his arm at t*, although he only does the former by doing the latter. There can be, on this way of looking at the matter, unintended causes as well as unintended effects of action, both of which might sometimes count as unintended actions by the agent. Smith can fire his neurones just as he can alert the prowler, both unintentionally.

Deflating the accordion isn't going to help the physical action theorist who wishes to identify trying with some brain activity. On the backwards-and-forwards accordion effect model, every unintended action (or action under its unintended description, but I shan't keep repeating this qualification) has to be built up from an unintended effect or an unintended cause of an intentional action. The prowler was alerted, so Smith alerted him; the neurones fired, so Smith fired his neurones. But this works only if the prowler being alerted or the neurones being fired are themselves either causes or effects of some intentional action the agent does, like his flipping of the switch in one case or his moving of his arm in the other.

But in the case of the totally paralysed arm, there is no other action, G-ing, such that it can be true that the agent performs a range of brain activity and the brain activity is an unintended cause of his G-ing intentionally. The point of the trying being allegedly naked is that there is no such action. If performing some brain movement is an unintended action, in the case of naked trying what would be the intentional or intended action in virtue of whose causes the agent can also unintentionally perform some brain activity? There is none.

So in non-pathological cases, it may be true that the agent fires some neurones, whether he knows or intends it or not, just as he has alerted the prowler whether he knows or intends it or not. Along with Wilson and Cleveland, I can accept that much. But specifically in the paralysed arm case, however, there are no grounds for taking the brain activity as intrinsic to any action the agent does. There is no accordion-like chain of actions, because there is no intentional action the agent does, backwards of which the agent might be said to fire his neurones unintentionally.

Although there is certainly brain activity going on in this case as in all others, he doesn't 'perform' a brain movement at all, let alone one about which he has a de re intention. The identification that Wilson and Cleveland propose assumes that we have grounds for thinking that there is such an action as firing one's neurones (or performing brain activity), and so that the trying is not naked. But there simply are no independent grounds for believing that the agent fires his neurones or 'performs' any brain activity in this sort of case. The brain activity could be an unintended action only if it is the cause of something else the agent does intentionally. But that necessary condition is no satisfied. The existence of activity in the brain of the agent does not stop his trying from being naked.

What exactly does the argument from naked tryings show? The mereological argument above purported to show that *no* act of trying (if there were such a thing) could be identified with a physical action or the mereological sum of physical actions or a conjunction of physical actions. The argument from naked trying might be construed as showing that only *some* tryings are not identical to physical actions. That is a weaker position and is compatible with a rejection of the conclusion of the mereological argument.

But I draw a stronger conclusion from the naked trying argument. With regard to the difference between successful and unsuccessful acts of trying, I said above: 'Why not say that the temporal part of his trying to stop the flood is identical to the lowering of the barrier when the agent successfully lowers the barrier, but not otherwise? This is a perfectly possible theory but it creates a partition among tokens of trying in an unexpected way that otherwise has no motivation. It commits us to two kinds of trying when from all appearances they seemed to be a homogenous class, and it still leaves us with the identification question for the tryings to lower the barrier in the case of failure.' To hold that some tryings are identical to physical actions (or conjunctions or sums thereof) but that only naked tryings are not, would create a partition among tokens of trying in an unexpected way that otherwise has no motivation. It commits us to two kinds of trying when from all appearances they seemed to be a homogenous class. And again it leaves us with no theory of naked trying. It seems plain that 'trying' is being used univocally in naked and non-naked cases. I infer that if the identification of a naked trying with a physical action fails, then the identification of any trying with a physical action fails.

Conclusion

The result of this chapter then is to support the view that there are naked tryings, tryings such that there are no physical actions, either world-side or inside-the-agent, with which they can be identified. Let me stress the obviously close connection between the physical actions by which one tries (when there are such) and what it is that one tries to do. That there is a close connection is surely obvious. The question is: what is the nature of that close connection, if not identification? My view is the most natural and simplest one: they are the actions by which the agent tries. Just as physical actions can have by-acts, there can be by-acts for trying. Just as agents can G by F–ing, so too an agent can try to G by F-ing. But this offers no comfort to a physical action theorist of trying. The conclusion is that there is no physical action (or sum of such) that the agent does such that his trying in the pathological case, or indeed in any case, is identical to that action or their sum.

This leaves us with the outstanding question of just what trying is, if not identical to any physical action. In the next two chapters, I address that outstanding question.

Notes

1. Jennifer Hornsby (1980) identifies trying as an internal event ('...[try-ings]are always internal events' (1980s, 45)) and hence places tryings on the inside of the agent. Other volitionists include Hugh McCann (1998), Paul Pietroski (2000), Brian O'Shaughnessy (1980) and Carl Ginet (1990).

2. Olivier Massin's particularist view of trying is more complicated: the trying is identified with an action done with a certain intention, i.e., Julie's trying to open the door=her pushing [of] the door with the intention of opening it (Massin 2013, and in private correspondence).
3. These issues are covered in Gozanno, Simone and Christopher Hill, editors, 2012.
4. Throughout the book, I call a theory of act individuation austere if it finds the multiplicity in the descriptions, so that 'his improving of the inhabitants' lives', 'his stopping of the flood', 'his closing of the sluice', 'his turning of the valve', and 'his bending of his finger' are all descriptions of a single action. A theory of act individuation is prolific if it finds the multiplicity in the actions themselves rather than in the descriptions. There are degrees of prolificacy: the most prolific theory holds that the above list names five distinct actions. A less prolific theory might hold that the list names less than five but more than one action.
5. Why the same result does not follow for substances, or for certain events and actions, is a long story, assumed to be true but not to be told here at any length. Briefly, two strategies are these: properties are (1) either time-indexed or world-indexed when ascribed for instance to a substance, (2) or ascribed not to the whole substance but to one of its temporal parts.
6. Peter Simons, *Parts: A Study in Ontology*, OUP, 2000, who disagrees.
7. Simon Evnine (2016) 'The times at which they are performed, therefore, cannot in general be essential to the identity of actions.'
8. William James describes the cases of the patients of Dr. Landry and Professor Strümpell. See William James (1950), 490–492.
9. See for example some of the literature, and quotations, in the note below this one.
10. Here are several recent major discussions of effort or exertion in which it is simply assumed that trying or attempting always also occurs and that it is not to be identified with exertion or effort:
    1. 'Exertion is accompanied by a sensation of strain and labour, a feeling that intensifies the harder a person tries', 'even if capacity is completely extinguished so that efferent activity is not possible (e.g., in paralysis), then no effort is felt even when intentionally trying to move', 'When people are trying to solve problems together, effort experiences can be the basis for unintended plagiarism' (Jesse Preston and Daniel Wegner (2008), quotes from 570, 571, 578 respectively).

2. Similarly in a second patient...futile attempts to abduct or extend the fingers were described as follows: 'My fingers felt normal but I could not move them. I knew what I was trying to do...but I could not feel any effort in it at all', 'To determine whether sensations of effort could arise when the limbs were not only paralysed but also insentient four patients with spinal transections were interviewed. These patients were aware of sensations of effort when first attempting to move their paralysed limbs...when specifically asked to try and move their limbs, patients said that the feeling of effort or heaviness remained', '...during the stage of complete paralysis of upper motor neuron type patients were aware of their failed attempts to move. But they did not feel the sense of effort...' 'Two patients, who suddenly became hemiplegic, without sensory symptoms, noted that attempts to move when movement first returned were accompanied by distinct sensations of effort or heaviness' (S. C. Gandevia 1982, quotes from 154, 155, 157).
3. 'Subjects with experimental paralysis of one limb experience strong sensations of effort when they attempt to move that limb...The same hypothesis would account for permanence of sensations of effort in all cases of distal paralysis, where corticofugal pathways are not altered' (M. Jeannerod 1995, 1429).

11. See Sarah Paul (2009) for a good discussion of the options for understanding intention.
12. See for example Thor Grünbaum (2008); Richard Taylor (1973), 82–85, 'The Paralyzed Man'; Timothy Cleveland (1997), chapter 6; George Wilson (1989), 151–167. Irving Thalberg is excessive in his judgment: 'Vesey ... rebutted several versions of it [that there is naked trying] ... Richard Taylor demolished an enticing reconstruction of it...Yet it comes back to haunt us...' (Thalberg 1983, 137). Indeed, so it does. And here I am, to haunt again.
13. There is a view that even belief has a phenomenology, that there is something it is like to believe that p. See David Pitt (2011).
14. That ubiquity thesis must be something like this, where 'F' ranges over physical actions types and 'x' ranges over physical action tokens: (TUT) (Nec) (x) (F) (if P does a token action x of type F intentionally→ P tries to F).
15. If he succeeds in F-ing in spite of his subjective certainty that he can't, it isn't the case that he has F-ed intentionally. (I defend this view more fully in Chap. 4).

16. Wilson begs the question when he argues for the proper use of 'performs' in connection with muscular contractions, which he says 'are part of the exercise of my normal control over my body' (p. 164), thereby conflating the idea of things an agent controls with the idea of causes of his control. The expression 'are part of' could be taken in either sense.
17. See also Michael Bratman (2006), 5–19.

Bibliography

Annas, Julia. 1977. How Basic are Basic Actions? *Proceedings of the Aristotelian Society* LXXVIII: 195–213.
Bennett, Jonathan. 1998. *The Act Itself*. Oxford: Oxford University Press.
Bratman, Michael. 2006. What is the Accordion Effect? *Journal of Ethics* 10 (1): 5–19.
Buckareff, A. 2007. Mental Overpopulation and Mental Action: Protecting Intentions from Mental Birth Control. *Canadian Journal of Philosophy* 37 (1): 49–65.
Cleveland, Timothy. 1997. *Trying Without Willing*. Aldershot: Ashgate Publishing Company.
Davis, L. 1979. *Theory of Action*. Englewood Cliffs, NJ: Prentice-Hall.
Duff, R.A. 1996. *Criminal Attempts*. Oxford: Oxford University Press.
Ehring, Douglas. 1997. *Causation & Persistence*. New York: Oxford University Press.
Evnine, Simon. 2011. Constitution and Composition: Three Approaches to Their Relation. *ProtoSociology* 27: 212–235.
———. 2016. *Making Object and Events*. Oxford: Oxford University Press.
Feinberg, Joel. 1970. *Doing and Deserving*. Princeton: Princeton University Press.
Gandevia, S.C. 1982. The Perception of Motor Commands or Effort During Muscular Paralysis. *Brain* 105: 151–159.
Ginet, Carl. 1990. *On Action*. Cambridge: Cambridge University Press.
Goldman, Alvin. 1970. *A Theory of Human Action*. Englewood Cliffs, NJ: Prentice-Hall.
Grünbaum, Thor. 2008. Trying and the Argument from Total Failure. *Philosophia* 36 (1): 67–86.
Hornsby, Jennifer. 1980. *Actions*. London: Routledge & Kegan Paul.
———. 1995. Reasons for Trying. *Journal of Philosophical Research* XX: 525–539.

James, William. 1950. *Principles of Psychology*. Vol. 2. New York: Dover Publications.
Jeannerod, M. 1995. Mental Imagery in the Motor Context. *Neuropsychologica* 33 (11): 419–432.
Lewis, D. 1986. *Philosophical Papers*. Vol. II. Oxford: Oxford University Press.
Lombard, Lawrence. 1986. *Events: A Metaphysical Study*. London: Routledge & Kegan Paul.
Massin, Olivier. 2013. L'Explication de l'action. *Analyses contemporaines, Recherches sur la philosophie et le langage*, no. 30, Vrin, Paris.
McCann, Hugh. 1975. Trying, Paralysis, and Volition. *The Review of Metaphysics* 28 (3): 423–442. Reprinted in McCann (1998), 94–109.
———. 1998. *The Works of Agency*. Ithaca: Cornell University Press.
O'Shaughnessy, Brian. 1980. *The Will*. Vol. 1 and 2. Cambridge: Cambridge University Press.
Pattaro, Enrico. 2005. *A Treatise of Legal Philosophy and General Jurisprudence*. Vol. 1. Dordrect, Netherlands: Springer.
Paul, Sarah. 2009. How We Know What We are Doing. *Philosophers' Imprint* 9 (11): 1–24.
Pietroski, Paul. 2000. *Causing Actions*. Oxford: Oxford University Press.
Pitt, David. 2011. Introspection, Phenomenality. And the Availability of Intentional Content. In *Cognitive Phenomenology*, ed. Tim Bayne and Michelle Montague, 141–173. Oxford: Oxford University Press.
Preston, Jesse, and Daniel Wegner. 2008. Elbow Grease: When Action Feels Like Work. In *Oxford Handbook of Human Action*, ed. E. Morsella, John Bargh, and Peter Gollwitzer, 569–586. Oxford: Oxford University Press.
Simons, Peter. 2000. *Parts: A Study in Ontology*. Oxford: OUP.
Taylor, Richard. 1973. *Action and Purpose*. Englewood Cliffs, NJ: Prentice-Hall.
Thalberg, Irving. 1983. *Misconceptions of Mind and Freedom*. Lanham, MD: University Press of America.
Wilson, George. 1989. *The Intentionality of Human Action*. Stanford: Stanford University Press.
Wittgenstein, Ludwig. 1984. *Notebooks 1914–16*. 2nd ed. Chicago: University of Chicago Press.

3

Trying in Some Way

What's in the Chapter[1]

In the Introduction below, I describe and categorise the verb 'to try', making a number of important distinctions and introducing ideas that will be important in the book, for example, the imperfective paradox. I turn to a Davidsonian-like argument that would seek to show that there must be particular acts of trying, in order to account for the adverbial qualifications in trying-sentences. (The argument has some similarities to one that he did produce, but is not itself attributable to him.) Most of the chapter then moves through various categories of adverbs, arguing that none of them requires acts of trying to account for the adverbs in these sentences. Along the way, I discuss the opacity of 'to try'. There is an important distinction between adverbs that occur inside the context governed by 'to try' and those that occur outside that context, and I show how that distinction is important for assessing the strength of those Davidsonian-like arguments.

Since naked trying might be thought to pose a particularly difficult challenge for my claim, I then apply the same arguments to cases of naked trying, to show that sentences about naked trying that have an adverbial qualification do not require the adjectival modification of an act of trying. In Chap. 2, I argued that it is true that agents can sometimes nakedly try to do something. But it does not follow from that claim, that when an agent nakedly tries, there is some particular, an act of trying that occurs (but one that is unaccompanied by any action).

I discuss some further considerations from Jonathan Bennett and Artemis Alexiadou that would support my view that there are no trying particulars. Finally, I look at, and dismiss, some examples that might force the conclusion that there are trying particulars in spite of the failure of the arguments from adverbial attribution: reference back, causation, attempts in law, and attitudes.

Introduction

In Chap. 2, I described two different views about trying: an inside-the-agent view and a world-side view. I argued against what is perhaps the most obvious world-side option in Chap. 2. I also argued against a physicalist form of the inside-agent option. Does that suggest that some other inside-agent option is preferable, perhaps a form of volitionism? I want to show that the inside-agent and world-side options are not exhaustive, and that there is a third option that needs careful elaboration and evaluation. Chapter 3 is preparatory and its goal is quite limited; it dismisses an argument that might be thought to support an important but unarticulated assumption made by both the inside-agent and world-side proponents. Chapter 4 will develop that third alternative fully and reply to objections to that alternative view.

Let's begin by asking this question. Are there any particulars, token tryings to do such-and-such? I am not asking what metaphysical sort such particulars would be, only whether there are any at all, of any kind. The particulars, if there be such, might be mental or physical; they might be events or actions (David Armstrong once proposed that they would be token non-actional brain events (Armstrong 1981, 75)). It is a widespread assumption, for the most part unargued, that there are such particulars, but with little accompanying consensus about the metaphysical kind to which such particulars belong. I am going to use the expression, 'a particularist theory of trying' for any account of trying that construes at least some trying-sentences to be about or to presuppose the existence of such particulars. These accounts of trying accept what I call Assumption (A):

(A) If P tries to F, then there is some particular, a trying to F (or, an act of trying to F), by P.

Indications of the prevalence of this assumption about trying particulars are to be found in such uses of 'trying', as when it is accompanied by the definite and indefinite article, or by its pluralisation: 'a trying', 'the trying', and 'tryings'. More explicitly, the same assumption is revealed in the use of expressions such as 'act of trying' or 'event of trying'. I mark no distinction of importance between the expressions, 'trying particulars', 'acts of trying', and 'events of trying'. If P is a type or property, then it must be metaphysically possible for P to have instances or tokens. But I don't think that it is metaphysically possible for there to be token tryings or trying particulars. So it follows that I don't think that 'trying to F' (the whole expression) names or refers to a type or property. 'F' or even 'Fs' (whatever is inside the context governed by 'to try to') may name a property, an action property, as in 'the agent is F-ing' or 'the agent Fs'. Grammatically, 'trying to F' is a predicate, and it can be predicated of an agent. But that whole predicate does not stand for a property. Chapter 4 will explain what I think saying 'some agent tries to F' comes to, if it is not ascribing a property to that agent. In denying (A), I am denying that trying-sentences entail that there is either a trying or an act of trying, etc. I return to these themes at the end of the chapter, in my discussion of the difference between nominal and verbal gerunds.

It is of course true that agents try to do things, and also true that trying is something they do, if that just means that they try. Chapters 3 and 4 collectively will show how none of those truths entail commitment to particular tryings, and will offer an alternative way in which to understand those truths. Why would anyone want to deny (A)? Is there any advantage in denying (A)? I think there are important philosophical gains to be made by its denial. If 'P tries to F' entails or presupposes that there is some particular, a trying to F by P, then a host of questions naturally ensue, about the identity of the trying, its relation to other particulars, what it is caused by and what it causes, its location (inside or outside the body for example as we have seen), whether it is a mental or physical particular, whether it has parts and if so, what those parts are, and so on. If, on the other hand, Assumption A were false, then the questions of exactly to what 'P's trying to F' refers, to what metaphysical sort it belongs, and questions about its causal status, its spatio-temporal properties, identity conditions, mereological features, and so on, would not even arise. Those would be, I submit, real advantages accruing to such a theory of trying.

The point of this chapter is only to address one influential philosophical argument that might be used to support Assumption A. I know of no philosopher who has actually used the argument, but that is in itself unsurprising, since Assumption A is almost never articulated, the only exception known to me is Anthony Duff 1967, who, like me, denies the assumption (see note 1). This chapter is meant to show that what I have called the influential argument would offer, on careful reflection, no support whatever for this assumption. The philosophical argument to which I refer, which we can fairly label 'Davidsonian', is itself hardly unassailable. But I do not intend in this chapter to assail it, only to dispute its application to sentences about trying in such a way that would yield tryings as a type of particular. I do not claim that Davidson himself ever used this argument in the case of trying-sentences, or even that he would have had he discussed the issue. I intend to show how to construe adverbial modifications in trying-sentences so that they provide no argument for assumption (A). Our addressing this assumption about trying in this chapter will also help us to address similar questions about causing-sentences in Chap. 7.

Philosophers who make assumption (A) in one form or another include Brian O'Shaughnessy (1973), Richard Taylor (1973), Hugh McCann (1975), Jennifer Hornsby (1980), O.R. Jones (1983), and many others. As we have seen in Chap. 2, some philosophers hold that these particulars belong on the inside of the agent; others place them on the world-side. But for these philosophers, tryings turn out to be some sort of particular, on whatever side they are placed. The particularist assumption is so widespread that it is not clear that one can find almost any philosopher writing about trying who does not accept it in one form or another, explicitly or implicitly.² This widely shared assumption is consistent with a large variety of otherwise incompatible views held by various philosophers on the nature of trying.

'Trying' can be followed either by a noun phrase or by an infinitive. These constitute two different senses of 'try'. In 'try' followed by a noun phrase, as in 'try the stew', 'try one's patience', or 'try the defendant in court', 'to try' has the sense of 'to sample' or 'to test'. In 'try' followed by an infinitive, as in 'to try to F', 'try' has the sense of endeavor or attempt. (In what follows, I use 'try', 'endeavour', and 'attempt' as near synonyms and mark no useful distinctions between them.) The two senses of 'to try' have nothing to do with one another. 'Trying' in the sense of sampling or tasting has no necessary connection with attempting or endeavouring. The ideas of success and failure differ in the two cases. In the second sense, if I try but fail to F, it remains true that I did try to F. My failure to F does not impeach the fact that I tried to F. In the first sense, if I fail, it can only be because I did not try at all. I will have failed to try the curry, for example. A person can certainly try in one sense without trying in the other sense. In what follows, both in Chaps. 3 and 4, I restrict myself only to the case in which 'try' is followed by an infinitive. As it is sometimes said, in this sense, 'try to' makes a verb out of a verb.

'F', in 'try to F', might not refer to an action; one can after all try to look pretty, to be good, or to be popular. But when it does refer to an action, the action can be either mental or physical. A person can try to row a boat, or try to add some numbers 'in his head'. Are there some mental actions with which no chance of failure is associated? Under what conditions will or would I succeed? If I can't fail, can I try? For example, if I try to think, doesn't it follow that I have succeeded to think just insofar as I have tried? Important questions indeed, but I have my work cut out for me just with physical actions that an agent tries to do. As in Chap. 2, and as I also will do in Chap. 4, in this chapter too I restrict my account to cases of trying to do physical actions.

Apart from the gerund 'trying', there is a derived or perfect nominal (perfect nominals are non-gerundive) formed from the verb 'to try': 'trials'. 'Trial' derives from the second sense of 'try' in which it is followed by a noun or noun phrase (and which I have excluded from discussion). I eschew any discussion of 'endeavour' as a verb or as a perfect nominal. Its grammatical behaviour is somewhat special. 'Endeavour' is a perfect nominal and as such it can be pluralised: 'P's endeavours to reduce personal injury claims was welcomed by the insurance industry' makes perfect sense. But as the quote from Hobbes in Chap. 2 showed, sometimes its singular use seems preferable when one might have expected a plural form: 'These small beginnings of Motion, within the body of Man, before they appear in walking, speaking, striking, and other visible actions, are commonly called ENDEAVOUR' (Leviathan, Chapter VI). In these cases, 'endeavour' behaves more like a mass noun than a count noun, making it somewhat similar to 'energy' and the likes: 'Endeavour is usually richly rewarded', and not 'endeavours', similar to 'many participants in the contest showed great energy', and not 'great energies'. I return to 'attempt' at the end of the chapter. In law, there are crimes of attempt: attempted murder, attempted rape, attempted theft, for example. One should not assume, without argument, that the sense of 'to attempt' in this specialised legal usage is the same as the sense in the more general usage that I will be or have been discussing. I will return to this question, later in this chapter.

Verbs can take imperfective aspect. How to characterise exactly what imperfectivity indicates is controversial: interior point of view, intrusitivity, ongoing or repeated occurrence, and other suggestions have been offered (see Robert Allen 1966, 218 and ff. for an early attempt at characterisation). For the needs of this book, we need only to indicate the form such imperfective aspect takes in English: 'is, was, or will be, verb-ing'. I shall mostly use, as imperfective aspect examples, verbs in the past or present tense (there is also an imperfect verb tense, not to be confused with imperfective aspect). Behind the contrast between perfective and imperfective aspect for verbs lies a metaphysical contrast between actions-in-progress and actions-as-completed, which is the justification for the focus on the grammatical contrast in this book. In Chap. 6, I describe how each of the pair in the metaphysical contrast relates differently to assignments of time.

When some verbs are used in imperfective aspect, the so-called imperfective paradox arises: for those verbs, if P was F-ing object o (imperfective aspect), it does not follow that he (ever) F-ed o. 'Closing' (in its transitive use) is such a verb. If P was closing the door, it does NOT follow that he ever closed the door. He may have been closing it but abandoned the task before the door was closed. Verbs like 'close', 'open', 'draw', and many, many others contrast with other verbs, like 'push', 'pull', and 'watering (the flowers)', that are not subject to the imperfective paradox: if agent P was pushing a cart during some interval of time (imperfective aspect), it follows that P pushed a cart in every subinterval of the time during which he was pushing it.

A good test for whether a verb passes the imperfective paradox test is this: does the perfective + 'throughout' make sense? If the verb does not pass the test, it is subject to the paradox. So for example, if the time over which P was pushing the cart was t-t*, then it is true that P pushed the cart throughout t-t*. So 'push' passes the test and is not subject to the paradox. On the other hand, if P was closing the door from t-t*, he has not closed the door throughout that time (that makes no obvious sense). True, he was closing it during that time, but he only closed the door at the end, if he finished the task, at t*. 'Close' in this usage fails the test and is subject to the paradox.

There are many other ways in which to classify verbs too, so let me just distinguish rather simply between telic verbs that have a specific endpoint (like 'to close' as above) and atelic verbs (like 'to push', as above) that do not.[3] When P closes the door, he can't be closing that door anymore once the door is closed (unless of course someone subsequently opens the door again and he has to re-close it, in which case there would be a second token closing of the door). On the other hand, when P pushes the cart, he could be pushing the cart forever. The token pushing episode has no specific endpoint, after which P can push no longer. A good test for a verb's being atelic is the 'keep-on-verb-ing test'. If in principle the agent can keep on F-ing endlessly on this token occasion of his F-ing, the verb is atelic. Of course, an agent can always keep on F-ing, whether 'F' is a telic or atelic verb, in the sense that the agent might F on other occasions. The agent can do it again. He can always engage in new episodes of F-ing. But that is not the sense the 'keep-on-verb-ing' test requires. That test asks: can the agent keep on extending this episode of his F-ing?

Is the verb 'to try' telic or atelic? Is it subject to the imperfective paradox or not? 'To try' does not fit the standard pattern, in which telic verbs tend to be subject to the imperfective paradox and atelic verbs do not tend to be subject to it. For example, as we have seen, 'to close (the door)' is telic and subject to the paradox; 'to push a cart' is atelic and not subject to the paradox.

First, like 'push (a cart)', 'try' is not subject to the imperfective paradox. If P is or was trying to close the door throughout a time period, it follows that he has tried to close it in every subinterval of that time. If P is or was trying, he tried. This is true whether or not 'to F' is itself subject to the imperfective paradox, whether P is trying to push the cart or trying to close the door. 'Try' passes the perfective + 'throughout' test. If P was trying to F from t-t*, P tried throughout that period to F, whether he succeeded or not in F-ing. True, P won't have finished trying in every subinterval, but he will have tried in every subinterval. So 'to try' is never subject to the imperfective paradox, irrespective of the verb that follows it.

That 'to try' is not subject to the imperfective paradox seems to me clear. But whether it is a telic verb deserves more careful attention. I think that the verb 'to try' is telic, when the second verb is telic, and atelic when the second verb is atelic. Take first a telic verb. If P is trying to close the door, he has reached the goal of his trying once the door has been closed. He can't keep on trying to F, once he has F-ed. So 'try' is telic in combination with 'close (the door)'. Then consider an atelic verb: if P is trying to push a cart, he might keep on trying forever, never reaching any natural conclusion. So 'try' is atelic in combination with 'push (a cart)'. (In Chap. 4, I argue that the agent has to be trying to F for as long as he is F-ing.) So 'try' has either a telic or atelic character, depending on the second verb's status.

Philosophers who think that tryings are particulars may have reasons for thinking that they are, other than the Davidsonian one, and I deal with some of those further reasons at the end of this chapter. As I mentioned above, I have no intention to subject Davidson's theory of events to any criticism, but only to dispute its application to trying-sentences in such a way that would require acts or events of trying. At the end of the chapter, mention is made of another reason, based on some work by Jonathan Bennett and Artemis Alexiadou, for believing that trying-sentences do not require acts of trying or any type of trying particular in their truth-conditions.

Since I am treating 'to attempt' as synonymous with 'to try', I will also need to say some things about that first verb too. It would be somewhat disappointing if 'to attempt' required particular attempts, even if 'to try' did not require particular tryings. That result would make the point I am making about 'to try' merely a peculiarity of grammar, with little or no metaphysical significance. Happily, I don't think that is the case.

Davidson's Argument

Donald Davidson's argument for the existence of events is widely known. The argument is straightforward and, in spite of dissenters,[4] still commands widespread acceptance. In spite of the dissenters, I will accept the general form of the argument here and do not seek to dispute it. My question will only be: can this argument also be applied to the case of 'to try'?

Davidson's argument is this: there are certain logical relations between sentences, principally commutation and simplification, which cannot be reconstructed without a commitment to events as part of the logical form of such sentences. The sentences are ones in which there is an adverbial qualification (either by adverbs or by prepositional phrases): 'P F-ed in a G-ish way', or 'P F-ed G-ly'. For example, to use part of one of Davidson's own examples:

(1) Jones buttered the toast in the bathroom, with a knife, at midnight.
(1) entails both (2) and (3):
(2) Jones buttered the toast with a knife. (By simplification)
(3) Jones buttered the toast at midnight, in the bathroom, with a knife.
 (By commutation)

Davidson argued that the inference from (1) to (2) and from (1) to (3) cannot be captured without recourse to events, in this case a buttering. What was grammatically an adverb becomes, once the logical structure of the sentence is revealed, an adjective of, or a prepositional phrase attaching adjectivally to, the corresponding action or event (assuming also a uniqueness condition: e.g., he buttered the toast only once). It was the one and only buttering that was done at midnight, with a knife, and in the bathroom.

If one uses this argument form and applies it to the case of 'to try', since there are some sentences like 'P tried to F G-ly', we might appear to be committed to trying particulars that are G. We can swallow Davidson's events of buttering, running, and kicking, along with the toast, but do we also have to thereby swallow trying particulars, i.e., trying events or actions? What of particular causings, since there also appear to be sentences with the form, 'P caused e G-ly'? In this chapter, I deal with the question of trying particulars; in Chap. 7, with the question of causing particulars.

A Note on Davidson's Logical Form Proposal

We have seen how imperfectivity works for verbs. How does it work for gerunds? There is a distinction that I will discuss in detail later in the chapter, between nominal and verbal gerunds. For now, let me just indicate the difference by example: 'the closing of the door' is a nominal gerund and behaves like a noun; 'closing a door' is a verbal gerund and is verb-like in its behaviour.

Do sentences with gerunds ever entail a sentence with the perfective form of the verb from which the gerund is formed? 'P was carefully watching P*'s closing of the door [the nominal gerund], but unfortunately P* never finished closing it, so it was never closed.' 'Closing the door [the verbal gerund] was very difficult for P*, so he gave up half-way and the door was never closed.' Both gerunds seem subject to the paradox. Alexiadou argues that the verbal gerund ('P's closing the door') is subject to the paradox but that the nominal gerund ('P's closing of the door') 'does not trigger aspect shift' (135). But I can see no reason to distinguish them on this score. No sentence using either of the gerundial forms of the transitive 'to close' entails that a door or whatever was ever closed. If a verb is subject to the imperfective paradox and is telic, both of its gerunds are also subject to the paradox.

What about the nominal and verbal gerunds formed from a verb that is not subject to the imperfective paradox and is not telic: 'The farmer's pushing the cart' and 'The farmer's pushing of the cart'? I think both gerunds do entail that the cart was pushed, and this is surely unsurprising given that the verb from which they are formed is not itself subject to the imperfective paradox.

The verbal gerundial (I will argue that there is no nominal gerund) of 'to try' ('his trying to F') conforms to the same pattern we saw with the verb 'to try'. Just as 'to try' is never subject to the paradox, whether the verb that follows it is or is not subject to the paradox, so too the verbal gerund is never subject to the paradox. If his trying to push the cart by himself was foolish, it does entail that he tried, and indeed that he tried foolishly. If his trying to close the door was also foolish, that also entails that he tried even though he never closed it.

It seems to me that this observation has a consequence for the Davidsonian proposal for the logical form of action sentences. For example, Davidson says that the logical form of (a) 'Shem kicked Shaun' (the Left Hand Side, LHS) is (b) 'There is an event x such that x is a kicking of Shaun by Shem' (the Right Hand Side, RHS) (Davidson 2001, 118–119). Surely this can't be quite right for telic verbs that are subject to the imperfective paradox. Consider 'P closed the door iff there is an event x such that x is a closing of the door by P.' The LHS sentence, 'P closed the door', entails that the door was closed, whereas, since the verb 'to close' is subject to the paradox, the gerundive use of 'close', i.e., 'closing', in the RHS does not entail that the door was closed.

Neither the verb in imperfective aspect, 'he was closing the door' nor the nominal gerund formed from that verb, 'there was a closing of the door' (on the RHS of the proposed scheme), entails that the door was closed. (In the terminology I will explain below, the RHS refers to an action-in-progress rather than an action-as-completed.) The closing might have been interrupted; 'closing' (the gerund) is like the verb from which it is formed; in its imperfective form, it is subject to the paradox, and so a door closing might not end with a closed door. So, the logical form of 'P closed the door' (the LHS) could not just be: 'There was a closing, of the door, by P' (the RHS). The LHS would presuppose success whereas the RHS would not.

There needs to be something more added to the RHS, for the RHS and the LHS to have the same truth values, something additional on the

RHS to capture the information that the door closing was completed. If the verb on the LHS has a perfect nominal form, using the prefect nominal (or derived nominal, as it is also called) rather than the gerund on the RHS might solve the problem: 'P closed the door iff there was a closure of the door, by P.'

But not all verbs have a perfect nominal form, for instance 'open' does not. Nothing stands to 'an opening' as 'a betrayal' stands to 'a betraying' or as 'a closure' stands to 'a closing'. Perhaps this is what we should say: 'P opened$_t$ the door [success assumed] iff there was an opening$_t$ of the door by P [success not assumed] and the door opened$_i$ [success assumed]'. But this won't be quite right either. After all, there might have been an opening$_t$ of the door by P, but one that P never brought to completion, and the door might have opened$_i$ anyway, but for some other reason. In that case, it won't be true that P opened$_t$ the door.

We would need to think about some sort of tie, causal or otherwise, between the two conditions on the RHS, between the opening$_t$ of the door by P and the fact that the door opened$_i$. I have a great more to say about this in Chaps. 5 and 6, but this is a problem, not for me, but for Davidson's logical form proposal, a problem that becomes apparent once we are clear about how the imperfectivity paradox affects gerunds and derived or perfect nominals (this issue has been discussed more fully in Szabó 2004, especially 44–45).

Adverbial Qualification

A useful three-way distinction between kinds of adverbial modification is made by Barry Taylor (Taylor 1985, 20–23) and I shall adopt it for my discussion. (The terminology he uses is not entirely standard.) There are sentence adverbs, phrase adverbs, and mode adverbs. By adverbial modification, I shall throughout the book include both adverbs and prepositional phrases used adverbially.

Sentence operators operate on whole sentences. If the adverbial qualification 'G-ly' is a sentence adverb, 'P F-ed G-ly' can be rephrased as, 'It was G that P F-ed'. Taylor adds the qualification that the terms following 'It was G…' should occupy referentially opaque positions. For example, 'he probably walked' can be rewritten as 'It is probable that he walked'.

Amongst other examples, modal and probabilistic adverbial qualifications are often, although not always, sentence adverbs. ('Aristotle is necessarily a man' is not equivalent to 'it is necessarily the case that Aristotle is a man'.) One would need to distinguish between de re and de dicto modality to get clear on when these modal adverbial qualifications are sentence adverbs and when not, but this is not my topic here.

If 'G-ly' is a phrase adverb, then 'P F-ed G-ly' can be rewritten as, 'It was G of P that he F-ed'. For example, 'he courageously led the charge' can be rephrased as 'It was courageous of him that he led the charge'. On some occasions, variants on 'of him' sound better, for example, 'for him'. (The same opaqueness qualification that Taylor added to sentence adverbs holds for phrase adverbs too.)

Finally, an adverbial qualification is a mode adverb if it is neither a sentence nor a phrase adverb. The Davidsonian argument applies at most only to mode adverbs and prepositional phrases. Davidson did not even think that his argument could be applied to all cases in which the modification was a mode adverbial qualification from a strictly grammatical point of view. Davidson's original sentence, from which (1) is a simplification, also contained the adverbs, 'slowly' and 'deliberately'. 'Slowly' is an attributive term on Davidson's account, whose treatment is otherwise specified (marking out exactly which adverbs are attributive is not an easy task, as we shall see). There is much more to come about 'slowly', and 'quickly', later in this chapter, and in Chap. 7, and more about attributivity immediately below.

What is an attributive adjective or adverb? Davidson's example is (4) 'Grundy was a short basketball player but a tall man'. 'Short' and 'tall' cannot be detached, so that (4) does not entail that Grundy was both short and tall (not short). Ordinary rules of detachment do not apply. In the case of nouns, the problem of attributivity arises only when a pair of adjectives is attributed to one and the same particular, such that if both were detached, the result would be a contradiction ('P is short and it is not the case that P is short').

There are many genuine cases of attributivity. But, as is well known, Davidson's 'austere' account of act and event individuation bloats the number of attributives. In the example he uses (Davidson 1967 (1980), 107) for actions, something is both fast for a swimming of the Channel and slow for a crossing of the Channel. If, on an austere theory, the crossing=the swimming, then on that account the best way to construe 'fast' and 'slow' is attributively, so that we do not get a single action that is both fast and slow (not fast). As has been pointed out elsewhere (for example, by Bennett 1988a, 193–206), far too many attributions of actions will now have to be construed attributively, given his account of act individuation. On a prolific account of act individuation, for example on one like the Goldman-Kim account (Goldman 1970; Kim 1976), the swimming≠the crossing, and so, for this case at any rate, no problem arises for 'slow' that requires it to be given an attributive reading. The swimming is fast; the crossing is slow.

I describe the austere and prolific theories of act individuation more fully in Chap. 6. There is also a prolific theory that is not the most prolific theory, a theory that Ginet calls 'the intermediate theory'. On an intermediate theory, not every difference in properties entails the non-identity of the actions so described. For example, on a plausible intermediate theory, suppose that the crossing=the night crossing, even though the crossing≠the swimming (Ginet 1990, 46–53).

An example of a bona fide case of attributivity, if we assume such an intermediate theory of event individuation, might be this: Suppose the crossing was slow, but as a night crossing it was fast (it's so much harder for a night crossing to gather speed). So one is forced in that sort of example, even on this intermediate theory, to say that a single action was slow for a crossing but fast for a night crossing. If we take this line, the lesson for an intermediate theory would be that at least some adverbs or adjectives are attributive in some contexts but not in others: 'slow' is not attributive in the swimming v. crossing contrast, since the swimming≠the crossing, but is attributive in the crossing v. night crossing contrast, since the crossing=the night crossing. Is that plausible? On the other hand, if we opt for the most prolific theory of act individuation, so that even the crossing≠the night crossing, it may be difficult to find any bona fide examples of attributive adverbs for action verbs, and thus there may be no case in which an adverb could be attributive in the context of one action verb but not in another. I will return to the discussion of an intermediate theory of act individuation in Chap. 6, when I discuss Goldman's views on (what I call) information deletion (Goldman calls it 'augmentation').

'Deliberately' imputes intention, and all such intention-related attributions, Davidson says, are to be construed as sentence operators (or as sentence or phrase adverbs, in Taylor's terminology). If he deliberately F-ed, then either it was deliberate that he F-ed or it was deliberate of him that he F-ed. I will exclude both intention-related adverbs and attributives (if any) from discussion in this chapter.[5]

I can now repeat the same question I asked before, but slightly sharpened to exclude cases of attributivity: the Davidsonian argument that seeks to reveal the logical form of sentences with non-attributive mode adverbial modifiers might offer a prima facie plausible argument for thinking that Assumption A was true. If P tried to F G-ly, and if 'G-ly' is a non-attributive mode adverb, then does it follow that there was an act of trying by P, a trying particular, such that it was G? This chapter seeks to answer that question negatively.

Types of Mode Adverbs

There is, as far as I know, no canonical way in which to categorise types of mode adverbs. However, Kirk Ludwig (Ludwig 2010, 40) has one such scheme for the categorisation of mode adverbs, and I shall make use of it in what follows, not only in this chapter but also occasionally throughout the book. He says: '[Mode] Adverbs and adverbial phrases are traditionally classified under the headings of manner ('carefully'), place ('in the kitchen'), time ('at midnight'), frequency ('often'), and degree ('very').' I also want to focus on an important subset of mode adverbs of manner and treat them separately so that they are salient: adverbs of speed like 'fast', 'slowly' and 'quickly'. My reason for so doing will become apparent later, and especially in Chaps. 6 and 7.

Since there is there no canonical categorisation of kinds of adverbs and prepositional phrases that attach to verbs, I know of no definite list that assigns, to each verb, the various categories of adverbs that might attach to it. So the chapter will have to proceed by example, with the hope that I include all the salient kinds of adverbial and prepositional qualification, and correctly give examples of each kind. How I intend to deal with the examples, however, is not ad hoc. It is driven throughout by an underlying metaphysical intuition.

What is that metaphysical intuition? Properties of course inhere in some sense in their subjects; in a single subject for non-relational properties, in multiple subjects for some relational properties (but not in all of them; I am thinking of the issue of so-called Cambridge properties, which will be a subject to be dealt with in Chap. 6). Grammar isn't always a good guide to metaphysics. Many sentences grammatically attribute a property to something, but only a moment's philosophical reflection shows that that can't be the metaphysical truth of the matter.

An oft cited and rather simplistic example is this: 'The average family has 2.2 members.' That sentence attributes no membership size to something called 'the average family'. The explanation is simple: there is no such thing that is referred to by 'the average family'. The sentence is shorthand for something longer, like: 'the number of people divided by the number of households today is 2.2.' The metaphysical intuition, with regard to alleged acts of trying, is that it would make no sense to attribute to them the properties that would be required by the conversion of the adverb modifying them to a corresponding adjective. In some of these cases, the idea that an alleged act of trying could have the sort of property which the adjective formed from the adverb would attribute to it seems to me to be incoherent. In such cases, I shall try and identify another, different candidate to be the bearer of such a property. There will be some residual cases in which such attribution does seem to be plausible for trying: a slow or a quick trying, for instance. One goal then of the chapter is to account for the few plausible-seeming cases without treating trying as a particular.

Implicit in the arguments of this chapter, and Chap. 7, is a distinction between a grammatical truth and a metaphysical one (as in the case of the average family). There are many cases in which 'try' takes an adverb and that may be a fact of grammar (just as a grammatical diagram of the structure of the sentence about the average family, a diagram of the kind one at least formerly did at school, would show that 'small' was an adjective modifying 'the average family'). But we do not always have to accept the grammatical truth as revealing a metaphysical one, as we will see on many occasions below. It is not necessary to introduce ideas such as deep structure, logical form, or whatever, to appreciate this simple point. I would like to keep this point as far as possible within the realm of the philosophically anodyne.

The Opacity of 'Try'

Let me begin with an important distinction for understanding how adverbial qualifications work in trying-sentences. The context that follows 'try' is opaque or, intensional (with an 's', of course). (I use the two terms, 'opaque' and 'intensional' interchangeably.) The contexts are opaque or intensional in the following three senses. (a) An agent can try to F, that is, try to perform a token act that is of the type, F, and fail. In such a case, it is true that he tries to F although there is no F-type token act at all that he does. (b) Further, suppose an agent Fs iff he also Gs. For example, using and somewhat enhancing an example borrowed from Aristotle (Aristotle, *Posterior Analytics*, A13, 78a23–78b15): it is nomologically necessary that celestial bodies twinkle iff they are near. So the agent can fly to a celestial body that is near iff he flies to a celestial body that twinkles. But he might be trying to fly to something near, without trying to fly to something that twinkles. Extensionally equivalent sentences (or even ones which are necessarily equivalent) cannot be substituted salva veritate within these contexts. (c) Finally, he may try to F (and succeed), but there is no specific token act of type F that he has in mind; any one from a range might do as well as any other and be counted as a success. When an agent P tries to F, he tries to do some action of type F; it is incoherent to think that there is some action particular, some token action, such that he tries to do *it*. If we assume that 'in a G-ish way' is the full description of how he is trying to F, then when an agent tries to F in a G-ish way (let 'G' be any finite list of features or properties, however long), 'an F that is G' is the name of a universal or an act type that he is trying to instantiate, such that in principle instantiating any instance of that act type, a G-ish F, will count as a success.[6]

Not all mode adverbial qualifications in trying-sentences occur *inside* the opaque contexts governed by 'try'. Consider two different readings for 'P tried to stop the flood at time t'. On one reading, 'at t' is the time at which P tried to stop the flood, whether he knew it or not. Stopping it at t wasn't something P tried to do; it was just as a matter of fact the time at which he did it. On that reading, the adverbial qualification is outside the opaque context. On a second reading, the 'at t' qualifies the sort of stopping that P tried to do; it was, as it were, an at-t sort of stopping of the flood that P tried to do, so it is inside the opaque context.

Most of the adverbial qualifications I consider with regard to mode adverbs other than those to do with speed, and spatial and temporal location, are of the second sort, and are construed as being inside the opaque context. I consider the first sort of mode adverbial qualification only when I deal with speed, and spatial and temporal, adverbial qualification.

The problem of opacity is not specific to 'try' or to my proposals about how to construe 'try'-sentences. Compare 'try' to 'see'. One can see a material object and one can see a hallucination or a mirage. Anscombe introduces helpful terminology (G.E.M. Anscombe 1965): certain verbs can take both intensional (with an 's' of course) and material (real) objects. A person can seek a real animal (a material object) or only a non-existent chimera (an intensional object).[7] (The problem of the ontological significance, if any, of intensional objects is not one I will pursue.) There is a whole class of verbs, often called intensional transitives, which have these same features as 'to try': seek, look for, hunt for, imagine, dream of, owe, want, desire, describe, talk about, refer to, need, ask for, demand, worship, blaspheme, curse, buy, sell, trade, bet, fear, love, loathe, hate, wait for, expect, plan, see, believe in, resemble, sound like (the list is Richards', with a few deletions: Richards 2001; see also Zimmermann 2006).

Davidson's inferences described above do NOT hold inside opaque contexts in the same way as they do outside opaque contexts. On a wide scope reading, if there is a frog such that I seek it, then there is an amphibian that I seek (this gives 'seek' wide scope). On this reading, there is also some particular frog that I seek, say Kermit. But, on a narrow scope reading, which is the reading that produces the opacity, if I seek a frog, so that 'frog' occurs within the context governed by 'seek', it does not follow by the rules of logic that I seek an amphibian. I might be biologically ignorant and not know what an amphibian is. Nor, to repeat the point in (c) above, on the narrow scope reading, must there be any particular frog that I seek. Any old frog might do equally well, if it is only true that I seek a frog, n'import laquelle.

How are we then to understand those adverbial qualifications that are inside the opaque contexts created by the verb 'try'? The verb 'try' is such an intensional transitive. To what extent can the sorts of inferences that Davidson was anxious to preserve for non-opaque contexts be preserved within opaque contexts? For example (I am assuming inside-the-opaque-context readings for the spatial and temporal qualifications in the examples below),

(1*) Jones tried to butter the toast in the bathroom, with a knife, at midnight.

Does (1*) entail (or otherwise licenses) either (2*) and (3*)?

(2*) Jones tried to butter the toast with a knife.

(3*) Jones tried to butter the toast at midnight, in the bathroom, with a knife.

Davidsonian-like inferences will not go through as a matter of logical form if we assume that all these adverbial qualifications are within the scope of 'try'.

How shall we describe the contents inside the 'try' context? Unlike 'seek', 'try' does not take a direct object (at least not in the sense of 'try' that I have specified above). I introduced earlier the place of universals or act types within trying-sentences: a person who tries is trying to instantiate some universal of action or some act type. The agent is trying to perform some token action of type F, for example. In (1*) above, one way in which to understand what the sentence says is that the act type Jones is trying to instantiate is an in-the-bathroom, with-a-knife, at-midnight, of-the-toast sort of buttering. We are not in this case attributing an adjective to a particular, but further specifying or refining the act type that we are trying to instantiate. How do trying to instantiate a toast-buttering and trying to instantiate a toast-buttering-with-a-knife relate? Since these act types occur within the opaque context, this is not the similar-seeming problem that Davidson or Kenny were addressing with their accounts, and the right answer to this question, whatever it may be, won't be in terms of an inference due to logical form.

These 'inferences' inside opaque contexts are not valid in the sense of logically valid. Issues about how we are to understand adverbial qualification within an opaque context are not issues that are special to the case of 'to try'. I will take a stab-albeit a borrowed stab-about how to address this problem that I think is plausible. But I want to stress that the question of the treatment of adverbial qualification within the context governed by 'to try' is part of a much larger problem; there is nothing, as far as I can see, that is a special or specific difficulty that arises in the case of 'try' that does not arise in the case of the other verbs on Richards' list that I quoted above.

As an example, take again the verb 'seek', which is on Richards' list. The basis for this (and here I rely in the rest of this section on some forthcoming work by R.M. Sainsbury[8]) is psychological: seeking a goldmountain, for example, is shaped by the subject's exercise of the complex concept GOLDEN MOUNTAIN, and this ensures that the concept MOUNTAIN also plays a role in shaping what he seeks. If he seeks a gold mountain, he seeks a mountain. Illicit inferences are illicit for the same sort of psychological reasons: for example, if a person is avoiding rather than seeking gold mountains, it does not follow that he is avoiding mountains. Unlike their valid cousins that take wide scope, the rules for these internal, narrow scope 'inferences' are much less clear, and nothing I say in this chapter depends on developing one view rather than another on this issue. Coming up with a set of rules about if and when these internal 'inferences' about trying to F G-ly are 'valid' is no part of what I want to do in this chapter. Whereas the inferences Davidson showed how to capture are uncontroversial, the inferences that are internal to opaque or intensional contexts are far from that and the rules we need for 'inferences' within the scope of 'to try' provide no exception from that unclarity about which 'inferences' are valid and why.

If this is on the right track, and if trying is aimed at act types and universals, trying to F G-ly is aimed at the act type F, and at the property or universal, being G, so that it is aimed at the act type, an F-that-is-G. Does it then follow that if a person tries to F G-ly, then he tries to F? It isn't always clear. Here is an example from Sainsbury (there is nothing original from me in this paragraph): does trying to dance gracefully entail trying to dance? In a way, yes, but on the other hand if a person had hoped that his lessons would teach him to dance gracefully (and he had no interest in just learning to dance any-old-way) but he was a poor learner and ended up dancing gracelessly, it would not do to say: 'but you at least tried to dance and now you do, so it's a part success!' If trying is defined by what would make it successful, for such a person, dancing gracelessly would not be a success of any kind. On the other hand, perhaps it is true that he was trying to dance, but it is only misleading to say this because another person might wrongly suppose that in learning how to dance, even gracelessly, he had succeeded at least in part in doing what he was seeking to do. However we answer this question, the key to the answer will not be in logic but in psychology.

Trying to F G-ly is to be construed as trying to perform some one particular action that will instantiate both the types, an F & a G. Trying to do an F that is G is certainly not trying to do F & to do something that is G, because the latter but not the former could be successful if the agent succeeded in doing a G-less F and an F-less G. Rather, what the agent is trying to do is an action that falls under a particular sub-kind of an F, namely one that is also a G.

In what follows, I speak often of various acts that an agent tries to do, or of another act by which he tries to do it. This is for ease of exposition. I leave it to the reader to interpret these claims in terms of the agent trying to perform some action token, such that a certain action type or property will be true of it.

Mode Adverbs of Manner

First, consider cases of mode adverbs of manner (including so-called instrumentals, like 'with a knife'). Since we are focusing only on the sense of 'to try' in which it is followed by an infinitive, (or a gerund, as in 'P tried F-ing'), there is always an explicit second verb on offer to take the attribution. In 'P tried to close the window carefully', assuming that 'carefully' is a mode and not a phrase adverb, it may be that what P tried to do was a careful window-closing. There is no need to hold that, in addition to the careful window-closing, the trying was also careful. The same can sometimes (but not always, as we shall see) be said of adverbs of speed. If P tried to close that window quickly, it might have been a quick window-closing that he was trying to do. I will discuss alternative accounts of speed adverbs later in the chapter, for not all of them behave in this suggested way.

What of instrumentals such as 'with a knife' in (1*)? 'With a knife' and its like also attach to the F-ing and not to the trying. It was, as it were, a with-a-knife buttering that Jones tried to do. The instrumental attaches to the act types or universals within the intensional context. The instrumentals do not attach to 'trying'. As for the question of how you obtain 'tried to butter' from 'tried to butter with a knife', the psychological answer adumbrated above for GOLDEN MOUNTAIN or DANCE GRACEFULLY works here as well, assuming it works there.

In 'P tried to F carefully', does the position of the adverb in the sentence make a difference? 'P carefully tried to F' does not seem to say that it was a careful F-ing that P tried to do. J.L. Austin noted that many adverbial attributions could be ambiguous between a phrase and a mode reading (Austin 1956, 198–200). Examples include 'softly', 'loudly', 'courteously', 'greedily', 'beautifully', 'neatly', and the like. 'He greedily tried to eat the banana' might be understood either as a phrase adverb, 'It was greedy of him to try to eat the banana' or as a mode adverb, 'he tried to eat the banana in a greedy manner'. Placing the adverb before the second verb suggests a phrase reading, but does not, I think, require it. 'He savagely stepped on the worm' might be construed as either saying something about the savage agent or as saying something about his savage worm-stepping. But when the adverb is to be construed as a mode adverb rather than a phrase adverb, whatever its position in the sentence might be, so that the sentences say something about his trying to step or his trying to eat, rather than about the agent, it says something about the type of stepping or the type of eating that he tried to do, and not about some alleged act of trying.

There are, to be sure, cases of trying in which the agent tries to do a basic or primitive action, an action that he tries to do but not *by* trying to do something else. But most of our actions are not basic in this sense and are done by doing something else (and one tries to do them by trying to do something else). Let's call the actions by which a person tries to do some action F, its 'by-acts'. As I said at the end of the last chapter, just as physical actions can have by-acts, there can be by-acts for trying. Just as agents can G by F–ing, so too an agent can try to G by F-ing (indeed, they can try to G by trying to F). Assume that, in the sentence 'he tried to F by doing E', 'by doing E' is also within the scope of 'try'. It can be true that P tried to do F by doing E, even when he failed both to F and to E. P might try to open the door by turning the handle, even when he not only fails to open the door but is unsuccessful in his handle-turning as well. In 'P tries to open the door carefully by turning the handle', a likely candidate for the careful manner is the opening's by-act, a turning, which was to be careful. But the opening of the door might be careful too, either in virtue of the turning having been careful or independently. One could insure this double reading of 'carefully' by the somewhat cumbersome: 'He tried to open the door carefully by carefully turning the handle.' The turning was careful and the door opening might have been careful, if it was, because the turning was. Or the opening might also be a careful opening independently of the manner in which he turned the handle.

Not all by-acts warrant an explicit mention in the trying-sentence. Consider again 'P tried to open the door carefully' (no mention of the turning). Many mode adverbial qualifications in trying-sentences, 'in a G-ish manner', really attribute a property to some implicit and unstated by-act, and not to any of the explicit verbs inside the 'trying' context, let alone some alleged act of trying. If P tried to open the door carefully, even though no handle turning is mentioned in the sentence, it might have been a handle turning that was to be careful, and P might not have cared whether the door opening was careful or not, as long as the handle turning was. In the case of trying to open the door by carefully turning the handle, the careful turning is likely to have been careful on purpose. But sometimes the acts by which an agent tries to do something are not done in that way on purpose; perhaps P tried to open the door by turning the handle but the turning was in fact very noisy, contrary to what he had hoped.

But suppose that the agent was not careful and neither the door opening nor the handle turning nor any other unmentioned by-act of the opening was careful, whether on purpose or otherwise. In such a case, it does not seem to me at all obvious what 'carefully' could really be contributing to the information embedded in the sentence. It is at this point that at least my metaphysical intuitions rise to the occasion: how could a particular act of trying, if there were such a thing, have the property of being careful in such circumstances? Or be courteous or graceful or beautiful or noisy? If one asserts that an agent P tried to F carefully, but then claimed that the property of being careful could not be ascribed to what the agent tried to do, nor ascribed to any of the acts mentioned in the sentence by which he tried to do it, nor to any of the implicit by-actions not explicitly mentioned in the sentence by which he tried to do it, nor even to the agent himself, then I cannot see what the assertion that P tried to F carefully could mean. The rejoinder that it could still be the act of trying itself that was careful, even in the absence of all these other indicators of carefulness, seems to have no substance to it.

Adverbs of Speed

Sometimes adverbs of speed function as phrase adverbs. 'P quickly tried to F' can mean 'It was quick of P to start his trying to F', or 'P was quick to start his trying to F', or some such. But even when construed only as a mode and not as a phrase adverb, adverbs of speed are ambiguous between two different readings. Suppose P asks P* to quickly dance with him. P could be asking P* to do either of two distinct things. P might be asking P* to dance a certain kind of dance, say a jitterbug rather that a sedate foxtrot. The dance should be a quick one. In this sense, a synonym for 'quickly' is 'fast'. Or P could be asking P* to start dancing sooner rather than later. In the latter case, P and P* might well do a sedate foxtrot but they will start that dance very soon. In this sense, a synonym for 'quickly' is 'promptly'. Let's call the first use of a speed mode adverb the 'intrinsic use': the second, the 'temporal relational use'. In 'P tried to dance quickly', both readings are within opaque context.

Let me tell a little story about Henry and Henrietta. This is a story I will use several times in the chapters that follow. Henry is keen on Henrietta. Henrietta has a fetish about doors opening too quickly, which annoys her, so she asked Henry to open a door slowly for her, the opening to finish no later than at a specific time. Henry is anxious to try and comply with her rather odd request. Moreover, there are several different processes by which Henry could get the door to start to open slowly (he can choose between various mechanisms, all of which lead to the door opening slowly) and these processes or mechanisms leading up to the slow opening of the door are of greater and lesser duration. But Henry is rather forgetful. He was in no hurry to get things going, dilly-dallying all afternoon, but once he noticed the time ticking by, he needed to select the process that took the least amount of time to start the slow opening of the door (even if 'slow' and 'quick' are attributive, this would not alter the point of the example). So Henry tried quickly to open the door slowly.

So (1) is true:

(1) Henry tried quickly to open the door slowly.

How to understand the placement of these adverbs? We know from the story that 'slowly' qualifies the door's opening (that is an intrinsic use, since it qualifies the kind of door opening it should be). What does 'quickly' modify? Could it be a phrase adverb? If it is Henry who is quick, he might have been quick off the mark, to start the process of the slow opening the door. But according to our story, Henry was a slowcoach in getting started. So slow in fact that he had to pick the quickest way to get the slow opening of the door started, in order for the opening to finish by the latest time Henrietta has set.

If anything is quick, it is because Henry made sure that he selected that process by which the door would start to open slowly and which would itself not itself take a long time to get that slow opening going. There appear to be three obvious things that might be considered for adverbial modification in (1): Henry, a door's opening, and the alleged trying. It can't be the door's opening, as that was slow, not quick. If it isn't Henry who was quick, doesn't it follow that there was a trying that was quick? That is of course exactly what I want to deny.

There may seem to be three things for modification in (1), but the story itself suggests a fourth possibility that construes 'quick' as a speed adverb in a temporal relational use rather than an intrinsic use. (1) presupposes that there was some process by which Henry tried to open the door. From the different options that Henry had for selection of the process that would lead to the door's starting to open, that one was chosen which was the one that would have the shortest duration. There is some unspecified trigger event at t that reminds Henry about what he is meant to do that the trying-sentence assumes but does not make explicit (he noticed the time, Henrietta reminded him, or some such), and the process of the door's opening starts at t*, and the temporal gap between t and t* was relatively short. (On the other hand, the opening finishes at t** and the temporal distance between t* and t** is relatively long.)

In this case, 'quick' does not serve as an adjectival modification of a trying; its use is only to describe the gap between two times. It is the temporal relational use of the adverb. Henry tried to insure a relatively short temporal gap separating the trigger event and the door's starting to open (and a relatively long gap separating the starting of the door's opening and the conclusion of the opening). The temporal relational reading for speed adverbs can occur both inside and outside the opaque context. In our story, Henry aimed for the temporal gap to be short, in which case 'quickly' is inside the opaque context. In a different case, it could be merely a truth about the gap between the two times, whether Henry was even aware of it or not, in which case 'quickly' would fall outside the opaque context. Unlike in our case, in this latter case, the quickness was no part of his plan, nothing at which he aimed, just an objective truth about what it was that he tried to do. The upshot is, once again, that we need no trying particular to bear the property of being quick.

Adverbs Outside the Opaque Context: Speed, Place, and Time

Like examples of adverbial qualifications of speed, adverbial qualifications of place and time can occur both within the opaque context and outside the opaque context. Adverbial qualifications of place and time comprise two additional sets of mode adverbs. In those cases in which they are within that opaque context, they raise no problems that we have not already encountered. The agent tried to do an act token of the type, (say) an-F-at-time-t or an-F-in-place-p. But how do we deal with trying sentences with the other reading, in which the adverb of space and time is outside the opaque context? Perhaps it was at time t in place p that P tried to F, although P did not try to F-at-time-t or F-in-place-p. Does any of this require us to assume that there is an act of trying, such that it has a temporal and spatial location?

An agent at time t and in place p tries to stop the flood (remember, in this example, 'at t' and 'in p' are not governed by 'try'). What happened in p at t? It was in p at t that he tried, but it doesn't follow from that, that p is where, or t is when, his trying was, because there are two better alternatives: either p and t are where and when whatever he did in order to stop the flood happened (turning the tap, perhaps, which is implicitly but not explicitly understood), or it is where the agent was when he did whatever he did do, in order to stop the flood. In these cases, there is a choice of alternative bearers of the spatial and temporal property. (I come back to time attribution a little later, in the section on naked trying.)

Adverbs of Degree of Effort and Frequency

Both effort and frequency come in degrees, and agents can display different degrees of effort and frequency when they try to do something. Agents can try hard, try half-heartedly, hardly try at all, really try, barely try, try one's best, and try successfully. (These may or may not be inside the opaque context, depending on how we specify the case.) To try successfully to F is to F because one has tried to F. To say of someone that he tried half-heartedly or whole-heartedly might be a way to describe his state of mind, as his lacking or having mental investment in or focus on what he was doing. If one hardly tries to F, there is nothing or almost nothing one does in order to F. 'He tried often' means that there were many occasions, an indefinite number, on which he tried. 'He tried rarely' means that there were very few times at which he tried. Again, no particular acts of trying or attempting are required. We have found it necessary to quantify over times in explicating these trying-sentences ('many times', 'few times'), and this is a topic to which I revert below. The point is this: these locutions do not require acts of trying in order for sentences with them to be true. It seems to me plainly incoherent to imagine that there could be a particular act of trying that had any of these qualifications ('hard', 'half-hearted', etc.) as its properties.

How are we to understand 'try hard'? Sometimes what one tries to do is not easy to do. For many of us, it is quite hard to always be nice to our enemies. But one might not try hard to be nice to one's enemies, even if it is hard to do. In understanding 'try hard', we want to understand what trying hard is, not what trying to do something that is hard to do is, like being nice to our enemies.

Trying hard can be a matter of frequency or effort or both. If one tries hard to F, then, e.g., one has to do many things in order to F or perhaps has to try to F repeatedly. That proposal for trying hard assumes that, in order for someone to try hard to F, either there must be repeated attempts by him to F or many other things he has to do in order to F. Both effort and frequency are evidenced by the number of times one tries. But might one hold that one can try hard to F even if there were only one occasion on which the agent tried to F and only one thing he had to do in order to F, so that the high degree of frequency and/or effort proposal for trying hard would fail?

So suppose one rejects my proposal for dealing with trying hard and thought that the adverb 'hard' attached directly to a trying particular after all. But in order to make plausible the idea that 'hard' attached directly to a single case of trying and that the agent just tried hard to F, without trying to do numerous other actions in order to F, one would have to say something about the difference there would be between a single case of trying hard (or to some other degree) and a single case of not trying hard (or not to that degree).

I can't see any plausible difference between any two such scenarios, trying and trying hard, if one rules out the conditions I have set for trying hard. What could the hardness of a trying to F consist in, if the agent tried only on one occasion to F and did only one thing on that occasion in order to F, and (say) F-ing was itself something he found it easy to do? Trying hard to F must show some level of increased frequency or effort compared to the norm for trying to F. Suppose you think that at least elevated effort could be marked physiologically in a single act. Could 'P tried hard' be understood as 'P's trying caused his heartbeat to increase, or caused him to sweat, or some such'? That seems to me to be hopeless.

Of course, when someone tries hard, it is often true that these physiological markers can be found. But there are, or can be, plenty of cases when an agent tries hard, without any of these physiological signs of increased effort: I might try hard to avoid fattening foods, be a good father, or whatever, in the absence of all such sweating, increase of heartbeat, and so on. Further, one can try to exercise in a gym, but not try hard to do so, and yet still have those same physiological markers present. Barring a counterproposal that I have not yet considered, I think that to try hard and to try to other degrees of effort and frequency are susceptible to the sort of treatment I am proposing. No trying acts as particulars are required to account for trying hard.

Naked Trying: Mode Adverbs of Manner, of Speed, and of Frequency and Degree

I return now to the issue of naked trying that I have discussed in some depth in Chap. 2. Naked trying poses a challenge to the view that adverbial qualifications of trying can always be understood in a way that does not require acts of trying. Recall that a trying to F is naked iff an agent tries to F but no token F-ing, nor any token action of a type that the agent does because (he believes that) a token action of that type will lead to his F-ing, occurs.

Examples of adverbial qualification within the opaque context present no special difficulty for the possibility of naked trying. Since the adverbial qualification inside the opaque context (including time, place, and speed mode adverbs) is merely to qualify the type of act that the agent is trying to instantiate, such qualification presents no difficulty for naked trying. There don't have to be any instances of the type of action the agent is trying to do, however qualified, on anyone's account.

But what of adverbs of speed in the naked case that occur outside the opaque context? If P quickly tried to F in a naked case, then 'quick' might be a phrase adverb, because it was quick of Henry to try, or Henry was quick to try. If it is a mode adverb, and if it takes its temporal relational sense, it must be a measure between the times of two occurrences or events. What two occurrences would the two times be times of? In the case of Landry's patient, if he quickly tried to raise his arm, the two occurrences would be (a) his receiving his instruction to raise his arm from the experimenter, presumably Dr. Landry, and (b) the onset of his (false) belief that he was raising it.

Are there any adverbs of frequency or of degree that can modify naked trying, and, if so, what do they modify? Dr. Landry's and Professor Strümpell's patients might have tried and failed repeatedly ('often', 'frequently') to raise their arms. Adverbs of frequency and degree can qualify 'try' in naked cases. But these were dealt with above, as involving no genuine adjectival qualification of a trying particular, and the same method of treating them applies in these cases of naked trying too. In the case of naked trying, one tries hard to F only if one nakedly tries to F on a number of occasions, or nakedly tries to do many things in order to F. How could one count the number of times at which Landry's patient nakedly tried? That number will be given by the number of times he acquires a distinct false belief that he has succeeded in F-ing, or, in case he knows that he has not or will not succeed, the number of times he acquires another propensity or disposition to have that belief.

Spatial and Temporal Qualification of Naked Trying

Two remaining possibilities for the adverbial qualification of naked trying outside the opaque context are the adverbial qualifications of time and place. In the William James account, Dr. Landry's patient tried to raise his arm in Landry's lab at some time t. Since no action ensued, which could be placed and dated at t in the lab, to what might 'in the lab' and 'at t' attach, if not an act of trying?

We have already said something earlier about adverbs of spatial location in the case of adverbial qualification outside the opaque context: it was in place p that he tried, but it doesn't follow from that that p is where his trying was, because there are two better alternatives: either place p is where whatever he did in order to stop the flood happened (turning the tap, perhaps, which is implicitly but not explicitly understood), or it is where P was. In the naked case, the first of the two alternatives is eliminated.

There was NO action that P did, so the first alternative is not available. But the second alternative is available: p is where the agent, P, was. Dr. Landry and his patient were in the lab. We do not need a trying act for the spatial location; the spatial location of the agent will suffice. The agent was in place p when he tried. But the 'at t' is more challenging for my proposal. It is only with the possible case of temporal qualification of naked trying that the view adopted in this chapter is to some extent revisionary.

What might it mean to give a time at which the naked trying occurred? Since there is no action to which the time can be attributed, no action available for the temporal qualification, and since I resist attributing the time to a trying, some other means will need to be found by which to capture the temporal information. I think that some of the revisionary proposals I am going to put forward have a long and otherwise well-motivated history. Many independent reasons can be adduced for such revisions, which allow them to escape the charge of being merely ad hoc.

There are several options available to deal with the problem of temporal attribution in a case of naked trying, of which I briefly mention four, but a detailed discussion of them and a reasoned choice of one over the others would take this chapter too far of course. The point to stress is that there are options, even in cases of naked trying, for dealing with temporal attributions, which do not require postulating any acts of trying.

The first option is rather radical; it requires a tensed view of semantics. The 'at t' attaches to 'true', so that it is true-at-t that Landry's patient tried to raise his arm. The second option has attracted many philosophers for other reasons; the temporal information about a naked trying could be captured by using an appropriate temporal part of an agent: 'the agent-at-t tried to F'. This option might be welcome to perdurance theorists, but anathema to endurance theorists. It does have the advantage of treating spatial and temporal adverbial qualification somewhat similarly, since both temporal and spatial adverbs would qualify the agent. But only perdurance theorists see that as an advantage anyway.

Third, one could treat times as objects over which quantifiers can range: 'the agent tried to F at t', where the whole predicate is '…tried to … at….', (timelessly) true of the triple: an agent, an act type or an act property, and a time (see Silverstein 1980, for a similar proposal). The idea is that 'at t' is no longer to be treated as an adverb at all, but that 't' names an object, which can be one of the relata of the triadic tried-to-at relation.

But, on this third proposal, how could one infer the conclusion that P tried to F from the premiss that P tried to F at t? This third proposal has some interesting similarity to Maria Alvarez' proposal for generating the predicate, 'caused with', that I deal with in Chap. 7. One problem she faces is explaining how one can infer 'x is caused' from 'x is caused with a knife', since '…is caused with…' is a dyadic relation and '…is caused' is a monadic predicate. If one abandons the idea that such inferences must always be legitimated by logical form, rather than simply by semantic truths, the problem might not be intractable. Fourth, one might treat temporal qualifiers as sentence operators, making them in effect sentence adverbs in Taylor's sense. Bennett proposed this treatment (Bennett 1988a, 201–203). Many adverbial modifiers must be treated in this way in any case ('probably', 'necessary', 'hopefully'), and, as Bennett says, such treatment 'can be smoothly extended to do all the work for temporal adverbs'.

None of these options is without some negative features. The first requires a non-orthodox semantics for truth. The second requires temporal parts of objects, perdurance rather than endurance. (I can't say that I am wild about that option for continuants, although I assumed in Chap. 2 that it works for events and actions as occurrents.) The third option appears to lose the inference from 'P tried to raise his arm at t' to 'P tried to raise his arm', since these will be distinct relational properties, with different degrees of adicity, as long as we try to validate that inference as one underwritten by logical form. But maybe the validation of the inference by logical form is in any case a vain hope, and semantics and/or psychology can take over where logical form fails.

What of the fourth option? In all cases of trying to act, whether the case is a case of trying to do a basic action or a non-basic action, it is not possible to decide a priori if the agent succeeded or failed to perform the action merely on the basis of the truth of the trying-sentence alone. Further, from the truth of the trying-sentence, one cannot even decide whether the action one tried to do was basic or non-basic, since any basic action is such that another token action of the same action type could be non-basic. So one can only tell a posteriori whether any case of trying is one of naked trying or not, since a naked trying has to be both a trying to do a basic action and a failure.

Since it would be very implausible to treat temporal adverbial qualification in different ways in failed attempts at basic action and in all other cases, all such temporal adverbial qualification should be treated in the same way. (It would be preposterous to be a perdurance theorist or to treat 'true-at-t' as fundamental only in some cases and to be an endurance theorist or to treat 'true' as fundamental in other cases, for example.) Although my strategy in this chapter has been to restrict the discussion of adverbial qualification as far as possible to the case of trying, without implying anything about what an account of adverbial qualification would be like for other verbs, these four alternatives for temporal qualification are best thought of as alternative accounts for temporal attribution quite generally, and not just for temporal attribution occurring outside the opaque context in trying-sentences.

Another Consideration

In this section, I want to mention another, independent consideration for denying the existence of trying particulars. The point arises from the work of many philosophers and linguists, but I shall focus on some work by Jonathan Bennett and, to a lesser extent, by Artemis Alexiadou. I will make use of this point repeatedly in the following chapters. It is an application to 'try' of some general views about gerunds.

In Jonathan Bennett's work on action, he contrasts (a) 'Quisling's betrayal of (and 'betraying of') Norway' with (b) 'Quisling's betraying Norway' (Bennett 1988b, 1–12). He says that, unlike (a), which is the name of an event and behaves in a noun-like fashion, (b) remains verb-like, even when it occurs in the subject position of a sentence. In (a), 'betrayal' is a perfect or derived nominal; 'betraying of' is a nominal gerund. In (b), 'betraying' (no 'of') is a verbal gerund.

Bennett's evidence for this claim is four-fold: (1) in (b), 'Quisling's' cannot be replaced by a definite or indefinite article ('the betraying Norway' and 'a betraying Norway' are ungrammatical), but can be so replaced in (a); (2) (b) takes only adverbs in the attributive position, whereas (a) takes adjectives in that position; (3) in (b), the gerund can be negated, tensed, and modalised by auxiliaries, but not so in (a); (4) finally, the gerund cannot be pluralised in (b), whereas both 'the betrayal' and 'the betraying of' can be pluralised in (a). Only the nominal gerund and the perfect nominal are referring terms and can give us particulars. The verbal gerund remains verb-like and does not. Alexiadou (2013) makes the same points in contrasting what he calls nominal and verbal gerunds; the differences between them are summed up in a table (Alexiadou 2013, 128). I find his table very helpful. In what follows, I adopt his nomenclature rather than Bennett's, since I find Alexiadou's more intuitive.

Terms like 'betrayal', where they exist, are derived (or, perfect) nominals, but not all gerunds have a corresponding derived nominal, like the correspondence between 'betrayal' and 'betraying'. There is no derived nominal for example that can be paired with 'the smelling of the rose'. 'The smell of the rose' names the object of the smelling (one smells a smell), and not an event of smelling. Alexiadou notes that the nominal gerund and the derived nominal are very similar in their grammatical behaviour, and suggests that nominal gerunds may be being replaced in English by the derived nominal form over time (134).

Derived nominals are themselves often subject to a process-product ambiguity. 'In the process-product shift, a word, often one ending in '-ion' or '-tion' ['betrayal' also falls into this category], may signify an activity or its result' (Clark and Welsh, 154). In 'P was horrified at Quisling's betrayal of Norway', it 'may be ambiguous …whether the actual process of [betrayal] or its result is meant' (154). In considering derived nominals and their relationship to the perfective form of the verb from which they are derived, it is important to be clear whether we are dealing with the product sense or the process sense of the derived nominal.

I think this ambiguity probably explains one's conflicting intuitions about derived nominals and perfectivity (I discussed gerunds and perfectivity above and will return to it several times subsequently in the book.) In the product sense, if 'P was horrified at Quisling's betrayal of Norway' is true, Norway had to have been successfully betrayed. There can't be a betrayal product until someone or something is successfully betrayed. In the process sense, the derived nominal seems little different from its corresponding gerunds, at least as far as perfectivity is concerned. P might have been horrified at Quisling's betrayal as it was in process, even though the steps Quisling took never ended in the betrayal product ever being completed. In the process since, P might have been horrified at the betrayal even if Norway was never in the end successfully betrayed.

I think that some of Bennett's and Alexiadou's claims are overly strong, especially the claim that verbal gerunds can take only adverbial modification and nominal gerunds can take only adjectival modification. For example, both 'Quisling's betraying Norway was unforgiveable' (the verbal gerund taking an adjectival modification) and 'Quisling's betraying of Norway was fast' (the nominal gerund taking an adverbial modification) both sound perfectly grammatical to my ear. But, whether I am correct or not in that last claim, the other differences between them are real, and do cumulatively indicate a striking contrast between the likes of (a) and (b).

Philosophers do not always keep the two distinct. Consider this sentence from Hornsby: 'Ann's carrying the suitcase *is* [her italics] the event of its being carried' (Hornsby 2011, 107). Since, in this sentence, the occurrence of 'is' is that of identity, a referring expression must flank both sides of the identity sign. On the right, Hornsby has 'the event of its being carried'. What is the referring expression on the left? 'Ann's carrying the suitcase' is a verbal gerund and does not refer. As formulated, the sentence is ungrammatical. The point in this case is trivial, and it does not affect anything important that Hornsby wants to say (so apologies for picking on her). But it serves as a reminder that these should be kept distinct.

What is striking is how closely 'P's trying to F', resembles (b) rather than (a), resembles the verbal gerund rather than the nominal gerund. 'P' cannot be replaced by a definite or indefinite article ('a trying to F' and 'the trying to F' are distinctly odd); 'P's trying to F' can be negated, tensed, and modalised ('P's having tried to F' and 'P's not trying to F' are both acceptable), and 'P's trying to F' cannot be pluralised ('P's tryings to F' makes no sense). Its logical behaviour makes it similar to the verb-like 'Quisling's betraying Norway' rather than to the noun-like 'Quisling's betraying of Norway' or 'Quisling's betrayal of Norway'. This certainly further suggests that there are no such things as tryings. Or, to put it somewhat more cautiously, what this suggests is that there can only be tryings if and insofar as verbal gerunds themselves had reference.

Metaphysical Significance

The points I am making in this section, have made earlier, and will make repeatedly later in the book, about perfective and imperfective verbs, and about nominal gerunds and derived nominal, might strike the reader as having only a grammatical interest. Not so. These distinctions have metaphysical significance. When I discuss actions and times in Chap. 6, I will have much more to say about this.

As we have seen, some action verbs are atelic: 'to run', 'to walk', 'to swim', 'to push' (Vendler's 'activities', Vendler 1962). They have no end point. So I focus in my remarks below only on telic verbs. An action, when it is designated by an action verb's nominal gerund, takes time, has duration, but, if the verb is telic, it can be completed at a time. So an agent's closing of a window or Quisling's betraying of Norway takes some finite amount of time, however short. That is what I call 'an action-in-progress'. If an action has a possible completion, the action-as-completed (or as-successful) takes place at a time: at some t, when there is the closure of the door, or when Norway is betrayed (perhaps the moment that the German troops are allowed access to the country), if these perfect nominal are taken in the product sense. The terminology of 'events-in-progress' and 'completed events' is due to Eric Marcus (Marcus 2012, 212–221).

Actions-in-progress and completed actions are not two particulars, or two kinds of action. There aren't two particulars: a closing of the door and a door's closure. There is only one action in each of these cases, which has both duration and an end point. (But see Marcus for an alternative view of the matter.) In the case of verbs that have no perfect or derived nominal (as 'to open'), the only way in which to indicate that end point is through an expression like 'the successful opening' or even 'the point at which the opening was successful, or was completed'. In the case of verbs with a perfect nominal, the perfect nominal, in the product sense, refers to the end point of the action, the time at which the action is successfully completed. In what follows, when I speak of an action at a time, I intend an action-as-completed. When I talk about an action's duration, I intend an action-in-progress.[9] Actions-as-completed happen only at a time. Actions-in-progress both have duration and also happen at times. P's closing of the window or opening of the door may have stretched from t1 to t5. But if P is asked by the judge to account for what he was doing at t3, in order to establish his alibi, P can truly say: 'M'lord, at t3 I was (busy) closing the window. I couldn't possibly have done the crime.'

It isn't easy to shoehorn all possible cases into the simple scheme that I have just offered. There will always be messy exceptions. (No doubt some more will occur to the reader.) For example, one of Vendler's examples (Vendler 1962) of an 'achievement verb' is 'to find'. One can find, or have found, a ten-euro note at a time t. Although 'to find' has an imperfective form, as in 'he was finding his life increasingly hard', it does not seem to have an imperfective form in the case of the note. It makes no sense to say that he was finding the 10-euro note over a stretch of time. He found it at t, but there was no stretch of time during which he was finding the ten-euro note, such that when he found it at t, he completed, or succeeded in, that finding. So perhaps we would do better to confine the claim above to telic action verbs that can take imperfective aspect in the particular example being considered. So the idea is that if an action verb in a sentence is both telic and in that the sentence the verb can intelligibly take imperfective aspect, then the verb's nominal gerund designates an action-in-progress and its perfect nominal, if it has one, designates an action-as-completed.

Lest it be assumed otherwise, it does not *follow* from the fact that a perfect nominal or nominal gerund can be derived from some verb, that that nominal or gerund necessarily does refer to some entity. Metaphysics takes over where semantics leaves off. To expand on what David Lewis says, (Lewis 1986, 241), it may be true that a certain mathematical sequence converges, but it does not follow that there is a converging of that sequence. (Lewis appears to accept that there might be such an entity, but says only that it can't be an effect or a cause.) It would, I think, be foolish to look for any entity to which 'the converging of the mathematical sequence' referred. Simon Evnine (2016, 231–232) argues a similar point for the special use of 'to make' required by his theory, and for 'refrain' and other verbs that might be thought to refer to so-called negative acts.

Apparent Counterexamples

References Back

Do verbal gerunds have reference? Bennett's conclusion above was that when the verbal gerund, 'Quisling's betraying Norway', does appear in a subject position (as in 'Quisling's betraying Norway was treacherous'), it refers to a fact, the fact that Quisling betrayed Norway. In that spirit, one can understand the genuinely referential instances of expressions that contain 'P's trying to F' as a part. So for instance, 'P's trying to F was disagreeable' can be construed as 'the fact that P tried to F was disagreeable'. On this construal, we have an ontology of facts, a metaphysical category for which I have argued elsewhere is required for a convincing account of explanation (Ruben 1990, 1992, second edition, 2012, 139–165).

The virtue of introducing facts is this: if 'he tried to F' does not commit us to an act of trying, neither does 'the fact that he tried to F' commit is to such an act. It commits us only to a fact. But since 'the fact that he tried to F' can be genuinely referential (or so I claim anyway), we can account for the cases in which a reference is being made in talk about trying, even though that reference is not to an act of trying.

Gabriel Segal (in private communication) has challenged my thesis about the nonexistence of any trying particulars with apparent cases of reference that do seem to require such trying particulars. Here are Segal's examples: (1) 'He tried to kill her. No one could explain that' (I have more to say about trying and explanation in Chap. 4), (2) 'He tried to kill her. But it did not work. She went on to live a hundred years'. In (1), what no one could explain was the fact that he tried to kill her. This is consistent with my general view of explanation, according to which explanation is of facts by facts, not of events by events. But even if that general view of explanation were rejected, there surely are some cases in which facts get explained, and (1) would be just such a case. It was a fact about his trying to F that could not be explained, not an alleged act of trying to F.

Many properties that can be ascribed to facts cannot be ascribed to events, and vice versa. My thesis about trying would only have a problem if there were an alleged property ascription in a trying-sentence that could not be ascribed to a fact about trying (or to a type of action within the scope of 'to try' or to the person who tries). For example, events, actions and persons can be treacherous, but one might hold that facts cannot be treacherous. Facts just aren't that sort of thing (if your intuitions differ from mine and you think that facts can be treacherous, my problem disappears). So what could we make of: 'P's trying to betray Norway was treacherous'? 'The fact that P tried to betray Norway was treacherous' won't do, for the reason already given. And let's assume that we are saying something other than that the betrayal itself was treacherous. Someone might be appalled both at his trying to do such a thing, as well as at what it was that he was trying to do. We have at least one obvious option. If what P tried to do, betray Norway, was treacherous, no need for a treacherous trying. It might have been that it was treacherous of P to have tried to betray Norway, which makes 'treacherous' a phrase adverb rather than a mode adverb.

(2) has a somewhat different solution. After all, it is not the fact that he tried to kill her that did not work; facts are not the sort of thing that either work or fail to work (again, if you think that facts can work or fail to work, my problem vanishes and I would not need to dispute your contrary intuitions). But consider this case once more. (a) 'The average family is smaller in size than it was 50 years ago.' It is a commonplace that 'the average family' is a faux-reference, the whole sentence being equivalent to something such as (b) 'The number of people divided by the number of households is a smaller number than it was 50 years ago.' No one, I take it, thinks there is such a thing as the average family. Now, the case is not changed if we say instead: (c) 'the average family is 2.1. It is smaller than it was 50 years ago.' 'It' in the second sentence is not a genuine reference back, since there is nothing to which it can refer. (c) as a whole, which is composed of the two sentences, also needs to be paraphrased into something like (b). There is no need to look for a referent to anchor

'it'. So too for (2) 'He tried to kill her. But it did not work.' It can be paraphrased into something like: 'He tried to kill her but he did not succeed in killing her.' Metaphysics guides insight into what language is telling us.

Causation

Causation is perhaps the single most serious challenge to a non-particularist account of trying. (a) If causation requires particular events to stand in the causal relation, and (b) if trying enters the causal order, then (if (a) and (b)) are true, mustn't there be trying particulars?

There is a way to deal with this: deny (a). Many who write on causation hold that the causal relation can (also) hold between facts. Bennett (1998) has a good account of this, and why fact causation is preferable to event causation, as being 'more informative' (Bennett 1998). If so, then the fact that a person has tried can be both cause and effect of the fact that other events have occurred. Some writers even allow 'mixed modes': the fact that someone has tried can be caused by events and can itself cause events. So trying could enter the causal order, but not as a particular. 'My trying to F caused my heart beat to increase' is equivalent to 'The fact that I tried to F caused my heart beat to increase.'

One might wonder how facts about trying could have causal power if there are no such things as tryings that have them. Quite generally, facts have causal powers, even if what the facts are about don't have them. The fact that 2+2=4 excited me is causal, in spite of the lack of causal powers of numbers. (For a more realistic example, consider a case in which the mathematical or logical truth is considerably more recherché.) Of course, in the case of trying, I assume that the fact that my trying caused such-and-such has whatever causal power it has no doubt because of some underlying neurophysiological state that I am in when I try. But that does not make trying a particular.

I'm not denying that there are philosophical theories that attribute a causal role to trying as a particular. A good example is Vihvelin (2013): 'I take trying to be a real event (or sequence of events) and logically independent of the action that it causes': 'Tryings are real events (or sequences of events), and like other events, they can be caused in a variety of different ways and they have a variety of different effects. A trying may be the cause of some movement of the person's body (intentional or not) or movement of the person's mind or brain (again, intentional or not)' (177–178 and ff.). On her view, trying is a stimulus condition for certain abilities: 'For a highly interesting subset of our narrow abilities, to have the narrow ability to do X is to have an intrinsic disposition to do X in response to the stimulus of one's trying to do X' (175).

It is NOT my intention to produce an argument against Vihvelin's detailed theory. But that is what it is, *a theory* of trying. I don't accept that theory, as is perfectly obvious from the entire drift of my argument about trying and particularity. Just think how odd it sounds to say that P's trying to F caused him to F, as Vihvelin asserts. It is commonplace to say things like 'P's desire for such-and-such got him [i.e., caused him] to F' or even 'P's desire to F was responsible for [i.e., caused] his G-ing.' But such locutions do not spring so readily to mind in the case of trying. The linguistic data, for what they are worth, don't come down squarely on her side rather than mine. Further, I think her claim that trying is 'logically independent of the action that it causes' is false, and my argument in the first part of Chap. 4 will address this point in some detail.

What of (b)? Trying could enter the explanatory order without entering the causal order. In Chap. 4, I return to a discussion of the role of trying as the explanans in an explanation: 'Why was P F-ing?' Answer: 'Because he was trying to G'. P might be searching in his bag because he was trying to find his keys. There are also quite a few examples of sentences that give reasons (as the explanans) for trying (as the explanandum) in an explanation (Hornsby 1995): 'His desire to find his keys was the reason why he was trying to remember where he put them' or 'She tried to lift the dumbbells as a way of impressing him with her strength'. Even if P's trying to find his keys explains in some contexts his searching in his bag, the former does not seem to cause the latter: what caused P to search his bag was, let us suppose, his desire to find his keys, not his trying to find his keys. An explanation using trying in either the explanans or the explanandum does not appear to be, at least straightforwardly, a causal explanation at all.

Still, I agree that there is a residue of cases that do seem undeniably causal: There must be some cases of explanation in which one is asking for the cause and not the explanatory reason why someone tried to do something: 'What on earth caused you to try to do something that stupid? I was drunk.' Other examples: 'His trying so hard caused him to break out in a rash'; 'His anxiety caused him to try all day to solve the issue'. In these cases, explanations by or about trying do enter the causal order. In these cases, denying (a) must be the fallback position.

You might ask: in light of this admission, why all the palaver of showing how adverbial modification in trying-sentences does not commit to trying particulars? Why not take the high road and just say that there are no trying particulars because there are only facts about trying to do something, and such facts about trying do not presuppose trying particulars? Why not: P tried to F G-ly is just something about the fact that P tried to F? Why need anything more be said?

First, without the work of this and the last chapter, it would be impossible to motivate such a view. Second, it won't work, because most of the cases of adverbial 'G-ly' in trying-sentences won't go over to G-ish facts about trying. Facts can't be graceful or cautious, slow or fast. But lastly, there is a point of greater importance. It is desirable to show just how few trying-sentences there are in which there are any even putative references required for their truth, either in causal contexts or in the other reference-back cases with which I dealt above. The reference-back and causal cases really constitute only a residual category.

Evaluations and Objects of Attitudes

Olivier Massin (also in private correspondence) reminds me that tryings can be the objects of attitudes which are, he says, typically directed at actions: intending to try, forbearing to try, deciding to try, undertaking to try. And trying can be the objects of evaluation, like actions. I think I can account for all of these cases without assuming that there are particular acts of trying.

When we evaluate trying, we needn't think of this as requiring an act, the act of trying, to which the evaluation attaches (as it does in 'a morally right action'). The evaluations of trying can be construed either as evaluations of the agent who tries or as requiring valuational sentential operators. 'It was good of him to try' evaluates the person and not the alleged act of trying. 'Trying to F is a good thing to do' can be construed as 'It is good that he tried to F'. The only case I can think of in which an evaluative word appears to attach to 'try' directly is when, as a means of encouragement, one says 'That was a good try'. But in those cases, necessarily non-naked (what would a good try be in a naked case, as opposed to simply a try?), one is evaluating the means one took to achieve a goal, typically unsuccessfully; for example, it was a good try to stop the flood, although he failed to stop it, because he took all the obvious necessary steps to stop it in a timely fashion, which turned out in the circumstances not to be sufficient.

Finally, consider two of Massin's other examples: deciding to try and intending to try. Deciding and intending are indeed attitudes, but they are propositional attitudes, directed not at actions but at propositions about action: 'P intended that he tries...', 'P decided that he will try...'. (There is some dispute about what exactly the propositional content of an intention looks like, but none of that dispute affects the point I am making.) If the proposition that P tries... or that P will try... does not require a trying particular, then there is no reason to think that introducing a propositional attitude toward that proposition would require one. I conjecture that 'forbear' and 'undertake', when they occur with 'to try', are propositional attitudes as well. An agent undertakes that he try, for example. I shan't defend that conjecture more fully here.

The Law: The Conduct Element in Attempts

First, I want to make some remarks about 'to attempt' generally, before turning to its application in the law. Unlike 'to try', 'to attempt' does have a perfect nominal. And unlike 'endeavours', 'attempts' is unmistakably a count noun. It has a plural, and its behaviour is noun-like, not verb-like. I do not propose to subject 'to attempt' to the same sort of detailed account I have been giving to 'to try'. All I want to claim here is that the non-gerundive noun, 'an attempt', is derived from the verb, 'to attempt', and that therefore locutions using the perfect nominal noun, 'attempt', can be analysed into verb formulations which in turn do not require the use of the noun formulations. The perfect nominal formulation is derivative; the verb formulation is primary. For example, 'this was his second attempt to F' means 'he has twice attempted to F', which in turn means something like 'he attempted to F at some t and he attempted to F at some t*, and t≠t*.' 'His attempt was dangerous' means something like 'It was dangerous to him [or, to someone else] that he attempted to F'. 'His attempt to F was careful' (and the like) is 'he carefully attempted to F', and then the same sorts of arguments I used to explain 'he tried carefully to F' without assuming trying particulars will apply, pari passu, to 'he carefully attempted to F' without assuming attempt particulars.

The question about attempting that I want to consider here is about attempts in the law and naked (as we might say) attempting, if there is such a thing. How does a non-particularist theory of trying (or attempting) account for criminal attempts? The problem is this: 'a bare intention [to commit a crime] is not punishable' (quoted in Duff 1996, 33), 'some act in furtherance of the intention is required' (Duff 1996, 33). Various courts at various times have identified differently what act ('the step') is required: a first step, a last step proximate to the crime, an irrevocable step, a significant step, a substantial step, an unequivocal step, and so on. For our purposes, we do not need to evaluate the competing candidates for the act required in order for a court to conclude that an attempted crime has occurred. What is of interest for us is only that some act or other seems to be required.

There are two different ways in which we might express this legal requirement. First, in the next chapter, I shall be defending an account, the (CTT), of what it is to try to do something that does not require any actual conduct element. Let's call that an account of the general idea of trying (or attempting). In the law, perhaps what it is that we find is a specialised account of trying or attempting-an account of a different but closely related concept, one that adds a requirement (a conduct element) to the general account. Although this would not be my preferred response, I think it is a perfectly plausible one. In many sciences (astronomy) for example, a common-and-garden idea, the ideas of a planet or a star for instance, is used, but requirements might be added or subtracted by the science to those in general use, in order for something to count as a planet or a star for the astronomer (e.g., our sun doesn't count as a star for everyday purposes-we only see the stars at night-but it is a star for astronomical purposes). Attempts might be like that for the law. On this response, attempts in the law do require some element of physical action, but the specialised concept of a legal attempt is not the same as the general idea of attempt or trying that is found in non-legal contexts and that general idea does not require any element of physical action. The former has a requirement additional to the ones for the latter.

But I think a more plausible response is what we might call 'evidentialist' (Yaffe 2010, 228–236). As Duff says (285), '...very few criminals will find themselves suddenly paralysed at the last moment...' and so 'subjectivists [Duff's term] could still justify a requirement for an overt act, not by appealing to the nature of trying itself, but rather by appealing to the evidential significance of overt conduct, and to the role of such a requirement in protecting us against intrusive policing' (this is not Duff's view, only a view he describes). On the evidentialist view, in principle there could be a case of a criminal attempt to F without there being any conduct element, but such cases would be rare indeed, so rare that there are pragmatic grounds for the law only to pursue and punish attempts in which is some conduct has actually occurred.

So the second way of responding to the conduct requirement for criminal attempts accepts the possibility of naked trying or attempting, however infrequent it might be, and would or could hold, if such an unlikely case were ever to arise, that such a suddenly paralysed criminal has indeed attempted a crime in the same sense in which an unparalysed criminal has, if the latter has taken some appropriate prior steps in pursuit of that criminal activity. However, on this evidentialist response, absent any action, we have either no evidence for the attempt, or only indirect evidence of some prior steps that might not be legally sufficient for prosecution. Further, there is an important norm in a liberal society for disallowing policing of mere thought and ideas, where there is no external behavioural result of what goes on in the alleged criminal's mind. So, on this option, the concept of an attempt in the law is the same as the general concept, but the law only adds an evidential condition for criminal responsibility.

Conclusion

This chapter offers an understanding of trying-sentences without requiring any trying particulars or particular acts of trying. It argues that Assumption (A) is false. I will present in the next chapter a positive account of the meaning of trying-sentences.

Notes

1. Many of the ideas in this chapter are taken from Ruben (2013).
2. One notable exception: Duff (1996): '…there is no 'it' that trying is: "to talk of trying is not to describe anything, but is merely a way of setting actions in a certain context".… 'Try' functions adverbially, rather than substantivally' (289). The quote within the Duff quote is from Heath (1971). I agree with Duff: no 'it'. I don't agree that they function adverbially. Hornsby says the same somewhere. I don't understand the claim.
3. I am influenced by Kenny's scheme (Kenny 1963). See also Mourelatos (1978).
4. The dissenters include Clark (1970), Horgan (1978), and Parsons (1972).
5. But see Parsons (1994, 44–45) for a different view on how to deal with attributives.
6. There is a lot of controversy on the nature of instantiation. See for example MacBride, Fraser (2005), 'The Particular-Universal Distinction: A Dogma of Metaphysics?', *Mind*, new series, Vol. 114, No. 455, 565–614.
7. Bratman (1987, 134) also speaks of intentional objects, but 'intentional' is with a 't' in his discussion.
8. Sainsbury should be credited with whatever is true in the following remarks on this topic and exonerated from any responsibility for anything false.
9. Compare: Vendler (1962), Kenny (1963), Mourelatos (1978).

Bibliography

Alexiadou, Artemis. 2013. Nominal vs. Verbal–ing Constructions and the Development of the English Progressive. *English Linguistics Research* 2 (2): 126–140.

Allen, Robert L. 1966. *The Verb System of Present-Day American English*. The Hague and Paris: Mouton & Co.
Anscombe, G.E.M. 1965. The Intentionality of Sensation: A Grammatical Feature. In *Analytic Philosophy*, second series, ed. R.J. Butler, 158–180. Oxford: Blackwell.
Armstrong, D.M. 1981. Acting and Trying. In *Nature of Mind and Other Essays*, ed. D. Armstrong. Brighton: Harvester Press.
Austin, J.L. 1956. A Plea for Excuses. *Proceedings of the Aristotelian Society* 57: 1–30. Reprinted in *Philosophical Papers*, 1970, second edition, Oxford, Oxford University Press, 175–204. Page references in text to the reprint.
Bennett, Jonathan. 1988a. Adverb-Dropping Inferences and the Lemmon Criterion. In *Actions and Events: Perspectives on the Philosophy of Donald Davidson*, ed. Ernest LePore and Brian McLaughlin, 193–206. Oxford: Blackwell.
———. 1988b. *Events and Their Names*. Oxford: Oxford University Press.
———. 1998. *The Act Itself*. Oxford: Oxford University Press.
Bratman, M. 1987. *Intentions, Plans and Practical Reason*. Cambridge: Harvard University Press.
Clark, Romane. 1970. Concerning the Logic of Predicate Modifiers. *Nous* 4 (4): 311–335.
Davidson, Donald. 1967 (1980). The Logical Form of Action Sentences, reprinted in his *Essays on Actions and Events*. Oxford: Clarendon Press, 105–118.
———. 2001. Aristotle's Actions, in Donald Davidson 2005, *Truth, Language, and History*. Oxford: Oxford University Press.
Duff, R.A. 1996. *Criminal Attempts*. Oxford: Oxford University Press.
Evnine, Simon. 2016. *Making Object and Events*. Oxford: Oxford University Press.
Ginet, Carl. 1990. *On Action*. Cambridge: Cambridge University Press.
Goldman, Alvin. 1970. *A Theory of Human Action*. Englewood Cliffs, NJ: Prentice-Hall.
Heath, P.L. 1971. Trying and Attempting. *Proceedings of the Aristotelian Society, Supplementary Volume* 45: 193–208.
Horgan, Terence. 1978. The Case against Events. *The Philosophical Review* 87 (1): 28–47.
Hornsby, Jennifer. 1980. *Actions*. London: Routledge & Kegan Paul.
———. 1995. Reasons for Trying. *Journal of Philosophical Research* XX: 525–539.

———. 2011. Actions in their Circumstances. In *Essays on Anscombe's Intention*, ed. Anton Ford, Jennifer Hornsby, and Frederick Stoutland, 105–127. Cambridge, MA: Harvard University Press.

Jones, O.R. 1983. Trying. *Mind* XCII (367): 368–385.

Kenny, Anthony. 1963. *Action, Emotion and Will*. London: Routledge & Kegan Paul.

Kim, J. 1976. "Events as Property Exemplifications". In *Action Theory*, ed. M. Brand and D. Walton, 159–177. Dordrecht: Reidel. Reprinted in *Supervenience and Mind: Selected Philosophical Essays*, Cambridge: Cambridge University Press, 1993, pp. 33–52.

Lewis, D. 1986. *Philosophical Papers*. Vol. II. Oxford: Oxford University Press.

Ludwig, Kirk. 2010. Adverbs of Action and Logical Form. In *A Companion to the Philosophy of Action*, ed. Timothy O'Connor and Constantine Sandis, 40–49. Chichester: Wiley Blackwell.

MacBride, Fraser. 2005. The Particular-Universal Distinction: A Dogma of Metaphysics? *Mind*, new series 114 (4555): 565–614.

Marcus, Eric. 2012. *Rational Causation*. Cambridge, MA: Harvard University Press.

McCann, Hugh. 1975. Trying, Paralysis, and Volition. *The Review of Metaphysics* 28 (3): 423–442. Reprinted in McCann (1998), 94–109.

Mourelatos, Alexander P.D. 1978. Events, Processes, and States. *Linguistics and Philosophy* 2 (3): 415–434.

O'Shaughnessy, Brian. 1973. Trying as the Mental Pineal Gland. *The Journal of Philosophy* 70 (13): 365–386.

Parsons, Terence. 1972. Some Problems Concerning the Logic of Grammatical Modifiers. In *The Semantics of Natural Language*, ed. Donald Davidson and Gilbert Harman, 2nd ed., 127–141. Dordrecht: Springer.

———. 1994. *Events in the Semantics of English*. Boston: MIT Press.

Richard, Mark. 2001. "Seeking A Centaur, Adoring Adonis: Intensional Transitives and Empty Terms". *Midwest Studies In Philosophy* 25 (1): 103–127.

Ruben, David-Hillel. 1990 (1992). *Explaining Explanation*. London: Routledge. Second edition (2012), Paradigm Publishers, Boulder, CO.

———. 2013. Trying in Some Way. *Australasian Journal of Philosophy* 91 (4): 719–733.

Silverstein, Harry. 1980. The Evil of Death. *Journal of Philosophy* 77 (7): 401–424.

Szabó, Zoltán Gendler. 2004. On the Progressive and the Perfective. *Noûs* 38 (1): 29–59.

Taylor, Barry. 1985. *Modes of Occurrence*. Aristotelian Society Series, vol. 2. Oxford: Basil Blackwell.
Taylor, Richard. 1973. *Action and Purpose*. Atlantic Highlands, NJ: Humanities Press.
Vendler, Zeno. 1962. Effects, Results and Consequences. In *Analytical Philosophy*, ed. R.J. Butler, 1–15. Oxford: Blackwell.
Vihvelin, Kadri. 2013. *Causes, Laws, & Free Will*. Oxford: Oxford University Press.
Yaffe, Gideon. 2010. *Attempts*, 72–105. Oxford: Oxford University Press.
Zimmermann, Thomas Ede. 2006. Monotonicity in Opaque Verbs. *Linguistics and Philosophy* 29 (6): 715–761.

4

A Conditional Theory of Trying

What's in the Chapter

In this chapter, I offer both a general argument showing why I think there could be no trying particulars, and I offer an account of trying-sentences that does not require such particulars. In Chap. 2, I argued against what I take to be the prima facie most plausible 'naturalistic' account of trying as a particular, the view that identifies trying with a physical action. In Chap. 3, I blocked one argument for the view that there were trying particulars of any sort. But of course none of this shows that tryings are not some sort of particulars other than physical actions. The purpose of this final chapter about trying is two-fold: (A) to offer an independent argument against any particularist theory of trying other than the one that identifies the trying with a physical action, for example, one that might identify it with a mental act or even with a mental event; (B) to offer an account of trying-sentences (the Conditional Theory of Trying, hereafer the CTT) that does not require trying particulars of any kind. The account in (B) meets the desiderata I set out earlier. It avoids having to answer questions about those alleged particulars, for example their mereological characteristics, their spatial or temporal locations (if any), their causal relation to physical actions, or alternatively their identity to physical actions. As a welcome (to me) by-product, it offers a natural way in which to understand naked trying. Even if (A) were unsuccessful as an argument, (B) would still stand as a contribution to views available for understanding what trying is. It would help to define the logical space of views one can hold about trying.

In (B), I state that account, (CTT), in an initial form, and offer various clarifications of what it says and does not say (for example, about the kind of ability my account requires). The remainder of (B) considers various objections to (CTT), some of which lead me to alter and improve the original formulation: fluky success; time-indexing, metaphysically impossible action, finks and reverse-cycle finks, the nature of blockers and preventers, intentions, and explanations that use trying. There are two sections on intentions. The first deals with the unintended consequences of action; the second responds to the claim that intentions play the same role in the economy of mind and action that (CTT) assigns to trying and hence makes my account redundant.

There is a lot of overlap between the argument in (A) and in (B), and the two sections make many of the same assumptions, but the arguments have different purposes. The first is a general argument against any particularist account of trying that attributes a 'bridging' function to such a particular. The second gives an account of what it is for an agent to try that does not make any particularist assumption.

(A) A General Argument Against Trying Particulars

Why might one wrongly think that the view of tryings and actions as non-identical particulars is an attractive one? Imagine an agent with beliefs, desires, intention, decisions, and whatever else on the inside of the agent you wish to add, except that the agent has not (yet) tried to do anything. Both in Chap. 2 and below, later in this chapter, I discuss the role of intentions, including proximate intentions, and how they don't get us all the way to action. We saw in Chap. 2 how Sarah Paul spoke of the need for a bridge from intentions to actions (Paul 2009). John Searle describes the gap between decision and action: '...the decision is not causally sufficient to produce the action ... you cannot just sit back and let the decision cause the action...' (Searle 2001, 14–15.) There is a gap between decision and action, and there is a gap between intention and action. Presumably, gaps need bridges.

Many volitionists, including Brian O'Shaughnessy (1980), David Armstrong (1981, 70) and Hugh McCann (1998), treat volitions and acts of trying as the same, or treat the former as a special case of the latter (McCann 1998, 104). Jing Zhu (2004) argues that volitions (replace his 'volitions' in the quotations in the paragraph below with: 'trying particulars') can bridge this gap between intentions and other mental states on the one hand and action on the other. Hornsby claims: 'Like intentions, the production of attempts mediates (causally, and conceptually) between a person's having reasons to do things and what she intentionally brings about.' (Hornsby 1995, 534).

So these volitionalist and related accounts invite us to think of trying as a 'bridge' *from* the various mental events that occur to agents or *from* the mental states in which an agent might be (viz., beliefs, desires, intentions, proximate or otherwise) *to* the action (when trying is successful). 'Some classical volitionists view volitions as being essential in bridging the ... gap, which translates thoughts into actual bodily movements by triggering the initiation of action' (Zhu, 179); 'Volition is thus postulated as a mediating executive process, by which an agent somehow puts (or tries to put) the relevant body parts into action in the execution of an intention' (Zhu, 179); '...volition serves as a conscious, executive activity with respect to intention and desire... This account neatly fills the gap between the mere having of reasons and intentions, and the occurrences of changes that are the results of actions. If this is correct, the connection between the two is through the agent's executive thought' (McCann 1998, 89–90).

In order to assess the plausibility of the bridging idea, let's start with the following Principle, which I name (HP) the 'H' being in honour of David Hume, since Hume claimed (Treatise, Book I, Part III, Section VI):

> (HP) 'There is no object, which implies the existence of any other if we consider these objects in themselves'.

Hume's Principle is worded in the singular, but it should be extended to claim that no number of particulars, $x_1...x_n$, requires the existence of any other distinct particular, x_{n+1}. Much of the discussion of Hume's Principle focuses on the question of necessary connection in general, since Hume used (HP) as a way of denying that cause and effect were necessarily connected (Wilson 2010, and further references therein). I will treat (HP) as about what Williams calls 'necessary existential connection' (Wilson 2010) and Correia calls 'rigid existential dependence': 'x cannot exist unless y does', i.e., Nec (Ex $\rightarrow$ Ey) (Correia 2008, 1014–1016). I'll speak of existential dependence and independence, omitting 'rigid' for the sake of brevity. When Hume adds 'if we consider these objects in themselves', he is of course thinking of objects and (what we could call) their intrinsic properties. Wilson also adds in her statement of (HP): there are no necessary connections between 'distinct, intrinsically typed, entities'. No one, I take it, disputes that there is a necessary connection (de dicto) between the cause of e and e, *in the sense that* it is necessarily true that if c causes e, e exists. If c is described as 'the cause of e', then from c's existence so described, it follows that e exists. But c is not intrinsically typed as the cause of e. So 'the cause of e caused e' is no counterexample to (HP). Hume's 'does not imply' is best understood to be about metaphysical possibility: there is some possible world in which the first, but not the second.

Correia's interests are quite different from mine; he is considering various attempts to characterise the asymmetric idea of grounding. For my purposes, asymmetry does not matter. The idea of existential dependence is non-symmetric. Co-dependence, or mutual dependence, is quite a standard idea. If x existentially depends on y, y may or may not existentially depend on x. x and y might be existentially interdependent. Following Wilson (2010, 607), we can distinguish between strong and weak versions of existential independence (she actually makes this distinction for the definition of modal distinctness): if only one of x and y can exist without the other, their independence is 'weak'; if both x and y can exist without the other, their independence is strong. (HP) asserts that even if there is a nomological connection between two events or objects, there is never a contradiction in assuming either one without the other.

Correia distinguishes between two forms of existential dependence, rigid and generic necessitation. Rigid necessitation holds between two specific objects; generic necessitation holds between an object and a fact. x's existence might necessitate only that something exists which has a certain property. Here is an example of generic necessitation: (s) necessarily, if statue s exists, then there must have been some sculpturer of s. (s) is about an object and a fact; it says that necessarily if a certain object exists, then some fact must obtain. (s) does not tie s to any particular sculptor, or to any other specific object. One might also believe that which particular sculpturer sculpted statue s is also metaphysically necessary, but that is not what (s) says. (HP) should be construed as a denial of rigid necessitation between distinct particulars. It is silent on generic necessitation.

(HP) is plausible, if the range of particulars to which it applies is appropriately circumscribed. Wilson says that 'Hume's denial of necessary connections between objects is ... more generally aimed at denying necessary connections between distinct entities of any ontological category fit to be causal relata (e.g., events)' (Wilson 2010, 597). Thus, I will restrict (HP) to substances and events. It certainly does not apply to properties. There are very many cases of non-identical properties that are necessarily connected: (a) determinable and determinate properties: Nec (x) (if x is red, then x is coloured). If (a) is true, then the properties of being red and being coloured are not strongly independent. (b) some geometric properties: Nec (x is trilateral iff x is x is triangular). If (b) is true, then the properties of being triangular and the property of being trilateral are not even weakly independent, since neither can exist without the other. There are other, non-geometric cases too, in which two properties are necessarily co-instantiated: 'Nec (x is extended iff x has a shape)' provides one such example. (A feature of all these cases is that it is a priori knowable that they are so connected.) Since I restrict (HP) to substance and events, I don't consider alleged counterexamples to (HP) in the case of sets, properties, numbers, tropes, or laws, for instance.

The application of (HP) to substances is relatively the most straightforward of its applications. By distinct substances in this context, I mean not only that the substances are not identical, x≠y, but also, if they have parts, they have no part in common (there is no overlap). They are disjoint. Constitution of an object by the aggregate of whatever makes it up does not provide a counterexample to (HP). Assume that an object≠that aggregate (if they are identical, the example is already ruled out by disallowing cases of identity). If an object is constituted by an aggregate or mass of particles, then neither requires the existence of the other. The object does not require that particular aggregate, even if it requires that there be some aggregate of particles that constitutes it, since the aggregate can go out of existence by losing a few molecules and by replaced by a different but very similar aggregate, while the table remains the numerically same table in spite of the change of aggregate. That is generic existential necessitation. Nor does the aggregate require for its existence the table, since, if losing its characteristic shape destroys the table, the aggregate of particles can remain the numerically same aggregate, but differently shaped or even by being widely dispersed.

In keeping with a common assumption about events, if (HP) covers the case of events, it should also cover the case of omissions, and should cover states, on the assumption that states are particulars (there are some strong reasons for not counting state as particulars (Marcus 2009)). On one plausible view, an event is the gaining or losing of a property, typically by an object (i.e., by a substance or by another event), at a time. Since we already have said that there are necessary relations between properties, it will follow that there are cases of existential dependence between some events: necessarily, the event, x's becoming triangular, exists iff the event, x's becoming trilateral, exists. So (HP) says this about events: no event e requires for its existence the existence of a second event, e*, if the properties that constitute e and e* are not themselves necessarily connected. (I would not use, in order to illustrate this point, the example of a determinable property and a determinate property, although they are necessarily connected, since-as I explain in Chap. 6—I think a strong case can be made for the view that, e.g., becoming red and acquiring a new colour can be two names for the same event, even on an otherwise prolific theory of event identity.)

Even with all these restrictions, (HP) isn't innocent. There are allegedly a number of counterexamples to it. I will discuss (and dismiss) two such alleged counterexamples: supervenience and necessity of origin (in one of its forms). First, let's consider supervenience. One event type, the acquiring of property M, supervenes on another event type, the acquiring of property P iff (Nec) (x) (y) (if x acquires property P & x acquires property M & y acquires property P, y also acquires property M). (Feel free to add additional necessity operators as you think they are required. I speak of 'acquisition' of properties to make the case one of about events rather than states). I assume that the properties M and P are not necessarily connected in any of the ways described above.[1] So, if acquiring M supervenes on acquiring P, than if the three token events, x's acquiring of P, x's acquiring of M, and y's acquiring of P exist, then necessarily the token event, y's acquiring of M, exits. That would constitute a counterexample to (HP).

That, or something like it, might be the correct account of one type of supervenience (there are many others) but it does not settle the question of whether there are any bona fide cases of it. These two propositions seem to be inconsistent: (1) there is no necessary connexion between non-overlapping events whose constituent properties are not necessarily related (HP as I have understood it); (2) given that a property M does supervene on a property P (or on a conjunction of properties P, and etc.), it follows that there is a necessary connection between the event of y's acquiring property M and the three events of x's acquiring property P, y's acquiring property P, and x's acquiring property M.

I think the best response is to retain (HP) and deny that there are any cases of supervenience between such events as in (2). It's easy to be sceptical about supervenience so characterised. Assuming that the case is not one of the events' constituent properties being necessarily connected, as they are for determinable and determinate properties, or triangularity and trilaterality, etc., why should there be any other case in which one thing's having two events occur to it and a second thing's having one of the two occur to it, require that the second thing have the second event occur to it as well?[2] What has whatever goes on with regard to y's P-wise twin x dictate what most go on with regard to y itself?

I share Horgan's scepticism (Horgan 1993; Ruben 2015). The strongest intuitions in favour of supervenience are to be found in ethics and aesthetics, and those are the very cases in which we are most inclined to think that we do not really find properties or events 'supervening' on a subvenient base. I leave to one side the use of supervenience with regard to physical and mental events, as being an intrinsically contentious application of the idea.

But if we conclude that whatever it is that does supervene lacks ontological reality, the explanation of why it may be true that that y is M-ish too in the circumstances envisaged above is more straightforward. Horgan's example is R. M. Hare's account of the supervenience of the moral on the non-moral (Hare 1964). In its bare bones, Hare is a non-cognitivist. Hare does not assume that there is a set of moral facts or properties distinct from the non-moral facts or properties, such that the former supervenes on the latter. Hare talks of the purposes to which moral discourse is put, and it is moral *discourse* ('the language of morals') that supervenes on non-moral discourse, not moral properties or events on non-moral properties or events. Claiming that x and y are both M-ish is not to claim that they have acquired some *property* M or that some tokens of an M-type event have occurred.

Horgan calls Hare's account 'irrealist', and one can see why, although this is not a term that Hare himself used. On Hare's view, moral language does not describe anything, neither any additional moral facts nor the descriptive facts on which such discourse supervenes. The discourse of morality does not 'connect' to reality in that way. It has a different purpose or function, on Hare's account: to commend certain actions or to prescribe them, not to describe them.

So Hare's view of morality is an irrealist (or non-cognitivist) view and the supervenience thesis is one about two discourses, one factual and the other used for teaching standards, not two areas or realms of reality whose properties or objects could require the existence of others. There is no property of goodness; there are properties, say P, Q, and R, in virtue of which we can call a particular object 'good' or a particular action 'right', but to call the object 'good' or the action 'right' is not to assert that the thing has another property, goodness, in addition to P, Q, and R or even that it has the property goodness such that goodness={P or Q or R}. The function of moral discourse is not to introduce properties or events or any particulars at all, but to commend things that have P or Q or R. As such, sentences of the moral discourse lack truth-values since they do not state that anything is thus-and-so. The irrealist view comes into its own in the explanation of the purposes of the second discourse, the supervening discourse. But the point for us here is that, so understood, supervenience does not challenge (HP). The events or properties in the subvenient base do not entail the existence of any supervening properties or events. It is discourses or fragments of language that supervene or are subvenient, not entities: neither properties, nor objects, nor events.

This way of approaching supervenience still has a question to answer: why should two language fragments relate in this way? I am not going to attempt to answer in full that question here, but presumably, in the case of this view of ethics for example, it has to do with consistency in our moral discourse and therefore our ability to teach ethical standards to others and to explain them to others and to ourselves. We put a premium on generalisation, in order to achieve a certain kind of intelligibility. Particularist views might work for causation, but they do not gain much traction in an account of explanation, for instance. It may be that no explicit generalisation is required for full explanation, but insofar as an explanans is about something having a certain property, the weight of generalisation is carried by the property mentioned in the explanans, and so no further explicit generalisation may be required in addition to that implied by the property (Ruben 1990 and 1992, second edition 2012, 186–189).

Somewhat analogously, suppose we held that a certain action a had non-moral properties P1…Pn, and action a was right, but that another action a* had the same properties P1…Pn as a, but that it was not right (and that no other non-moral properties were relevant to the rightness or wrongness of actions a or a*). Someone to whom we were trying to teach moral judgment would be at a loss to know how to morally categorise a third action a** that had the same non-moral properties, P1…Pn. Right or not right? Nor would anything about our own judgments about a and a* help us to make a judgment about that third action, a**. Nothing about our evaluations of a and a* could help to form a standard or principle by which to judge the moral worthiness of a**. This can all be spelled out, presumably, without any commitment to thinking that moral judgment is about the moral properties that actions might have. It is about consistency of moral judgment. The claim I am making is conditional. If one thinks that the moral supervenes on the non-moral, then the above seems to me to be the only convincing way in which to interpret the claim. Realism about moral properties (and I would add, realism about psychological properties too) requires some account other than supervenience.

Second, let's consider necessity of origin. There are many ways in which to word a claim that might be called 'the necessity of origin'. If we limit the examples to organisms, including of course persons, it might be alleged that an organism o could not exist unless a certain zygote had existed, or a pair of gametes, or a specific sperm and egg. But following Kripke's original suggestion, I will construe necessity of origin in terms of the parents of a person: if a person p exists and p has parents p_1 and p_2, p could not exist unless p_1 and p_2 existed. Assuming that the relation, '… could not exist unless … existed' is transitive, p's existence will metaphysically require the existence of every one of his direct ancestors, however far back. Some of p's indirect ancestors won't even be persons (they could be slugs or sloths or whatever), but presumably they will have had to exist as well, in order for p to exist, for as long as it is true that the organism(s) from which another comes is its 'parent' organism(s).

Thus understood, I don't think that there is much by way of support by 'intuitions' for the necessity of origins. It is easiest to see some problems with necessity of parentage by considering the case of a person no longer alive, say, Julius Caesar (P. Mackie 2009, 93–117). Why should something existing or occurring before a person is born be taken as metaphysically necessary for that person but nothing existing or occurring during his life (or even after his lifetime) taken as metaphysically necessary for him? And even were we to accept the temporal asymmetry in necessity of antecedent existences or occurrences rather than the necessity of post-birth existences or occurrences, why should we select antecedent items only to do with parentage? Why not place or time of birth? These are rhetorical questions, but they prompt us to try and find, if we can, something special about parentage as necessary for the identity of a person, rather than other facts about the person that occur before, during, or after his birth.

We seem to be able to consider what Caesar's life would have been like if Gaius Marius (his uncle by marriage) had been his father rather than Gaius Julius Caesar (David Wiggins 1980, 116, n. 22), just as we can consider what his life would have been like had he not crossed the Rubicon. We can ask how Kafka's outlook in his writing might have changed had he not been 'of Jewish descent and upbringing' (Michael Dummett 1973, 132). It is true that Dummett's observation does not necessarily question the doctrine of the necessity of parentage; after all, Kafka could have had the same parents but they, in turn, not be of Jewish descent and upbringing either. But his parents had parents too, and, in order to construe Dummett's supposition in such a way that it does not bring the necessity of parentage into question, all of Kafka's ancestors would have to fail to have been of Jewish descent and upbringing rather than just not exist. Further, none of Kafka's siblings would have been of Jewish descent and upbringing, nor any of his parents' siblings, and so on for all the siblings of all of his ancestors. In the end, in order to give content to Dummett's supposition about Kafka without changing his parentage, we would have to assume that almost all of the Jews of a long-ago generation were not in fact Jewish. The far simpler and more plausible choice is to give content to Dummett's supposition by imagining that Kafka had different parents.

It may be that we give greater weight to considerations of parentage in specifying the identity of a person than we do with other considerations, and, if so, this is something that Mackie (2009, 116–117) calls 'the tenacity of origin'. But the weighting is only relative, not absolute. Tenacity leaves us with the possibility of being able to consider what a person (or other biological organism that has parents) would have been like had it had different parents. Tenacity of origin offers no counterexample to (HP).

In his statement of (HP), Kris McDaniel (2007, 135) restricts its application further, to fundamental relations. (He applies it to the occupation relation.) Being the parent of is not likely to be a fundamental relation. Without more being said about which relations are fundamental and why that is so, it is hard to be sure whether (HP) so restricted would avoid these alleged counterexamples to (HP) altogether, thereby rendering my defence of (HP) from them unnecessary. The relation of existential independence seems like a convincing example of a fundamental relation, on any plausible account of fundamentality of relations, so perhaps McDaniel's further restriction would be helpful to my case.

However plausible a restricted (HP) is as a general principle (and I think it is very plausible when properly circumscribed and apparent counterexamples are dealt with), its application to the example of trying and action seems to me to be amongst its strongest cards. Suppose you think that a trying (for instance, P's trying to F) is a particular and that an action (P's F-ing) is a particular and that these two particulars are distinct (they are neither identical nor do they overlap). If trying were to serve as a bridge, trying must be existentially independent of whatever it is to which it leads, and whatever it leads to must be existentially independent of it. But is trying an existentially independent particular in this way, either weakly or strongly? I am going to argue that trying and acting are not existentially independent relative to one another, so they can't be particulars distinct from one other.

Let me make several points first about my argument in this section. First, I assume that the laws of nature are contingently true, not necessarily true.[3] I acknowledge that there is a view that this is not so, but it is a view that I will disregard in what follows. Second, the argument in section (A) proceeds under the assumption of determinism. In section (B), I discuss a certain amendment to my account of trying that would be required if determinism is false. I think that that same amendment would work here as well. Third, I'm assuming that the necessity of causal origin is false. Fourth, the argument that I will sketch for trying bears some resemblance to some bad arguments about reasons and causes being 'logically distinct', due for example to A.I. Melden and others, that Davidson successfully demolished long ago (A.I. Melden 1961; Davidson 1963 (1980), 13). Whatever the resemblance might be, I believe that my argument will escape that demolition. Fifth, in this chapter and in the remainder of the book, I assume that actions are particulars. I have more to say about that assumption in Chap. 7. Finally, I am going to conduct the discussion in (A) of this chapter as if (TUT) were not true. Why? Not because I have any doubts. If (TUT) is true (as I believe it is), that already makes the idea that action and trying are distinct particulars dubious, since they could be at best only weakly independent. Since there are many who would dispute (TUT), it is safer not to employ it in (A) of this chapter, and this only makes my work in this section harder.

The argument I am going to produce about trying particulars can be usefully contrasted with a structurally similar argument for particular events that are causes and effects. The conclusions of the two arguments, however, are different; the contrast is instructive.

A Conditional Theory of Trying

Suppose three events, e1, e2, and e3, such that e2 is 'the bridge' by which e1 causes e3; that is, e1 causes e3 via causing e2, the latter of which causes e3. e2 would have to be a distinct particular, neither identical with nor overlapping either e1 or e3. e2 can't be identical to either e1 or e3, because nothing causes itself or is caused by itself (theological exceptions perhaps notwithstanding). And e2 can't overlap e1 or e3, because it would then cause or be caused by part of itself. One might think of two new events, e1-minus the e2 part, or e3-minus the e2 part, but then e2 no longer overlaps either of them.

When P struck a match at t, suppose he caused it to light at t*. That token striking, e2, and that token lighting, e3, are distinct event particulars, and they are existentially independent: there are possible worlds which contain that same token striking but not that same token lighting (or any token lighting), and possible worlds which contain that same token lighting but not that same token striking (or any token striking). (This can be rephrased into counterpart theory, for those who prefer.) But that still leaves another possible existential independence we need to think about.

In lots of those possible worlds that contain the striking but not the lighting, the match might be wet, the wind very strong, oxygen might be absent from the air in the vicinity, the strike pad on the box may have lost all its red phosphorus. Lots of the particular circumstances that accompanied the striking when it did cause the lighting might be missing, so that many of those possible worlds might fail to contain at least one such particular circumstance. That would explain why many of these possible worlds are worlds that contain that same token striking but not that same token (or any) lighting.

Consider the conjunction of all those conditions, k (k includes states, events, absences, etc.) such that it is *nomologically* necessary such that when e2 (our original match striking) occurs & k obtains, e3 (our original lighting) occurs. The set of all metaphysically possible worlds s in which we are now interested incudes all those worlds that contain e2, the original match striking, *and* in which all of the conditions listed in k obtain. No nomologically necessary condition for the match's lighting is missing, such that the lighting, in conjunction with all those nomologically necessary conditions, is nomologically sufficient for the match's lighting. We are going to exclude from s those possible worlds that contain e2, the original match striking, but in which any of the conditions listed in k fails to obtain.

What can we say about this set s of such possible worlds? Will the token lighting occur in all of them? No. Many of the possible worlds in s will be ones in which the match's lighting also occurs, but at least one world in s must still fail to contain that match's lighting. Why? It is metaphysically possible for our match to have been accompanied with all the conditions which were nomologically necessary for its lighting, but still the lighting does not occur. Such worlds may have laws different from our own, or maybe there is some other explanation (a small miracle?). But it is always metaphysically possible for a match to be struck in conditions nomologically sufficient for lighting, but no lighting to ensue.

How would an analogous argument work for trying and acting, if trying were conceived of as a particular, bridging the gap between the agent's mental states and action? Suppose that there were a trying particular, say P's trying to F, that served as a nomic or causal bridge from P's mental states and events, m, to his token action a, P's F-ing. I quoted Vihvelin (2013) in the last chapter as claiming: 'I take trying to be a real event (or sequence of events) and logically independent of the action that it causes'. P's trying to F would have to be a distinct particular, neither identical with nor overlapping either m or his F-ing.[4] To start with the obvious: there can be a trying to F by P without there being a F-ing by P. Alas, agents often don't manage to do what they try to do.

As in the case of causes and effects, there are circumstances that accompany trying, and that are required for a successful outcome. In (B), I will spend a great deal of time listing and explaining them-they will be the antecedent conditions of the subjunctive conditional that constitutes my account of trying. But just to list the main relevant ones here: the agent has to have the opportunity to act, the skill to act, the know-how, there can be no preventers or blockers to his acting as, for instance, occurred to Dr. Landry's and Professor Strümpell's patients, there can be no finks or reverse-cycle finks at work, and so on. If you feel so inclined, add any other conditions you fancy (as long as the condition does not by itself entail that P's F-ing occurred), and call their conjunction k. So now consider the set of metaphysically possible worlds s*, in which P tries to F and *all* the conditions in k obtain. In at least many of the possible worlds in s*, P's F-ing also occurs. But if P's trying to F were a distinct particular that could provide a 'bridge' from P's mental states to another distinct particular, P's F-ing, P's F-ing would have to be existentially independent from the conjunction of P's trying to F and circumstances k. That means that at least some possible world in the set s* would have to include P's trying to F and circumstances k, but *not* include P's F-ing. If these are really distinct particulars, P's trying to F and circumstances k can't jointly rigidly necessitate P's F-ing.

Bridges can go nowhere, but could a trying particular in circumstances k really go nowhere? My claim is that a thought experiment that attempts to imagine a metaphysically possible world in which there is a particular, a trying to F by P in k, but no F-ing by P, will fail. If, in circumstances k, a particular, call it 'e', identified by some particularist account of trying as an act of trying, occurs but the agent still does not act, neither the agent nor we would have any reason to believe that e was an act of trying.

For any particular e, imagine that e occurs, but that nothing whatever prevents or blocks the agent from acting, the agent is able to act, has the opportunity and know how, etc. On what grounds would we want to accept e as a trying? (This thought experiment should not be confused with one in Chap. 8, in which the agent does not act, because in that that experiment, the agent does not have the opportunity to act; not all of the circumstances in k obtain.) I appreciate that my argument has an evidentialist or verificationist ring to it; one could argue that something *could be* a particular act of trying even if we had no possible grounds for believing that it was one. However, the argument is meant to be a challenge to produce any grounds that we might have for identifying, in the circumstances imagined in the counterexample, any such e as a particular and distinct act of trying, and, in light of the inability to offer any such grounds, at least the argument invites a reconceptualisation of what is going on in such a case.

Recall Grünbaum's argument in Chap. 2: he challenged us to distinguish between an idle wish and an attempt in the naked case. I think I met his challenge. But if one produced the same challenge here, the same reply that I gave there does not work. After all, in the naked trying case, we could identify the reasons for which the attempt was naked. There were physiological or other reasons for which Dr. Landry's and Professor Strümpell's patients' attempts were naked. But in the case we are now considering, there would be, ex hypothesi, no such explanation, since all the nomologically necessary conditions for the agent to F would have been fulfilled. I think that the right conclusion here is that, whatever e is, if it is a particular, it could not be a trying. If it were, there would be a metaphysically possible world in which one tries in circumstances k but fails to act. But there is no such metaphysically possible world; so trying cannot be a particular that is existentially independent from a distinct, non-overlapping particular action. (I will argue later that the same argument cannot be applied to the case of intentions, since for them there is such a metaphysically possible world.)

If we think of endeavouring or trying as a particular of the sort that a suitably restricted (HP) covers, this bridge strategy described above must be a mistake. The bridge envisaged from other mental states to trying and from trying to action would provide a nomological, causal connection. If two particulars are only nomologically connected, it is metaphysically possible for one to occur without the other. (HP), as circumscribed, tells us that nomological necessity is the tightest connection there can be between distinct particulars of the sort we are considering. So, if the thought experiment is right (and given (TUT), which I bracketed until now), the connection between trying in k and acting is not just nomologically necessary, but is metaphysically necessary, in both directions. There is no metaphysically possible world in which an agent tries to F in k but fails to F, and no metaphysically possible world in which an agent Fs but does not try to F (that is (TUT)). Trying (in k) and acting are not existentially independent (not even weakly, let alone strongly) in the way in which non-identical, non-overlapping particular events or substances are. Since I assume that actions are particulars, it must follow that there can't be any trying particulars.

The same point, that trying cannot be a nomological bridge in the way envisaged by many particularists, can be generalised to apply to some non-particularist views of trying as well. Consider Gideon Yaffe's view of trying in his 2010: trying requires both commitment, commitments inherited from intentions and therefore subject to the same canons of rationality (this constitutes his main disagreement with Bratman), and guidance. On his view, commitment and intention on their own are not enough for trying; the element of guidance is absolutely essential to distinguish trying from intending. 'The idea that trying involves more than a commitment to success is motivated by the observation that a person can be committed to something-can have, in fact, an intention-based commitment to it-and not be trying to do it at all' (Yaffe 2010, 90); 'Intention, therefore, is not sufficient for trying' (91). Note also that Yaffe also holds (as do I) that: '…trying need not be, itself, an action' (91). One can try to do a basic action and fail. He doesn't speak of naked trying, but he would accept, I think, that there could be the sorts of cases of trying described by William James and elsewhere in the modern scientific literature.

What sort of account can Yaffe offer of guidance, in the face of the possibility of trying-but-with-no-ensuing-action? On his view, in order for there to be guidance, and hence trying, the agent's intentions must cause something, even if not any action. '…there is guidance by a commitment if and only if the intention that constitutes the commitment non-deviantly causes an event … no matter where we stop the sequence of events caused by an intention … we meet the necessary and sufficient condition on guidance…' (92). In the case of action failure, the agent can be said to try if, for example, his intention-based commitment only causes his presynaptic nerve to release acetycholine [sic] that is not then received by the postsynaptic muscle nerve (92). So, in order for the guidance required for trying to take place, the intention must at least start some non-deviant causal chain, which in the successful case would have led to the action that the agent is trying to do.

On Yaffe's view, trying is not a particular. It's more like this: the agent can be said to be trying to F when his intention initiates and gets to *some* specific point on the causal chain (call whatever point is chosen on the chain 'point p') that would lead to the intended action in the case of a successful trying. There is no suggestion by Yaffe that point p=the trying. Rather, the causal chain arriving at some point p is a condition of its being true that the agent tried.

But I don't think this can be right, for the same reason I gave above. Call the release of acetycholine by the presynaptic nerve 'the release'. But now we can say the same thing about the release (and about causal chain's reaching any other point p on the causal chain one cares to identify) that we said above about trying. The release, or the chain's reaching p, is a particular event. It is metaphysically possible that the release occurs in circumstances k (so there is no nomological reason why the causal chain does not continue to action), but yet the agent does not act. On Yaffe's view, the agent has tried (because of the occurrence of the release or the chain's having reached point p) but it must be, on my view, metaphysically possible that the release occurs, or p is reached, in circumstances k and still the agent does not act. But since I claim that it is not metaphysically possible that one try in k but not act, one can't be said to have tried in virtue of the release occurring or point p's having been reached.

I believe that in every case of trying there will be some causal chain from mental states to action. To repeat something I said in Chap. 2: we are not like the Strawman in The Wizard of Oz, who can act without a brain. Even imagine that it is a nomic truth that the causal chain at least reaches the release event, or point p, whatever and wherever p is, whenever an agent tries. But, in the light of the argument above, that the release occurs when the agent tries might be a nomic truth, but it can't be the truth-maker for 'P tried to F'. Trying can't be a particular event on the causal chain, nor can it be true that someone has tried in virtue of some particular point on the causal chain having been reached (Yaffe's version), even if there is such a particular occurrence in all nomologically possible cases.

Looked at in this light, the view that there are particular acts of trying (or events or states, but there is no need to keep repeating these additional possibilities in what follows), existentially independent from the actions the agent is trying to do, must be a mistake, if it just adds to the agential story yet another particular, a trying or an act or event of trying. No particular that is not identical to the action could ever get the agent metaphysically close enough to the action that he was trying to do. So, if trying does get an agent metaphysically closer to the action that he is trying to do, and yet is not identical to, or does not overlap with, that action, trying must not be just another particular.

Rejection of the particularist view of trying, both the inside-the-agent version that identifies tryings as mental acts or as brain states or events, and the world-side version which identifies them with physical actions at the surface of the body or beyond, leaves us with something of a puzzle about what trying adds to the action story. Just what does 'P tries to F' add that would otherwise be missing? What function, if not reference to some sort of particular, does 'P's trying to…' perform? On the conditional theory that I develop below, there will be a metaphysically necessary connection (other than identity) between trying and physically acting, in a way for which a merely nomological tie that might link two distinct acts or events cannot account. The theory will also show how trying does come metaphysically closer in some way to the action, when there is one, than any additional particular not itself identical to the physical action could do.

(B) The Conditional Theory of Trying

What I shall now try to do is to offer an analysis of 'P tries to F in circumstances k at time t' in terms of a subjunctive conditional. This might be found to be surprising, since subjunctive conditional analyses are more frequently offered for dispositional terms like 'fragile' or 'flexible', and 'P tries to F…' isn't an obvious candidate to count as dispositional (Choi 2005, 2009). I can only point out that there is a philosophical tradition of offering analyses of what appear to be non-dispositional concepts in terms of subjunctive conditionals. Two obvious examples spring to mind: (1) the phenomenalists' account of material objects: 'There is really a door in front of me iff if such-and-such visual appearances should be sensed, then such-and-such tactual appearances would be sensed' (Roderick Chisholm 1966, 193); (2) a compatibilist account of free will: 'P chose to do F freely iff if P had decided to choose to do something other than F, P would have done something other than F.' I don't mention either of these analyses as particularly compelling ones, but only in order to show that the tradition of philosophical analysis that uses subjunctive conditionals to elucidate ideas that are not obviously dispositional hardly begins with my (CTT) below. If you think that offering a conditional analysis for trying (and indeed similarly for material objects and for free will) is a sufficient condition for counting trying to act as a disposition, although it did not at first sight appear to be one, so be it. In that case, trying to act would count as a disposition.

As a first shot (this isn't the final formulation by any means), the analysis of 'P tries to F' (where F-ing is a physical action type; I offer no account of mental action, if there is such) that I propose is this:

> (CTT) P tries to F at t in circumstances c iff in the closest possible world to the actual world in which at t P has whatever ability is required in order to do F in c, knows how to F, and has the opportunity to F in c, and there are no blockers or preventers to his F-ing in c, then Fs intentionally or is F-ing intentionally at t in c.

In what follows, I refer to 'P tries to F' as the LHS; to the subjunctive conditional, as the RHS. In the consequence of the RHS, in (CTT) and in later formulations, 'then he will F intentionally in c' or 'then he Fs intentionally in c' means that there is some action token of type F that he does or will do. There will always be more than one such token action that would fit the bill.

(CTT) is a subjunctive conditional. The closest possible world in which all the conditions listed in the antecedent of the RHS obtain might of course be the actual world. I disregard questions about possible ties for the closest possible world; there may be a set of equally closest worlds. (CTT) is intended as an alternative to any theory on which trying is a particular.

In terms of the anti-particularist argument of section (A), the argument that there is no metaphysically possible world in which an agent tries to F in circumstances k but fails to F, another way of stating the same idea in terms of (CTT) is this: if the agent tries to F, then the LHS of (CTT) is true. If all the circumstances in k obtain, then the antecedent of the RHS is true. In which case, there is no metaphysically possible world in which the agent fails to F. Note that it is metaphysically impossible for the agent to try to F in k but fail to F; but the subjunctive conditional on its own only asserts that in the closest possible world to the actual world [NOT in all metaphysically possible worlds] in which circumstances k obtain, the agent Fs. In section (A), I referred to the circumstances that, along with trying, were jointly metaphysically sufficient for success as 'conditions k'. Those circumstances are enumerated in the antecedent of the RHS.

'Conditions c', on both sides of (CTT) are the ones that help us identify which case of P's trying to do something is being subject to the analysis. For example, in a case that will arise below, it helps us identify which of P's many possible golfing putts is the one under current investigation.

Another form of (CTT) has 'try' in imperfective aspect. I have expressed (CTT) in present tense; the obvious adjustments should also be made for past, and future tense, both for perfective and imperfective aspect. But more on that below.

(CTT) explains how the trying gets us closer to the action than any state or event or act of trying could. Trying is on the very verge of acting, as it were, conceptually or metaphysically, and not just nomologically, speaking. The idea conveyed by (CTT) is that if a person tries, he 'almost' acts ('almost' because his acting is conditional on the antecedent conditions being satisfied). Perhaps this is what Vesey had in mind when he wrote that when the agent tries, '…as far as he, or the mental side of him, but not necessarily his arm, is concerned, he moved his arm' (Vesey 1961). Vesey might have been thinking of it this way: when the agent tries, then, on the agential side of things everything is in place, in order for him to act. What remains is only that he should act.

This account of trying works as well for naked trying as it does for any other trying. In naked trying, there is no actual action. On (CTT), trying requires no actual action; it only requires that there would be an action given some set of circumstances, at least one of which would be merely counterfactual in the case of naked trying. (CTT) makes no assumption that the agent actually does anything. It merely asserts that under certain specified conditions, the agent would do something. In a closest possible world in which all the antecedent conditions are satisfied, which might of course be the actual world, he acts. But that is consistent with his naked trying in the actual world, if in the actual world some of those antecedent conditions are not satisfied.

Time and (CTT)

Let me explain how I think time works in (CTT) and why I have expressed the consequent of the RHS in a disjunctive form. I assume that an action always takes time. No action is instantaneous and no action can occur only 'at t', if 't' is an instant of time. An action can be completed at an instant: the window may have closed at t. But if P closed the window, his closing of the window is an action that took some finite amount of time and whose terminal point might have been at t. It is always in order to ask, 'How long did it take you to F (to close or to open the window)?' (I disregard the case of interrupted actions with non-contiguous parts: even when P is photocopying his paper, he might break for a coffee but if asked what he is doing, he might still say truthfully that he is (in the midst of) photocopying his paper.) To be sure, there are achievements and accomplishments (Mourelatos 1978; Kenny 1963), but they are the terminations of actions that take time, and it is on the latter that I wish to focus. I discuss and extend the idea that actions take time at the very end of Chap. 6.

In the case of verbs subject to the imperfective paradox, a person may have been opening or closing a window from t1 to t10. But that is consistent with it being false that he opened or closed the window, if the window never opened or closed. So we won't say of P that he opened or closed the window until the window opened or closed at t10. But that should not make us think that his action only occurred at t10. It didn't. It took from t1 to t10.

Just as actions stretch over a finite period of time, so does trying to act. When an agent tries, he tries over a period of time; let's say that he tries from t1 to t10. He commences trying at t1. Since 'try' is never subject to the imperfective paradox, it is true that he tried at each time within that stretch. He tried at t1 and he tried at t10 and he tried at all times between those two times, if he is acting at all those times. But it is also true that if he tried at some specific t, there must have been some finite stretch of time, however short, over which he was trying, a stretch that includes t. Since the closing of the window will have taken time, a person will have had to try to close it over the time he took to close it.

How we deal with temporal maters will differ somewhat in the case of telic verbs that are subject to the paradox of imperfectivity and in the case of atelic verbs that are not subject to that paradox. Consider two of our old verb friends as indicative of atelic and telic verbs respectively: 'pushing' and 'closing'. I take these two verbs as indicative of a large class of similar verbs but I am not committing myself that in matters regarding time, there might not be other variations that I have not considered. However, the expectation on my part is that even if there are other variations, those variations will not compromise the central idea behind (CTT).

Let's start with an atelic verb that is also not subject to the imperfective paradox: 'push'. If P pushes the cart from t1 to t10 (he stops because he has become bored with the pushing), then P tries to push the cart from t1 to t10. He starts trying to push it at t1. He finishes trying to push it at t10, when he finishes pushing it. At every time between t1 and t10, he is pushing it (the imperfective), or he has pushed it (the perfective), and at every time between t1 to t10, he is trying (imperfective) to push it or has tried to push it (perfective). So, if 'F' is an atelic verb not subject to the imperfective paradox:

> (CTT-not subject to paradox) P tries to F in circumstances c at t iff in the closest possible world to the actual world in which at t P has whatever ability is required in order to do F in c, knows how to F, and has the opportunity to F in c, and there are no blockers or preventers to his F-ing in c, then Fs intentionally at t in c.

Now consider a telic verb that is subject to the paradox: 'open'. P tries to open the window from t1 to t10 (who would have believed that there is so much to do in order to get the blasted window finally to open!). At any time between t1 to t10, he is trying to open the window. But between t1 to t10, he may be opening the window but it may not be true that he has opened the window. He only opened the window at t10, when the window opened. So,

> (CTT-subject to the paradox) P tries to F in circumstances c at t iff in the closest possible world to the actual world in which at t P has whatever ability is required in order to do F in c, knows how to F, and has the opportunity to F in c, and there are no blockers or preventers to his F-ing in c, then at t P is F-ing intentionally at t in c or P Fs intentionally at t in c.
>
> (In subsequent formulations, I won't reproduce both versions of (CTT)).

There is a way to misunderstand the analysis offered by (CTT) and how time plays its part (this misunderstanding is responsible for many objections to (CTT) that I have heard). Suppose I have decided and intend to commence trying to F at t2, but that at t1 I have not yet commenced trying, which I will do only later at t2. But at t1 (which might be years before t2), might not the antecedent of the RHS already be true (all the antecedent conditions could already be met regarding ability, opportunity, and so on, at t1) but yet the consequent false? Doesn't that contradict my analysis?

For the RHS to be true, it isn't enough that all the antecedent conditions are satisfied (that, I think, is the essential error in this misunderstanding). The RHS is a subjunctive conditional; the claim is not that the antecedent entails the consequent, so that necessarily the consequent is true *whenever* the antecedent is. Sometimes the consequent is false even though the antecedent is true? When is that? If, by hypothesis, I am only going to commence trying to F at t2, so that I am not trying to F at t1, then I am only going to intentionally F at or after t2. At t1, I won't be F-ing. But if I am not acting at t1, the RHS may have a true antecedent at t1 but it will have a false consequent at t1, so it will be false at t1. That is, the RHS is false at t1, not true, just as the LHS is false at t1 (because I'm not trying either). It's true that I'm not F-ing at t1, but I'm not trying at t1 to F either. The analysis remains correct: it has a false LHS and a false RHS (because the RHS has a true antecedent but false consequent).

Gideon Yaffe has another additional clause in the antecedent of his conditional, restricting P from changing his mind: assuming t5 is the time of the intentional action (I have altered the times in Yaffe's example), '…[person] D does not (at least until after t5) change his mind…' (Yaffe 2010, 94). Do I also need a no-change-of-mind clause in the antecedent of (CTT)? I don't think this is necessary.

Suppose that P changes his mind about F-ing at t4, without finishing whatever it was that he set out to do by t5. It is true, in that case that he tried and was trying to F until t4 but not thereafter. So I can't see that we need a clause explicitly ruling out change of mind. He was trying to F until t4 as long as he was F-ing until t4. He was no longer trying to F after t4 since he was no longer F-ing after t4. He tries to F at all times at which he is F-ing; he stops trying to F (the LHS will be false) when he stops F-ing (the RHS will be false because it will have a false consequent), when he changes his mind.

Just as one can stop running a race in the middle of the race, so too one can stop trying to run the race before the race is finished. As long as he is running the race, he is trying to run it (and similarly for 'pushing' and 'closing'). If he changes his mind about running it, he stops trying to run it. As long as the LHS and the RHS of (CTT) have the same times, the change of mind is automatically taken care of. Whenever the agent was trying or tried, at that time or for that stretch of time, the antecedent conditions held and he was acting or acted. Just as one can begin to try and stop trying, one can begin to act and stop acting. As long as these are co-ordinated in (CTT), no counterexamples arising out of change of mind successfully challenge the account. No additional clause is required.

Some Further Clarifications

For physical action success, the person must have whatever ability is required in order to do what he is trying to do. Ability marks the area of what the agent has to be like; opportunity, preventers, and blockers mark the area of what the world must be like. I do not think there is a sharp distinction between a person's lacking the ability to do something and there being a blocker to his action, but surely there are clear cases of both.[5]

I have added to (CTT) a separate antecedent condition: 'knows how to F'. One might, not entirely implausibly, stretch ability to include such know-how, but it seems to me safer to add it as an explicit, additional requirement. There are many very bad ways of trying to do F, so bad that one could never do F by trying in that way. Many of these bad ways relate primarily to lack of the agent's knowledge. If P does not know how to get to Edinburgh from London and leaves London, crossing the Channel, P will never get there. The additional clause 'knows how to F' is meant to rule out cases like that.

I'd like to say as little about ability as I can get away with (for a fuller and rich discussion of these issues, see Clarke (2015), whose terminology I mostly follow) and Maier (2014, 2015, 131), and similarly I would like to say as little as possible about the connection of ability to issues of free will and determinism. The ability required in (CTT) is narrow ability.

This includes what Clarke calls general ability (skill and competence,) but also includes 'the psychological and physical capacity to use' such things (Vihvelin 2013, 11). In what follows, when I refer to 'ability', I mean to be referring to what Clarke calls narrow ability. There is a sense in which I am still not able to F (say, write a letter), even if I have the narrow ability, but lack paper, pen, and ink, or if someone is holding my arm still. But I include those things separately, as lack of opportunity or as preventers and blockers.

There is also a distinction between a general sense of 'ability' in which it is applied to act types and a particular sense in which it is applied to particular actions (Honoré 1964, 463–468). (Maier 2014 calls these general abilities and specific abilities.) In (CTT), the sense in play is the particular or specific, since we are considering trying to do an act token of some type on some specific occasion. We are not considering an ability to do actions generally of some type.

There are various analyses of ability on offer in the literature, for example a conditional account, a causal powers account, and the restricted possibility account. I have no reason as far as this chapter goes to opt for any one or the other, with one proviso. Sometimes conditional (and other) accounts use 'trying' in the antecedent of the subjunctive conditional that is meant to be the analysans for 'P is able…': 'P is able to F iff if P tried to F, P would F.' An example of an account of ability which uses trying is that by Kadri Vihvelin (2013, 175, ff). (Vihvelin also takes trying to be real events with causal powers; I mentioned this in Chap. 3, but more on that below.) Obviously, no conditional account of ability that uses 'try' in the antecedent of the conditional (or anywhere in the analysans of ability) will be consistent with (CTT). 'P is able to F iff (if (if P has the ability, etc. to F, P intentionally Fs), then P would F)' is nonsense.

We need to distinguish between doing something well and being able to do it at all. In many cases, the idea of ability needed by (CTT) is a very basic idea, as in the term 'motor abilities' for example. There is a much less basic idea of ability, sophisticated ability we might say, as being able at tennis or chess for example. Not everyone who has enough ability to play chess has the ability in chess playing in the sophisticated sense of 'ability'. A person might be able to play chess however poorly, simply because he knows the rules for moving the pieces on the board, and he might repeatedly play tennis in order to build his ability to a sophisticated level. Ability comes in degrees.

Following Yaffe (2010), I include (narrow) ability and opportunity separately. Some accounts of ability build opportunity into the idea of ability itself, thereby yielding a more inclusive notion of ability, appropriately enough called 'wide ability'. Maier for example (2015, 129–130) thinks that there are at least these two different ways of conceptualising ability. The contrast is between 'properties of agents that undergird and ultimately explain their options on particular occasions' on the one hand, and 'a certain pattern of options across a range of possible scenarios' on the other. An option is an action that is in my power to perform here and now: there is nothing 'between [the agent] and the deed' (123). Assuming that I have understood correctly what he is saying, the first way of thinking about ability is closer to the one I use as 'narrow ability'. His second way of thinking about ability is closer to what I have included in opportunity.

How does (CTT) relate to the so-called ubiquity of trying thesis (TUT), the idea that whenever an agent intentionally acts, he tries to do what it is that he does do intentionally, even in the absence of special circumstances like difficulty of task, need to expend extra effort, and so on? I think the ubiquity of trying thesis is true, as I said in Chap. 2, and that the arguments adduced in its favour show this (Hornsby 1980, 34–36). That ubiquity thesis must be something like this, where 'F' ranges over physical actions types and 'x' ranges over physical action tokens: (TUT) (Nec) (x) (F) (if P does a token action x of type F intentionally→P tries to F).[6] But does (CTT) entail (TUT)? It depends.

In the RHS of (CTT), the antecedent does not of course entail the consequent (if it did, we would be trying to everything we had the ability, opportunity, etc. to do!). However, does the consequent of (CTT) entail the antecedent? That is, if he acts intentionally, does it follow that all those antecedent conditions were satisfied? One might think so. After all, if he acts intentionally, surely he had the opportunity and ability to do what he did and nothing prevented or blocked him from acting. What better proof of possibility is there than actuality? If the consequent of (CTT) does entail the antecedent, then a fortiori the subjunctive conditional on the RHS of (CTT) will be true whenever the consequent is true. In that case, the agent tries (the LHS will be true). So, if we can assume entailment of the antecedent of the RHS by its consequent, and if an agent does do something intentionally (so that the consequent is true), then, according to (CTT), he tries to do it-and that is what (TUT) asserts.

But is there an entailment of antecedent by consequent on the RHS? I think the key question resolves around ability and cases of fluky success. Austin (1979), in discussing such a case, says that 'it follows merely from the premise that he does it, that he has the ability to do it...'. But there are intuitions aplenty for the view that a single success, if it could not be followed by similar successes, is not sufficient for ability, and if so, the entailment from the consequent to the antecedent of the conditional on the RHS of (CTT) would not be valid. Maier (2014, 11) suggests that both sets of intuitions could be reconciled by the distinction between specific and general abilities. The agent who flukes into successfully F-ing intentionally may have had the specific ability on that occasion without having the general ability to F. I'm not sure that is right.

Consider the fluky success of the wanna-be golfer, who wants to hole the ball in the cup, intends to do so and tries to do so. Poor chap, he has no ability to speak of, but he hits the ball, and the ball goes into the hole only because of a series of incredible and unlikely coincidences: the ball hits a tree t a long way from the hole, so that its path is diverted from what it otherwise would have been to a path that leads it to another tree, t*, which again diverts its path so that it finally drops into the hole. It seems that the golfer has intentionally holed the ball, albeit not by means of the plan he had envisaged. Imagine that the trees were only planted there yesterday. Had the trees not happen to have been placed there yesterday, instead of tomorrow as originally planned, the ball would have ended up nowhere close to the hole. Did the golfer have any specific ability even on that one occasion to get the ball into the hole? If there can be fluky success of such a single intentional action, this would show that the consequent on the RHS did not entail the antecedent.

J. L. Austin introduced the idea of an executive failure (Austin 1979, 218n). This is the idea of a fluky failure rather than a fluky success. A talented golfer misses an easy, short putt, one similar to ones he has done countless times before. He tries and fails, but kicks himself because he could, really could, have sunk it, or so he thinks. It isn't that he could have done it had conditions had been different; he can sink a putt like that in precisely the conditions that then prevailed (or again, anyway, so he thinks). But he didn't. Case like this can easily be multiplied. A professional footballer tries to make an easy goal from only a short distance. He has the relevant ability if anyone does and he has the opportunity to make the goal. Nothing stands in his way; there are no apparent blockers or preventers. But he misses. In these cases, isn't the LHS true (the golfer and the footballer certainly try) but the RHS false, since the antecedent of the RHS is true but the consequent is false? So it seems that (CTT) fails. I'm going to argue that in the case of a fluky failure, the antecedent conditions can't have been satisfied.

Gideon Yaffe has provided a completion counterfactual for 'P tries to A' somewhat similar to mine, but he says that his counterfactual is a 'test' for trying, not an analysis of it (Yaffe 2010, 94–95).[7] I discussed some aspects of his account of trying above. Even so, thinking about his completion counterfactual provides a useful foil for developing (CTT) as an analysis of 'P tries to F'. Yaffe adds the absence of executive failure to his list of conditions in the antecedent of the conditional. Should I have added it too?

What should we say about such cases? Perhaps the golfer didn't really have the ability, even the specific ability required on this occasion, to sink such a putt (or the footballer to score the goal, but the two examples make the same point), but that is strange, because the golfer seemed to have whatever abilities were required to sink putts just like it. Perhaps he didn't have the know-how, but one does not generally doubt the know-how of a professional golfer each time he misses an easy putt. The golfer knew how to sink it, but failed to do so. There is no doubt that he had the opportunity. Nor can we just put it down to 'executive failure', because that appears to be merely a fancy term for a *ceteris paribus* clause: if he has the opportunity to F, has the ability to F, has the know-how, and there are no blockers and preventers to his F-ing, then he does F intentionally unless he doesn't. And that would be vacuous.

In a deterministic world at least at the level of human action, his missing the putt (or the goal) can't just be a random occurrence. If 'random' means 'there is no reason for', then nothing is random in that sense in a deterministic world. There must be some difference, however small, between the putts he sinks and the ones he doesn't. It might be some tiny difference in the lay of the land that he did not take into consideration, some almost trivial difference in wind speed or direction, some small way in which he did not align his body correctly. That difference must be caught by some difference in the antecedent conditions in the (CTT), between those cases in which he successfully sinks the putt and those cases in which he does not.

I think we need to distinguish between the ability, know-how, and opportunities (viz., the circumstances) the golfer had on this specific occasion at a gross level of sameness and at a more micro-level of sameness when compared to other occasions on which he has made the putt. When the gofer is exasperated because he thinks he has sunk the same putts in the same circumstances c, he is using a gross criterion for sameness; in fact, to understand his failure, we would need to use a much more refined criterion of sameness in order to understand why on this occasion he failed to sink the putt. In the ordinary course of life, we rarely if ever bother to use the more refined level of description of opportunities and ability, in order to decide exactly where the fault leading to the failure lies, but we do know it must lay somewhere. (In fact, in the increasingly and overly commercialised world of professional sport, much more attention is being devoted to these micro-differences.)

So a fluky failure can't be truly random in the sense that there will be no reason for the fluke. There must be some difference between this putt-sinking failure and the other putt-sinking successes, even if we will never know what it is. Perhaps he did not have the ability (even the basic ability) to adjust his swing to the specific and unusual circumstances of this hole; perhaps he was momentarily distracted from adjusting his swing correctly by a loud noise; perhaps the pitch of the green was slightly different than he supposes (that would count as a difference in circumstances). I see no reason to complicate (CTT) by adding an additional clause about executive failures. What else could an executive failure be, if not one of these micro-differences in ability, or opportunity, or know how, or the presence of a blocker or preventer, between when he succeeds and when he fails?

A Conditional Theory of Trying 133

What if we don't live in a deterministic universe? If so, considerations of probability will have to be introduced into (CTT). That might be desirable in any case. It only might be probable to some degree r (say, where r is less than 1 but considerably greater than 0.5) that the golfer will sink his putt. Perhaps we could then explain Austin's executive failures with some probabilistically modified form of (CTT). Even though all the antecedent conditions were satisfied, there remained a chance that he would not sink the putt.

The thought is this: (CTT_i) The golfer, P, tries to F iff in the closest possible world in which all the antecedent conditions are satisfied, the golfer has a probability r of successfully sinking his putt: P tries to F iff (in the closest possible world in which all the antecedents are satisfied, Prob (P's sinking of his putt=r)). The probability in (CTT_i) is unconditional probability.

The right-to-left inference might be thought to fail. Suppose it is true that in the world in which all of the antecedent conditions are or were satisfied, the golfer has probability r of sinking his putt in that world. But having a probability r of sinking the putt isn't the same thing as trying to sink it, so how could it follow that the golfer has actually tried, just because he has some probability r of sinking it? I think it does follow, and I now explain why.

Why would it be true that if all the antecedent conditions are or were satisfied, the golfer has probability r, where r<1.0, of success? Recall in the deterministic case the possible confusion of thinking that the antecedent of the conditional entails the consequent. It does not. (CTT) says that in the closest possible world with antecedent conditions satisfied, the conclusion is true. (CTT) is a subjunctive conditional, not a logically necessary conditional. That's why, as I said above, that, in the deterministic case, all the antecedent conditions in the subjunctive conditional *could* be true but the person never act, because he has not even tried. A person doesn't necessarily act just when or because the antecedent conditions are all satisfied. When he doesn't act (so the consequent of the conditional is false and therefore the RHS is false), it follows that he hasn't tried (the LHS is false). When the subjunctive conditional is true (true antecedent, true consequent), one can infer that the golfer has tried. It is not the case that all golfers placed in those antecedent circumstances mentioned in the antecedent of the RHS of (CTT) sink their putts, whether they try or not!

The same reasoning works for the indeterministic case, (CTT$_i$). If all the antecedent conditions are satisfied, that doesn't confer a probability of degree r of a successful putt-sinking to the golfer. What does then confer that probability on him for sinking it? Parallel to the deterministic case, in the indeterministic case too, all the RHS antecedent conditions could be satisfied but the golfer not have probability r of sinking his putt. The golfer may have the know-how, the narrow ability, the opportunity, and there may be nothing that blocks or prevents him from sinking the putt, but he may not have probability r, or indeed any probability, of sinking it.

Why? What would be missing is that he may not have tried to sink it. He has probability r of sinking the putt only if he tries to do so. So when the indeterministic subjunctive conditional is true (true antecedent, true probabilistic consequent), one can infer that the golfer has tried. The only difference between the deterministic and the indeterministic cases is that the consequent of the latter attributes a probability of success to the golfer, rather than simply states that he succeeds in sinking it. If the golfer had not tried, there would have been a true antecedent but a false consequent on the RHS, false because there would have been nothing that would have conferred the probability r of success to the golfer's putt. It is not the case that all golfers placed in those antecedent circumstances mentioned in the antecedent of the RHS of (CTT$_i$) have a probability r of sinking their putts, whether they try or not! (I'm deliberately repeating the point of the final sentence in the paragraph before the last, but altered for the probabilistic case).

Objections to (CTT)

(1) Let's return to the idea of a fluky success. Here is a special case of it. Suppose (I take the case from Hornsby 1995) that Edie wants to persuade an onlooker that there is some stone too heavy for her to lift: 'She has no reason to lift it, taking that to be impossible. But she has a reason to try and lift it: when she tries and fails, she demonstrates the impossibility,

which is what she wanted to do' (526–527). Hornsby's conclusion is that one can have a reason to try to do F without having a reason to do F. Hornsby assets that 'she cannot have intended to move it, because she knew that she couldn't move it' (528). How would this affect my analysis?

Assume that the LHS is true: Edie tries to lift the stone. But assume also that Edie was in error about what she could do; it wasn't impossible for her to lift it. She tried to lift it (so Hornsby would say) and, to her great surprise, she succeeded. She lifted the stone. However, 'despite the fact that *move it* was exactly what she tried to do, she would certainly not have moved it intentionally' (530). The RHS would have a false consequence (the moving was not intentional) but a true antecedent, so the RHS would be false, even though the LHS is true. Bad news for (CTT).

There are two assumptions in Hornsby's example that could be challenged: (a) P did not move the stone intentionally; (b) P did try to move the stone. She says that her argument for (a) 'relies on intuition…' (537, fn. 14). She says that it would be counterintuitive to say that someone did something intentionally that she believed it was impossible for her to do. I agree.

But what of (b)? Hornsby agrees that 'there are philosophers who hold that anything which an agent believes it to be impossible to do…is something that it is impossible for her to try to do'. But she dismisses this, on the grounds of her capacity account of trying.

I will challenge (b). I think that our judgements about trying to F and F-ing intentionally will go together. If P thinks there is even the slightest chance of his F-ing, he can try to F and, if he does, he has F-ed intentionally. But if Edie really believe that there is no chance of lifting the stone whatever, zilch, that it is really impossible for her to F, then if Edie does F to her great surprise, then it is true she has not F-ed intentionally but then she has not tried to F either. Hornsby's view is what one might call a 'hybrid' response. It breaks the link, because it supposes that Edie tries to do something but when she succeeds, her doing is not intentional, in light of her negative beliefs about her possible success. I want to retain that link.

In the case Hornsby describes, Edie is trying to show the onlooker that it is impossible for her to lift the stone. There seem to be two possible descriptions of Edie's case. (c) One could say that Edie is trying to show the onlooker that the stone is too heavy for her to lift by trying to lift it, or (d) (Adam's suggestion, 1986) that Edie is trying to show the onlooker that it is impossible for her to lift the stone by going 'through the motions that she goes through when she tries to lift it believing that to be possible.' On (d), it is not true that she is trying to life the stone.

I agree with Adams. I think Edie did *not* try and lift the stone. She only tried to convince the onlooker that she could not lift it, not by trying to do so, but by going through movements similar to those she would have gone through had she tried. Of course, the onlooker may falsely believe that Edie is trying to life the stone, when she isn't.

It is possible to hold that she tried to do both; it is possible that she tried to convince the onlooker that it was impossible for her to lift the stone by trying to lift the stone. But I don't think that is the most natural way in which to describe the case. She tried to convince the onlooker by actually doing something, tugging at the stone perhaps, and given (TUT), it follows that she tried to tug. So she tried to convince the onlooker that it was impossible for her to lift the stone by tugging (and trying to tug) at the stone. She tried to convince the onlooker that it was impossible, by acting as if she could do it, so by imitating as far as possible the actions a person would normally do when they lift stones.

Isn't Edie likely to say: 'Look, I tried to lift it but it did not budge'? She might indeed say that, but it is a matter of appeasing the onlooker by taking on his perspective for the sake of replying to him. The onlooker thought she could do it and so the onlooker thought that she could (and did) try to lift the stone. But that is a pragmatic concession to the onlooker's point of view. The onlooker falsely believed that Edie could try. What Edie might have said is: 'You, but not I, thought that I could try to life the stone, but it did not budge'. The truth is that she did not try because she believed that it was impossible for her to lift it.

Hornsby's rejoinder to Adams is actually to accept (d), the second description above, of such a case, but to argue that that is the same description ('going though the motions...etc.') one would give when she does *not* believe the stone to be impossible to lift. Her conclusion: 'going-through-the-motions-of-one-who-believes-that-lifting-it-is possible can *be* trying to lift it' (533). So on Hornsby's reply, Edie is trying to lift it even when she believes it to be impossible, because her trying to lift it=the motion(s) she makes, whether she believes it to be possible or not.

Her reply to Adams appears to depend on a type of physical motion theory of trying that identifies trying with some physical motion. Suppose that (a) one goes through motions m when one believes that lifting the stone is possible. So the argument would run like this: it could be that (b) one goes through the same motions m when one believes that lifting it is impossible. If trying to lift the stone=m, then Edie has tried in both cases, whether she believes it possible or impossible for her to lift the stone.

Unsurprisingly, in the light of Chap. 2, I don't accept a physical motion theory of trying any more than I do a physical action theory of trying. Tokens of different types of tryings can be identical to tokens of the same type of movement. (This is the 'reverse' of multiple realisation.) I can try to offer a libation to the gods, I can try to spill excess wine from my glass, I can try to impress you with my largesse, and so on, all by making token movements of the same type. So I think that Hornsby's reply to Adams fails. Edie has tried to convince the onlooker; she has not tried to lift the stone, even if the movements would be of the same type in both cases. Sameness of movement in the two cases does not insure sameness of what it is that one is trying to do.

(2) It is clear that agents can try to do the metaphysically impossible. Poor Hobbes spent a long time trying to square the circle, because he falsely believed that he could. An agent might try to do something even if he believes there is only some very small chance that he will succeed.[8] Unlike Edie above, Hobbes thought he had a chance of success, in spite of the metaphysical impossibility of what he was trying to do.

But trying to do impossible actions causes a problem for my analysis. A standard view (there are others, though) is that all conditionals with metaphysically impossible antecedents are vacuously true. If so, it would seem that all of us, and not just poor Hobbes, have been trying to do an indefinitely large number of impossible actions, whether we knew it or not.[9] Since the RHS of (CTT) would be vacuously true for impossible actions, it follows that agents have been trying to do these impossible actions without knowing it. Lewis rules out such cases by restricting his analysis of causation, for example, to cases in which the conditional is non-vacuously true, but, for (CTT), I prefer to deal with this objection in a more explicit way.

The conditional theory of trying is tailored for actions that one can do, if the agent and the world co-operate. But with trying to do the metaphysically impossible, we have a category of actions that are impossible to do, whatever the agent and the world are like, and some allowance needs to be made for that. The thought behind the emendation we need is this: what the agent can both try to do (and succeed in doing) is some action that he falsely believes that it is necessary that he do, in order to do some further action that we, but not he, know is metaphysically impossible. I suggest:

> (CTT*) P tries to F in c at t iff (1) if it is a metaphysically possible to do token actions of type F, then in the closest possible world to the actual world in which at t (a) P has whatever ability is required in order to do F in c, (b) has the opportunity to F in c, (c) knows how to F in c, and (d) there are no blockers or preventers to his F-ing in (c), then P Fs intentionally or is F-ing intentionally at t in c & (2) if it is metaphysically impossible to do token actions of type F, but there is a range of action types r such that it is metaphysically possible to do token actions of the types in r, then in the closest possible world in which at t (a) P believes that the token actions of the types in r are ways in which to do F in c, and (b) if P has whatever ability is required to do actions of the types in r, (c) knows how to do actions of those types, (d) P has the opportunity in c to do them, and (e) there are no blockers or preventers in c to P's doing them, then P does some token action of some type in r intentionally, or is doing that token action intentionally, at t in c.

This alteration will cover cases of metaphysically impossible non-basic actions. It would not cover metaphysically impossible basic action, if there were any. I cannot think of a plausible example of an action that could be counted both as metaphysically impossible and basic. (I assume that a conjunction of basic actions is not itself a basic action: simultaneously raising one's left hand and lowering one's left hand, which is a conjunctive action that is metaphysically impossible to do, for example.) There are many nomologically impossible basic actions that an agent might try to do: bend his thumb backwards, for example. But metaphysically impossible basic action seems like an empty category.

(3) Suppose someone proposes a conditional analysis of a wire's being live: 'x is live iff if x were touched by a conductor, x would conduct electricity.' Now imagine a dead wire connected to an electro-fink which is a devise that senses when the conductor is about to touch a wire, and which then always makes the dead wire live. The wire is in fact dead but in the circumstances in which it would be tested, it becomes live. So in the analysis of 'x is a live wire', the LHS is false but the RHS is true; hence the analysis fails. In the case of the dead wire, the conductor touching the wire initiates a process that makes the consequent true, but in an unexpected way, and hence makes the conditional statement true, in spite of the falsity of the LHS.

This sort of case is referred to in the literature on dispositions as the case of a finkish disposition. Another case is that of a reverse-cycle finkish disposition. In this case, the LHS is true but the RHS is false. A reverse-cycle fink attaches to a live wire but if it senses that the wire is about to be touched by the conductor, it insures that the wire becomes dead. The general lesson doesn't just strike against analyses of dispositions of course. It also strikes against conditional analyses of categorical statements like (CTT), if there are such.[10]

David Enoch uses a case similar to that of a finkish disposition to provide a counterexample to Gideon Yaffe's 'test' for 'P tries to F',[11] but I will apply Enoch's counterexample to (CTT). 'Think, for instance, of a case where one (intuitively) doesn't try, but only because one believes that if one were to try, one will fail' (Enoch 2012, 23). The person doesn't try to F because he does not have the ability to F and believes truly that he does not have that ability. The idea is that this person is very good at assessing what he is able to do. This is why, when he doesn't have the ability, he believes that he does not have it. This is also why in the closest possible world in which he does have the ability to F (or anyway so says Enoch), he also believes that he has that ability. So the LHS is false (he doesn't try in the actual world because he believes that he does not have the ability) but the RHS is true (in the closest possible world, *if* he has the ability (and also believes that he has it), and the other conditions are fulfilled, he does F). The counterexample is a case of a fink at work.

We can also construct a reverse-cycle fink counterexample to (CCT*) as it now stands. Suppose that it is true that the person tried but did not succeed in F-ing because he did not have the ability involved in F-ing, although he believed that he did have it. (He isn't so good at assessing his ability in this case.) But there is a counterfactual intervener lurking (probably a cousin of Frankfurt's counterfactual intervener (Frankfurt 1988, 1–10)) and if he sees the person about to succeed, he injects him with a drug so that he no longer wants to do F (or alternatively, so that he no longer believes that he has the ability). So it is true that he tries but in the closest possible world in which he does have the ability, etc., but which includes the involvement of the counterfactual convener, he doesn't do F, because the counterfactual intervener injects him so that either he believes that he is not able to F or stops him from wanting to F.

I don't know if there is some general fix that can be used to save conditional analyses (whether of categorical or dispositional statements) more generally. I shall deal only with the conditional analysis of trying, and I shall ask if we can fix (CTT*) to avoid counterexamples that arise from finks and reverse-cycle finks. As I said at the beginning of the chapter, 'trying' is not obviously at any rate a dispositional concept. So even if Choi is right that dispositions are not intrinsically finkable (Choi 2012), we should expect both extrinsic and intrinsic finks and reverse-cycle finks in the case of the apparently categorical 'P tries to F'. The case from Enoch of finking was an intrinsic fink; the case of reverse-cycle finking that I gave was extrinsic. Not that the distinction here between intrinsic and extrinsic is crystal clear (the reverse–cycle fink is really both intrinsic and extrinsic), but it does not matter for our purposes. Since 'P tries to F' is a categorical statement, albeit one that has a conditional analysis, both finking and reverse-cycle finking are possible.

In both of the alleged counterexamples, the agent has different mental state in the closest possible world w* than he has in the actual world w. In the case of finking, he believes that he does not have the ability to do A in the actual world; in the closest possible world, he believes he does have it, as a result of having the ability. In the reverse-cycle fink case, he wants to do F (or believes that he has the ability required to do F) in the actual world; he loses the desire to do F (or loses the belief that he has sufficient ability to do F) in the closest possible world as a result of the intervention by the intervener. Both counterexamples to (CTT*) require a change in the agent's mental states between w and w* (where this might include only a change in their relative strengths rather than by their total deletion or addition).[12]

Why should these counterexamples all require a change to the agent's mental states? We are dealing with cases of intentional human action in the consequent of the conditional. Suppose the agent does not try to F in the actual world but there is a fink attached to him, so that, in the closest possible world, if the fink senses that if he has the ability to F, has the opportunity to F, there are no preventers and blockers, it causes him to do F intentionally anyway, in a way that does not run through changes in his mental states. Suppose some causal loop in finking or reverse-cycle finking cases that bring about the truth or falsity of the consequent, but which doesn't run through any of the desires, intentions, wishes, beliefs, motives, or whatever of the possible world agent. But in that case, such a loop that 'made' the agent do F in spite of his mental states would rob F of being an action, or at least rob it of being an intentional one. The agent's body could be made to move in certain ways, but he could not be made 'to act intentionally', contrary to his total motivational state.

In order to deal with the finking example, the version of (CTT) that we need holds constant the agent's belief in the actual world that he does not have the ability to F, and so, generalising, what we need is this:

> (CTT**) P tries to F in c at t iff (1) if it is a metaphysically possible to do token actions of type F, then in the closest possible world to the actual world in which at t (a) P has whatever ability is required in order to do F in c, (b) has the opportunity to F in c, (c) knows how to F in c, and (d) there are no blockers or preventers to his F-ing in c, (e) P's total mental states includes all and only the same states (beliefs, desires, intentions, emotions like fear, pride, and hope) that he has in the actual world, then P

Fs intentionally or is F-ing intentionally at t in c & (2) if it is metaphysically impossible to do token actions of type F, but there is a range of action types r such that it is metaphysically possible to do token actions of the types in r, then in the closest possible world in which at t (a) P believes that the token actions of the types in r are ways in which to do F in c, and (b) if P has whatever ability is required to do actions of the types in r, (c) knows how to do actions of those types, (d) P has the opportunity to do them, and (e) there are no blockers or preventers to P's doing them, and (f) P's total mental states includes all and only the same states (beliefs, desires, intentions, emotions like fear, pride, and hope) that he has in the actual world, then P does some token action of some type in r intentionally or is doing that token action intentionally at t.

For example, if the agent tries to F but fails to F at t in w because, say, he lacks the ability to F, the RHS of (CCT**) is about that agent's *same* mental states *at t*, but now in a different world w*, a world in which he has the ability he lacked in w, but retains the same mental states in w* at t that he had in w at t. It is crucial to note that the requirement of 'sameness of mental states' does not rule out the way in which temporally extended actions require informational updating as the action unfolds diachronically, across time. The sameness requirement compares the mental states of an agent in different worlds at the same time. Within a world, the agent's mental states can change over time, but those changes must be matched by the same changes over time in the other possible words.

The requirement for all his mental states to remain the same is more than sufficient; some subset would have been enough. But to single out the just-sufficient subset of mental states with a qualification like 'relevant to his F-ing' might seem question-begging and as far as I can see, the stronger requirement of 'all the same mental states', although it is more than is needed, is harmless enough and does not generate any new counterexamples to the analysis. I also include all of P's motivational states and not just P's reasons for action for instance, since he might be motivated to act out of non-rational emotions, passions, and so on.

Is my addition ad hoc, merely to save an otherwise inadequate analysis, or is there any justification for it? I think there is a justification for it. I

A Conditional Theory of Trying 143

think that what we want to know, when an agent tries, is what that very same agent, motivated in the same way in which he was actually motivated, would do under certain, possibly otherwise changed, circumstances (note that the agent's abilities belong to the circumstances in this sense and not to the agent, since they, unlike the agent's mental states, can vary from actual to possible world). What we want to preserve is what the agent, given the mental states that he is in fact in, would do in certain new situations. The motivational profile of the agent is what must be held constant across possible world scenarios.

This solution is similar to part of the one Lewis offered for cases of finking in the analyses of dispositions (Lewis 1997). Lewis points out that the following two counterfactuals are consistent (Lewis 1997, 150):

If it were that p, then it would be that non-q.
If it were the case that p and q, it would be that r.

In the case of dispositions, and as a rejoinder to finking cases, Lewis uses this fact to argue that, in an analysis of the fragility of glass, it can both be the true that if x's stimulus condition were to occur (if the glass were struck), and x were to retain its non-dispositional base for the disposition that it has in the actual world, then the response would occur (the glass would break), but if the stimulus were to occur (if the glass were struck), the basis would not be retained (because it is finked by a sorcerer, or whatever).[13]

In my analysis of trying, the retention of the set of the agent's mental states plays a similar role to that played by the dispositional basis in Lewis' account. In the closest possible world in which the agent both has the ability, know how, and opportunity to do F (p), and retains the same mental states that he has in the actual world (q, which includes his believing that he does not have the ability), he would not do F (r); however, in the closest possible world in which he has the ability, know how, and opportunity (p), he does not have the same set of mental states (not-q, which now includes that he does believe he has the ability), and as a result of this, he would do F. '…the supposition that p and q is more far-fetched, more 'remote from actuality' than the supposition just that p. But we are not forbidden to entertain a supposition merely because it is far-fetched' (150). It is both true that if kangaroos had no tails, they would fall over and that if they had no tails but were supplied with NHS crutches, they wouldn't.

(4) I doubt whether we can construct an exhaustive list of possible blockers and preventers, but such blockers or preventers might include: physical restraints of various kinds and degrees of severity, causal connections in the world not working as normally expected, and objective conditions in the world that stand in one's way. Remember that, under 'blockers and preventers', we only want to consider conditions that are not already covered by ascribing the agent the narrow ability to act. (Drugs, alcohol, and mental illness, for example lessen or destroy an agent's capacity to act and hence count as a disability rather than a preventer.) But if this is all we can say about preventers and blockers, there is a worry that we trivialise the analysis: if, whenever a person who tries and who has the ability, know how, and opportunity to do F but fails to do F, we cite the presence of a preventer or blocker, has one said anything more than he does F unless he doesn't?

Can we say something that limits the range of what counts as a preventer or blocker to save the analysis from triviality? I think we can. Dowe gives an analysis of 'A prevented C' (Dowe 2001). I remain neutral on its details but the main thought (slightly amended) is that when A prevents C from happening, there is a third thing, B, such that (i) A and B occur but C does not, (ii) B initiates a process leading to C, (iii) there is a causal interaction between A and the process initiated by B, and (iv) if A had not occurred so that the interaction had not taken place, that process initiated by B would have led to C. The thought is that B gets going, just as it should, B has initial causal efficacy or umph, but the intervention of A stops the process initiated by B from leading to C. B gets blocked or prevented on its way to C. B gets derailed by A from getting to C.

The application of this to my account of trying requires an alteration. 'A' is the blocker or preventer, whatever that might be. 'C' is the possible action that fails to occur. To what does 'B' refer? 'B' does not refer to an act of trying, because there is no such thing. On my account, if there is a blocker or preventer, when one tries, there is some process that would have led to the intentional action if there would have been no blocker or preventer, but there is no reason to commit to what initiates that process or what the stages on the process are before it would have reached C. 'B' surely refers to the motivational or other mental states, whatever they may be, in the light of which the agent tries. The competing views on what these might be are well-known. But I think we can remain non-committal on their precise identity.

Dowe complicates the analysis to cover cases of what he calls over-prevention and pre-emptive prevention, and then extends the analysis further to cases in which the blockers or preventers are absences or omissions. But the point remains that there is always a causal requirement: in order to argue that there is a preventer or blocker in the neighbourhood, there is always a requirement to actually find some causal process that would have led to C, but which was interrupted, and to identify what it was that interrupted it. Because of this requirement, the 'no preventers or blockers' escapes the triviality of a mere *ceteris paribus* clause.

(5) There are a number of objections to (CTT**) that centre on the role of intentions. I have already set out some of my views on intention in Chap. 2. I argued that Landry's patient could have the proximate intention to act, not know about the conditions that prevent his acting, whatever they might be, and yet be surprised that he had not acted. If he is surprised that he has not acted, it is because he tried but failed, not just because he intended or proximately intended to act. In (A) of this chapter, I spoke about the gap between intention and action. That said, there are more issues about intentions and intentionality that require addressing. I do not aim to develop anything even approaching a comprehensive account of intentions; I only want to say enough to explain to some extent how intentions fit into my account of trying.

The first objection to (CTT**) that focuses on the role of intention in action is the problem of foreseen but unwanted consequences of action. When I run a marathon, I know that I will also wear down the rubber soles of my shoes. Let's assume that the wearing down of the soles is something I do not want to happen (I'll have to buy a new pair all that much sooner), but I regard it as a necessary evil that is far less important than my running of the marathon. The wearing down is a foreseen but unintended consequence of my running. But, says Michael Bratman (1987, 122–127, 133–138), my wearing down of the soles is an intentional action, even though I do not intend to wear the soles down. Bratman uses the case to argue against what he calls the Simple View: that if P does F intentionally, then he intends to F. I don't want to dispute his arguments against the Simple View more generally; in particular what I say here would or could leave his famous video game case untouched. I only want to dispute its application to the case of unwanted but foreseen side effects of the action one does intend to do.

If Bratman were correct, the RHS of (CTT**) could be true: in the nearest possible world in which the agent has the ability, knows how, and the opportunity, to wear down the rubber on his soles, and there are no preventers or blockers, his wearing them down is an intentional action. But I think it would be generally agreed that this is not something he tried to do. If only he could, he would avoid doing it. So the LHS of (CTT**) would be false, but the RHS true. Hence, the case of wearing down the rubber soles would be a counterexample to (CTT**).

My reply is that I do not think that the runner's wearing down the rubber soles of his shoes is intentional. Is there more to be said beyond swapping intuitions about whether this action is intentional or not? Here is a consideration that I find persuasive, although I accept that in the end a determined opponent could simply reject it too. What both sides of the dispute would agree is that, in Bratman's case, the wearing down of the soles is foreseen. Suppose a second case in which the wearing down of the soles is unforeseen (the runner is a physics illiterate). No one thinks that in the unforeseen case the wearing down is intentional. But the only difference between the first and second cases is the difference between the action being foreseen and unforeseen. I cannot see why that difference should amount also to a difference between intentional and unintentional as well. Why should adding the fact that the action is foreseen convert the case from a case of an unintentional side effect to an intentional action? We have a perfectly good way in which to describe the difference between the two cases: foreseen and unforeseen action. Why add the distinction between unintentional (or nonintentional) and intentional action to that first distinction?

In the first case, I knowingly wear down the rubber; in the second case, I do so unknowingly. There is nothing to be gained from collapsing the three-way distinction between unintentional and unforeseen actions, unintentional and foreseen actions, and intentional actions, into only a two-way distinction, by including all foreseen actions within the category of intentional actions. Bratman himself suggests that one could argue that there is a category of voluntary but nonintentional action: spontaneous action (126; see also Bishop 1989). Elsewhere, philosophers have spoken about deliberative action. All of these categories open up possibilities for understanding in other ways the case of wearing down the rubber of the soles, as unintentional or non-intentional but foreseen.

What argument does Bratman use for classifying foreseen side effects as intentional? A central point in his case is that so doing is to identify 'ways of acting for which an agent may be held responsible ... This is why it seems natural to classify as intentional my wearing down my sneakers. After all, as Sidgwick notes.... "we cannot evade responsibility for any foreseen bad consequences of our acts by the pleas that we felt no desire for them"' (Bratman 1987, 124). But I think that this argument supports my view rather than his. By eliding distinctions, we are able to make fewer nuanced moral judgements. With a fuller typology, viz., intentional, foreseen but not intentional, unforeseen and unintentional, we are more likely to make the careful and differentiated judgements of responsibility that we require.

Von Wright's claims that there are no 'clear criteria for deciding' whether a foreseen action that an agent does is intentional or not. But in a reverse of Bratman's view, he says that the distinction is of 'a moral nature' and that whether such an action is intentional or not depends on whether the agent can be blamed (Von Wright 1971, 90). Bratman's argument is that a virtue of ascribing intentionality to a foreseen action is that it permits us to hold the agent responsible. Von Wright's argument is that we start by deciding which actions are the ones for which agents are blameworthy and are foreseen by them, and ascribe intentionality to those. So, on his view, some foreseen actions an agent does will be intentional and some not, depending on the question of the attribution of blame.

But even his view, if correct, would pose a problem for (CTT**), since it allows some intentional actions that the agent does not try to do. Suppose P is utterly negligent in buying running shoes with a very poor quality rubber that he foresaw would wear down quickly. He can be blamed for their purchase. Imagine that the wearing down of the rubber has some serious unfortunate consequence. On von Wright's view, since he was both blameworthy and foresaw the outcome, his running down the rubber on the soles of his running shoes was intentional. Still it is nothing he tried to do. So, on this view, there could be cases in which (CTT) had a false LHS and a true RHS.

Von Wright's theory would have to deal with clear cases of actions for which an agent is blameworthy but were not intentional, even though the outcome was foreseen. If a doctor saves the lives of many patients, which he can do only by letting one other patient die, the doctor is responsible (blameworthy?) for the second death, and foresees that it will occur, but surely does not intend it. There are many consequences of a person's actions, both foreseen and for which the person is blameworthy, but which are not intentional. So I don't find von Wright's reversal of explaining intentionality by responsibility rather than responsibility by intentionality at all plausible, and I think my insistence of a distinction between only-foreseen-but-not-intentional action and intentional-and-foreseen action is the right way to reply to a Bratman-like challenge to (CTT**).

(6) Another objection to (CTT**), connected to intentions, might be this. Recall from Chap. 2 that a proximal intention is an intention to do something now, at once. Alfred Mele has claimed: '…an agent who … proximally intends to A … will A intentionally (beginning) straightaway, unless something prevents his doing so or thwarts his efforts', '…the mental and physical architecture of any being capable of intentional action is such that when such a being acquires a proximal intention to A, an immediate effect is the triggering of appropriate actional mechanisms, unless something prevents it' (Mele 1992, 72, 167). (Mele adds lack of ability to the list of preventers or blockers.) And 'The Final Account' (192): 'In all cases of overt intentional action, the acquisition of a proximate

intention triggers appropriate actional mechanisms-unless they are already operating-and the intention causally sustains their functioning' (192; there are a few more tweaks but these are not relevant to the discussion here).

Strictly speaking, there is no contradiction between this view of proximate intention and my view of trying: it can be true both that P entails R and that Q entails R. Moreover, Mele is clearly talking about a nomic connection between proximate intention and action; I have made it clear that I am speaking about a metaphysically necessary connection between trying and action. It is difficult to integrate or even compare the two accounts, but it is hard to get away from the suspicion that one, if true, undercuts to some extent the other. If his view of proximate intention were correct, it would remove much of the point of the view of trying I have defended. Put it this way: if proximate intention nomologically could get an agent all the way to intentional action in the absence of obstruction, what need would remain for the agent's trying?[14]

But I don't think that intention can get one nomologically all the way to action, in the way Mele supposes. *Pace* Mele, in Chap. 2, I gave several examples of what might come between intention, even proximate intention, and intentional action, other than preventers and blockers: inertia, forgetfulness, procrastination, boredom, ignorance, memory loss, distraction, and inattention. Such cases, as I explained in Chap. 2, assume some temporal gap, however small, between the intention and the intended action. Here is Sarah Paul again (Paul 2009, 19): 'We are not divine agents; there is a gap for us between intending and doing.'

But perhaps the strongest cases that show why it is not true that intentional actions are the immediate effects of proximate intentions, assuming only no blockers or preventers (as Mele says), are cases of final stage weakness of the will (Bishop 1989, 117–120). Some cases of weakness of the will are cases in which we fail to form the right intentions, given all our beliefs and desires about what it is on balance best for us to do. But cases of so-called final stage weakness of the will are cases in which we do form the appropriate intentions, even intentions to do something right now, conforming to our beliefs and desires about what is best on balance for us to do, but in which we fail to act on these intentions and do not merely replace them with alternative intentions on which we do act. It is not as if we change our minds about what to do. We have dealt with change of mind separately. The final stage akratic agent intends to F, after weighing and considering all his options. All things considered, he thinks that the best thing for him to do is to F. He does not then intend to do something else, to G, instead of intending to do F, because in that case his intention to do G would have merely replaced his intention to do F. He would have a vacillating will rather than an akratic one. The final stage akratic intends to F, does not F, and does not replace his intention to F with any alternative, competing intention.

When John Bishop discusses (and dismisses) the possibility of final stage akrasia, the possibility of a break between the proximate intention and the action (and without replacement by another, alternative intention), he concentrates on the case in which the agent does something else: '…final stage akrasia is possible only if merely voluntary action is possible too' (183). The only alternative Bishop can think of is that the final stage weak-willed action is not intentional action, hence not based on any final evaluative practical judgement, but is merely a nonintentional voluntary action (if there were such a thing, and Bishop thinks there isn't).

There is something uncompelling about the idea of an agent's having a proximate intention to F but his G-ing intentionally instead, without having an intention to G. Bishop's suggestion, although one he dismisses, is that the agent has a proximate intention to F but instead Gs voluntarily (but not intentionally). Bishop does not consider another, rather more plausible, alternative, the one in which the agent fails to act on his proximate intention, say to F, and there is no alternative action at all that he does instead. It is true that some count omissions as actions as well, and this is not a debate into which I wish to enter. It's just that using the case of inaction makes the argument that there are, or can be, cases of final-stage weakness of the will more plausible.

In William James' famous example (James 1950, 524), a person has decided (and intends; James' word is 'resolves') to get out of bed, but when it is time to do so, surveying the prospect of leaving his warm bed for a cold room, he does nothing. In James' example, the chap eventually does rise, but only after an inexplicable delay, and there is nothing in the example that would rule out the possibility of his not arising at all. At some point, we may want to withdraw our ascription to him of the intention to rise, but he can retain that intention for a long time while he remains in bed, perhaps until he falls asleep again. I think this is a case of a failure of an intention, a proximate intention to rise, to issue in intentional action. Or is it, as Bishop might say if pressed, only a case of a person dropping his intention to rise and acquiring instead an intention to remain in bed (the latter of which does issue in intentional inaction)? Perhaps in the end one is only swapping intuitions about the case, but at least I can enlist James on my side. Although James never uses the term 'intention' in this discussion (there is only one reference to intention in either of the two volumes of his famous *The Principles of Psychology*, and that reference is to the intention to speak, in Volume I), I think it is fair to extrapolate what he would say about intention from other things that he does say.

James says that our activity is 'paralysed' in such a case. A 'struggle' is going on in the man's mind, which prevents our intention from being effective (keeps 'our idea of rising in the conditions of wish and not will'). There is no suggestion that when the person does not rise at first, as he has decided to do, but finally does manage to do so, that there have been two changes of intention, from an intention to get up to an intention not to get up and then back again to an intention to get up. James says: 'The moment these inhibitory ideas ceased [the expectation of the cold room], the original idea [to arise] exerted its effects.' It wasn't that two contradictory intentions were contending against one another. The phenomenology of the case is otherwise.

I can see nothing convincing in the view that the person in James' example changed his mind, having first intended to get out of bed, and then intended not to get out of bed, and finally (again) intended to get out of bed if and when he finally arises. I don't think that anyone not otherwise in the grips of a philosophical theory about intention that dictates that view would be tempted into re-describing the phenomenology of the example differently from the description James offers. He retains his intention to get out of bed throughout the episode, whether in the end he gets out of bed or not. His not getting out of bed is just a case of inertia, or procrastination, or final stage weakness of will.

The point of the example is merely to demonstrate that a proximal intention, even one that is neither changed nor dropped, does not necessarily lead to an intentional action in the absence of a preventer or blocker, as Mele claimed. If one has a proximate intention, as long as there is some finite time between it and the commencement of the intended action, the intended action can fail to ensue, even when all the conditions mentioned in the antecedent of the subjunctive conditional on the RHS of (CTT**) are satisfied.

But note that no such story can be told about his trying. Once one is trying, no space remains for a weak or forgetful or distracted or lazy or procrastinating will. In trying to F, even in the naked case, an agent is beyond an intention, on his way to F-ing, going from whatever complex of mental states that precede the action and moving towards that action; he does F intentionally, if he possesses the requisite ability to do F, has the opportunity and the know how, and if nothing stops him from so doing, and this is not so with proximate intentions. Even in the naked case, it isn't forgetfulness or weakness of will or inertia or distraction or forgetfulness or procrastination that prevents one from acting; it is some sort of a preventer or a blocker that intervenes and stops Dr. Landry's patient from successfully acting.

Couldn't memory loss, weakness of the will, distraction, procrastination, inertia, lack of know how, or forgetfulness, just be counted either as preventers or blockers, or even as failures in the agent's narrow ability, thereby challenging my distinguishing between the accounts of proximate intention and trying? Calling any of these former conditions a preventer or a blocker would stretch the concept beyond recognition. The preventers and blockers (or failures of narrow ability, etc.) render someone's trying unsuccessful; memory loss, weakness of the will, distraction, inertia, procrastination, or forgetfulness can insure that the agent doesn't even try. So my (CTT**) is an analysis of 'P tries to F', and not of 'P intends to F' or even of 'P proximately intends to F'. Intending is simply one step further away from acting than is trying.

Overall, the story I would want to tell about action and its antecedents would go something like this. An agent will be in many relevant mental states prior to his trying, and typically that will include having an intention to F (or, remembering the video game player introduced by Bratman, another closely related intention). (I am not of the view that every intentional action must be preceded by some intention, but let that pass.) The mental states needed, in order for the agent to move beyond mere proximate intention, even just to try to do that action, may be a pot pourri: attention, constancy of purpose, robustness of memory, determination, strength of will, single-mindedness, concentration, persistence, clarity of purpose, perhaps even absence of self-deception. I don't think that there is some final definitive list of all the mental states or events that might be relevant, so I would not evaluate the chance of finding some law-like generalisation connecting proximate intention to the agent's trying very high.

When all of these mental states are in place, including any absences of other mental states (perhaps lack of confusion, for example) if relevant, the agent then tries to F intentionally. But of course, on (CTT**), that just means that if he has the narrow ability, know how, opportunity, and there are no blockers, etc., he Fs intentionally. As I said earlier, I have no doubt that there must be some complex, underlying brain state which he is in, and in virtue of which the conditional statement, (CTT**), is true of him. But that complex, underlying brain state, composed of disparate parts, each of which underlies a different condition or absence required for the intention to progress, is not a particular to which 'P's trying to F' refers.

So, in terms of (CTT**), compare its RHS as an analysis of trying and what it would be like if it were an analysis of intending, given what I have said. Could the RHS of (CTT**) be an analysis of 'P proximately intends to F'? No. Imagine an incontinent or lazy or distracted proximate intender, P. In such a case, P intends, proximately, so the LHS is true. But is it true that, in the closest possible world in which he has the ability, no blockers, and so on, *and* also has the same mental states that he has in the actual world, he Fs? Not necessarily. The RHS could be false, because it could have true antecedent and might have a false consequent. Since he remains lazy or incontinent or distracted or a procrastinator or whatever, he fails to F (or even try to F). But as an analysis of 'to try', there is no difficulty. If he tries to F, then for sure he was not in fact incontinent or too distracted or too lazy or too forgetful, did not procrastinate, etc., so that he did try, and projecting those same mental states of P into the nearest possible world insures that P does act, does F, when the antecedent conditions on the RHS are met.

Return for a moment to James' reluctant riser. I've used the example only to argue that even proximate intentions may not result in action or in trying to act. But how does (CTT**) deal with such a case? As it stands, (CTT**) is formulated to cover only actions, but not omissions to act or negative actions. I'm not committed to that extension. But let's assume that it should and could be extended to cover these cases of omissions as well. In most cases of this kind, there is no pressure to break the link between trying and intentional action (i.e., intentional omissions) for which I have already argued. If a soldier tries to stand still on parade and not move, he stands still intentionally.

James' case though is different. (In what follows, I use 'not rising' and 'remaining in bed' interchangeably.) The reluctant riser has an intention to rise, no intention not to rise, but does not rise. He does nothing. Is there still a link between trying and intentionally omitting to act, on the view of James' case for which I have argued? If his remaining in bed were intentional, even in the absence of an intention to remain in bed, the RHS of (CTT**) would be true. The RHS would have a true antecedent and a true consequent. He has the ability and opportunity to remain in bed; there are no preventers or blockers to his remaining in bed, and so on. And he would remain in bed intentionally. On the other hand, if his remaining in bed were not intentional, but, say, merely voluntary, the RHS would be false. The RHS would still have a true antecedent but now a false consequent.

In order to decide whether either choice presented a difficulty for the version of (CTT**) extended to omissions to act, we should have first to decide whether the LHS of (CTT**) was true or false in such a case. Did the reluctant riser TRY not to rise? Since the reluctant riser was trying to rise, insofar as he was trying to do anything at all, it seems far-fetched to attribute to him trying not to rise. If, on the other hand, the reluctant riser *did not* try not to rise (so a false LHS), then his non-rising must *not* be intentional-perhaps only voluntary, thereby yielding a corresponding false RHS (it will have a true antecedent and a false consequent). The only scenarios that provide a problem for (CTT**) would be if either (a) the reluctant riser is trying not to rise or yet his not rising is not intentional (true LHS; false RHS), or (b) it is false that the reluctant riser is trying not to rise and his not rising is intentional (false LHS; true RHS). Both of those combinations seem to me to be implausible.

A further virtue of holding that in James' case the reluctant riser was NOT remaining in bed intentionally is that it saves the (TUT), which only covers intentional action. If he were remaining in bed intentionally, (TUT) would entail that he was trying to remain in bed, and as I have said, that is a very implausible attribution to him in the circumstances.

(7) The idea that someone tried to do something plays an important role in explaining actions. For this, I want to look at (CTT) in is simplest form, no asterisks allowed. All the additional complications, both about impossible actions and about sameness of mental states in the actual and possible worlds, couldn't be part of any ordinary explanation. It's too complicated; it is a philosophers' construction. But the unadorned (CTT) might be explanatory in the ordinary course of events, or so I will argue. I am not aiming at providing a complete account of explanations by trying but aiming merely to give some indication of how (CTT) and explanations about trying might interact.

In general, it is not at all clear that in an analysis, or in an identity, the analysans and the analysandum, or the identified and the identifier, must be equally good at explaining or being explained by the same things. '… explains….' is not an extensional context, so that identities, or the two sentential sides of a biconditional analysis, are not necessarily substitutable salva veritate. 'Tully brilliantly denounced Cataline' does not explain why 'Cicero was the greatest Roman orator'. But let's accept the burden that the RHS of (CTT) should explain whatever (the LHS) explains. What does trying ever explain?

Why is some agent, P, F-ing? Here are three different ways in which we might explain why an agent is acting: (a) Sometimes the answer is in terms of a further objective goal; 'P is F-ing in order to G'. (b) At other times, the answer is in terms of a goal that P believed he could achieve, 'P is F-ing because he believed he could thereby G'. (c) And at still other times, it is in terms of what P was trying to achieve, 'P was F-ing because he was trying to G'.

Why was P searching in his bag? Answer (a): because the keys are in P's bag. Answer (b): because P believed that the keys are in his bag. Answer (c): because P was trying to find the keys in his bag. On some occasion, all three answers might be true. But which explanation we select to offer on a particular occasion is a highly pragmatic matter. Can we give some indication of why we chose one of the answers rather than the others on some particular occasion?

When are we likely to plumb for answer (c)? I have committed myself to (TUT), that whenever someone Fs intentionally, it follows that he is trying to F. I have rejected the view that 'he is trying to F' is *true* only when the agent did not F easily or straightforwardly, or thought he might not be able to F, although it might be that those are the only occasions on which it is appropriate or not misleading to say that he was trying to F. However, it does not also follow that whenever someone Fs intentionally, it follows that his trying to F is always a good, or the best, explanation of why he is F-ing. Either of: (a) 'because the keys are in his bag' or (b) 'because he believes the keys are in his bag', may be much better explanations in straightforward circumstances.

The restrictions that some philosophers wrongly place on the truth of the view that if a person Fs intentionally, then he tries to F, restrictions that turn out to be only conversational implicatures, are best seen as conditions for when someone's trying to F is a good or the best explanation of his F-ing. So, it is when trying to F is not easy or not straightforward or we or the agent doubts his ability to F, that explanations in terms of trying, like (c), are more desirable than explanations like (a) and (b).

To answer the question of why someone is searching their bag with the explanation that he is trying to find the keys in his bag, does suggest that he is struggling, finding it hard to find them, or there is something in some way awkward or exceptional about the case, or there is some doubt about his eventual success. Perhaps P is not really good at searching his bag, so he struggles, or the bag doesn't really provide the opportunity for an easy search because it is too deep or, lacking pockets, everything is jumbled together, or something is impeding P in searching, like a broken zip fastener or a recalcitrant clasp, or P regularly fails at bag-searches because of insufficient know how, so we doubt his success on this occasion.

If this were not so, it would be a better explanation just to say that he is searching because the keys are in his bag or that he believes that they are there. If (c), an explanation in terms of trying, is better justified as an explanation in some cases compared to (a) or (b), there must be some difference in the circumstances in which the explanations are proffered. The cases in which explanations like (c) are justified are just the ones, I submit, that those who wrongly reject (TUT) place on the truth condition for trying-sentences.

But 'because he is *trying* to find the keys in his bag' is a better explanation of his searching his bag in the limited circumstances I have specified than are the alternative explanations, we can see why (CTT) is as good an explanation as the trying explanation is, in exactly the same limited circumstances. If we have doubts that the situation is not easy or straightforward, explaining why he is rooting in his bag by saying that if he has the ability or know how to find the keys in his bag, and if nothing prevents or blocks him from finding them, etc., then he will find the keys in his bag, is as appropriate an explanation as explaining why he is searching his bag by saying that he is trying to find the keys in his bag. Both address the same doubts about the circumstances of his rooting.

On any specific occasion c, on which the trying-explanation is offered, it will be unlikely that *all* the circumstances listed in the antecedent of (CTT)-the opportunity, the narrow ability, the know how, the circumstances, the searcher's state of mind-would be exceptional and call for the trying-explanation. Perhaps P is perfectly capable of searching but it is the zip fastener on the bag that is proving awkward (it is the circumstances that are awkward). If (CTT) is the explanation for his searching the bag in c, we are being given an information overload, because his current searching is being given an explanation in terms of (CTT) that includes additional information, that would cover other cases as well, for example if he were struggling because of lack of narrow ability or know how.

But the explanation in terms of trying does that as well. It also provides informational overload. To explain someone's bag-searching by saying that he is trying to find his keys also does not itself single out the one respect out of several possible that might be causing difficulty for the bag search. (CTT) and the trying explanation match, because the same explanation could be given by both (CTT) and the trying sentence in the situation in which the difficulty of the search arose from an awkwardness of any one of the antecedent conditions of (CTT), i.e., P's fumbling rather than the poor design of the bag or from something being in his way. Their information overloads match.

Notes

1. I use 'M' and 'P' as the dummy names of the two properties, since those are the ones used so often in the discussion of the alleged supervenience of the mental on the physical. But I use these as the dummy names of any two properties whatever, as long as they are not a priori necessarily related, as are triangularity and trilaterality.
2. I'm not suggesting that the relation between, e.g., something's being triangular and it's being trilateral is best thought of as a case of supervenience. Being trilateral does not supervene on being triangular (or vice versa) even though (a) it is a necessary truth that if x is triangular and x is trilateral and y is also triangular, then y is trilateral. But (a) follows from the simpler (b), the necessary truth that if y is triangular, then y is trilateral. x does not even get a mention in (b). (a) just has some irrelevant information in it about x, irrelevant form the point of view of the relation between y's trilaterality and y's triangularity. If 'p' entails 'q', adding additional but unnecessary premises to 'p' does not invalidate that entailment. Similarly for having a shape and being extended and many other examples.
3. For an alternative view, see Sydney Shoemaker (1980).
4. There certainly are accounts of trying that make it a part of the action. Suppose the trying and the action overlap. How might we model this suggestion? I assume that parts can exist without the wholes of which they are the parts. Either (a) the trying must be a part of the whole action or (b) the action must be part of the whole trying. Neither alternative really alters the question we are asking.

    (a) It would not be enough for the trying to be a proper part of the whole action. Suppose the trying part occurs. Call the remainder of the whole action, action-minus. We would still want to know whether there was a metaphysically possible world in which the action-minus part could fail to occur when the trying part occurs.

(b) Suppose the action is a proper part of the trying, so if the whole trying occurs, so must the action. That won't answer the question either. Call the whole trying minus its action part a trying-minus. So both the action and the trying* are proper parts of the trying. We would still want to know whether there was a metaphysically possible world in which the action part could fail to occur when the trying-minus part occurs.

Whatever virtues a mereological view of trying and action might have more generally (I think very little), thinking about trying and actions mereologically, as one being a part of the other, isn't going to help us in understanding trying as a particular whose function it is to bridge the gulf between other contents of the mind and action. We are going to face exactly the same questions, whether we do or do not adopt the mereological view just described.

5. In the case of basic action, it may be that we do not normally speak of the ability required to do a basic act. But it is literally true that we normally do have the narrow ability to perform our basic actions. If one can have the narrow ability required to do a basic action, it must be true that one can fail to have that ability. And this is indeed so. I am in the fortunate position of having the narrow ability to wiggle my ears, which is a basic action for me. But if you are not one of the cognoscenti, you unfortunately don't have the same ability to do it as I have.
6. The expression, 'P does a token action x' has its problems. One does not 'do' actions or 'perform' actions, although I have used this expression several times in previous chapters; one just acts. But the antecedent in the formulation of (TUT) that I offer can be re-expressed without the offending locution; it's just that the replacement makes it harder to include an expression both for the token and the type.
7. Actually, Yaffe takes as the LHS of his biconditional 'the [relevant] intention motivates the person' to F but as far as I can see, this is equivalent for him to 'the person tries to F', or anyway so I will treat it for my purposes.
8. Kirk Ludwig argues that an agent can intend to do something that he regards as impossible (Ludwig 1992). I suppose that (a) if one can intend what one believes is impossible, a fortiori one could try to do what one believes to be impossible. But I have just argued against the antecedent of (a). Bratman argues that trying is not subject to the same consistency and agglomeration demands as is intending (Bratman 1987, 135–138).

This suggests that (b) one could try to do what one believes to be impossible but not (knowingly) intend to do it.
9. For a contrary view about conditionals with impossible antecedents, see Daniel Nolan (1997).
10. In the literature on the analysis of dispositions, in addition to finks and reverse-cycle fink, there are antidotes (or maskers) and mimickers. Some substance is a poison iff if a person were to ingest it, it would be fatal. But that can't be correct: there are maskers. If the poison were ingested, and the person given an antidote, the poison wouldn't be fatal. The antidote masks the effects of the poison. A plate is fragile iff if it were dropped, it would break. But that can't be right: there are mimickers. A mimicker brings about the effects in lieu of the disposition. Consider a plate made of styrofoam, that isn't fragile. But if the Hater of Styrofoam hears the plate whenever dropped, and tears it to shreds as a consequence, then when dropped, it will break in spite of not being fragile. A mimicker is parallel to a fink; in both cases, the conditionals are true in spite of the falsity of the LHS. An antidote is parallel to a reverse-cycle fink. In both cases, the conditional is false in spite of the truth of the LHS. Finks and reverse-cycle finks may change the dispositions things have when the stimulus condition occurs; maskers and mimickers leave the dispositions intact but block the standards response from occurring.

My own account of trying in effect deals with maskers under the heading of preventers and blockers. Can there be maskers and mimickers of trying, as there can be with dispositions? 'Whereas Martin's so-called 'finkish' cases featured an object gaining (or losing) a disposition when the activation conditions for that disposition obtain, masking and mimicking cases made use of the external factors to interfere with the connections between dispositions and their associated conditionals' (Troy Cross 2012).
11. Enoch, David, 2012, 'Comment on Yaffe's Attempts'; Yaffe, Gideon, 2012, 'Reply to Enoch, Dahan-Katz, and Berman'. Enoch's counterexample is modeled on one by Mark Johnston (1993). The pertinent examples that create trouble for counterfactual analyses are in Johnston's Appendix 1 and Appendix 2, 119–121.
12. Yaffe understands Enoch's counterexample differently than Enoch does. 'A person ... might be convinced that he will fail to C should he try, and so not try. And he might be incapable of shedding this belief, and might be incapable of acting unless he tries. And so it might be the case that he

lacks the ability to act thanks to the belief. But it might also be true that if he had the ability to act, and so no longer thought that he would inevitably fail, then he would try and go on to succeed' (2012, 67). But this seems to say that the agent's belief that he does not have the ability to C causes him to not have the ability to C, rather than conversely.
13. An example in which something in the actual world is held constant in a subjunctive conditional is provided by Cian Dorr (2008): 'If it were the case that ...[the axioms of abstract objects] and the concrete world were just as it actually is, then it would be the case that S.' (Dorr 2008, 37).
14. Compare the view by Adams and Mele's on distinguishing between trying and intending. See Adams and Mele (1992) and also Michael Bratman (1987).

Bibliography

Adams, F. 1986. Intention and Intentional Action: The Simple View. *Mind and Language* 1 (4): 281–301.
Adams, F., and A. Mele. 1992. The Intention/Volition Debate. *Canadian Journal of Philosophy* 22 (3): 323–337.
Armstrong, D.M. 1981. Acting and Trying. In *Nature of Mind and Other Essays*, ed. D. Armstrong. Brighton: Harvester Press.
Austin, J.L. 1979. Ifs and Cans. In *Philosophical Papers*. New York: OUP.
Bishop, J. 1989. *Natural Agency*, 117–120. Cambridge: Cambridge University Press.
Bratman, M. 1987. *Intentions, Plans and Practical Reason*. Cambridge: Harvard University Press.
Chisholm, Roderick. 1966. *Perceiving: A Philosophical Study*. Cornell: Cornell University Press. Originally published 1957.
Choi, S. 2005. Do Categorical Ascriptions Entail Counterfactual Conditionals? *Philosophical Quarterly* 55 (220): 495–503.
———. 2009. The Conditional Analysis of Dispositions and the Intrinsic Dispositions Thesis. *Philosophy and Phenomenological Research* LXXVIII: 568–590.
———. 2012. Intrinsic Finks and the Dispositional/Categorical Distinction. *Nous* 46 (2): 289–325.
Clarke, Randolph. 2015. Abilities to Act. *Philosophy Compass* 10: 893–904.

Correia, Fabrice. 2008. Ontological Independence. *Philosophy Compass* 3 (5): 1013–1032.
Cross, T. 2012. Recent Work on Dispositions. *Analysis* 72: 115–124.
Davidson, Donald. 1963 (1980). Actions, Reasons, and Causes, reprinted in his *Essays on Actions and Events*. Oxford: Clarendon Press, 3–19.
Dorr, C. 2008. There are No Abstract Objects. In *Contemporary Debates in Metaphysics*, ed. T. Sider, J. Hawthorne, and D. Zimmerman, 32–63. Oxford: Basil Blackwell.
Dowe, P. 2001. A Counterfactual Theory of Prevention and 'Causation' by Omission. *Australasian Journal of Philosophy* 79: 216–226.
Dummett, Michael. 1973. *Frege: Philosophy of Language*. London: Duckworth.
Enoch, D. 2012. Comment on Yaffe's Attempts. *Jerusalem Review of Legal Studies* 6: 20–35.
Frankfurt, Harry. 1988. Alternate Possibilities and Moral Responsibility. In *The Importance of What We Care About*. Cambridge: Cambridge University Press.
Hare, R.M. 1964. *The Language of Morals*. Oxford: Oxford University Press.
Honoré, A.M. 1964. Can and Can't. *Mind* 2 (292): 463–479.
Horgan, Terence. 1993. From Supervenience to Superdupervenience: Meeting the Demands of a Material World. *Mind* 102 (408): 555–586.
Hornsby, Jennifer. 1980. *Actions*. London: Routledge & Kegan Paul.
———. 1995. Reasons for Trying. *Journal of Philosophical Research* XX: 525–539.
James, William. 1950. *Principles of Psychology*. Vol. 2. New York: Dover Publications.
Johnston, M. 1993. Objectivity Refigured: Pragmatism Without Verificationism. In *Reality, Representation, and Projection*, ed. J. Haldane and C. Right. New York and Oxford: OUP.
Kenny, Anthony. 1963. *Action, Emotion and Will*. London: Routledge & Kegan Paul.
Lewis, D. 1997. Finkish Dispositions. *The Philosophical Quarterly* 47 (187): 143–158.
Ludwig, Kirk. 1992. Impossible Doings. *Philosophical Studies* 65: 257–281.
Mackie, Penelope. 2009. *How Things Might Have Been*. Oxford: Oxford University Press.
Maier, John. 2014. Abilities. *Stanford Encyclopedia of Philosophy*.
———. 2015. The Agentive Modalities. *Philosophy and Phenomenological Research* XC (1): 113–134.
Marcus, Eric. 2009. Why There are No States. *Journal of Philosophical Research* 34: 215–241.

McCann, Hugh. 1998. *The Works of Agency*. Ithaca: Cornell University Press.
McDaniel, Kris. 2007. Extended Simples. *Philosophical Studies* 133: 131–141.
Melden, A.I. 1961. *Free Action*. London: Routledge & Kegan Paul.
Mele, A. 1992. *Springs of Action*. Vol. 72, 167. New York: Oxford University Press.
Mourelatos, Alexander P.D. 1978. Events, Processes, and States. *Linguistics and Philosophy* 2 (3): 415–434.
Nolan, D. 1997. Impossible Worlds: A Modest Approach. *Notre Dame Journal of Formal Logic* 38: 535–572.
O'Shaughnessy, Brian. 1980. *The Will*. Vol. 1 and 2. Cambridge: Cambridge University Press.
Paul, Sarah. 2009. How We Know What We are Doing. *Philosophers' Imprint* 9 (11): 1–24.
Ruben, David-Hillel. 1990 (1992). *Explaining Explanation*. London: Routledge. Second edition (2012), Paradigm Publishers, Boulder, CO.
———. 2015. Beyond Supervenience and Construction. *Journal of Social Ontology* 1 (1): 121–141.
Searle, John. 2001. *Rationality in Action*. Cambridge: The MIT Press.
Shoemaker, Sydney. 1980. Causality and Properties. In *Time and Cause*, ed. P. van Inwagen. Dordrecht: D. Reidel Publishing Company.
Vesey, G. 1961. Volition. *Philosophy* 36: 325–365.
Vihvelin, Kadri. 2013. *Causes, Laws, & Free Will*. Oxford: Oxford University Press.
Von Wright, G.H. 1971. *Explanation and Understanding*. London: Routledge & Kegan Paul.
Wiggins, David. 1980. *Sameness and Substance*. Oxford: Basil Blackwell.
Wilson, Jessica. 2010. What is Hume's Dictum, and Why Believe It? *Philosophy and Phenomenological Research* XXX (3): 595–637.
Yaffe, Gideon. 2010. *Attempts*, 72–105. Oxford: Oxford University Press.
———. 2012. Reply to Enoch, Dahan-Katz, and Berman. *Jerusalem Review of Legal Studies* 6: 51–78.
Zhu, Jing. 2004. Intention and Volition. *Canadian Journal of Philosophy* 34 (2): 175–194.

5

Causing and Doing

What's in the Chapter

What is the relationship, if any, between doing something and causing it to happen? The idea of an intrinsic event plays a central part in formulating an answer to that question. I therefore start by explaining what an intrinsic event is. The expression, 'intrinsic event', is not innocent; I explain it as best I can here, but the remainder of the book returns repeatedly to this idea and further clarifies it.

Philosophers and linguists interested in the question of the relation between doing and causing often refer to, and often conflate, two claims. The theses are distinct although related. I don't think that the conflation is harmless. Since one of the claims, which is often referred to as Causative Alternation (CA) in the linguistics literature, is an indisputable truth of semantics and the other, (PT) (for 'Paraphrase Thesis') is a controversial philosophical analysis, its conflation with the semantic thesis lends a degree of credence to that analysis that it does not deserve. A theme of the chapter is the need to separate out views on the semantics of verbs from views about the metaphysics of action. Note 5 details some examples of that conflation. They are not always carefully separated in either the linguistics or the philosophical literature. I am not asserting that any philosophers or linguists explicitly state that the first thesis entails the second; they do not. But many simply slide from one to the other without carefully separating them.

After distinguishing the two, I will argue that (CA) is a claim about the semantics of ergative verbs, and, although indisputably true, does not have any interesting philosophical implications on its own. The second claim, the Paraphrase Thesis, (PT), is a view in the metaphysics of action. It says, roughly, that an agent acts iff he [but note: he, not his action] causes some event, for instance, e, and e is then said (in many cases) to be intrinsic to that action. (PT) is false. Since it entails a biconditional, it has two parts: a left-to-right entailment and a right-to-left entailment. In this chapter I examine only the right-to-left entailment. I state and look at counterexamples to the right-to-left entailment, and clarify some matters about the causation that is required by (PT). Much of my discussion focuses on the question of who is the doer (or doers) of the action when more than one person helps to insure that some consequence occurs, or participates in the generation of that action. I leave the left-to-right entailment until Chap. 6.

I distinguish the expressions 'P caused such-and-such', 'P was a cause of such-and-such', and 'P was the cause of such-and-such'. I also introduce a distinction about causation in order to support my dismissal of the right-to-left entailment: remoteness of cause and partiality of cause. I compare my view with one by David Lewis on the same question, and, finally, in an appendix to this chapter, I briefly mention a third thesis, the Derivation Thesis (DT), which is an empirical hypothesis in the linguistics literature about how a sentence about what an agent does is 'generated' from a sentence about what he causes, only in order to distinguish it from the philosophical analysis (PT), with which it might be confused.

Intrinsic Events

I want to begin by introducing the idea of an intrinsic event. I will say a few things about it now. The brief introduction will have to suffice for now. In a way, Chaps. 5 and 6 are in essence about intrinsic events, even when it is not immediately obvious that this is so. But it is important, I think, to *begin* to get clear about this idea before I begin the discussion proper of causing and doing.

As far as I know, it was Von Wright who first introduced into the literature the idea of an intrinsic event (1977, 39–41): 'To every act (of the kind which we are here considering) there corresponds a change or an event in the world.' The act is defined as the act of 'effecting' such and such change. 'For example, the act of opening a certain window is, logically the act of changing…the world in which this window is closed to a world in which in which it is open'. Von Wright rightly limits his claim to acts 'of the kind which we are here considering'. What follows won't be true for all actions and their verbs; there will be a lot in due course about how we limit these claims.

Von Wright confusingly uses the word 'result' (and not the expression 'intrinsic event') of an act to mean the 'change corresponding to the act or the end-state'. To simplify a bit, the result of the action of opening the window is either the window's opening or the state of its being open. He says that the relation between the act and is result is intrinsic. 'An act cannot be truly called an act of opening the window unless it ends (results) in the window's being open'. The intrinsic tie between the act and the result is contrasted with the extrinsic causal relation between the act and a consequence. His example of the latter is that a consequence of the opening of the window might be the lowering of the room's temperature. Alvarez and Hyman (1998), Hugh McCann (1998), and many others, adopt von Wright's distinction between the results of action and their causal consequences: 'An action is of such and such kind if and only if its result is of the corresponding kind…' (McCann, 233). '…I do not think that actions cause their results' (Alvarez 1999, 217). Actions don't cause their results ('result' in von Wright's sense); actions cause effects; an action's result is 'internal' or intrinsic to the action.

The use of von Wright's distinction is near ubiquitous in the philosophy of action, even though the terms used to refer to intrinsic events differ between authors. What von Wright calls an 'event result', Davis (1979) calls 'a doing-related event'. John Bishop (1989) uses the expression 'an intrinsic event' and it is his terminology I mostly follow in this chapter, although I also speak of 'an event result' subsequently (I take 'intrinsic event' and 'result' to be synonyms for these purposes). Still others have called it 'the associated event'. 'Result' (as well as his unfortunate use of 'effecting' above) might wrongly suggest a causal idea, which is precisely what von Wright does not wish to maintain. The intrinsic event supplies the identity conditions for the type of action of which the token action is an instance. 'Each type of action is a bringing about by the agent of a specific type of event or state, and this is what counts as the event- or state-type intrinsic to that action. For example, the rising of an arm is the type of event intrinsic to the action of raising one's arm' (Bishop 1989, 105).

The above seems to be a reasonable survey of some of the uses of this distinction. Let's try to impose some order on it. First, in von Wright, Alvarez, and Hyman, it is clear that the intrinsic event is a token event; only Bishop says that the intrinsicness relation is between action types and event types (I now will indicate transitive and intransitive verbs with the appropriate subscript, 't' or 'i'):

(1) When P's token act f is of action type F (e.g., a moving$_t$ of his arm), it is metaphysically necessary that a token event e must occur, of type E (e.g., a moving$_i$ of his arm). Token event e is said to be that token action f's intrinsic event or result. The use of 'intrinsic' is meant to indicate that the tie between the token action and the token event is not contingent. An intrinsic event or result of an action is not among that action's causal consequences.
(2) In the most favourable case (there are less favourable cases), the action type F, and the token action f, and the event type E, and the token event e, can be picked out by the transitive and intransitive uses of the same verb, sometimes with minor grammatical adjustments.
(3) A token action's intrinsic event gives the identity conditions for the type of action of which that action is a token. Von Wright says that 'An act cannot be truly called an act of opening the window unless it ends (results) in the window's being open…'.
(4) What is the relation between the agent (NOT the action) and the intrinsic event? Alvarez and Hyman say that 'Agents cause the events their actions result in.' These claims look causal, positing a contingent relation between agent and intrinsic event (assuming that the causal origin of an event is not a necessary property of the event). Each could exist without the other.

(5) The view that the causal relation is between the agent P and the intrinsic event e, (4), is consistent with the view that that claim is merely shorthand for the claim that some agent P-involving event c caused e. (However, Alvarez and Hyman, and many other causal agent theorists reject that shorthand view. I am not building that rejection into my understanding of 'P caused e', except towards the very end of Chap. 8.)

I want to make it clear that in this, and in subsequent chapters, it is not my intention to subject agent causalism to any sort of thorough review or investigation. There is widespread disagreement amongst agent causalists about what event it is that the agent causes (a bodily movement, a mental event, a brain event), or even whether it is a simple event, rather than a more complex entity such as an event plus some mental state for example, that is the second relatum of the agent causal relation. There is also a distinction between agent causalists who are offering an analysis of action and those who are offering an analysis of free action. A good survey of some of these differences can be found in Timothy O'Connor (2011). In any case, agent causalism is NOT my target in the book. The RHS of one of the claims I discuss below, (PT), is expressed in the terms of an agent causing an event. I discuss the account to be given of 'P caused e', without assuming that 'P caused e' presupposes that that sentence cannot be given an analysis in terms of ordinary event causation, which is a thesis of agent causalism.

Causative Alternation

The first claim that I mentioned goes by several different names. Typically it is called 'causative alternation' (hereafter, CA) and I continue to use that designation, even though I think that the use of that name lends itself to confusion between it and the substantive philosophical analysis claim about action. I don't agree that there is anything causal about causative alternation. (It's called 'causative alternation' because the sentence containing the transitive occurrence of the verb entails a sentence containing an intransitive occurrence of the same verb. The latter sentence is about an event, and (PT), not (CA), says about that same event that the agent causes it. This, I think, is one of the sources of the conflation between (CA) and (PT)).

Causative alternation is a type of transitivity alternation. (CA) simply registers the fact that certain action verbs (called 'ergative verbs') can occur both transitively and intransitively, and such that that the transitive form entails the intransitive form: e.g., that 'he broke$_t$ the window' entails 'the window broke$_i$' (and similarly for the verbs in present tense and taking imperfective aspect, as long as both uses of the verb, on the LHS and the RHS, are in the same tense or aspect). I refer to the intransitive form of the verb as 'the intransitive alternate' of the transitive form. It is also referred to in the literature as the 'anticausative' form of the verb. It's to these verbs and the actions they designate that von Wright's claim about intrinsic events should be limited.

Thus, Hornsby (1980, 2), whose formulation I shall use as standard: '…a verb is in the intended class if, and only if, it supports inferences on the following pattern:

$$(CA) \text{FROM}: aV_T b \quad \text{TO}: bV_I\text{'}$$

Where 'P' names the agent of the action, I shall say that the action, P's V_t-ing (of) b (e.g., P's opening$_t$ of the door), is the truth-maker for the LHS of (CA), and that the event, b's V_i-ing (e.g., the door's opening$_i$), is the truth-maker for the RHS of (CA). If the sentences on the LHS and RHS of (CA) are in imperfective aspect, this is correct. P's opening$_t$ of the door is indeed the truth-maker for 'P is (or was) opening$_t$ the door', and the door's opening$_i$ is the truth-maker for 'the door is (or was) opening$_i$'.

Recall the discussion in Chap. 3 on A NOTE ON DAVIDSON'S LOGICAL FORM PROPOSAL. Suppose the sentences on the LHS and RHS are in perfective aspect: 'P opened$_t$ the door' and 'the door opened$_i$'. Unlike the imperfective forms, both assume success. However, in the case of verbs subject to the paradox of imperfectivity, the nominal gerundial forms do not assume success. Making P's opening$_t$ of the door and the door's opening$_i$ the truth-makers does not take into account the variation in aspect between the sentences and their gerundial truth-makers. The 'fix' in this case is to impose a further condition of success on the truth-makers. The problem will also arise in case there is a derived nominal on the RHS (e.g., 'there was a closure of the door'), depending on whether it is taken in the process or product sense.

The causative alternation thesis merely claims that certain verbs have both a transitive and an intransitive use and the former entails the later. The causative alternation claim is an indisputable and hence undisputed fact about certain verbs in English. However, the grammatical distinction on its own is of little interest to philosophers. What is of interest to philosophers is that the transitive form implies agency (whether by a human agent or a nonhuman agent, if such there be), whereas the intransitive form does not imply agency, so that the converse of (CA) is false. As Hornsby puts it: '…in the cases that interest me, there appears to be no hope of founding the intransitive on the transitive' (1980, 125). Parsons says: 'It is also important in analyzing the logic of these examples that the intransitive alone does not imply any form of the transitive' (Parsons 1994, 106). The claim then is that the LHS (left-hand side) of (CA) entails the RHS (right hand side), but that the RHS does not entail the LHS.

Linguists debate which of the two is derivationally prior: '…what is the derivational relationship between the alternants, i.e., is the causative version derived from the anticausative version via a process of causativization, or is the anticausative version derived via a process of detransitivization; alternatively, are both derived from a common base?'[1] The derivational question discussed by linguists is *not* the derivation claim made by philosophers, and it is only the latter that I am discussing here. (I have something to say, albeit not very original, about the empirical derivation question discussed by linguists in the appendix to this chapter.) In the logical sense of derivation, it is clear that the LHS does not derive from the RHS, since the latter can be true but the former false. Yet among linguists the same derivation is at least an open question. 'Derivation' must therefore bear two different senses in the discussions by philosophers and linguists.

For philosophers, the important contrast is between activity and passivity, between change that is agent-driven and change not driven by an agent. First, I intend 'agent-driven' as something more than just agent-involving. 'The bruise that appeared on Tom's body' involves Tom, who is an agent, but does not involve him *as* an agent. Change that is agent-driven involves the agent qua being an agent. Second, the token intrinsic event, b's V_i-ing, is in fact agent-driven, simply in virtue of it being an event that is intrinsic to the agent's action, but (a) there could be, indeed presumably are, other tokens of the same type, a V_i-ing of b, which are not agent-driven by any agent, because not intrinsic to the action of any agent. (a) is sufficient by itself for concluding that the RHS does not entail the LHS. I call (a) 'the weaker claim'.

I think that philosophers who speak of intrinsic events sometimes assume (b) as well: (b) the token event intrinsic to an action could have failed to have been intrinsic to that token action, perhaps by being intrinsic to no action at all. I refer to (b) as 'the stronger claim'. Is it possible for that token intrinsic event to have occurred but not the action to which it is intrinsic? Of course, if an intrinsic event occurred but the action to which it is intrinsic had failed to occur, we would not call the former 'an intrinsic event' anymore. But (b) would claim that that very same token could occur, however named.

(CA) says that *if* the token action occurred, then it follows that its token intrinsic event also occurred. That gives a one-way necessary connection, from action to intrinsic event. But it does not obviously rule out (b), the possibility that if the action had not occurred, the same token event could still have occurred, but now intrinsic to no action or perhaps even to some other action, because directed by another agent or by no agent. Is the one-way necessary connection enough to make the intrinsic event intrinsic? In the next chapter, we will see what is problematic about (b), and in fact I do not accept it, but for now let's use both (a) and (b) in order to characterise what is meant by an 'intrinsic event'. (a) is about different tokens of the same event type; (b) is about whether the property of being intrinsic is an essential property of that very token.

Might there be a non-causal model for (b)? A non-causal model for (b) might be the relationship of wholes and their parts. If one assumes that parts are essential to the wholes they compose but that wholes are not essential for their parts, consider the whole w that is the sum of p1 and p2. If w exists, p1 must exist. But if w did not exist (say because p2 didn't), p1 could still exist, independently as it were. p1 could be a part of a different whole or a part of no whole. Similarly, if one were to think of the action as the whole and the intrinsic event as one of its parts, then even if the action had never happened, that intrinsic token event could have still existed. If (b) were true (remember, I don't think it is), that would also block the inference right-to-left, since the event which is in fact intrinsic to a token action might still have existed but without being intrinsic to that token action, if the action had failed to exist.

Whether we accept only (a) or both (a) and (b), the intransitive form of the verb in which we are interested, 'something V_i-ed', must imply this: it is metaphysically possible for something to V_i, (e.g., the door to open$_i$, the window to break$_i$), and no agent V_ts that thing (no agent opens$_t$ that door or breaks$_t$ that window). Not quite all cases of grammatically transitive-intransitive pairs are such that the intransitive form meets this requirement. For example, 'Parliament passed$_t$ the law' entails 'the law passed$_i$', and the latter uses the intransitive form of the verb (to be distinguished from 'the law was passed$_t$', which uses the passive transitive form of the verb). Yet if the law passed$_i$, some agency is required for that event to have occurred; no law can pass$_i$ unless some body passes$_t$ it. In a case Hornsby cites, 'the toothpaste sold$_i$' uses a grammatically intransitive verb, but it entails a sentence using the transitive 'to sell$_t$', since if the toothpaste sold$_i$, someone must have sold$_t$ it (see also Levin 1993, 29). I (like Hornsby) exclude in what follows examples like 'to sell' and 'to pass', even though they have an intransitive causal alternate, and I therefore include only those ergative verbs whose intransitive causal alternates are consistent with the absence of agency. Grammar is not a foolproof guide; we need our metaphysical intuition at work too. The example of Parliament passing the law is also a helpful reminder that the idea of an agent can include more than just individual persons or non-human creatures.

Many philosophers, including Parsons (1994), Hyman (2015), Alvarez (1999), Mayr (2011), and others, are inclined to expand the idea of agency far beyond animate beings: '…these events are caused by nerve cells and muscle fibres, which are agents themselves, with their own distinctive powers. These powers in turn are activated by events caused by more minute agents' (Hyman 2015, 41–42). Hyman, for instance, expands agency to include all substances insofar as they exercise causal powers (Hyman, 39–42), so the question becomes: what counts as a substance?

If all of these things are counted as substances and hence as agents, the range of events that do not involve agency will be drastically reduced. Since the closing$_i$ of the door could still be brought about by something other than an agent even on Hyman's account, say some gust of wind may have caused it to close rather than a substance, 'the door closed$_i$' (the RHS of (CA)) on its own still won't entail the transitive LHS ('Some agent closed$_t$ the door'). 'The door closed$_i$' is consistent with the closing of the door being brought about both by an agent (i.e. on this view, a substance) and only by an event. But since for example loose hinges surely count as substances, 'the door closed$_i$ because of its loose hinges' would, I suppose, entail 'The door's loose hinges closed$_t$ the door'. If that is what the expansion of agency entails, it has an odd result. Much more on this problem in Chap. 7.

The intransitive form of an action verb should not be confused with the passive form of the transitive verb. 'He broke$_t$ the window' entails (3) 'the window was broken$_t$ by him' and hence entails, by deletion, that (4) 'the window was broken$_t$'. (4) uses a transitive verb form, not an intransitive one. However, as I explain in Chap. 7 in discussion of a proposal by Maria Alvarez, this does not mean that 'the window was broken$_t$' is elliptical. It is a complete sentence in its own right, entailed by the longer sentence. So although 'the window was broken$_t$ by him' entails, by deletion, 'the window was broken$_t$', 'the window was broken$_t$' is a complete thought on its own.

(3) and (4) use the transitive form of 'break', albeit in the passive voice. In cases in which there is genuine causative alternation, a sentence like 'he broke$_t$ the window' can be paired with (5) 'the window broke$_i$', and (5) uses a genuinely intransitive form of the verb.[2]

The Paraphrase Thesis

There are several distinct but related doctrines discussed by some linguists and philosophers alongside causative alternation (CA), and not always clearly distinguished from it.[3] The one that interests me is the paraphrase thesis (PT).[4]

(PT): For ergative verbs, P V$_t$ (transitive) object o iff P caused o to V$_i$ (intransitive). The RHS of (PT) should be adjusted for tense or aspect, to match changes in tense or aspect on the LHS.

For example, P closed the door iff P caused the door to close; P was growing the flowers iff P was causing the flowers to grow; P opens the window iff P causes the window to open, etc. Notice that (PT) employs the verb, 'to cause', on its RHS. It is not clear on (PT) as stated, when an agent causes an outcome, whether the agent is meant to be a cause or the cause of that outcome. Nor is it clear when an agent causes an outcome, whether the agent is meant to be the whole cause or a part of the cause of that outcome. In short, what is not clear is how we are to move from a verb to a noun formulation of 'cause' in (PT). This is something that shall occupy me later in this chapter.

The paraphrase thesis claims that there is some class of verbs, ergative verbs, for which the paraphrase thesis is true. (PT) is intended to apply to all verbs (or, to such verbs when combined with a specific object: more on that qualification later) meeting these conditions: (a) the verb is an action verb, (b) it is transitive, and (c) it has an intransitive counterpart (it is an ergative verb), and (d) the intransitive use does not imply that any agency is involved. One can try to extend the (PT) to other verbs as well, for example those not meeting (c), but (a)–(d) comprise its core application.

What, if any, support does (CA) give to (PT) or (PT) give to (CA)? Hornsby (1980, 126), having endorsed (CA), then supports (PT) as follows: 'the slots for events revealed here [causative alternation] permit a very old suggestion to be cast in a new form. It has been said that 'wake up Rachel' means 'cause Rachel to wake up'. But now one can say that Rupert's waking up Rachel is his causing her waking up…' (Hornsby 1980, 126). Hornsby doesn't explain how it is that (CA) is meant to lend credence to (PT), which is, I think, the interpretation one should give to her remarks. Although (PT) does not follow from the causative alternation thesis, if the transitive verb V_t has an intransitive alternate, V_i, then in 'caused b to V', it is 'V_i' that belongs in the V-slot. Nothing of great interest follows immediately from the mere fact that certain action verbs have a transitive form and an intransitive form, not even when the derivation in (CA) is added to that fact. Even if 'the boy broke$_t$ the window' entails 'the window broke$_i$', that thought does not further entail on its own anything about the analysis or meaning or paraphrase of 'The boy broke$_t$ the window' as 'The boy caused the window to break$_i$'.

I have expressed (PT) as a biconditional, which is the weakest form in which to consider it. As a purported analysis, it should have some sort of necessity attached to it, but I shan't discuss any such addition. Instead of 'paraphrase', some linguists talk of synonymy or sameness of meaning and some qualify 'paraphrase' rather oddly with 'roughly'. The literature that advances this proposal speaks less often of 'meaning' and more typically of 'paraphrase', although it sometimes also describes this second doctrine as a truth of semantics, or of the two sentences being synonymous (Cruse 1972, 520), rather than being a philosophical analysis in the conventional sense. Parsons says that 'the transitive form of the verb has roughly the same meaning as "cause to V", where "V" is in the intransitive form' (Parsons 1994, 106). Martin and Schäfer (2014, 209) use the same odd qualification, 'roughly', as Parsons: 'Their transitive use roughly means "cause to v-intransitive".' Levin (1993, 26–27) says: '…the transitive use of a verb V can be paraphrased as roughly "cause to V-intransitive".'[5]

I am extremely doubtful that (PT) could have the status of a semantic truth. A strike against such an idea derives from an application of one version of Moore's famous open-question argument (Moore 1966, 15–16). (Q1) 'Did P cause the flood to stop iff P caused the flood to stop?' is not an open question. But (Q2) 'Did P cause the flood to stop iff P stopped the flood?' is an open question. Understanding the meaning of all the constituents of (Q1) settles the question of its truth. Not so for (Q2). Since (Q2) is an open question even when all the meanings of its constituent parts are understood, 'P stopped the flood' can't just *mean* 'P caused the flood to stop'. Moore's open-question argument is hardly uncontroversial, and there is an enormous literature discussing it. Possible counterexamples to it might include mathematical assertions about whose truth we are unsure (Goldbach's Conjecture?), but (arguably) if such assertions are true, and thus really are mathematical theorems, their meaning is given by the axioms from which they follow.

So, it might be said, we could consider it as an open question about the truth of the assertion in such a case ('Given all the axioms, is it really true that p is so?'), although nothing of interest follows about a difference in meaning between the assertion, that p is true, and the axioms from which it follows (except of course the assertion that p is true might only be part of the meaning implicit in those axioms). But our case is nothing like that; there is no long, tortuous, and 'hidden' route from 'P caused the flood to stop$_i$' to 'P stopped$_t$ the flood' that might derail our semantic intuitions, as there might be in the case of Goldbach's Conjecture. I do think that a perhaps suitably modified and qualified open question argument points to a problem any semantic construal of (PT) must face.

This argument assumes that (Q2) is an open question. Is that so? As we will see, there are many philosophers and linguists who argue for and against (PT). For those who argue against (PT), could it really be the case that they have misunderstood the meaning of some of the key terms in (PT)? But even in the case of those who argue in favour of (PT), it is hard to reconcile that fact with the idea that (PT) is true in virtue of its constituent meanings. If (PT) were a truth of semantics, arguments should be otiose. No one can argue for the view that vixens are female foxes or that bachelors are unmarried adult males (assuming that these are semantic truths), if they have grasped all the constituent terms involved. What I do in this chapter is to produce counterexamples to (PT) when it is understood as a biconditional. If the biconditional fails to be true, a fortiori the RHS of (PT) cannot provide the full meaning of its LHS (although that by itself is consistent with the RHS providing *part* of the meaning of the LHS, although I don't accept that either).

Not all philosophers fail to see that (PT) is a piece of substantial philosophy, and not a linguistic or semantic truth that somehow follows from (CA): 'The way I propose to formalize action sentences...is guided by a particular conception of agency: to act is to cause or bring about an event...' (Alvarez 1999, 218). I agree with Alvarez about the status of (PT), although I don't agree with her about its truth. (PT) is a purported philosophical analysis of action sentences, not a truth of semantics or an analytic truth, and my discussion of (PT) in what follows assumes this to be so.

What about support in the other direction, what can (PT) do for (CA)? Might it be that an analysis like (PT) could explain why the inference represented by (CA) is sound? Donald Davidson argues that the (PT) explains why the (CA) is true: '...if John breaks a window, something he did caused the window to break. This obvious analysis explains what would otherwise be a mystery: the relation between the transitive and the intransitive forms of many verbs; here, for example, the transitive 'break' means 'cause to break'...' (Davidson 2001, 287). Davidson explicitly says that (PT) explains why the inference in (CA) is valid. I leave it to linguists to assess this suggestion, but it seems to me very unlikely that an 'obvious [assuming that Davidson means 'philosophical'] analysis' could support a grammatical or semantic truth.

I have been careful to limit the claim of (PT) to ergative verbs. If we aim for a full analysis of action sentences, the analysis would need somehow to be extended to the case of non-ergative action verbs (like 'push' and 'pull'), ones that do not meet condition (c). I return to this issue at the very end of Chap. 6. But here is one way in which I believe that such an extension *fails*. Consider John Hyman's remarks on 'swim' (Hyman 2015, 35). 'But English is not always so cooperative.... For example, 'Byron swam the Hellespont' reports an act, but we cannot paraphrase the sentence in a way that brings out its causative meaning simply by substituting a dictionary definition of the verb 'swam'. Even so, to swim the Hellespont is to cross the Hellespont by swimming, and therefore by moving-i.e., causing movements of-one's limbs' (Hyman 2015, 35). Alvarez (1999, 226–227) makes the same sort of move and hers is somewhat more plausible: 'a walk…[is] an event which has occurred when someone's body has traversed space as a result of certain leg movements'. So, they are proposing that in the absence of an intransitive alternate, we might simply substitute some description of the bodily movements made by the swimmer or walker after the verb 'cause' on the RHS of (PT).

I disagree. It is indisputable that if one swims, it follows that one moves one's limbs in some characteristic way (although it might be hard to describe in a noncircular way the many ways in which one might move one's limbs when swimming). No doubt, if someone walks, it follows that they have traversed space as a result of leg movements. Even though true, it is not clear that this observation is a truth of semantics and, if it is not, it is not easy to see how it could be brought in support of (CA), which is a semantic truth. But the problem with their proposals runs deeper. Suppose that 'to swim the Hellespont' is 'to cross the Hellespont by swimming, and therefore by moving (i.e., causing movements of) one's limbs' is true, even necessarily true. However, because 'swim' and 'walk' have no intransitive alternate form, substituting the way in which one moves one's limbs in the appropriate slot on the RHS of (PT) makes for failure of right-to-left entailment.

Why? The description of the movements on the RHS is too generic to permit right-to-left entailment, even if it preserves left-to-right entailment. If agent P causes his limbs to move in a way characteristic of swimming or walking, it certainly will not follow that P is swimming or walking. Imagine that P is suspended from a crane, out of water, and moves his limbs in that way. P won't be swimming. P's action of swimming needs a context, for example a pool or other body of water and P needs to be to be immersed in the water. Imagine someone who uses those same leg movements that are characteristic of walking, to pedal a bike while standing up off the seat. He will have traversed space as a result of those leg movements but he will have cycled, not walked.

What the intransitive alternate of an action verb does, and the generic descriptions of the bodily movements cannot do, is to import, along with the movements, the necessary context to insure that the physical movements are those of a swim or a walk, and not of some other action that may have the same characteristic movements. In the absence of an intransitive alternate form, nothing placed in the 'V_i' slot, in 'P caused b to V_i', will license an entailment from the RHS to the LHS of (PT). The extension of (PT) to non-ergative verbs will fail in the RHS to LHS direction, since from the fact that P is causing something characteristic of b's being F_i-ed, it won't follow for the reasons given above that P F_t-ed b.

Finally, a note on sentences ascribing agent causation. Throughout the book, I assume that what I say is consistent both with the view that in general agent causation sentences are irreducible and with the view that they are always reducible to, because always merely elliptical for, sentences about event causation. But doesn't my view really require irreducible agent causation? Consider P's moving$_t$ of his arm. Assume that token, the moving$_t$ of P's arm, is a basic action. But suppose 'P caused his arm to move$_i$' were elliptical for 'Some act of P caused his arm's moving$_i$'. But what act could that be? If it is some act by which P moved$_t$ his arm, then, contrary to hypothesis, his moving$_t$ of his arm is not a basic action. If, on the other hand, it is just P's moving$_t$ of his arm, then we have a case of self-causation. I do not know if the causation relation is irreflexive or merely non-reflexive, but even if the latter is the case, we certainly do not want to be saddled with this sort of self-causation in action theory.

But I do NOT maintain that, on the reducibility option that I am claiming is consistent with my view, 'P caused his arm to move$_i$' would be elliptical for 'Some act of P caused his arm's moving$_i$'. Rather, it would be elliptical, I imagine, for 'Some P-involving event caused P's arm's moving$_i$.' In that wide sense of 'event' and 'involvement', the event might be an action or it might be a non-actional event, for example a brain or other neurological state or a mental state (an intention or a belief-desire pair, or whatever). In the case of a basic action, the P-involving event would certainly not be another of P's actions. I stress, though, that I am not arguing that agent causation is reducible in this way, but only that the view that it is, is consistent with my other views about action in this book and in particular with my discussion of (PT).

Failure of the Biconditional RHS to LHS for Ergative Verbs

I now address the biconditional, (PT), restricted to cases of ergative verbs. In offering counterexamples, it is important not to simply swap my intuitions for those of the authors with whom I disagree. When I do base my argument on intuitions, I will try to do two things.

First, I will use only examples that I think are less controversial, by switching examples from quoted authors were necessary. For example, I regard the use of 'kill/die', the example that figures in much of the literature, as problematic and not at all typical, for three reasons. (a) 'to kill' is not an ergative verb and I will confine my examples to ergative verbs. 'to kill' has no intransitive alternate; (b) I think that 'kill' evokes intuitions, irrelevant to the issue at hand, that more mundane or pedestrian examples do not evoke. Many intuitions about 'kill' versus 'cause to die' are complicated by questions of indirect responsibility, negligence, and by the distinction between commissions and omissions. The more pedestrian the example, the better[6]; (c) action verbs can be more and less specific about the kind of action that is involved. For example, 'to poison' is more specific than 'to kill'. There are many ways in which to kill someone, poisoning being one of those ways. I think one's intuitions are more reliable about the sort of cases that I will discuss, the more specific the verb is, and I will chose examples that are as close as possible to a description of a specific kind of physical action. Second, where there is a clash of intuitions, I will back mine up with some supporting argument about such cases. In the end, perhaps some residue of the mere clash of intuitions must always remain, but that is not to say that a supporting case for the intuitions can't be made, even if the case is not definitive.

The main argument against the right-to-left inference in (PT) is that the RHS can be true but the LHS false in some indirect cases in which an additional agent is involved.[7] These are second-agent counterexamples. Both Hyman and Hornsby deal with these sorts of cases, and try to preserve the RHS to LHS entailment, but they do so in very different ways.

It might be alleged, says Hyman, that '…if one causes a man's death by hiring an assassin, one does not kill the man oneself' (Hyman 2015, 37–39), although ex hypothesi he has caused his death. So, according to this objection, a person, in this case the employer of a hitman, can cause the death of another without killing him. If the objection were to stand, it would show that there was no (RHS) to (LHS) inference after all.

Hyman rejects this line of argument and his reply to this sort of objection is to argue that, appearances notwithstanding, the LHS is true when the RHS is: '…we are comfortable saying that Louis XIV built Versailles, that Hitler bombed London, and that Stalin killed millions, while acknowledging that they did not do these things with their own bare hands' (H, 39). Presumably, this should lead us to agree that, in the case of the hitman for example, in addition to the hitman's employer causing the death of his enemy (the RHS is true), it is literally true that this employer of the hitman killed his enemy as well (the LHS is also true), so that the enemy had at least two killers-the actual assassin and the hitman.

There certainly can be cases in which more than one agent does the same thing, even though the hitman case is, in my view, not such an example. There are at least two kinds of cases of what we can call joint action, or co-agency. Consider the case of building a ship that I mentioned in Chap. 2: construct the hull outline, fix the planks, put pitch in the joins, paint the result, fix a mast, run up a sail, and so on, and finally-voila!- a ship. A number of agents can jointly build the ship, each by doing one or more of the distinct token actions that is part of the overall shipbuilding plan. There is a single token episode of shipbuilding, but it has stages and, assuming he works alone, only one agent does each stage or part of that shipbuilding. The pitching of the joints, perhaps, is the pitching of the joints only by P, even though P does the shipbuilding along with others. They are all co-agents of the shipbuilding, but P is the sole agent of the joint-pitching. That is one sort of case. In another sort of case, two agents can jointly be the co-agents of a single token action. Suppose two bell-ringers, P and P*, are each pulling$_t$ the rope that is attached to a bell, so that both are ringing$_t$ the bell. In this case, there is a single token act of bell-ringing$_t$, the agents of which are both P and P*. In cases of joint action in which both agents are required and one agent alone could not have successfully acted, defenders of (PT) must speak of the joint actors as each partially causing the outcome (I return to this idea of partially causing more fully later.)

To return to Hyman's example, it seems obvious that more than one agent could be the agent of the same killing, as in the case in which two agents together hold a vial of poison and pour its contents into the victim's mouth. Or, to replicate the pattern of the ship building example, one could hold the victim down while the other pours the poison into the victim's mouth. Both have killed him. But I think that, in addition to the co-agency of joint action, there are cases of aiding and abetting an action, participating in it (as the criminal law quote in note 6 states), without being even a co-agent of the action. That I think is the case in the hitman and his employer example.

Hyman considers the reply that the employer does not strictly speaking kill his victim, but says that so saying is merely to insist that 'strictly speaking kill' means 'kill personally or with one's own bare hands' and that we can all agree that the employer of the hitman did not do that. My own view of this example is that 'Stalin killed millions' is not a literal truth at all but is an example of hyperbole, a façon de parler. What the hitman did literally was not to kill his enemy but to have his enemy killed on his behalf. I defend this judgment more fully in what follows.

Hornsby's reply (Hornsby 1980, 127–128) to the same kind of case, in which each of two people do something that causes a boat m to sink, is to accept that the LHS is not true in at least some cases of indirect causation, so that at least sometimes the indirect causer is not the actor or doer of the deed (so the LHS is false in the imagined case for the indirect causer). But she adds a further condition to the RHS, thereby making the RHS false as well in the case of the indirect causer of the outcome, by requiring that only the agent whose action is causally most proximate to the caused event counts as the doer of the action (Hornsby, 127–128). 'Where two people each performed actions that caused the sinking of m, the one who sank m was he whose action was causally more proximate to m's sinking' (127). In the case she considers, Penny orders Paul to sink a dinghy, which he does. Hornsby's fix requires that Penny is the dinghy sinker only if Penny's ordering Paul to sink the dingy is a cause of the dinghy's sinking (as indeed it is), and any action other than hers that also caused the dinghy sinking caused her action as well. Her action, the ordering, has to be the action causally most proximate to the sinking. But Paul's action, although it also caused the sinking, did not cause Penny's action, so Penny's action was not the one causally most proximate to the sinking. Penny did not sink the dingy (Paul did). On Hornsby's analysis, Stalin did not kill Zinoviev for instance (so the LHS is false), although he did cause Zinoviev to die (but in spite of his having caused Zinoviev to die, the RHS is false because of the added condition). On Hornsby's amended analysis, only Ivan the Executioner, who was the proximate or direct agent of Zinoviev's death, killed Zinoviev.

With Hyman and Hornsby, we have two different and contradictory responses to the relation between indirect or mediate causation and agency. On Hyman's account, indirect causers are also doers, so (PT) needs no alteration. (Hyman does not discuss whether there are any limitations that need to be placed on the indirect causers who also qualify as doers.) On his account, there might be many doers of a single action, because many causers of the event that is intrinsic to the action. On Hornsby's account, almost all the causers are not doers, only that causer who is most proximate to the resulting intrinsic event is the doer. Unless two or more causers are tied for most proximate, only one causer is a doer.

There is a famous case introduced into the literature by Jerrold Katz, the Wild West Story (Katz 1970, 253, fn. 31), slightly enhanced and altered in my retelling. The local gunsmith (call him 'Smithy') faultily repairs a sheriff's gun. Soon thereafter, the sheriff, who is the fastest gun in town and who always wins gunfights, has a gunfight with the slowest gunslinger in town, but his gun jams, as a result of the faulty repair, so that he is killed by the slow gunslinger. Katz' claim is that Smithy caused the sheriff's death but did not kill him, and I agree. Since the gunslinger and not Smithy is the most proximate agent to the killing, Hornsby's (e) would correctly select the gunslinger and not Smithy as the killer. Hyman presumably would, or anyway could, accept that both the gunsmith and the gunslinger killed the sheriff.

I said above that killing and dying introduce extraneous issues that cannot be generalised, both because of the failure of ergativity, because of issues of moral and criminal responsibility, and relative 'distance' in degree of generality from a specific action. Negligence is obviously a feature in Katz' story. So let me offer an example that uses the ergative verb, 'to ring'. The case will be much less exciting. No deaths, no injuries. Boring. The case I want is this. The bell ringer intends to ring$_t$ the bell and so pulls$_t$ on the rope. Smithy walks by and notices that the rope is snagged on a nail. He doesn't much like snagged ropes, regarding them as unaesthetic, so he unhooks the rope from the nail, thereby allowing the bell to ring$_i$.

There is nothing special about 'ring'. Similar cases could be made using 'hang [a picture]', 'rotate', 'turn', 'snap', 'grow', the list is very long (Beth Levin 1993, 26–32). The closer the verb is to specifying a specific physical action, the less likely one is to conflate aiding or helping someone's do something with doing the deed oneself. That's yet another of the problems with the example of 'kill' that makes any lessons learned from it ungeneralisable; it is too far removed from specifying any particular physical action by which the killing took place. So many token actions of wildly different types can count as a killing: a poisoning, an electrocuting, a hanging, a garrotting, a guillotining, a shooting, and so on. Whatever 'intuition' there is for Stalin's having killed Zinoviev, there is a lot less for Stalin having shot$_t$ him, rather than for having him shot$_i$ by someone else.

When I introduced (PT) at the beginning of the chapter, I noted that it was unclear how we are meant to infer from 'the agent causes....' to 'the agent is a (or the) cause' (the counterpart of (PT) expressed using 'cause' as a noun rather than as a verb). I shall now have to address those questions.

What is clear is that on (PT), every case of a person's causing an event (where the event is describable using the intransitive form of an ergative verb) is a case of acting (with that event intrinsic to that action), and every case of acting is a case of that person [note: NOT his action] causing the event intrinsic to the action. (PT) requires a one-way correspondence between doers and causers: To simplify matters, I won't consider uncontroversial cases of joint action. If (PT) is true, (a) there will always be the same number of causers as doers because (b) each causer is identical to a doer, and each doer is identical to a causer.

What I want to do now is to introduce some distinctions, and offer some arguments, to show why both (a) and (b) are false. I want to distinguish between doers of action (that includes the possibility of co-doers of a joint action), providers for an action, enablers of an action, encouragers of an action, and commanders of an action (the list is not intended to be exhaustive of the ways in which persons can relate to actions. There are surely other ways.). I think our ordinary conceptual scheme allows various people to be related causally to actions in at least these different ways. Not all those who participate in some action are the agents of that action. It is simply wrong and misleading to collapse these distinctions and treat everyone in some way causally connected with an action to be connected with it in the same way, say as a doer or agent of the action. Doers, providers, enablers, encouragers, and commanders can all be part of the causal history of an action, and hence participants in the action in some way, but in different ways, which explain their different roles vis-à-vis action.

Take a provider first. In order for the bell-ringer to ring$_t$ the bell, someone had to provide the bell, the rope, and so on. No bell ringing$_t$ without bell and rope. If Smithy cast the bell, then Smithy was the provider of the bell, a necessary condition for the bell-ringer's ringing$_t$ it. Smithy certainly has an honourable place in the causal history of that token bell ringing$_i$, but not as a bell-ringer. A repairer is also a provider (the gunsmith is Katz' original example). Suppose Katz' Smithy forges the bell, produces a rope that leads to the bell, and (let us add) hoists the bell aloft. The bell-ringer on the ground then pulls$_t$ the rope. The bell rings$_i$. Let's say that the provider and the repairer are participants in the generation of that action, but without being the doer or agent of that action.

Second, remember that the rope snagged on a nail and Smithy released the rope. In this case too, Smithy is also part of the causal history of the ringing$_i$ of the bell, and so participates in its generation, but now as someone who enabled the action to occur, but not as the bell-ringer. One can aid or enable someone to do something, for example in his rotating$_t$ a disc, or be a participant in the disc's rotating$_i$, not by putting one's hands on it and rotating$_t$ it with him (that's joint action), but rather by, say, putting the pole in place on which the disc is to rotate$_i$. What else could 'aiding' or 'enabling', or 'participating in' mean? The concept of aiding or enabling is a causal idea. Aiding or enabling is in such a case a matter of (partly) causing, i.e., being *a* cause of, that rotation$_i$, without actually rotating$_t$ the disc.[8]

A third example includes encouragement and discouragement, carrots and sticks. On many occasions, others encourage one to do something, often by offering incentive or rewards. On other occasions, discouragement is offered by way of threats and disincentives. Encouragers and discouragers too play a role in the causal generation of actions (or omissions), but no one is a doer of an action simply by encouraging or discouraging someone to do it. On some occasions, the encouragement takes the stronger form of a command or an order. John Austin (1998) held that all positive law took this form: '…laws or rules, properly so-called, are a species of command' (Austin, 13). If the Sovereign commands P to do F, and P F's as a result of being commanded, the Sovereign's so commanding is one of the causes of P's F-ing. Call the one who commands, 'the commander'. To apply this distinction to one of the cases that Hyman invoked, Stalin was the commander of the killing of Zinoviev. Stalin did not kill him. Only Ivan did. But Stalin certainly commanded it, and hence participated in Zinoviev's death. Stalin was a cause of Zinoviev's death, without being his killer. There is also a weaker idea, permitters of an action, those who might allow an action to occur due to their inactivity, by not stopping it although they could have done so, and that too is a form of causality, causality by omission.

Somewhere amongst the encouragers, discouragers, and commanders, are the authorisers of action. Hobbes, in discussing natural and artificial persons, distinguishes between 'the person [who] is the actor; and he that owneth his words and actions is the AUTHOR' (*Leviathan*, Chapter XVI). Smithy might own the bell, and so suppose the bell-ringer needs the go-ahead from Smithy, in order to ring$_t$ it. Smithy authorises (as Hobbes has it, is the author of) the bell-ringing$_i$ without being the actor, the bell-ringer. In this case too, Smithy is a part of the causal history of the bell-ringing$_i$, is a cause of the bell-ringing$_i$, but without ringing$_t$ the bell.

So we have agents who are providers, enablers, encouragers, permitters, commanders, authorisers, and more, in addition to the action's doer(s). All are causes of the action, because all are part of the causal history of the bell-ringing$_i$; all are participants in the generation of the action, without necessarily being the agent of the action in question. (I deal below with a challenge to counting them as causes.)

These distinctions and arguments will support my view that in the bell-ringing case, and of course in countless others with a similar structure, both Smithy and the bell-ringer caused the bell to ring$_i$, but only the bell-ringer rang$_t$ the bell. I don't want my view to rest merely on my intuitions about the case, although I do think that the intuition that Smithy did not (even unintentionally) ring$_t$ the bell merely by unhooking the snagged rope is very strong. Hopefully the arguments and distinctions will raise my view above the level of mere intuitions about the examples.

I have used, until this point, the idea of an agent as a possible or potential agent-someone who could be the agent of an action even if he is not so. For example, in my remarks about naked trying, I called the naked trier an agent, even in the case in which there was no action that ensued. (Indeed, I argued that there was no exercise of agency at all in such a case.) No harm done. But let me be clearer now about my usage, although I mentioned this already in the Introduction: I want to introduce the idea of the doer of an action in contrast to a participant in that action. The agent who acts is the doer of the action. There may be other agents on the scene-possible or potential agents-but the action itself might *not* be attributable to them as their action. They are participants in the generation of the action but they are not necessarily doers of that action. There will be many agents on the scene who participate, but often only one of them may be the action's sole doer.

Remoteness and Partiality

I have argued above that there are more causers of an action than doers of it, so that (a) is false. In this section, I will offer counterexamples to the right-to-left entailment that show that there are cases in which there is an agent causer (or causers) but no doer at all. This counterexample provides another reason for holding that (a) is false. We don't have in such a case the same number of causers and doers: one, or more, causers, but no doers. Let me state at the outset that the argument of this section won't convince everyone (as if any arguments ever do), in part because the distinction I require is based on an idealisation. But I will do my best to extract the lesson from it that I think is pertinent to the overall argument of this chapter.

We need a distinction between partiality and remoteness of cause. Both remoteness of cause and partiality of cause affect the confidence we have in saying that the agent V_t-ed b when he caused b to V_i. In what follows, I assume that the relation, being the full cause of, and the relation, being part of the cause of, are both transitive. I assume that transitivity holds both for event causation, fact causation, and agent causation (in the last case, transitivity has to be understood in a way somewhat different from the standard way). The assumption has, to be sure, its detractors, but it is a plausible assumption.

As time goes by, the effects of an agent become swamped by yet more independent causal factors, marking the contributions of many more agents, or non-agential conditions, and thereby making the original agent an increasingly partial causal factor of an outcome. This is what I intend by 'partiality'. Many different causal chains involving many agents or independent non-agential conditions meet at the point of an event. As more and more independent causal factors enter into the aetiology leading to an event, we become less and less willing to think of that event as an event intrinsic to an action of only one of the agents. 'Why is THAT agent the one whose action it is and not the others?' becomes a fair question. But we also become less and less willing to think of the event as an event intrinsic to an action of any agent whatever.

Like causation itself, partial causation is transitive, but partial causation comes in degrees. One event e can be a major part-cause a second event f when not many other causes contribute to f's occurrence. As more events in addition to e become causally necessary for an outcome g, further down the causal line from f, e becomes a more minor part-cause of g than it was for f. But regardless of the weakening, partial causation is a transitive idea. The relation of being-a-major-part-cause-of is certainly not transitive.

But remoteness of cause raises a different issue. To see pure remoteness at work, as it were, abstracted from issues to do with partiality, we need to eliminate the complication that arises from additional and independent causal chains or agents participating in the production of an effect. To make the case as clearly as possible one of remoteness rather than partiality (and I agree that such a case is an idealisation, in the same sense that a closed system is an idealisation), suppose that the causal chain c, leading from the agent to some event remote in time, forms a (relatively) closed causal system, so that as few as possible other independent agents, or even events from some chain other than c, participate in the causation of that event. Let's consider chains on which the agent is a remote, distant cause of an event, g and such that at least no other agents figure anywhere on that causal chain that leads to g. It could be that we judge that the rest of g's causal story is composed of background conditions for g rather than further causes of g.

Joel Feinberg's 'accordion effect' addresses these kinds of examples (Feinberg 1970, 134). We have already met the accordion effect in Chap. 2, when I argued that it could go inside, as well as outwards from, the agent. His accordion effect is not limited to the case of ergative verbs, but in the main I shall confine my discussion to them. He described the accordion effect as: 'We can, if we wish, inflate our conception of an action to include one of its effects…Instead of saying that Peter did A… and thereby caused X in Y, we might say something of the form "Peter X-ed in Y"; instead of "Peter opened the door causing Paul to be startled," "Peter started Paul".' The example with which Feinberg works is not relevant for (PT) as stated, since 'startle' has no intransitive alternate ('to be startled' is not an intransitive, but a transitive passive).[9] But if we picked a better example, like 'to ring', Feinberg's accordion effect seems to be very similar to the right-to-left entailment of (PT), except that Feinberg's formula is 'P's acting and thereby causing an event', rather than simply 'P caused the event'.

Think of a very convoluted Heath Robinson or Rube Goldberg device, with loads of bells and whistles, which eventually leads to an unforeseen and unintended consequence g, which might even be a movement of the same agent's body if the route to get there is sufficiently indirect. At some point we cease to be willing to build the causally remote and unforeseen g that he has caused into the description of his (perhaps unintentional) action as its intrinsic event. Suppose a person sets off a self-contained chain of events that leads to a bell's ringing a thousand years later. Suppose that the person cannot reasonably foresee the bell's ringing, and certainly does not intend it. The person is a very remote cause of the bell's ringing$_i$, no one else has had a hand in its ringing$_i$, and so he has remotely caused, however indirectly or mediately, the bell to ring$_i$. But he has not rung$_t$ the bell, intentionally or unintentionally. So we have another case of a remote causer who is not a doer even of an unintended action. Or so I say. If this is right, then we have a token event that is remotely caused by an agent, but such that no one does any action to which this event would be intrinsic. We have a causer but no doer whatsoever.

Not everyone will agree with this way of describing things. David Lewis is one such. He thinks that even a very remote effect can be intrinsic to what one does, but only if it goes through what he calls an insensitive chain (more on insensitivity below). 'A lethal Rube Goldberg machine may work in many steps, it may be full of thousand-year fuses...', but still the person who starts the machine working may be the killer of the person who dies a thousand years later (Lewis 1986, 184–188.) Once again, I think the example of 'to kill' distorts our intuitions, in this case because of issues about responsibility. As before, I want to stick to boring and mundane examples, like startling someone (Feinberg's example) or ringing a bell and I will amend the case where appropriate accordingly. Lewis himself limits his claim only to 'kill' and 'cause to die' in any case.

He speculates that his account might work for causatives in general but he does not commit himself to the generalisation of his view to other causative verbs. But ignoring Lewis for a moment, if we switch from killing to bell ringing, we will get our intuitions more reliably responsive only to the causation issue, and not to questions of responsibility.[10] King Canute of England sets the machine going in the year 1018 (amazing, his access then to such advanced technology). In 2018, the bell rings$_i$. The bell is on a Lewisian thousand-year fuse.

But it seems to me pretty clear in this case that, whether or not the causal chain is relatively insensitive (I explain insensitivity below), King Canute did not ring$_t$ the bell in year 2018 as a consequence. Lewis disagrees. But how do we adjudicate two conflicting intuitions about action in the wake of the thousand-year wiring of the bell? The legal situation that I now cite is only intended by me to be suggestive; it does not clearly distinguish agency from responsibility or liability, or remoteness from partiality. But for what it's worth, this is the situation: It was, and still is in some jurisdictions, a principal of criminal law that if a potential agent does something that causes another's death long thereafter (formerly, it was a year and a day in English law), the agent has not killed him, but had he died in exactly a year, he would have killed him. In tort, remoteness is in many cases a test for liability, and the remoteness typically takes the form of a chain of events whose outcome the agent could not reasonably foresee. Partiality of cause, as well as remoteness of cause, no doubt is part of the reasoning in such cases, but the law did not insist that the case be one of partiality as well as, or instead of, remoteness.[11] Imagine that the fuse King Canute lit in 1018 has been burning, protected in amazing casing and undisturbed, for all this time. When the thousand year fuse starts the bell ringing in 2018, so we have a case of (almost pure) remoteness rather than partiality, I don't believe anyone should be inclined to say that Canute rang the bell.

Suppose, like Lewis, you think that Canute did ring the bell (let the chain be insensitive, as he requires). When did Canute ring$_t$ the bell? He must have rung$_t$ it either in 1018 or 2018 or sometime in between. I don't think that anyone can ring$_t$ a bell before the bell rings$_i$, and I will argue for this at length in the next chapter. Although I am going to argue that one can ring$_t$ a bell, for example, long after his body has ceased to move in the relevant ways and when he is expending no further effort (and I'm not even going to rule out decisively the possibility of acting after one's death), I think that the idea that Canute rings$_t$ a bell in 2018, when he died in 1035, is implausible in the extreme. Of course, this argument will only appeal to those who date a completed action in the way I propose. But the alternative is also not very enticing: that Canute rang$_t$ a bell 1000 years before the bell rang$_i$. I think the right answer is that Canute did not ring$_t$ the bell at all, either intentionally or unintentionally, either in 1018 or in 2018. Canute was a remote cause of, or remotely caused, the bell ringing$_i$ but he did not ring$_t$ the bell.

Why did the Law draw the line between a year versus a year and a day? My view is that the distinction between what an agent does, whether intentionally or unintentionally, and what he merely causes, is vague, and that the vague distinction can be precisified when required by the law, or for important ordinary purposes. This means that the idea of remoteness is vague. There may be no sharp cut off point at which we say that up to that point the agent has V$_t$-ed b (intentionally or unintentionally, foreseen or unforeseen) and after that point the agent has only caused b to V$_i$. ('V' can now be either an ergative or a non-ergative verb like 'to startle'.) Sometimes the unintended and unforeseen consequences of what one does are intrinsic to some (unintentional) action one does, and sometimes not. There may only be a spectrum on which we grow increasingly less inclined to attribute the action to the agent, as he becomes a more and more remote and partial cause of an outcome, with no real decisive cut-off point. If the causal chain leading to the consequence, b's V$_i$-ing, is a deviant causal chain, we may be even less likely to say that the agent V$_t$-ed b. Suppose Canute imagined that the fuse would work like a normal fuse, but because of some quirk in background conditions, the fuse extinguishes but then relights due to the sun's heating of the sheath in which it is encased. Did Canute still ring$_t$ the bell in 2018, when a deviant causal chain is operative?

If this is right, then one may say that an assertion like 'Agent P V$_t$-ed b' may be vague; there may be cases for which it is neither determinately true nor determinately false. I think that it is the vagueness of the idea of action that is responsible for the fluctuating and variable intuitions we have about such cases. Different people's intuitions will differ and one's own intuitions seem sometimes to be unstable, just as it would be if we asked different people to classify the men they meet as bald or not bald. But just as there are clear cases of when a man is bald and when he is not bald, so too there are clear cases when an agent causes but does not act and clear cases when he does act. The inference from the RHS to the LHS of (PT) is not valid.

'Remoteness' is, as I said, highly context-sensitive. Here is a case from Jewish Law that makes that point rather dramatically. The case won't appeal to everyone, and it too depends on my way of dating a completed action (as I said, the arguments for this appears in Chap. 6). It is this: it is forbidden to light a light on the Sabbath. Intentionally so doing is (biblically) a capital offense. Even an unintentional violation requires sacrificial expiation. But I can set a time clock one minute before the Sabbath commences, at t, and the light will light, one minute after the commencement of the Sabbath, at t*, and I will have violated no law, not even unintentionally. On the assumption that the time of an action is the time I propose, it must be that I do not light$_t$ the light at t*, although the light lit$_i$ at t* and I caused it to do so. 'Remoteness' is indeed context-sensitive; in the context of Jewish Law, a remote effect can be one that occurs on the Sabbath when its initiating cause was just before the Sabbath.

I have been arguing against two claims: (a) there will always be the same number of causers as doers; (b) each causer is identical to a doer, and each doer is identical to a causer. I will focus on (b). If (b) is true, then so is (a). Examples and the discussion above show that (a) is false (many causers but only one doer; one causer but no doer). But they also show that (b) is false, since some of the causers (the commanders, the encourager, the provider, etc.) are not identical with any doer. But I agree that each doer is someone who causes the outcome. 'Someone who causes'? What does that mean? Why do we think that the enabler, the commander, providers, encouragers, and so on are causers at all? To be sure, they are part of the causal history of the bell's ringing, but is everything in that causal history a cause?

A Cause, the Cause

We need to be clear about the idea of causation in 'P causes…'. In (PT), as I have said, we are given no explicit instructions for converting 'P causes…' ('causes' as a verb) to something of the form 'P is…a/the cause…' ('cause' as a noun). If P causes e, is P *a* cause of e, *the* cause of e, *a part-cause, a whole-cause, the full* cause of e, or what?

I can't undertake to be faithful to every theory of causation on the market. But I intend to make my remarks faithful to many of the most prominent theories of causation. I will use two such theories as a way of organising what I want to say. I will look at some assumptions made about causation by John Mackie and David Lewis, in order to answer the question about the idea of causing being used in (PT).

First, suppose 'P causes e' means 'P is the full cause of e'. That is not a very plausible idea and surely can't be what 'P causes e' is meant to mean in (PT). On David Lewis' account, the full cause of e (he does not use that expression) includes the whole causal history of e, stretching back no doubt to the Big Bang. 'Roughly speaking, a causal history [of some event] has the structure of a tree' (David Lewis 1986, 214–217). For Lewis, all the points on the causal history are events, including omissions. At the node on the tree that represents the event e, causal chains converge and diverge. In our world, the causal history of an event is either 'infinite or merely enormous.' Either way, it is a very replete structure, with lots of other nodes on it. Each event is 'the culmination of countless distinct, converging causal chains', stretching over a very long period of time. No single (non-conjunctive) factor, agential or otherwise, could be the full cause.

John Stuart Mill says that 'The cause…is the sum total of the conditions positive and negative' for the event's occurrence (Mill 1970, Book 3, Chapter 5, Section 3) and John Mackie (1974, 63–64) adds that 'there is no good reason why we should not go further and equate 'the cause…' with the complete disjunction of conjunctions…It is this that is both necessary and sufficient for the effect….as causes have often been assumed to be.' For Mackie, as for Mill, that sum total not only includes events but also situations, standing conditions, and absences. The full cause works against an assumed background, the causal field, ('in F'), and 'these will not figure as conjuncts [in the antecedent conditions]...' (Mackie 1974, 63; more on this below). In any particular case, we don't count any event or condition in the field as a cause, although each is necessary for the effect along with the causes, but what events or conditions belong in the assumed field and not treated as causes itself varies, and depends on what our interests are in explaining the event. Something that we consign to the field in one investigation may shift to being one of the causes in another investigation, or even in the same investigation, should our explanatory interests alter.

The take-home so far is only this: In 'Agent P caused e', at least on the accounts of full cause above, an agent P cannot be the full cause of e. This is utterly obvious. 'But what is ordinarily called a cause, or what is referred to by the subject of a causal verb, is practically never anything like this [full cause]....what is typically called a cause is an inus condition or an individual instance of an inus condition...' (Mackie 1974, 64). The whole causal history of an event e, or the disjunction of conjunctions of conditions necessary and sufficient for e in field F, provides innumerable events, states, conditions, omissions, processes, (and we can add) agents, and so each of the latter can count as *a* cause (one of the innumerable causes) of e. So suppose agent P is *a* cause of e. But so also might non-agential conditions, or other agents, be *a* cause of e too. So let's say that every event or agent that has a place on a given event e's causal history (and not consigned merely to the causa field) is *a* cause of e. The provider, enabler, encourager, permitter, or commander can also be *a* cause of e.

But sometimes we speak of *the* cause of an event, rather than *a* cause of the event. We don't mean by that definite article that the cause in that sense is the full cause. If someone says that e1 was the cause of e, another says that e2 was the cause, and still another says that the cause was e3... 'I do not think any of them disagree with me when I say that the causal history includes all three. They disagree only about which part of the causal history is most salient for the purposes of some particular inquiry' (Lewis, 215). Or as Mackie points out, selecting the cause from the many causes can be taken 'as reflecting...' the 'conversational point, the sorts of use to which they are likely to be put' (35). Our interests, as is often remarked, influence these decisions. The selection of *the* cause (when there is but one that is selected from the many candidates) is made on pragmatic grounds: when experts declare a short-circuit to be the cause of a fire, they 'are saying in effect that the short-circuit is a condition of this sort, that it occurred, that the other conditions which, conjoined with it, form a sufficient condition were also present, and that no other sufficient condition of the house's catching fire was present on this occasion' (Mackie 1965 (1993): 34). So to call something in the causal history of e 'the cause of e' rather than 'a cause of e', signifies only the type of interest or perspective we have concerning the explanation of e's occurrence.

On Mackie's account, selectivity enters at two different points: (a) the choice of what is a cause of e and what is only part of the causal field in which e occurs; (b) the choice of the cause of e from the several causes of e. 'There is admittedly some logical redundancy in the two treatments... But at present my object is ...to analyse our ordinary thinking about causal sequences, and I believe that this does contain the two separate elements I have tried to describe' (36–37).

Some have distinguished two kinds of cases of selectivity (Gorovitz 1965): the context of occurrence and the context of inquiry. In the first kind, we envisage two different situations that have different structures. The presence of oxygen and the faulty wiring were both necessary for the fire, but in a standard situation we may cite the faulty wiring as the cause; in another situation, in a special laboratory where precautions had been taken to exclude oxygen from the environment, we might cite the presence of oxygen as the cause. In this first kind of case, there are objective differences between the two situations that underwrite the two different judgments of what is the cause.

In the second kind of case, different observers might make different judgments about what is the cause in a single situation, depending on their interests. The Indian farmers might identify the cause of the famine as the draught but the World Food Authority might identify the cause as the Indian Government's failure to build up food reserves (Menzies 2012, 354). This last kind of selectivity is (as Menzies says) enquiry-dependent. Both kinds of selectivity can affect choice of doer v. mere causer, but it is enquiry-dependent selectivity that will be most important for my argument.

Reflecting on the various different ways in which agents can participate in the causal history of an action, there is more than one way in which to participate in that history. Might one argue that these agents who are not the doers of the action are not amongst the action's causes either, but only amongst its necessary background conditions? As we saw, what counts as a background condition versus a cause (let alone what counts as *the* cause versus *a* cause) shifts as our interests or purposes of our enquiry shift and different factors become salient in the causal story that we want to tell. But I think it is easy enough to describe cases in which all of these characters-the enabler, the provider, and so on-become the focus of our concern and attention and hence are a cause of the action rather than only a causally necessary background condition. When Smithy unsnags the rope, he is not just part of the background conditions for the bell's ringing. He is, I think, a cause of its ringing$_i$.

Indeed, that is exactly what has happened in the case of Stalin's alleged killing of Zinoviev. I have argued that Stalin did not kill Zinoviev, but only commanded or ordered his killing, and so that he was amongst the causes of it, and hence a cause of the killing. To further demote Stalin from being a cause of Zinoviev's death, to being only a causally necessary background conditions seems quite misguided. There were, to be sure, *some* merely background conditions in this example; some of the agents might have only been part of what Mackie called 'the causal field'. An example might be (thinking now only of agents) the courier, Boris, who brought Stalin's execution order to Ivan. If Boris had not done so, Zinoviev would not have suffered that particular death that he did suffer, although he might have suffered a different death. Borris' bringing of the order might count in the normal way as a causally necessary condition and not a cause of Zinoviev's death, although even so one could retell a different story on which the bringing of that order was a cause of the death by attributing to it some sort of causal importance or salience that it otherwise lacked.

On the other hand, in the sense of '*the* cause' that also reflects the pragmatics of explanation, the selection of the cause depends on what we want to focus on. The important question will be: which agent (assuming it is some agent and not some non-agential condition) from the many who are in some way causes of the result, or figure in its causal history, is the one and only one who is singled out on some occasion as *the* cause of the bell's ringing$_i$? It would be a pragmatic decision how to single out which agent was *the* cause of the outcome from the many agents participating in the outcome's causal history and each of whom is a cause of that outcome. It is plausible to hold that in the Stalin-Zinoviev example, Stalin is *the* cause of Zinoviev's death, and Ivan only a cause, in spite of Ivan being the deed's doer. Given the facts of the case, Stalin was the main and most important participant in that death, and inherits all or most of the responsibility for it, but he was so without being the actual agent of the death. What is clear is that our real concern and interest in this case is with Stalin, and not with Ivan, who was only a small cog in a rather extensive and loathsome machine.

Imagine that we are undertaking a study of how bystanders who are proactive and can spot problems that might impede action can be crucial to outcomes. The bell ringer routinely rings$_t$ the bell; there is nothing noteworthy in that. He does it thrice daily. But remember that Smithy spotted the snagged rope and released it. That was not routine and was noteworthy. Our focus would now shift to Smithy as the one who was the cause of the bell's ringing$_i$. Smithy is *the* cause in whom we are interested. Yet the bell-ringer surely remains the doer. Smithy does not become the doer, just because he becomes the pragmatic focus of the investigations as *the* cause of the bell ringing$_i$. The doer, at least in this case, is the bell-ringer, who operated the rope, willingly and knowingly, with no coercion or compulsion. Smithy is the causer, who *really* brought about the bell ringing$_i$, because he is the agent in whom we are interested and provides the focus for our investigation. It is true, of both the bell-ringer and Smithy, that they were each *a* cause of the bell ringing$_i$. But if asked who was *the* cause of the bell's ringing$_i$, an acceptable answer in these imaginary circumstances would be that Smithy was the cause, and that the bell-ringer, the doer, were not the cause, although it remains true that they were both a cause. The bell-ringer is the doer (that is not a pragmatic matter), but even so, Smithy might be the cause of the bell-ringing$_i$.

The view of causation I have outlined, in Mill, Mackie, and Lewis, assumes that there is no real metaphysical distinction (only a pragmatic and shifting one) between an event's being a causally necessary condition for e's occurrence and its being a cause of e (add for Mackie and Mill to 'events': 'conditions, etc.') or its being the cause of e. If my grandparents had not married, I would not be writing this book. Does that make them a cause of my writing? The answer is that it does, unless their marriage is consigned to the causal field. To deny that would be to deny the transitivity of causation (and of causally necessary condition), since there will surely be a causal chain leading from their marriage to my writing. 'The supposed distinction between conditions and causes can be adequately accounted for in these two ways: an alleged condition which is not called a cause, although if in the circumstances it had not occurred the result would not, either is part of the field presupposed in the view of the speaker…(and so is not a cause in relation to this field) or is a cause, but mention of this fact happens to be irrelevant…to some current purpose' (Mackie, 36).

The claim that the enabler, for example, was *a* cause of the event is plausible. It's when one converts the claim back to the verb form that doubts tend to arise: 'the enabler caused the bell-ringing$_i$.' That might sound less promising. The enabler was *a* cause of the event, but it might strike one as more problematic to say that the enabler caused the event. But I think that that doubt only arises because in saying that the enabler caused the event (verb form), we immediately might hear that as suggesting that he was not just *a* cause, but was *the* cause, i.e., that it is in him whom we are principally interested. Unlike in the example I gave in which Smithy was the focus of our interest when he unhooked the snagged rope, more often than not the enabler, or any of the other causers who are not the doer, won't be the focus of our interest. If we stick to the 'a cause' or 'the cause' form (the noun forms), I think we can see that it is true that the enabler (or the provider or the encourager or the commander etc.), along with the doer, is *a* cause of the event e, along with lots of other causes too, and each of them could be *the* cause of e, should our explanatory interests be directed onto him.

Not everyone agrees with the Mackie-Lewis view on pragmatic or conversational selection (Mackie, 35) of causes and conditions. Menzies is one such. He claims that 'the whole approach is highly questionable' (Menzies, 355) and offers three arguments against this approach. The first two arguments have little weight: the selectivity does not have to be 'capricious or invidious' as he charge. There may be inter-subjective principles for this selectivity. Nor are we given any independent reason to believe that the difference between 'a causal condition', 'a cause', and 'the cause' must be non-pragmatic, 'central and crucial to the concept of causation'. The second 'argument' is just a re-assertion of what needs to be demonstrated. But it is worth pausing briefly over his third argument, which is this: the Mackie-Lewis view makes 'a cause' primary, and 'the cause' derivative (obviously he is addressing only the 'the cause'/'a cause' contrast, not the 'cause'/'condition' contrast, although the section of his article is entitled 'Causes vs. background Conditions'). But, he argues, 'the expression of 'the cause of the explosion' does not usually mean 'the most salient among the factors that count as a cause of the explosion'. Rather the direction of explanation is the other way: 'the expression "a cause of the explosion" is understood as meaning "one of the causes of the explosion"...' (355).

How exactly to put Menzies point? The view he wants to deny is that (a) *the* cause is to be explained as (b) the one from many causes (each of which is *a* cause). The direction of explanation is, he says, the other way: (b) *a* cause is to be explained as (a) one of *the* causes. But the argument is invalid. 'The' is being used ambiguously in the two instances of (a). In the first (a), 'the cause' is, in the context in which it is being used, intended as a uniquely identifying description; the single most salient cause in the circumstances. In the second occurrence of (a), 'one of the causes', 'the cause' is just the plural definite article for count nouns, as in 'the causes of the war are listed on p.8', which means '(x) (x is a cause of the war→x is listed on p. 8)'. 'One of the causes is listed on p.8' can be true when actually many of the causes are listed there. There may be a conversational implicature that only one is, but that is not part of the truth-conditions of the assertion. If I assert that one of the causes is listed on p.8, and then add: 'oh look, other causes are listed there too', what I first said is not thereby rendered false.

So Menzies alternative proposal does not even address the same point as the view he denies addresses. There does not seem to be any way of explaining 'a cause' by means of 'the cause', where the 'the' is a uniquely identifying referring term. So I agree with Mackie: In contexts of enquiry, we pick out '*the* cause' from a situation in which there may be many causes, and/or conditions and we do using principles of selectivity that are pragmatic, that relate to the interests or purposes we have in inquiring about the cause of something.

But wait! Why can't the choice of doer be pragmatic too, and if so, might not the pragmatic selection of *the* (one and only one) causer match the pragmatic choice of the action's (one and only one) doer (assuming it's not a case of joint action)? Both (a) and (b) would be true after all. The number of causers (in the sense of '*the* causer') and doers would match and the doer=the causer. If P*, the rope unhooker, is *the* causer, maybe P* is also *the* doer, the latter also being selected on pragmatic grounds. P would still be *a* cause of the bell ringing$_i$, but only the enabler P* (on this supposition) is *the* cause of the bell's ringing$_i$ (pragmatically selected) and so only P* rings$_t$ the bell (also pragmatically selected). P, who is *a* causer of the bell's ringing$_i$, along with loads of other causes and causers, is neither *the* (one and only pragmatically selected) cause of the bell's ringing$_i$ nor the (one and only pragmatically selected) agent who rings$_t$ the bell. This disenfranchises P, the agent who (we may have wrongly thought) rang$_t$ the bell, from ringing$_t$ the bell; he is only another cause in the causal history of its ringing$_i$.

I think that the idea of pragmatic choice of the doer that parallels the pragmatic choice of the causer is an absurdity. In the case of action, the doer(s) comes attached to the action. This is a metaphysical point, not an epistemic one. I can know that someone rang$_t$ the bell, so I can know that there was a bell ringing$_t$, without knowing who it was who rang$_t$ it. Maybe the ringer wore a disguise or maybe I am behind a partition. But if that I so, I can only give a partial and incomplete description of the token action. But what isn't possible is that we can uniquely identify some token action, such that it is metaphysically possible that it might be the action of either one agent or of another. Helen Steward makes a similar point, although in a different connection: 'Thinking of actions like particular butterings…. rather suggests that they are particulars that an agent may or may not choose to bring about' (Steward 2012, 37–38). On the contrary, actions come with a specific agent 'built in'. Actions come with agents already attached; one agent in the case of individual actions, multiple agents in the case of joint action. It is one thing to argue for agent-expansion to second or even more agents beyond the obvious agent(s), as Hyman did for instance. It is quite another to argue for agent disenfranchisement, to try and pose the possibility that the prima facie agent of an action isn't even really the action's doer at all, on the grounds that choice of the doer must also be pragmatic, to match the pragmatic selection of the causer.

Unlike Hyman's, Hornsby's 'fix' for the second-person counterexamples we discussed earlier was to require the doer not just to be the causer but the most proximate causer, and, baring tie scores, this would justify both (a) and (b), amended to cover only the most proximate causer, since the one most proximate causer (if no tie scores) would be the sole doer, and the number of causers and doers would therefore be the same (again, discounting joint action). But her view will not produce the right result in the case of the bell ringing. I don't think that proximity or immediacy of cause is the key here. Smithy's action is the more proximate cause since he unsnags the rope from the nail. Smithy still has not rung$_t$ the bell even though his unsnagging action is a more proximate cause of its ringing$_i$ than is the bell-ringer's pulling of the rope. So Hornsby's solution that selects the proximate causer of the event as the deed's doer won't work either. The most proximate causer is not necessarily the doer.

To make Hornsby's view yield the right result for the case of Smithy, Smithy would be the bell ringer only if his unsnagging$_t$ of the rope is a cause of the bell's ringing$_i$ (as indeed it is), and any action other than his that also caused the ringing$_i$ caused his action as well. (That is what it would mean for it to be proximate to the bell ringing.) What other actions are on the table, as it were? Not the ringing$_t$ of the bell (by whomever), because the ringing$_t$ of the bell cannot cause the bell's ringing$_i$. So it must be the rope pulling$_t$. But the rope pulling$_t$ did cause the unsnagging$_t$, and that makes Smithy the bell-ringer after all. There is no doubt that the ringer's pulling$_t$ of the rope is less proximate to the bell's ringing$_i$ than is Smithy's unsnagging$_t$.

Is there a response she can offer to this counterexample? Could she agree that Smithy isn't ringing$_t$ the bell, but only, she might say, because he is not, in my example, the most proximate cause of the bell ringing$_i$ after all? Perhaps Smithy is proximately causing something else other than the bell's ringing$_i$ (perhaps he is only allowing the bell ringer to ring$_t$ the bell) and only mediately causing the bell's ringing$_i$. So the causal chain might be this: the bell ringer pulls$_t$ the rope; Smithy unsnags$_t$ the rope; Smithy allows (or causes?) the bell ringer to cause the bell's ringing$_i$; the bell ringer causes the bell to ring$_i$. The idea is to get causation by the bell ringer back into the causal picture *after* Smithy's unsnagging$_t$.

This proposed reply, admittedly somewhat farfetched, raises more questions than I can answer here. Causal proximity isn't the same as temporal proximity, but it is still important to have an idea of how to date these occurrences. Nor is it clear *what* an allowing or a causing is (much more on causing in Chap. 7). But one possible rejoinder is this: Smithy's allowing or causing the bell ringer to cause the bell to ring IS his unsnagging the rope. And no doubt about it: the unsnagging$_t$ is causally subsequent to the rope pulling$_t$. Another way of conceiving of the situation is this: the bell ringer, by pulling$_t$ the rope, initiates a causal process that runs, say, from t1 to t5, when the bell rings$_i$. Suppose Smithy unsnags$_t$ the rope at t4. True, since the bell ringer is engaging in a causal process, so that his causing the bell to ring$_i$ can stretch from t1 to t5 (more on dating of actions-in-progress in Chap. 6), at t4 he is also causing the bell (eventually, at t5) to ring$_i$. But this would make Smithy, who unsnags at t4, a joint agent of the bell's ringing$_t$ along with the bell ringer, but that is wrong: Smithy is not a joint agent of the bell-ringing. The only way in which Smithy could allow the bell ringer to ring$_t$ the bell is by unsnagging the rope, and that may well be the last thing, or joint last thing, on the causal chain leading from the pulling of the rope to the ringing$_i$ of the bell. There is no getting around the fact that Smithy may be the proximate, or joint proximate, cause of the bell's ringing$_i$ without ringing$_t$ the bell.

I think the upshot here is that causing is one thing, doing is another, and that they can come apart. I don't mean to assert that doers are not always also causers; only that not all causers, Smithy for example, are doers. First, in a case of remote causation, a very remote causer of an event may not be the doer, on the grounds that in such a case, there is no longer any doer at all. Second, enablers, providers, encouragers, commanders, and so on, are also causers of e. But they are not doers of e. If there are many causers and only one doer, then *eo ipso* we have many causers who are not doers. If only one causer (only one who is *the* cause of) and one doer, they may not be identical, since our selection of the agent who is *the* cause from the multiple agents who are *a* cause of e can vary, depending on various pragmatic considerations. But the attachment between a token action and its doer is invariable and not pragmatic; it is metaphysically necessary that a token action has the doer it does have.

David Lewis on Doing and Causing

In Postscript C to his famous article, 'Causation' (Lewis 1986, 184–188), David Lewis discusses the difference between killing someone and (merely) causing his death. I will use the 'kill'/'cause to die' pair in what follows, since he uses it, in spite of my disquiet about using it as the paradigm example for the relation between causing and acting. But since Lewis does not expand his claim to other causative verbs, it would be inappropriate to switch his example to an ergative, verb.

Lewis mentions a list of possible restrictions on the causal chains that end in a death and which might make the initiator of the chain a killer as well as a causer: single step causal dependence; shortness of causal chain; high probability of outcome; simplicity of causal chain; foreseeability of the consequence; absence of intermediate human involvement. He says that none works either on its own or in combination with the others. Lewis says that one can kill someone in the absence of any or all of these restrictions. One can kill when the causal chain is long, complex, when the outcome is improbable, unforeseeable, unintentional, and when the killing is via the involvement of a third party.

Lewis proposes a different way in which to draw this contrast between killing and causing death: 'I suggest a different way to distinguish the right kind of causing…' that is also a killing (186). When an effect depends on a cause, it will depend on other circumstances as well. Striking the match caused it to light, but if the wind would have been stronger or the match itself had been wet, or the oxygen in the air had been absent, striking the match would not have caused it to light. So let us say that the match's lighting, caused by the striking, is *sensitive* to the absence or presence of all these other circumstances.

Sensitivity is a matter of more-or-less. Sometime a causal connection is sensitive to any small perturbation in circumstances; if the circumstances had not been just so, the potential cause would have failed to bring about the effect. A causal chain is sensitive if it consists of steps that are sensitive.

But at other times, the causal chain is relatively insensitive. To use Lewis' own example, when a person shoots another point blank and causes his death, relatively little change (only 'some very remarkable difference') would alter the outcome. There are fewer things to go wrong and of the things that could go wrong, they mark a greater departure from the normal. For example, the bullet might shatter in mid-air. In this case, the dependence of the effect on the cause is relatively insensitive and so the shooter not only causes the death of, but also kills, his victim.

So causing the death counts as a killing when the causation is of a relatively insensitive kind. Very sensitive causal chains yield causings of death that are not killings. Lewis' proposal uses terms like 'relatively' or 'comparatively'. This makes the cut-off between causing death and killing vague, and this is to be welcomed, since it is a feature of my view too. Lewis points out that his proposal also can explain why some of the possible restrictions mentioned above are obviously relevant to some extent. For example, other things being equal, shortness and simplicity make for insensitivity, and insensitivity makes for foreseeability.

How does Lewis' proposal compare to mine? Lewis' sensitivity condition bears some resemblance to partiality. The more insensitive a causal chain is, the more the event initiating the chain is a less partial cause of the outcome, more like the whole of the cause (ceteris paribus). Using the sensitivity/insensitivity contrast, Lewis proposes to give an account of the difference between killing and causing death: an agent A kills B if (and only if?) A relatively insensitively causes the death of B. Lewis' proposal is going to produce a lot more doers than I have conceded, at least in the cases of insensitive but remote causal chains (remember his case of the thousand-year fuse). We agree that there are some causers who are not doers where sensitive causal chains are involved.

Lewis' proposal that makes insensitivity the key to the distinction has difficulty with cases that involve a third party. Take Lewis' own case in which A gives B a box of poisoned chocolates, B then unsuspectingly serves him to a guest, C, and C dies. Since the chain is insensitive, both A and B kill C. The case has the same structure as the employer and the hitman. As I have said before, I have no problem with the thought that more than one person can kill a third. Here is a bona fide case of joint action poisoning: the box of poisoned chocolates is heavy, so if both A and B hold box and together tip the chocolates from the box into C's mouth, both A and B have killed C.

On Lewis' view of the poisoned chocolate case, we have multiple causers and multiple doers, at least in the case of a relatively insensitive chain. He thinks that A (and B?) are causers of C's death and killers of C. But it is not true that, in the case of the poisoned chocolates as Lewis describes the case, that A has killed C, as he claims (he is assuming that such a chain from A to C must be insensitive). Lewis' judgment about such cases simply erases the distinction between a doer and a provocateur, or between doing on the one hand and aiding and abetting the doer on the other (at least in an insensitive chain example). In cases like this, liability and moral blame don't neatly follow the causing/doing distinction. In such circumstances, the person who actually did the killing unintentionally (suppose he did not know about the poison in the chocolates) can be less culpable than the person who got him to kill but didn't do the killing. But B has unintentionally been the sole killer of C.

Lewis concedes that the case *seems* to be different if A gets B knowingly to kill C. Suppose B knows that the chocolates are poisoned. When B knowingly kills C by giving him the chocolates given to him by A, A no longer kills C, only B does, according to Lewis. But why for Lewis should it be the case that A does kill C (and B does too?) when B gives C the chocolates unknowingly but A does not kill C (but B does) when B gives the chocolates knowingly? One might have thought that the degree of sensitivity in the causal chain was the same in both cases. How does whether or not B knows what he is doing affect the sensitivity of the causal chain?

Lewis's reply to this objection is complex and two-fold. First, 'I reply that indeed that might be so [the chain is equally insensitive in both cases], and nevertheless we might speak as if it were not so' (187). That is, in truth even when B knows about the poison, A does still kill C because the chain is insensitive (and B also does or does not kill C?). That is, the chain is equally insensitive both when B knows and when B does not know, according to Lewis, because the chain is, and A knows that it is, not going to be effected by B's knowledge. It's not going to make any difference to hard-hearted B. B is an incorrigible badie. So the chain is equally insensitive and if A kills C in the one case (B does not know), then A kills C in the second case too (B does know).

However, it is, on this view, disrespectful on the part of A to treat B's readiness to *knowingly* kill as 'stable and durable, inexorable and insensitive to fortuitous circumstances of the case'. (Note that 'inexorable' has been slipped in for the first time. The relative insensitivity was not meant to be the same as inexorability.) On this first reply, A remains the killer, but if we deny that A is the killer, it is only because 'we are paying the thug [B] a gesture of respect-insincere, undeserved, yet unsurprising' by treating the causal chain *as if* it were sensitive to B's ability not to do what A wants him to do. So the chain may in truth be insensitive but, in respecting B as an agent, we treat it as if it were sensitive, remaining open to B not to pass on the poisoned chocolates and in spite of our secure knowledge that he will not avail himself of that option.

It is not clear what the take-home is meant to be on this first response. On Lewis' first reply, A is *in truth* the killer (or one of the killers?) whether or not B knows that the chocolates are poisoned, even if we do not wish to *say* this in the case in which B knows that the chocolates are poisoned. That is, the chain is insensitive even though we don't want to say that it is. But all this seems wrong headed. In the case in which B knowingly gives C the poisoned chocolate that A has supplied, it is simply the case that A is NOT the killer, although he retains a prominent causal role in the killing, regardless of what it might be opportune to say, and even though the causal chain displays the same amount of insensitivity in both cases.

Drug dealers (choose an especially toxic example of a drug) knowingly cause a lot of deaths, but they do not kill people by supplying the drugs to those who kill themselves by using them. The law recognises this. When drug dealers are punished, it is for drug dealing and not for murder. The law in various jurisdictions differs, regarding who is an accomplice to a deed, who the principal actor of the deed, and what constitutes common purpose. Both intentionality and foreknowledge play roles in these cases. I don't intend to examine those legal ideas here. Suppose an unsuspecting C is given toxic drugs and does not know that what he has been given is dangerous. My claim is limited: in a case in which A gives dangerous drugs to B, knowing what the results of so doing are likely to be, and B knowingly or unknowingly gives them to an unsuspecting C, if anyone kills C, it must be B and not A. In one case, B kills intentionally and in the other unintentionally. A has committed a crime, but killing is not one of them. A is an enabler of, or a provider for, but not a doer of, the killing of C.

As I have repeatedly insisted, the case would be clearer if one switched the example to something boring and pedestrian, like bell ringing$_i$. The following example has the same simple structure but abstracts away from those inevitable issues of liability and responsibility that come with killing: A hands B the rope that B will use. Suppose A knows that B's pulling on the rope will lead to the bell's ringing$_i$. The chain from A to B to the bell's ringing$_i$ is, let us suppose, insensitive. Who rang$_t$ the bell? B did, whether or not B knows that his pulling on the rope will lead to the ringing$_i$ of the bell. When B does not know, his bell ringing$_t$ will be unintentional (or unintentional under that description), but it will be just that: one of his, B's, unintentional actions. A did not ring$_t$ the bell, in spite of it's being true that he gave B the means to ring$_t$ it. So Lewis' approach does not work for causatives generally (he did not claim that it would), quite apart from its failure to deal adequately with the 'kill'/'cause to die' pair. But I think it is fair to extrapolate the somewhat clearer intuitions from the bell's ringing back to the killing.

Lewis' second reply runs like this. In truth, A is NOT the killer of C when B knowingly gives C the poisoned chocolate (and it's not just the case that we treat A as if he is not and B as if he is). The truth conditions for 'kill' are not just a matter of insensitive causation. An exception would need to be made for the case in which the insensitive causal chain runs through an additional agent's knowing involvement, as it did in Hyman's and Hornsby's examples. On this second reply, we have a causer, (A), who supplies the chocolates, but who is not a doer, for whatever reason, so Lewis and I would be in agreement about the failure of the right-to-left entailment of (PT) in such a case.

I think that a difficulty with Lewis' proposal is his account of sensitivity and insensitivity.[12] He appears to assume that a causal chain is, *de rerum natura*, either sensitive or insensitive. I don't think that that is so. Sensitivity is a matter of how the causes on the chain are described. Take the case again of shooting someone at point-blank range, but imagine two further facts about the case: (1) the shooter has some sort of palsy; (2) there is a row of people who are lined up, only one of whom is to be shot. It may be that the shooting leads insensitively to someone's being shot ('only some very remarkable difference in circumstances would prevent [someone's] death'), but leads sensitively to the death of the specific person P who in the end is shot (it could have so easily been someone else, given the shaking the palsied shooter was displaying). The shooting of P is insensitively the death of some person in the line but sensitively the death of P in particular. On Lewis' view, the shooting would be one of my actions described in one way but only something I cause when described in another. I don't think this is the conclusion that Lewis wants.

One last point about Lewis' proposal. If it were true that P could kill someone by lighting a thousand-year fuse, the view would face the standard problems of time and date of actions, but with a special vengeance. Either P kills the victim at t when he is alive, or at t+1000 years, the time of the victim's death. On the first option, he kills the victim 1000 years before the victim dies; on the second, he might kill the victim 1000 years after he, P, dies. A similar example can be constructed that gives us two options about the place of the action. I will discuss these options in the next chapter.

The message of this chapter is consistent with the following view. If one thinks in terms of Venn diagrams, cases of agents' causing events can be represented as a large circle in such a diagram; cases of agents' acting can be represented by a smaller circle entirely within that larger circle. That picture captures the thought that there are many cases in which one causes some event e to occur without one's E_t-ing. The purpose of the next chapter is to evaluate whether this is the correct picture of the relation between events and actions.

DT: The Derivation Thesis

I have discussed (PT), which I take to be a philosophical analysis of action. There is, as far as I can tell, another distinct thesis discussed by linguists. It is not a philosophical thesis at all. It is an empirical hypothesis. I call it the 'derivation thesis', in the linguists' non-logical sense of derivation: (DT) '…sentences like [Floyd melted the glass] derive from deep structures like [Floyd caused the glass to melt]' (Lakoff 1965). My main interest in this discussion is to differentiate (DT) from any philosophical analysis, like (PT).

As I mentioned before, there is a disagreement amongst linguists about whether the sentence with the transitive verb is basic and the causal sentence with the intransitive form of the verb is derived, or vice versa (or whether they are both generated from a common source). The Derivation Thesis, on which I now wish to comment briefly, holds that the derivation (or generation) is from a sentence about what an agent causes to the sentence about what he does. I have not addressed this view elsewhere in this book. Other than the few remarks I want to make now, I am not competent to enter into this non-philosophical discussion. Unlike the case with (PT), the relevant literature assumes that the 'deep-structure sentence' and the derived sentence are meant to have the same meaning, and that any adverbial qualification in the deep-structure sentence must be accounted for in the derived sentence in a straightforward way.

What I want to do is to review and restate more fully some of the counterexamples to this derivation thesis. The counterexamples are not new (they were discussed extensively by Fodor (1970, 1975, 130–131, especially fn. 23) and by others), but I expand somewhat on their discussion. I follow convention by using (*), in this section of the chapter, to indicate a sentence either of dubious grammatical acceptability or of semantic oddity. Given the counterexamples, and the uncertain status that (DT) has in linguistics, it would be an error to try and support (PT) by citing as evidence (DT).

The derivation failure of a sentence about what the agent does from a sentence about what an agent causes is often most salient when adverbial modifiers, both to do with time and manner, are added to a sentence. Therefore, these counterexamples are not counterexamples to any form of (PT), which as stated makes no provision about how to treat adverbial modification on the two sides of (PT). As far as (PT) goes: 'P caused o to V_i iff P V_t-ed o' could be true, even if 'P caused o to V_i F-ly iff P V_t-ed o F-ly' were false. The adverbial modifications that 'distribute' in sentences that are equivalent often do so in more complicated ways than any such simple model would allow. Here is an example: 'A football team wins a match iff it scores more goals than the other side' states a true equivalence. (It is even an analytical truth about football.) Now add the adverb 'elegantly' to the left-hand side: 'A football team wins a match elegantly'. We cannot 'plug in' this adverb in any clear way on the right hand side and still get a true biconditional: Winning elegantly is not the same as scoring goals elegantly, or scoring more elegant goals than the other side. For 'winning elegantly' we would need a much more complex sentence on the right-hand side.

So although the counterexamples that follow won't work as counterexamples to (PT), as it is currently formulated, I think (and the important point is that the linguistics literature assumes) that they work as counterexamples to (DT), which is about how the meaning of a surface structure sentence gets 'generated' from the meaning of a deep structure sentence. Katz' example of the sheriff and the gunslinger (Katz 1970, 253, fn. 31) is put forward by him in a discussion of (DT). On the view of an interpretative semantics type of grammar that he is discussing and dismissing, 'kill' is said to be *synonymous* (my italics) with 'cause to die'. At the end, I will also mention a few other counterexamples to (DT) that do not depend on adverbial modification, and these, but only these, might well also be counterexamples to (PT).

To briefly recap the story I first told in Chap. 3: Henry is keen on Henrietta. Henrietta has a fetish about doors opening too quickly, so she asked Henry to open a door slowly for her, the opening to finish no later than at a specific time. Henry is anxious to comply. Moreover, there are several different processes by which Henry could get the door to start opening slowly (he can choose between various mechanisms that lead to the door opening slowly) and these processes or mechanisms leading up to the commencement of the slow opening of the door are of greater and lesser duration. But Henry is rather forgetful and laid back. He is almost horizontal. He was in no hurry to get things going, dilly-dallying all afternoon, but once he noticed the time ticking by, he needed to select the process that took the least amount of time to start the slow opening of the door.

Assume that (1) is true, given the story just told:

(1) Henry quickly caused the door to open slowly.

I shall argue in Chap. 7 that in this context, 'quickly causing' is really an adjective that modifies a pair of times, t and t*, that between them set the beginning and end points between Henry's starting to cause the door to open and the door's starting to open, and that says of them that they are close in time. This is what I called in Chap. 3 the temporal relational use of an adverb of speed, the broad outlines of which were described in that chapter. But in Chap. 7, I will expand on the application of this idea specifically to the case of 'cause'. But this won't be important for the point I am making here.

If a sentence with a transitive verb, 'V_t,' could be derived from a deep structure, namely, the causative sentence that uses the intransitive form of the verb, 'V_i,' then we should be able to derive from (1) either (1a) or (1b) or (1c) (this requirement is accepted, as far as I am aware, by the linguists who discuss the alleged derivation):

Either
(1a) Henry opened the door slowly;
Or,
(1b) Henry opened the door quickly.
Or,
(1c) Henry opened the door slowly and quickly.

(1c) seems incoherent. How could the opening be both slow and quick?

Making it attributive won't help, because (1c) appears to say that it is both slow and quick and both qua an opening. One might wonder if the placement of the adverb makes a difference:

(1d) Quickly Henry opened the door slowly.

But (1d) is no better than (1c). (1d) still has the opening being both slow and quick, because there is nothing else for the adverbs to modify (if it is a mode adverb and not a phrase adverb). Adverbs must modify a verb, and there is only one verb in any of the candidate-derived sentences, including (1d), for the two adverbs in (1) to modify. (I will explain in Chap. 7 what adverbial modifications of the verb 'cause' amounts to.) For the reader who thinks that (1d) does help in capturing my story, I submit that that is because he reads (1d) as if it is asserting: Henry did something quickly that lead to the door opening slowly. But that of course is not what (1d) says. Neither (1c) nor (1d) makes any sense unless two verbs are at least implicitly understood (say, 'did' and 'open'), so that the sentences are construed as saying something that they don't explicitly say.

I have some difficulty in deciding whether, on the story told, either (1a) or (1b) is true. If they are not, we have a counterexample to (DT). But even if one of them were true, it would suffer from information loss compared to (1). Since both (1a) and (1b) suffer information loss when compared to the causative from which they are allegedly derived, neither (1a) nor (1b) can be equivalent to, or synonymous with, (1).

The problem is obvious and offers a method for generating many counterexamples to (DT). The causative has two verbs, in the case to hand, 'cause' and 'open'. The allegedly derived sentence has only one verb, 'open'. If both verbs are adverbially qualified in the causative, the derivation is bound to fail, as there will be information loss in the derivation, since there is only one verb in each of (1a)–(1d).

Other counterexamples use temporal qualification, and they work similarly, whatever view we take about the timing of an action. Both Fodor (1970, 422–423) and Smith (1970, 105–106), construct counterexamples using time. Here is one such example, taken from Smith:

(1) On Friday the secretary caused the documents to burn all up on Saturday (it was a Saturday-burning$_i$).

Perhaps the secretary lit a 24-hour fuse. There is controversy about whether the secretary burned$_t$ the documents on Friday or Saturday (I discuss this in the next chapter). But the counterexample works whichever option is chosen, since my argument turns only on information loss and not on any dating discrepancy between the causative and the sentence allegedly derived from it. Documents can burn (completely) only once, so they can't burn all up on both Friday and Saturday. If (2) were to entail:

(2a) The secretary burned$_t$ the documents (all up) on Friday.

The information about something having happened on Saturday is lost, and if (2) were to entail:

(2b) The secretary burned$_t$ the documents (all up) on Saturday.

The information about something happening on Friday is lost.

There are a few more counterexamples, discussed by linguists, that don't rely on adverbial modification that I want to mention. The two below have an interesting implication, which, as far as I am aware, has not been discussed more generally in the philosophical literature. Unlike the information-loss counterexamples that I have just discussed, these may be counterexamples to (PT) as well, if they are counterexamples to (DT).

Both Cruse (1972) and Smith (1970) provide something like a categorisation of the counterexamples and the rationale behind them. Here are two from Cruse:

(3) John caused the sparks to fly.
(3*) John flew the sparks.
(4) John caused his mirror image to move (by changing his position vis-à-vis the mirror).
(4*) * John moved his mirror image.

(4) depends on 'move' taking as its subject something that is not a straightforward physical object. Cruse's own example uses 'shadow', but I have substituted 'mirror image' since my intuitions are clearer in the case of a mirror image. One might argue that (4*) is not ungrammatical or nonsensical, but I find that suggestion farfetched. As with all intuitions, intuitions about these matters may differ, so I concede that this would be by itself a weak argument against either (DT) or (PT). (3) seems to me to be a much stronger example.

What is interesting to my mind about both (3) and (4) is that if the counterexamples work, they work not just because of the verb involved, 'to fly' or 'to move', but only because and when the verb is combined with one specific kind of object rather than another. One would not get a counterexample with 'John caused the airplane to fly$_i$' or 'John caused his hand to move$_i$'. This suggests that whether or not either derivation works for any specific verb does not depend on the verb alone, but the verb in combination with an object. Even if you thought that 'he flew$_t$ the airplane' and 'he moved$_t$ his hand' derived (in either or both the linguists' 'generational' sense or the logical senses) from 'he caused the airplane to fly$_i$,' and 'he caused his hand to move$_i$,' respectively, surely you should not also be committed to thinking that 'he flew$_t$ the spark' and 'he moved$_t$ his mirror image' could be derived (in either the generational or the logical sense) from 'he caused the spark to fly$_i$,' and 'he caused his mirror image to move$_i$,' respectively, although both verbs are ergative verbs.

Compare in the same vein 'Agent P broke$_t$ the window' and 'Agent P broke$_t$ the world record'. (The same contrast between these two sentences would arise if 'break' were replaced with 'shatter'.) The first use of 'break' has a causative alternate but the second does not. When P breaks$_t$ the world record, *the world record does not break$_i$, although it certainly is broken$_t$ (the passive form of the transitive verb). This might suggest that even for (PT), whether (PT) is true for an ergative verb sometimes depends not just on the verb but also on which object the verb takes. Perhaps a reply to this might be that the verb 'break' in these two sentences is ambiguous, and really signifies two different verbs. I think that this is a difficult question and would involve carefully distinguishing between metaphor and change of sense.

But that ambiguity certainly does not seem to be true in the case of 'fly'. In 'P caused the airplane to fly' and 'P caused the sparks to fly', 'fly' seems to have the same meaning in both sentences, and yet one of the sentences appears to entail a sentence that uses 'fly' in the transitive and one clearly does not do so.

Notes

1. Fabienne Martin and Florian Schäfer (2014, 210).
2. Both Levin (1993) and Smith (1972) provide a good account of English verbs in general and in particular an account of the ones for which causative alternation yields appropriate pairs. There are certainly some verbs that lack a transitive form: 'arrive', 'blossom', 'die', and 'wilt'. More importantly, there are many transitive action verbs that have no intransitive alternate (in English): 'dance', 'push', 'slice', 'read', 'go', 'eat', and, as

we have just seen, 'sell' 'The waiter cleared the table' has no intransitive alternate, since 'the table was clear' uses an adjective and not an intransitive verb form, and 'the table was cleared' is only the passive of 'clear' and not an intransitive (Hovav and Levin 2012, 7–8). Similarly, 'he read the book', 'he poisoned the president', 'he pushed the door', 'he injured the soldier', and 'he danced the rhumba' do not have as their intransitive alternates: 'The book was read', 'the president was poisoned', 'the door was pushed', 'the soldier was injured', or 'the rhumba was danced'. The latter are merely the verbs in their passive voice, entailed by 'the book was read by someone', 'the president was poisoned by someone', 'the door was pushed by someone', 'the soldier was injured by someone', and 'the rhumba was danced by someone'. 'John holds the candle' is acceptable, but 'The candle holds' is ungrammatical, so that 'holds' has no intransitive alternate.
3. After a discussion of verbs in what she calls 'the change class', i.e. the class verbs for which (CA) is true, and which includes 'burn', Carlotta Smith (1970, 105–106) goes on to deny that the 'The secretary caused the documents to burn' is a paraphrase (is 'not fully periphrastic' for) of 'The secretary burned the documents' (105). So she unsurprisingly accepts (CA) but rejects (PT). It seems clear that one can accept the causative alternation claim without the paraphrase thesis.
4. Philosophers other than the ones I discuss in the text that subscribe to some form of (PT), include: Bach (1980, 114), Von Wright (1977), Chisholm (1964), Bishop (1983).
5. I want to describe some examples by linguists and philosophers of the conflation between (CA) and (PT). First, the linguists. Some linguists do not separate their account of (CA) from (PT). Schäfer, in discussing (CA) (2009, 642) adds what is in effect (PT): '…verbs like English 'cause' or 'make' are often used to paraphrase the meaning of lexical causatives' ('The boy broke the window' can be paraphrased as 'The boy caused the window to break)'. In Beth Levin's account (1993, 27), causative alternation is itself described as: a verb V_T can be paraphrased as 'caused to V_I.' In Martin and Schäfer (2014, 209), causative alternation is described similarly, as holding that such verbs in the transitive use roughly mean 'cause to v-intransitive'.

Some philosophers similarly conflate the two theses. Zeno Vendler (1972, 210–216) starts by giving instances of causative alternation (CA): 'John grows flowers' and 'the flowers grow'. But he goes on to sum up this observation by proposing 'the following transformation' principle

(1972, 211): '(A1) $N_iC\ (N_jV)$-N_iVN_j'. (We don't need to worry about the details of his principle and what each letter in the formula signifies.) As an example of (A1), Vendler says that a statement such as 'N caused the flowers to grow' is 'transformed into' 'N grows flowers'. Vendler's transformation principle speaks only of some sort of inference from the RHS to the LHS of what I have called (PT), but the point I want to make here is only the tendency to conflate (CA) and the issue of causation. (Actually, what Vendler seems to conflate with (CA) is not (PT) but (DT)-see the appendix to this chapter.)

Alvarez & Hyman note the ambiguity of the transitive and intransitive forms of a verb, like 'to move', and explain causative alternation, but say, in a footnote on the same page, that the transitive form is called 'a causative', (*not* because 'A moved B' implies 'B moved', which is the reason they should have given), but because 'A moved B' implies 'A caused B to move'. That is not (CA), but half of the biconditional of (PT) (Alvarez and Hyman 1998, fn. 9, 223). In John Hyman's *Action, Knowledge, and Will* (2015, 35–36), there is a section entitled 'Causative/Mutative Alternation' (i.e., causative alternation), but in it he discusses not only causative alternation but also and mainly the (PT). So it seems that it is common that there is no careful separation of (CA) and (PT) in many discussions, in the philosophical and linguistics literature. (CA) is not about causation at all; it is only about the relation between two forms of a verb. There is quite simply nothing explicitly about causation in (CA) as it stands, in spite of its being called 'causative alternation'. It is obvious that the inference claimed in (CA) is not the same as the inferences alleged in (PT), either from (LHS) to (RHS) or from (RHS) to (LHS).

6. In the criminal law, being an accessory or an accomplice to a crime is often tantamount to being guilty of the crime. So if we say, for example (the case that I consider in the text) that Stalin killed millions, our use of 'kill' may be reflecting only our attribution to him of the responsibility for their deaths rather than a genuine attribution of agency. An accessory to a crime constitutes:

> *In* **Criminal Law**, *contributing to or aiding in the commission of a crime. One who, without being present at the commission of an offense, becomes guilty of such offense, not as a chief actor, but as a participant, as by command, advice, instigation, or concealment; either before or after the fact or commission.*

The criminal law can make someone in addition to the agent responsible, or co-responsible for the commission of a crime. Such a person is referred to as 'a participant', which I take to be a category, distinct from being an agent. The law appears to acknowledge that there are ways to participate in a crime without being the agent who actually performs the criminal act.

7. The question of direct and indirect causation is dealt with in great depth by Fabienne Martin and Florian Schäfer, 'Causation at the syntax-semantics interface', 237–244, in Copley and Martin 2014.
8. Lawrence Lombard (1990) gives an account of enabling. On his view, enablers are not generally the causes of the events they enable. This would introduce an interesting complication into my account here, but its effect would be to produce an even stronger argument for distinguishing between doers and enablers.
9. A case sometimes considered in the literature, as a counterexample to Feinberg's accordion effect has to do with promotion: A promoted B iff A caused B to be promoted. But A can cause B to be promoted by getting some third party C to promote B. The example seems to me to be a good candidate for being a counterexample to Feinberg's accordion effect, as Atwell argues (Atwell 1969, 337). It falls outside the range of examples I want, because 'to promote' is not an ergative verb. Feinberg's accordion effect is not limited to ergative verbs.
10. Ad Neeleman and Hans van de Koot (2012, 85–90 and ff) have an interesting alternative suggestion for replacing the direct/indirect causation contrast as the explanation of the difference between doing and causing. They are commenting on the original Katz case, already quoted, in which the gunsmith produces a defective gun, thus allowing the gunslinger to shoot the sheriff. Suppose the gunsmith intentionally sabotaged his repair, since he had a grudge against the sheriff and wanted him dead. In this case, N & K argue that 'the gunsmith killed the sheriff' is true, because the gunsmith is accountable, responsible, for the death. 'Responsible' in this context does not mean 'causally responsible'; it must mean 'morally responsible' or 'legally responsible'.

But this can't be right, which was my point in note 6. No one thinks that an agent's being morally responsible for event e is sufficient for that agent's E_t-ing, rather than just causing e (see Hart and Honoré, 64 and ff, for examples). One example is this: an occupier is responsible for the injury done to a passer-by as a result of a defect in his property, say a

falling chimney, even if he had no reason to believe the defect existed or had any opportunity to repair it. The property occupier caused the injury to the passer-by by his omission, but he did not injure him, in spite of being morally or legally responsible for the injury. Fockner (2013) introduces the topic of responsibility in his understanding of the accordion effect.
11. Hart and Honoré (1985), 403–405, for the year-and-a-day rule. Their chapter IV, 84–108 provides a good overview of the kinds of causal questions that need addressing in the law. The entire book is locus classicus for causation, action, and responsibility, from a legal perspective.
12. Gavriel Rosen suggested this example to me.

Bibliography

Alvarez, Maria. 1999. Actions and Events: Some Semantical Considerations. *Ratio*, new series XII (3): 213–239.
Alvarez, Maria, and John Hyman. 1998. Agents and Their Actions. *Philosophy* 73: 219–245.
Atwell, John E. 1969. The Accordion Effect Thesis. *Philosophical Quarterly* 19 (77): 337–342.
Austin, John. 1998. *The Province of Jurisprudence Determined*. Indianapolis: Hackett Publishing.
Bach, Kent. 1980. Actions are Not Events. *Mind* 89 (353): 114–120.
Bishop, J. 1983. Agent-Causation. *Mind* 92: 61–79.
———. 1989. *Natural Agency*, 117–120. Cambridge: Cambridge University Press.
Chisholm, Roderick. 1964. The Descriptive Element in the Concept of Action. *Journal of Philosophy* 61: 613–624.
Cruse, D.A. 1972. A Note on English Causatives. *Linguistic Inquiry* 3 (4): 520–528.
Davidson, Donald. 2001. Aristotle's Actions. In *Truth, Language, and History*, ed. Donald Davidson. 2005. Oxford: Oxford University Press.
Davis, L. 1979. *Theory of Action*. Englewood Cliffs, NJ: Prentice-Hall.
Feinberg, Joel. 1970. *Doing and Deserving*. Princeton: Princeton University Press.
Fockner, Sven. 2013. What is the Accordion Effect: Harmonizing Bratman's Principles F and D. *Springer Plus* 2: 279.

Fodor, J.A. 1970. Three Reasons for Not deriving 'Kill' from 'Cause to Die'. *Linguistic Inquiry* I: 429–438.
———. 1975. *The Language of Thought*. Cambridge, MA: Harvard University Press.
Gorovitz, Samuel. 1965. Causal Judgments and Causal Explanations. *Journal of Philosophy* LXII (23): 695–711.
Hart, H.L.A., and Tony Honoré. 1985. *Causation in the Law*. 2nd ed. Oxford: Oxford University Press.
Hornsby, Jennifer. 1980. *Actions*. London: Routledge & Kegan Paul.
Hovav, Malka Rappaport, and Beth Levin. 2012. Lexical Uniformity and the Causative Alternation. In *The Theta System*, ed. Martin Everaert, Marijana Marelj, and Tal Siloni. Oxford: Oxford University Press.
Hyman, John. 2015. *Action, Knowledge, & Will*. Oxford: Oxford University Press.
Katz, Jerrold. 1970. Interpretative Semantics vs. Generative Semantics. *Foundations of Language* 6 (2): 220–259.
Lakoff, G. 1965. On the Nature of Syntactic Irregularity. Mathematical Linguistics and Automatic Translation, Report No. NSF-16, Computational Laboratory of Harvard, Cambridge, MA.
Levin, Beth. 1993. *English Verb Classes and Alternation*. Chicago: University of Chicago Press.
Lewis, D. 1986. *Philosophical Papers*. Vol. II. Oxford: Oxford University Press.
Lombard, Lawrence. 1990. Causes, Enablers, and the Counterfactual Analysis. *Philosophical Studies* 59: 195–211.
Mackie, John. 1965 (1993). Causes and Conditions. *American Philosophical Quarterly* 2 (4): 245–264. Reprint in Sosa and Tooley (eds.), Causation (Oxford 1993). 33–55.
———. 1974. *The Cement of the Universe*. Oxford: Oxford University Press.
Martin, Fabienne, and Florian Schäfer. 2014. Causation at the Syntax-Semantics Interface. In *Causation in Grammatical Structures*, ed. Bridget Copley and Fabienne Martin. Oxford: Oxford University Press. Part II, chapter 9, 209–244.
Mayr, Erasmus. 2011. *Understanding Human Agency*. Oxford: Oxford University Press.
McCann, Hugh. 1998. *The Works of Agency*. Ithaca: Cornell University Press.
Menzies, Peter. 2012. Platitudes and Counterexamples. In *The Oxford Handbook of Causation*, ed. Helen Beebee et al., 341–367. Oxford: Oxford University Press.
Mill, John Stuart. 1970. *A System of Logic*. London: Longman Group.

Moore, G.E. 1966. *Principia Ethica*. Cambridge: Cambridge University Press.
Neeleman, Ad, and Hans van de Koot. 2012. The Linguistic Expression of Causation. In *The Theta System*, ed. Martin Everaert, Marijana Marelj, and Tal Siloni, 78–100. Oxford: Oxford University Press.
O'Connor, Timothy. 2011. Agent-Causal Theories of Freedom. In *The Oxford Handbook of Free Will*, ed. Robert Kane, 2nd ed., 309–328. Oxford: Oxford University Press.
Parsons, Terence. 1994. *Events in the Semantics of English*. Boston: MIT Press.
Schäfer, Florian. 2009. The Causative Alternation. *Language and Linguistics, Compass* 3 (2): 641–681.
Smith, Carlota. 1970. Jespersen's "Move and Change" Class and Causative Verbs in English. In *Linguistic and Literary Studies*, ed. Mohammad Ali Jazayery, Edgar C. Polomé, and Werner Winter, 101–108. The Hague: Mouton Publishers.
———. 1972. On Causative Verbs and Derived Nominals in English. *Linguistic Inquiry* 3: 136–138.
Steward, Helen. 2012. *A Metaphysics of Freedom*. Oxford: Oxford University Press.
Vendler, Zeno. 1972. *Res Cogitans*, 210–216. Ithaca: Cornell University Press. Appendix II.
Von Wright, G.H. 1977. *Norm and Action*. London: Routledge & Kegan Paul.

6

Doing and Causing

What's in the Chapter

In Chap. 5, I argued that the RHS of (PT) does not entail the (LHS). But does the LHS entail the RHS? When a person acts (and the action verb is an ergative verb), isn't it trivially true that he causes, i.e., that he is a cause of, the event intrinsic to the action, trivially true that he brings that very event about? (Remember, it is consistent to hold that the relation between an action and its intrinsic event (if it has one) is non-causal and necessary, but that the relation between the agent and the event intrinsic to his action (if it has one) is causal and contingent.)

Thus far, in terms of Venn diagrams, the results of Chap. 5 are consistent with the following picture: a large circle represents the class of cases in which an agent causes something to occur. A smaller circle entirely inside the larger one represents the class of cases in which the agent acts. All doings are causings but not all causings are doings. Is this the picture that best represents the relation of doing and causing? It is this question that this chapter addresses.

I do hold that the LHS of (PT) entails the RHS. But in order to explain and develop this, I need some preparatory work first. I start by discussing the extensionality of the causal relation. I then look again at (CA). Should we understand the LHS and the RHS of (CA) as being about two particulars or as using two descriptions of a single particular? I describe one-particularism as the view that takes the second of those options. I strengthen the case for one-particularism by looking at the idea of Cambridge changes (and hence Cambridge actions). I examine two obvious counter-arguments to one-particularism: (a) that, on an action chain, an action doesn't cause another action, but it only causes the event that is intrinsic to its successor action on the chain, if it has one; (b) Alvin Goldman's view, shared by many others, that would imply that one-particularism gets the time of an action wrong.

So I address the main question of this chapter, the LHS to RHS inference of (PT), only at the end of the chapter, in light of these discussions and the distinctions I have made. I also return to the question in Chap. 8. I can only ask the reader to be patient. There will be method in the madness. I promise.

Causation: Extensionality

The relata of the causal relation might include: facts, events, tropes, states of affairs, and mixes of the same. In Chap. 3, I suggested that fact causation might be one way to deal with certain apparent counterexamples to my non-particularist account of trying. I am catholic in my views about causal relata. But I certainly think there is such a thing as event causation; sometimes, statements of the form, 'event c caused event e' are true. In 'P caused e', the second relatum of the relation is an event. That in any case is the form in which (PT) has been expressed and defended by the philosophers I have been considering, so that is the form in which I have been, and will continue to, consider it.

I assume that such event causation as there is, is extensional, and in particular that the context following 'cause' is 'extensional: co-referential expressions-singular terms with the same denotation … are substitutable within it without changing the truth-value of the whole, "salva veritate", i.e. …Leibniz' law holds for it' (Haack 1978, 246). If 'Person P caused b to V_i' is merely shorthand for 'Some P-involving event c caused b to V_i', then trivially 'P caused b to V_i' is extensional too, since agent causation would only be a particular sort of shorthand expression of event causation. But suppose that it is not elliptical, that 'P caused b to V_i' is an assertion of agent causation that is not reducible to any statement of event causation. The context following 'P caused…', even on the non-reductive agent causal reading, is extensional. I can see no reason why agent causation of events should not be extensional if event causation of events is. (I use 'extensional' and 'transparent' interchangeably.)

After all, agent causalist theorists usually stress that both event and agent causation are kinds of a single idea of causation in some more basic, univocal sense that allows for both variants. Many agent causalist theorists claim this. Here is one example: '…agent causation … is (or involves) exactly the same relation as event causation. The only difference between the two kinds of causation concerns the types of entities related, not the relation' (Clarke 1995, 207). If the only difference between the two types of causation is in the types of relata, then if one is extensional, the other is too. So, whether or not agent causation is sui generis or reducible to event causation, and on whatever criterion of event identity one wishes to adopt, if the event, b's V_i-ing is identical to c's V^*_i-ing, then, if 'P caused b to V_i' is true, it follows that 'P caused c to V^*_i' is also true. If P caused the window to open and the window's opening=the largest aperture in the house's increase in size, then P caused the largest aperture in the house to increase in size. The view about the extensionality of both causal variants, agent and event, might be reinforced by a reminder of the difference between causation and causal explanation, the latter not being extensional, and the two ideas sometimes being conflated.

Is fact causation extensional for terms with the same denotation? If P caused the fact f, that b V_i-ed, and if the fact f, that b V_i-ed, is identical to the fact f*, that c V^*_i-ed, then P caused the fact that c V^*_i-ed. There is a different question about under what conditions fact f and fact f* are identical (see Chapter V, Ruben 1990 (1992), and 2012). Is the fact that b V_i-ed identical to the fact that c V^*_i-ed, only if b=c and if V_i-ing=V^*_i-ing? There are both fine-grained and coarser-grained accounts of facts. This will turn out to be is a question about the extensionality of facts, not a question about the extensionality of fact causation, so it is not a question that I will address here.

Returning to (CA)

Recall that the inference that typifies ergative verbs is this (I have been using Jennifer Hornsby's formulation (Hornsby 1980, 2)):

$$(CA) \text{FROM}: aV_tb \quad \text{TO}: bV_i$$

The idea is that the token event that makes 'bV_i' true, b's V_i-ing, is a change, such that some other tokens of the same type might not be agent-directed, however remotely. I call such agent-undirected tokens 'mere events'. Every agent-directed event, and so every event intrinsic to an action, has or could have a look-alike mere event partner, a veritable event doppelgänger: I can move my body and my body can move as a result of a spasm. I can close a window and the window can close on its own. Some types of events might have only mere event tokens. For the type, the explosion of a supernova, I imagine that there is no token supernova explosion that is intrinsic to anyone's action. No one can explode a supernova. This is, I suppose, a continent truth, if it is a truth. Is there a type of event such that it is metaphysically impossible for any of its tokens to be an event intrinsic to some finite agent's action? I don't know for sure, but to simplify matters below, I assume there is not such a type of event.

To recap from Chap. 5: Hornsby: '…in the cases that interest me, there appears to be no hope of founding the intransitive on the transitive' (Hornsby 1980, 125), and Parsons: 'It is also important in analyzing the logic of these examples that the intransitive alone does not imply any form of the transitive' (Parsons 1994, 106). So from the fact that some token event of any type occurred (but where the type is a type expressed by the intransitive form of an ergative verb), a V_i-ing$_i$ of b, it never follows that some agent acted, that PV_tb. (Alert readers will remember exceptions from Chap. 5: the verbs 'sold' and 'pass', so the claim needs to be appropriately qualified.) Given only the information that there is a token V_i-ing of b, one can't know whether that token is (1) a mere event or (2) an event only caused by the agent but not intrinsic to any of his actions (as argued in Chap. 5), or (3) an event intrinsic to the agent's action, since there could be tokens of the type, a V_i-ing of b, of all three kinds. This is what I've called the weaker claim in Chap. 5. Only the weaker claim was needed in order to secure the lack of entailment from the RHS to the LHS of (CA).

However, there is a stronger claim too, which I described in Chap. 5. The stronger claim is this: the very same token or particular which makes 'bV_i-ed' true, a particular which is in fact intrinsic to the token P's V_t-ing of b, could have existed without having been intrinsic to that same (or maybe to any) token action. Or: there are some tokens or particulars which makes sentences like '$b\ V_i$-ed' true, particulars which are in fact NOT intrinsic to any action, but which could have been intrinsic to some action. That is a question of whether the property of being intrinsic or not intrinsic to a token P's V_t-ing (of) b is an essential property of the token b's V_i-ing. In the course of this chapter, I want to be able to answer that question.

It seems to me that the most important question to ask about (CA) is this: we do not yet know whether or not these two descriptions, 'P's V_t-ing of b' and 'b's V_i-ing', are two descriptions of the same truth-maker or are descriptions of two different truth-makers. (CA) does not imply that there are two particulars, one that makes 'PV_tb' true, and a second that makes 'bV_i' true. (CA) does not say that when someone acts (and when the action verb is ergative), an event occurs, *in addition to* the action, so that there must be two non-identical (but perhaps overlapping) particular items, an action and another event, related in some way other than by identity. Perhaps they are just two different descriptions of only one particular.

But could (CA) be about two such particulars? Let's call that view 'the two-particulars view'. On the two-particulars view, the LHS of (CA) would be made true by an action; the RHS would be made true by a non-actional event. On the two-particulars view, these are not identical, even if they overlap. Let the RHS event be the moving$_i$ of the agent's body. On the two-particulars view being considered, the action must be something other than (just) that bodily movement$_i$, since it's the bodily movement$_i$ that makes the RHS true. On that two-particulars reading, since (CA) claims that the existence of the first particular entails the existence of the second, the second must be a proper part of the first, in some suitable sense. But what might that first particular be, beyond just that bodily movement$_i$ that makes the RHS of (CA) true? How shall we understand 'P's moving$_t$ of his body', the truth-maker for the LHS of (CA), on a two-particulars account of (CA)? I will mention two theories of action that support the two-particulars reading of (CA).

On one response, the action is some whole (call this the mereological view) that makes the LHS of (CA) true; that whole action includes as a proper part an intrinsic event, e, and it is e that makes the RHS of (CA) true. The action might start inside the agent with some appropriate mental state, an act of will or volition, or an intention or a belief-desire pair (perhaps caused by the agent, on one version; or perhaps caused by other agent-involving events, on another version), and continue with the bodily movement$_i$, and on still other views, perhaps continue even beyond the bodily movement$_i$ to other events beyond the agent's body that the agent causes. On the mereological view, necessarily, if the action occurs, then so too does its intrinsic event, since it is a part of that token action. Necessarily, if the whole action, which includes intrinsic event e, occurs, then e occurs. The necessity is this: suppose the action=the sum {a&b&e}. Necessarily, if the whole sum occurs, then e occurs. Such a view could explain the inference embodied in (CA). The action is not identical to the event, so there are two particulars, but they are overlapping particulars, e and the sum that includes it.

But a different response is forthcoming if we adopt the view that the action is *the causing* of the event (call this view 'the causing view' for short). Necessarily, if the causing of the event occurs, the event occurs. Even if the relation between P and the token event is contingent, so that that very token event could have occurred even if P had not caused it (assuming no necessity of causal origin), it is still necessarily true on this second view that if P acted, i.e., if P did cause event e, then e occurred. Hence, the causing view would justify or explain the inference in (CA). Of course, if you think that an action is the causing of some event, then you can't also think that the action=event caused.[1]

In both cases, on both the mereological view and the causing view, the event intrinsic to the action, for example, b's V$_i$-ing, is a proper part or a component of the action, albeit in two different ways; if the action exists, so too does the event. But both views require a two-particulars reading of (CA). On the mereological view, the action is a whole and the intrinsic event is one of its parts. On the causing view, the action is a causing of an event by an agent and so the event must be one of the components of the action.

Suppose you think that the action is one thing (a whole, or a causing), the bodily movement is another, as both of these two-particulars theories assert. Here is a simple thought: as hard as one looks, one can only see one thing, the bodily movement. So either the action gets at least partly driven inside the agent (so that's why you did not see it!), or it gets identified as the causing, (so that's why you did not see it, because who could ever see a causing, in addition to a cause and an effect?), with all the attendant problems that that last view faces, problems that I explore in the next chapter.

I don't aspire to demonstrate that every two-particulars view must be wrong (although I think they are, in both suggested forms). My main aim is to sketch an alternative account of action in this chapter. My goal in this chapter is not to refute two-particulars theories of action but to create the logical space for a distinctive one-particular theory of action.

But I will say quite a lot in Chap. 7 about one of the two options for a two-particulars view, that actions are causings of events, so the causing and the event caused count as two. I won't deal with the mereological version of the two-particulars view that identifies the action with some 'internal' goings-on plus the bodily movement. The mereological view can take several different forms; in the form in which it postulates an agent's mental states as what it is that is additional to the intrinsic event, I think it overpopulates the mind of the agent (Ruben 1995, 2003, Chapter 4).

The One-Particular View[2]

We need to distinguish between events and the descriptions we happen to use in order to describe them. From the fact that 'b's V_i-ing' is a description of something that includes no agent-directed information, it does not follow that it is the description of something that isn't agent-directed. If the agent has acted, so that 'P V_t-ed b' is true, then 'P's V_t-ing of b' (the action description) and 'b V_i-ing' (the event description) might refer to that same item, an action, but the latter by using a description of that action that has no agent-directed information in it. Let's call this view 'the one-particular view'. The one-particular view sharply distinguishes between a metaphysical relation between two particulars (the two-particulars view) and a semantic relation between two descriptions we use in describing one particular (the one-particular view).[3]

There is a difference between having a description with no agent-directed information included in it being true of something, and that thing's *not being* agent-directed. 'b's V_i-ing' is a description that includes no agent-directed information about whatever it is that it is true of. On the one-particular view, it is true that this token moving$_i$ of P's finger, the one that is the event intrinsic to P's action of his moving$_t$ of his finger, *is* agent-directed, even though the description 'the moving$_i$ of P's finger' contains no information about that agent-directedness, because the action is agent-directed and the intrinsic event *is* that action, just differently described. Unlike *being described* as agent-directed, *being* agent-directed is a property of a particular (full-stop), however described; it is not a description-relative property of that particular.

Not only is it true, but also it is necessarily true that the token intrinsic event is agent-directed. An action is such that it is necessarily agent-directed; if there is some token event *identical* to that action, it must also be necessarily agent-directed too. The weaker claim described in Chap. 5 is true: *other* token events also described as 'a V_i-ing of b' could exist even if no action existed to which they were intrinsic. But token identities are metaphysically necessary; if e is a token event intrinsic to some action a, and if token action a=token event e (one-particularism), then in every world in which e exists, e is intrinsic to a. It's metaphysically impossible for the token event to exist without the token action whose token intrinsic event it is. (For those who prefer counterparts to transworld identity, it is trivial to alter these formulations accordingly.) To be sure, the subscripts, 't' and 'i', indicate a grammatical distinction, but a grammatically intransitive description can be a description of an action. Of the two views described in Chap. 5, the stronger, (b), cannot be sustained on the one-particular view. The relation of being intrinsic-to is a metaphysically necessary relation between a specific token action and the token event intrinsic to it (if there is one), namely itself, since identity is a necessary relation. The intrinsic tie of which von Wright spoke is indeed intrinsic; the identity of the token intrinsic event and the token action explains the necessity of the relation of being intrinsic to, at least in the case of actions and their intrinsic events.

Like the mereological and causing views, one-particularism can also account for the inference in (CA). It is certainly true that the action description is more informative about the particular that occurred than is the event description. Add any piece of information to the LHS of (CA) and the LHS will be even more informative: 'P's moved$_t$ his finger on a Wednesday' will also entail 'agent P's finger moved$_i$'. So we can say that the LHS of (CA) refers to a particular that is agent-directed, namely, an action, and that the RHS of (CA) redescribes the same action, with some information about it deleted. When an agent acts, on the one-particular view, the event referred to by 'b's V$_i$-ing' is the agent's action, albeit described as an event with no information about its being agent-directed as part of that description. Since one-particularism holds that these two descriptions refer to the same action (or event), and yet one description contains information about the agent and his agency and the second does not, I can accept only an account of act or event individuation consistent with this result. On the Kim-Goldman (Kim 1976; Goldman 1970) account of act individuation and identity, if two event or action descriptions have different subjects, or refer to different times, it is intuitively plausible, I think, that they must refer to non-identical particulars. But it is not similarly plausible that two descriptions, one of which has information about the subject deleted and the other of which retains that information, cannot both be about one and the same particular. I discuss such an 'intermediate theory' of event and action identity at more length below.

I don't want to give the impression that my version of one-particularism is only true for some special category of basic action. (A basic action is an action that initiates an action chain, so that it is not done by doing any other action.) What's true for basic actions like movings$_t$ of fingers is also true of non-basic actions like stoppings$_t$ of floods. Suppose we have a case of agent P stopping$_t$ the flood. A decompositional two-particulars view factors that into two parts, (a) the agent's action (perhaps his moving$_t$ of his body or his causing); (b) some event external to the agent, the stopping$_i$ of the flood, which is somehow intrinsic to the action (caused by the agent, or part of the action whole). One-particularism accepts that *all* actions are identical to their intrinsic events, if they have one.

Suppose we have a case of agent P stopping$_t$ the flood. How could the two-particulars view be wrong? Wasn't there an external event, the stopping$_i$ of the flood, as well as the action? What exactly is being denied by the one-particular view? First, we need to keep types and tokens clearly distinguished. Some flood stoppings$_i$ really have nothing to do with an agent. Many tokens of flood-stopping$_i$ are events that are indistinguishable from actions. Sometimes such look-alike floods stop$_i$ by themselves. I have been referring to such token events that are not agent-directed in any way as 'mere events'. Furthermore, sometimes an agent causes a flood to stop$_i$ but does NOT stop$_t$ the flood (as per my previous arguments in Chap. 5). Perhaps the event is causally too remote from the agent, or the agent too partial a cause, or a third party is involved in the causal chain leading from the agent to the event. Events that are caused or part-caused by an agent but not intrinsic to that agent's action, I call 'extrinsic events'.

Consider some particular occasion on which the agent did stop$_t$ the flood. In that case, the flood-stopping$_i$ was his stopping$_t$ of the flood. The flood-stopping$_i$ is not a proper part of his action. It *is* his action. But isn't the flood 'external' to the agent? Aren't there two things, the agent and the flood? Yes, of course there are. But it does not follow from the fact that the agent and the flood are two, that 'P's stopping$_t$ of the flood' and the 'flood's stopping$_i$' are not just two descriptions of the same token item. Since, on my view, a token action=its token intrinsic event, by the indiscernibility of identicals, whatever is true of the one must be true of the other. Therefore, whatever causes and effects the event has, so must the action have as well.

As far as I can see, the one-particular view is compatible with many (although not all) views about the logical form of action sentences. It introduces no new complexities. If the reader thinks that Davidson's proposals on the logical form of action sentences have it about right, then this proposal is consistent with that.[4] The one-particular view certainly avoids some of the complexities that arise with other proposals that reject Davidson's approach, for example Alvarez' proposal to quantify only over the events intrinsic to actions and not the actions themselves (Alvarez

1999; see Chap. 7). On the other hand, nothing in the one-particular view requires specifically Davidson's approach.

If someone stopped$_t$ the flood, it follows that there was a stopping$_i$ of the flood. That's of course just the indisputable (CA). If one thinks of this inference as an inference from the more informative to the less informative, it is of the same sort of inference that most bothered Kenny (1963, 151–170). This particular inference cannot be shown to be valid as a matter logical form. So what? I cannot see that that is any more problematic than the inference from 'x is red' to 'x is coloured'. That inference does not appear to be due to logical form, but from the meanings of the sentences themselves, as specified by whatever is the correct semantic theory of such matters. The validity of the inference in (CA) depends on information-loss, as in a case of 'red' and 'coloured'. The premise of the inference contains more information than the conclusion, and that explanation of the validity of the inference is consistent with one-particularism.

Are actions events? Various theories of action will handle this question differently, so I don't think that there is any theory-neutral way in which to answer the question in a substantive way. On my view, actions *are* intrinsic events (but are neither mere events nor extrinsic events). On the standard theory of action, that actions are events caused non-deviantly by the mental states that rationalise them, actions are events because every action is identical to some event with a certain causal history. On the causing theory, actions are events if causings are events, since actions are causings. It is a matter of dispute amongst causing theorists of action whether causings are events or not. This dispute is the subject of the next chapter.

On the other hand, eschewing substantial answers, some philosophers classify actions as events as a matter of definitional fiat. There are countless examples of this in the action literature. Here are two: 'If A and A' are one and the same action, then they are one and the same event' (Goldman 1970, 13); 'Doings are events' (Davis 1979, 6). Actions or doings for Goldman and Davis are a subclass of events. No honest philosophical effort is involved in such a classificatory decision. It is just a terminological fiat, not what I called above a 'substantive' answer. (This isn't intended as a criticism of Goldman's or Davis' view, just an observation about them.) I can't see that anything hangs on this matter of definitional choice. That is just to use 'event' in a very wide and theory-independent usage. I am indifferent about that merely terminological decision.

The One-Particular View and Act Individuation

One consequence of the one-particular view is that it places many of an agent's actions far from his body and distant from him in time. It places many of an agent's actions out in the world. How plausible is that? In order to answer that question, I need to take something of a detour. I will first make out a case for one-particularism. Afterwards, I will bring out what some take to be its counterintuitive consequences and defend one-particularism from those criticisms. I think that some of those criticisms depend on some 'orthodox' views about action, often repeated but rarely defended, but which have little independently to recommend them. But first, before I switch to defensive mode, let me offer the positive case.

Token action a=token action b iff .... Well, iff what? An agent, P, bends his finger, turns the valve, closes the sluice on a dam, stops the flood, and thereby improves the lives of the inhabitants living downstream. P did each action on the list by doing its predecessor (if it has one). A list of this sort describes an action chain (a lot more on action chains to come.) How many things did P do? How many actions are there on this chain?

The alternative theories that attempt to answer this question are well known. The most austere theory says that P did only one thing, and that what the list above provides are five different descriptions of one token action. An action is, on one version of austere theory, a moving$_t$ of the body, variously described.

The most prolific theory says that, in the list above, P performed five different actions. Each action description on the list is a description of an action different from the action any other description on the list describes. A prolific theorist finds the plurality in the action, not in the description.

In Chap. 3, I described Ginet's intermediate theory (Ginet 1990, 46–53), and initiated a discussion of it above. On an intermediate theory, not *every* difference in properties entails a difference in actions with those properties. For example, on one plausible intermediate theory, merely substituting for a property that an action tokens, another property with more detail included in it than in the first property, does not automatically require commitment to another action token. To borrow an example from Chap. 3, P's crossing of the Channel might be identical to P's night crossing of the Channel, even though the property of being a Channel crossing and the property of being a Channel night crossing are two different properties.

The one-particular view requires some sort of prolific theory of action individuation, even if not the most prolific one. Suppose P stops the flood by turning the valve. If P's turning$_t$ of the valve=the valve's turning$_i$, and if P's stopping$_t$ of the flood=the flood's stopping$_i$ (as they are on the one-particular view), and since it seems undeniable that the event, the turning$_i$ of the valve≠the event, the stopping$_i$ of the flood, it follows that the turning$_t$ of the valve≠ the stopping$_t$ of the flood. I have argued for such a prolific theory of act individuation elsewhere and find this consequence of the one-particular view welcome (Ruben 2003, Chapter 1). I want now to expand on my defence of a prolific theory (but not necessarily the most prolific theory), when combined with one-particularism.

But why not the most prolific theory? Consider P's turning$_t$ of the valve and his turning$_t$ of the green valve. P's turning$_t$ of the valve=the valve's turning$_i$. P's turning$_t$ of the green valve=the green valve's turning$_i$. So far, so similar to the first case. But it does not seem undeniable, as it did in the first case, that the turning$_i$ of the valve≠the turning$_i$ of the green valve. These events might be identical, on some plausible theory of event individuation. If they are identical, then there is no difficulty in holding that P's turning$_t$ of the valve=P's turning$_t$ of the green valve. If the intrinsic events are identical, then the actions, which are themselves identical to those intrinsic events, will also be identical.

More strongly, one-particularism requires an intermediate theory and a rejection of the most prolific theory, since it claims that two different descriptions can refer to the same particular. Goldman's theory of action individuation, on the other hand, is a most prolific theory, but I don't think we need to accept it. Goldman's theory of act individuation (Goldman 1970, 1–20) is designed only for the identity conditions of actions. (I'll extend this discussion to the case of an action and its intrinsic event below.) In the course of his discussion (Goldman, 2–4, 28–30), he considers one variety of the possible relations between the multiple actions on an action chain that he calls 'augmentation generalisation'. Examples include: 'running' and 'running at ten miles per hour': 'extending one's arm' and 'extending one's arm out of the window': 'saying "hello"…' and 'saying "hello" loudly'. '…If F and F' are distinct [i.e., non-identical] act-properties, no exemplifying of F is identical with any exemplifying of F' (Goldman, 11). The properties of saying hello and of saying hello loudly, the properties of extending one's arm and of extending one's arm out of the window, and the properties of running and of running at 10 mph, are different act-properties. Goldman accepts the 'seemingly counterintuitive' (his own words) results that because these phrase-pairs express two different properties, they are the names of two 'distinct' action tokens. He admits that these cases are 'not as intuitively as attractive as' his other examples of two-properties-so-two actions (28). Goldman admits that his theory, applied to these types of cases, 'may seem counter-intuitive at first, [but] I think it is one with which we can live' (13).

That is to say, on his view, if two properties are related by (what I have called) information deletion, and if they are properties whose tokens are actions, they must be properties of two distinct act tokens. There will be a close relationship between such distinct act tokens, a relationship that Goldman seeks in the course of the section on augmentation generation to describe. But they are distinct act tokens nonetheless. He also notes the telltale fact that, unlike for the other relations between actions that he discusses, actions related by the augmentation relation are not related by the 'by'-relation.

If the view is so intuitively unattractive, why does Goldman hold it? He argues that its 'main defense lies in its superiority to the other alternatives' (29). I think that that superiority is spurious. He lists two reasons why the actions expressed by such phrase-pairs can't be identical: (a) they have different causes and effects; (b) in one case, 'driving to house h at 70 mph in a 60 mph zone' and 'driving to house h', the former act has a property that the second lacks: the first is 'a violation of the law' and the second does not have that property.

Goldman says that P's saying hello loudly may be partly caused by P's tense emotional state, but that tense emotional state is not part of the cause of P's saying hello. But I don't think that that is true. P's tense emotional state WAS a cause of his saying 'hello', whether or not we explicitly qualify that by saying the way in which it was done. Further, P's driving to h was in violation of the law, whether or not we include in its description that feature in virtue of which it was a violation. Here, as elsewhere, we need to keep firmly in mind the difference between explanatory descriptions and non-explanatory descriptions. I can't explain *why* P's driving to h was a violation unless I include in the description of the driving information such as that it was done at 70 mph in a 60 mph zone; but the driving to h was a violation nonetheless, even though describing his driving merely as a driving to h won't explain why it was a violation. The point here is not just to swap intuitions about what to say in such examples. I merely make the point that there are perfectly good ways to understand the data for which Goldman is trying to account without multiplying the actions such phrase-pairs refer to, especially when, on his own admission, to do so is so unintuitive. My purpose here is not to disprove Goldman's most prolific theory, but merely to stake out a claim for an intermediate theory, a theory less than the most prolific theory, which is what I think that one-particularism requires.

True, Goldman says nothing about the identity of an act and an event, as does one-particularism, but it would be a natural extension of his most prolific view to deny that an action, such as P's turning$_t$ of the valve, could be identical to its intrinsic event, the turning$_i$ of the valve, since the two properties are different, one of which carries augmented information relative to the other. In general, the most prolific theory denies act token identity in cases of information deletion or augmentation, and, if applied similarly to an action and its intrinsic event, it would reject one-particularism as well. Goldman even denies that 'John marrying Mary at t' and 'Mary marrying John at t' pick out the same act token, and I assume that, a fortiori, he would deny the identity claim in the case of events expressed by converse relations ('John becoming taller than Mary' and 'Mary becoming shorter than John'). Notice that Goldman's examples are in the main, although not entirely, cases of syntactic deletion, or detachment: 'John's extending his arm out of the window' and 'John's extending his arm'. My claim of action or event identity-in-spite-of-information-deletion covers cases of semantic deletion as well: 'o's turning green from red' and 'o's turning colour', or 'P's turning$_t$ of the valve' and 'the valve's turning$_i$'. How do we know that the latter is a case of semantic deletion? That is exactly what (CA) tells us. My point is that information deletion in referring expressions is not incompatible with the identity of the act and/or the event to which the expressions refer.

To what position is the one-particular view committed concerning the time and place of P's action, whose intrinsic event is at a time and place distant from the time and place where P is? Recall the distinction from Chap. 3 between actions-as-completed and actions-in-progress. Throughout the following discussion, unless otherwise indicated, I am speaking only of actions-as-completed, not of actions-in-progress (I have a separate discussion below of the later). This is so even when I use the imperfective form of the action verb, or the nominal gerund derived from that verb. Many action verbs don't have a perfect nominal by which to refer to the action-as-completed in any case, so no easy way exists in those cases to refer to the action-as-completed that avoids the nominal gerund. So, for example, when, in what follows, I speak of the time at which P's stopping$_t$ of the flood occurred, I mean thereby the time at which he stopped$_t$ it. That's the action-as-completed or the action-as-successful. I will make it explicit below when I want to speak about the action-in-progress.

There is a version of prolific theory that I will consider later, that places the time and place of all of P's actions, basic and non-basic, where and when P basically acts, where and when P moves his body for example. But that is not the sort of prolific theory I want to defend. One-particularism places the actions of the agent at the times and places of the intrinsic events of those actions, and these will usually be times and places far from P when and where he basically acts.

As most readers will be aware, placing and dating all of P's actions where P basically acts, and placing and dating P's actions where their intrinsic events are placed and dated, both have apparently counterintuitive consequences. Suppose it is at time t and in place p that P moved$_t$ his body, which is what caused the flood to stop$_i$. So P V$_t$-ed b (P stopped$_t$ the flood). But if bV$_i$-ed at t* in p* (the flood stopped$_i$ at t* in p*), how do we date and place P's stopping$_t$ of the flood? The spatial and temporal location of P's stopping$_t$ of the flood must be either at t* in p*, when and where the flood stopped$_i$, or at t in p, when and where he moved$_t$ his body, or at some time and place between those two times and places.

It is odd to say that P V$_t$-ed b *before* b V$_i$-ed at t* and in p*. How could someone stop$_t$ a flood before the flood stopped$_i$? On the other hand, if P V$_t$-ed b only when b V$_i$-ed at t* in p*, we might be committed to saying that P did something, like stop$_t$ a flood, after he died, or anyway long after his body ceased to move in any way relevant to the flood, and in a place in which he never was. Suppose that I bend$_t$ my finger at t in London, the flood stops$_i$ at t+six hours in Edinburgh, but I die at t+three hours on my way to Edinburgh, which I never reach, no doubt having become ill from finger strain induced by all that finger bending. I will have stopped$_t$ the flood after I have died. How could that be? (I assume for this case that I do stop$_t$ the flood and not just that I cause it to stop$_i$. The stopping$_i$ of the flood is intrinsic to my action and not just an extrinsic event that I cause. If you don't like this example, just shorten the distance between the time and place of the intrinsic event and my finger bending$_t$.)

There are bullets to bite on either choice. I have argued elsewhere that the time and place of an action is the time and place of its intrinsic event (more strictly, the time and place one will assign it under description as an intrinsic event). If b V$_i$-ed at t* in p*, and if P V$_t$-ed b, he did so at t* in p* (Ruben 2003, Chapter 1) and not before then, and not anywhere else. I explain why below, in my discussion of Geach and Cambridge events and actions.

I don't think there are any knockdown arguments either for or against one-particularism's dating and placing of actions. But perhaps one might be more inclined to accept this result if a distinction is carefully drawn between two different expressions: 'I saw P stopping$_t$ the flood' and 'I saw P's stopping$_t$ of the flood'. In 'I saw P stopping$_t$ the flood', the direct object of 'saw' is the agent, P, and whatever it is that I saw must be at whatever place the agent was, since it is the agent whom I saw. That will be at t and in p. 'I saw P stopping$_t$ the flood' should then be construed as 'I saw P, who was stopping$_t$ the flood'. But if the agent was at t in p, so that is when and where I saw him, didn't I see him doing whatever he did, at t in p as well? Yes and no. 'I saw P's stopping$_t$ of the flood at t in p' is either literally false (because one cannot see him stopping$_t$ the flood before the flood stopped$_i$, nor can one see all the way from London to Edinburgh), or be understood as the truth that I saw P, who to be sure was at t in p, doing something or other at t in p that caused the flood to stop$_i$ at t* in p*.

On the other hand, in 'I saw P's stopping$_t$ of the flood', there isn't the same prima facie pressure to date anything I saw to time t or to place anything I saw at place p, because the object of 'saw' is 'the stopping$_t$ of the flood', not 'the agent, P', the former of which need not be placed and dated where the agent is. The relation of the agent to his stopping$_t$ is one of (what we might call) ownership of the action. The fact that the action is at t* in p* does not entail that the action's owner is in that same place and at that same time, rather than earlier and elsewhere. A person can own many things distant from him in time and place (property for instance), and some of P's actions might be amongst those things. It is true that P may have tried to stop the flood at t and in p, and we decided in Chap. 3 that, in spite of the fact that there is no particular that is a trying, one might date when and where someone tried by the time and place where and when he was.

One-particularism is an improvement, I believe, on my earlier view of the relation between an action and its intrinsic event (*Action and Its Explanation* 2003). In that earlier formulation, I unwisely denied the inference from '$aV_t b$' to 'bV_i'. As I said in Chap. 5, (CA) is indisputable. So I should not have disputed it. I denied the existence of events intrinsic to actions, in the case of basic action. Even then, the alleged relation between two particulars, an action and its intrinsic event, puzzled me, but I made the mistake of denying that there was an intrinsic event in cases of basic action. I could see that the answer 'two particulars' was problematic, even if they overlap, but I should have considered the possibility of the identity of the action and its intrinsic event rather than the elimination of the intrinsic event.

'What is left over if I subtract the fact that my arm goes up from the fact that I raise my arm?' (Wittgenstein 1953, section 621). In that earlier book, I thought that, for basic actions, the answer to Wittgenstein's question was that the action itself would be left over, since there was nothing there to subtract. How would I now answer his famous question? The answer is: nothing would be left over, since if you subtract the arm going up, you take the action away and there is nothing left.

Randolph Clarke said about my earlier view: 'Ruben makes some rather odd claims in the course of stating his view, including the puzzling assertion that 'when a person bends his finger, it is false that his finger bends, only true that he bends it' (Clarke 2010, fn. 21, 540)'. One-particularism does not deny the inference; it simply says that the LHS and the RHS of the inference refer to the same item. When a person bends his finger, his finger bends, but his bending$_t$ of his finger=his finger's bending$_i$. I hope Clarke does not find this view equally puzzling or odd.

Real Change and Cambridge Change

Peter Geach introduced into the literature a distinction between real change and Cambridge change (1981, 318–323, 1969, 66–67, 70–73, 98–99). A real change is a change as ordinarily and intuitively understood. The change in a schoolboy if he comes to admire someone he did not admire before, the change in a woman when she gives birth to a sixth child, the change in an object when its colour changes, are all real changes.

Real changes, when they are relational, often[5] pair in some way with Cambridge changes: the change in Socrates every time a fresh schoolboy comes to admire him, the change in the number six each time it becomes or ceases to be the number of someone's children,[6] the change in Adam and Eve each time they acquire a new descendant. The change in the schoolboy and the birth of my eldest daughter are real changes; the change in the number 6, the change in Socrates when he comes admired by yet another schoolboy, and Adam and Eve's descendant-gains of my children are only Cambridge changes. What makes them 'Cambridge' changes in these things?

Cambridge change pairs break down into at least two different types. (The reader interested in my somewhat fuller account of Cambridge change should see my 1988, although I have changed my mind about many of the claims made therein.) The first type, which is the only one that interests me here, includes cases like admiring and being admired by, becoming taller than and becoming shorter than, and eulogising and being eulogised by. Let's say that, e.g., the schoolboy's coming to admire Socrates and Socrates' coming to be admired by the schoolboy, or Macron's eulogising of Napoleon and Napoleon's being eulogised by Macron, provide an 'active-passive' pair of change descriptions, both of which refer to a *single* token change, when the descriptions are related by simple grammatical transformation between active and passive voice, but also extended to capture cases of straightforward converse relations, like 'before' and 'after' or 'above' and 'below', for example.[7] (Spatial relations are explicitly excluded from the account on offer, both here and in much of the literature that discusses Cambridge change.)

In cases of converse changes, it is often difficult to tell from a single sentence whether both relata really change or, if only one does, which one it is that really changes. For example, suppose x becomes taller than y. It follows that y has become shorter than x. But was it because x grew taller than y or because y grew shorter than x, or both?

For cases of this type of Cambridge change, 'Cambridge' or 'real' do not denote two kinds of changes, but rather refer to two different senses in which the multiple subjects of a *single* relational change may change. Concerning a single change with two (or more) subjects of change, one subject may change really and the other may change only in a Cambridge fashion. The change itself is able to enter the causal order: Macron's eulogising of Napoleon has causes and effects, and so it follows that Napoleon's being eulogised by Macron has the very same causes and effects, since both 'Macron's eulogising of Napoleon' and 'Napoleon's being eulogised by Macron' are two descriptions of the same change.[8]

Geach, as far as I am aware, never offered an account of this difference between real and Cambridge changes. I think that the basic idea is that somehow there is an asymmetry in terms of their dependence on one another, between what changes really and what changes in a Cambridge fashion. The Cambridge changer depends on the real changer changing in some way non-relationally, in a way in which the later does not depend on the former changing in some way non-relationally. In order for Macron to eulogise Napoleon, Macron must undergo some non-relational changes; in order for Napoleon to be eulogised by Macron, no non-relational change in Napoleon needs to be assumed.

The new schoolboy's coming to admire Socrates takes place in London in 2018. But then Socrates' coming to be admired by the new schoolboy must have the same time and place, for there is only one change, described first actively and then passively. Since in such a case there is only one change, it has to be dated and placed either in London in 2018 or in Athens ca. 2400 years ago. Either the schoolboy had to come to admire Socrates in Athens ca. 2400 years ago, or Socrates had to come to be admired by the schoolboy in London in 2018.

The first option is absurd. So Socrates changed in 2018, by obtaining another remote admirer, and if anywhere, where that remote admirer lived (say, in London). This is so despite the fact that Socrates died almost 2400 years ago in Athens, and never travelled to England. The correct placing and dating of Socrates' Cambridge changing is taken from the placing and dating of the partner's real changing, or the partner real changer, in this case that of his remote admirer in London in 2018. No one should want to date or place Socrates's remote-admirer-gain by the dating and placing of the 'grounding' act of his brilliance in Athens, or by any other way in which Socrates was or by any way in which he acted, so long ago and so far away, for which he is admired, rather than by the date and place of the remote admirer, the schoolboy.

Let's return the discussion specifically to actions. The same account that I gave above, I think, holds for actions. Indeed, it would be surprising if there could be Cambridge changes, but no Cambridge actions. I will again restrict my discussion of the puzzle about the time and place of actions only for ergative action verbs that are subject to the imperfectivity paradox.

I think that the import of asserting that a Cambridge actor only Cambridge acts is only that there is no further effort he must expend in doing that action. I will elaborate that point below. But that is a question about *the actor*. A different question is whether the Cambridge action is itself a particular, capable of entering into the causal order of things, and to that there must be an unambiguous answer: yes, just as it was in the general case of Cambridge changes. It must be, since on one-particularism, the Cambridge act is identical to its intrinsic event, and that event is certainly capable of entering into the causal order. The Cambridge action is in no way a second-class ontological citizen; it only imputes a Cambridge change to the agent.

Reconsider in this light my action, my stopping$_t$ of the flood. There is my bending$_t$ of my finger (cf: Socrates' displays of his brilliance in Athens). There is also a subsequent pair of 'partner' changes: the flood's stopping$_i$ and my stopping$_t$ of the flood (cf: Socrates coming to be admired by the schoolboy, the schoolboy coming to admire him). So, there are three 'elements' to consider in both cases: (a) the initiating or grounding act, my bending$_t$ of my finger, which is a real change in me, dated (let's say) at t and placed in p, just as Socrates' displays of his brilliance in Athens were real changes in Athens long ago; (b) a different action, my stopping$_t$ of the flood. That action, (b), is my Cambridge action, just as Socrates' gaining a new admirer was a Cambridge change in him. My stopping$_t$ of the flood is a Cambridge action because no real, non-relational change subsequent to my finger's bending$_i$ need have happened to me. Finally, (c) there is the flood's stopping$_i$ at t+6 hours in a location remote from me, which is a real, non-relational change in the flood, just as the schoolboy really changed in London in 2018 when he came to admire Socrates. Remember that in cases of these 'partner' changes, (b) and (c), there is in truth only one change, but two things can be said to change in one sense or another (really or only in a Cambridge fashion). The schoolboy's coming to admire Socrates=Socrates coming to be admired by the schoolboy; my stopping$_t$ of the flood=the flood's stopping$_i$. (The latter is of course one-particularism.) In the case of my flood-stopping$_t$, the real change is in the flood, the Cambridge change is in me. So, on the one-particular view, my stopping$_t$ of the flood=the flood's stopping$_i$, a single particular, described as either my Cambridge action (because I only Cambridge change) or as a real change in the flood (because the flood really changes). One-particularism is continuous with a very plausible view of Cambridge change.

So, my stopping$_t$ of the flood, (b) above, takes its temporal and spatial locations from the flood's stopping$_i$, (c), just as Socrates's gaining another remote admirer took its date and place from its 'partner' real change, the schoolboy's coming to admirer him in 2018 in London. My stopping$_t$ of the flood no more has the place and date of the initiating change, my finger bending$_t$, (a), than does Socrates' coming to be admired have the time and place of the initiating event, whatever happened to him, or whatever he did, in Athens so long ago (whatever display of brilliance that it was that convinced the schoolboy to admire him so long thereafter). These Cambridge actions, like Cambridge changes generally, do not take the spatial and temporal locations of their initiating events. On the contrary, they are placed in space and in time (if temporally placed at all) by the spatial and temporal positions of the real changes in their relational partners. Many, perhaps most, of an agent's actions can be placed at a spatial position distant, far removed, from that of his body. Most of my non-basic physical actions are Cambridge actions.

The challenge to the specific version of prolific theorist that I am defending is to account for the fact that I may be credited with acting at a place where I am not, and after I stop moving my body in any relevant way. The reply is that these are my Cambridge actions, since they presuppose only Cambridge changes in the actor. This way of placing and dating real and Cambridge changes makes perfectly good sense on the one-particular view. The one-particular view requires the Cambridge theory of actions to be plausible.

Typically, in the case in which the action chain follows the accordion effect outwards from the agent's body, when P Cambridge changes, there are no further real changes in P himself, but rather only in whatever it is that P changes. The real changes are in the flood, the door, the sluice, the dam, the lives of the downstream inhabitants, or whatever. But there are other sorts of cases too. What shall we say in the case in which P really does change, for example when he moves$_t$ various parts of his own body, but only by moving$_t$ other parts of his body? Suppose I move$_t$ my left arm by rotating$_t$ it with my right arm. My moving$_t$ of my left arm is not basic, since it is done BY my moving$_t$ of my right arm. After I expend effort in moving$_t$ my right arm, no further effort is required on my part to move$_t$ my left arm. But my moving$_t$ of my left arm in such a case does not presuppose only a Cambridge change in me either. Both my moving$_t$ of my left arm and my moving$_t$ of my right arm presuppose real changes in me. Neither non-basicness of an action nor failure of need for further effort in action is a metaphysically sufficient condition for my action's being a Cambridge action that presupposes only a Cambridge change in me, even though an action's being a Cambridge action is sufficient for it requiring no further effort on the part of the actor, and for it to be non-basic.

'To change' is an ergative action verb too, and since it is a transitive verb, it needs an object: from 'P changed$_t$ o', one can infer that 'o changed$_i$'. On the one-particular view, 'o's changing$_i$' is therefore another description for 'P's changing$_t$ of o'. In the case in which o is one of P's own bodily parts, and in which P moves$_t$ his bodily part o but *not* by doing anything else, are two things changed, P and o, both changers really changing? In this special case in which P changes the position of parts of his own body but not by doing anything else, only one thing really changes, because a change in o is a change in P. P is changing himself.

If we distinguish between real and Cambridge specifically for action, it can be true that agents *can* act, Cambridge act, after they cease expending any effort relevant to the task, and at locations they have never occupied. *When* did P (finally) manage to stop$_t$ the flood, ring$_t$ the bell, open$_t$ the door, or close$_t$ the window? Poor chap, he managed to pull it off, to do it, only after he was expending no more effort on these tasks and his mind was elsewhere. *Where* did P (finally) manage to stop$_t$ the flood, ring$_t$ the bell, open$_t$ the door, or close$_t$ the window? Poor chap, he managed to pull it off, to do it, only in Edinburgh where the flood stopped$_i$, where the bell rang$_i$, where the door opened$_i$, and where the window closed$_i$, but he wasn't there to learn of his eventual success. He may have had to learn of his success in an indirect manner, by report.

So one *can* continue to act after ceasing to expend any effort (note that 'to expend effort' is, like 'to push a cart', not itself subject to the imperfectivity paradox, so does not itself raise the same puzzle that verbs that are subject to it raise). We tend, albeit wrongly, to associate the idea of effort with our idea of action. How can Cambridge action be any sort of action, since, as Bennett pointed out, the agent expends no effort additional to the effort expended in the first act, say in his bending$_t$ of his finger? (Bennett 1973, 315–323). To that extent, the observation is simply correct: there is further action without additional effort. I act (and it is not just that new descriptions become true of my single act), yet without exercising any more effort beyond what I did when I bent$_t$ my finger

(1997). There are many other examples in which I act without exercising effort: I stand at the photocopy machine and print out a paper. Most of the time I am standing at the photocopier, expending no effort, merely watching the paper being produced. But it is true, even during those intervals, if asked what I am doing when I am standing where I am, I can truly reply that I am printing my paper. I can be printing my paper, and expending no further effort than I did when I set the printer to work. To be sure, this case has dissimilarities as well as similarities with the case of Cambridge action, but my point is only that we are used to the idea of action without effort, and Cambridge action does not seem exceptional in that regard.

After all, as I claimed in Chap. 4, every action, unless it is described by an action verb implying successful completion ('I closed$_t$ the door at t but still it took me a while to close$_t$ it'; 'I stopped$_t$ the flood at t but still it took me a while to stop$_t$ it'), even the bending$_t$ of one's finger, takes some time—that is, it's not something a person can do AT a time, but something that's done OVER time. It can only be *completed* at a time. I can stop$_t$ the flood at t*, but I can be involved in the stopping$_t$ of it *from* when I bent$_t$ my finger at t *until* the flood stops$_i$ at t*. (See below on more on this way of dating actions.)

In many cases, there will be gaps over that temporal expanse from t to t* in which no bodily movement$_t$ by the agent will be occurring. One might argue that there is a KIND of effort involved in standing at the copier and watching to see that all goes well. There's also oversight of the process, and readiness and ability to intervene as necessary. But it seems that (a) I can be printing my paper when I am doing none of these things. I can be in another room, not watching nor ready to intervene and still, if asked to do something else, I can truthfully reply that I can't do something else because I am busy printing my paper. Perhaps this could be spelled out by counterfactuals: if I wanted to exercise oversight, or to intervene, I could do so. But it also seems that (b) in many cases of Cambridge action, the same watching, oversight, and readiness to intervene can be present, of course within limits, or similar counterfactuals could be formulated. I bend$_t$ my finger at t, I stop$_t$ the flood at t*, and perhaps it is true that I am stopping$_c$ it over the temporal expanse between t and t*, just as I am printing$_c$ my paper over an analogous temporal expanse. I might watch what's going on between t and t*, and I might be able act to eliminate at least some obstacles that I see arise during some of that time.

Can a person act even after his death? That is an even somewhat stronger view, which might appeal only to the very strong-hearted. But one might want to restrict the idea of Cambridge action to cases in which the agent remains alive and conscious, and where there is at least some possibility of the agent's watching, oversight, or readiness to intervene in the process he initiates. One might say that if P moves$_t$ his hand at p and at t, and stops$_t$ the flood at p* and at t*, P should be able to watch, oversee, or be ready to intervene in the process between t and t*, that extends from the first action to the second (David Mackie 1997). I am reliably informed that a dead person cannot alter the course of a process or change or control a process that he may have set in motion before his death. The thought that I can often or usually oversee, intervene, or whatever, or could do so if I wanted to, might be made more plausible by recalling my view from Chap. 5 that very distant effects are typically extrinsic events, not intrinsic events to actions. P's causing an extrinsic event has no such restriction to alive or conscious initiators. If P can do none of these things, watch, oversight, etc., perhaps then the stopping$_i$ of the flood is only an extrinsic event that P causes and not an event intrinsic to an action of his stopping$_t$ of it. I said in Chap. 5 that, pace David Lewis on 'killing', King Canute did *not* ring$_t$ the bell after a lapse of one thousand years. If King Canute did not ring$_t$ the bell, although the bell rang$_i$ in 2018 and Canute caused it to do so, then eo ipso we don't have to say that a dead King Canute could act in 2018. (I assume though that Lewis would, unlike me, place Canute's bell ringing$_t$ in 1018, not 2018).

I leave it as an open question here, whether Cambridge action should have any spatial or temporal distance restrictions placed on its limits, other than the vague ones already in place differentiating action from only causing an event. Cambridge changes generally have no such restrictions (Adam and Eve will gain another remote descendant for as long as humankind exists), but Cambridge actions are more likely candidates for having some such restrictions placed on their reach. If there were to be such further restrictions, death and permanent lack of consciousness seem like plausible candidates. My argument in the last chapter was that as effects of what an agent does become increasingly remote, we become increasingly disinclined to treat those events as events intrinsic to some action by that agent. And I also said that it was vague where the line between action and causing an extrinsic event is to be drawn. But if you think that King Canute does ring$_t$ the bell (you would in fact be agreeing with a natural extension of David Lewis' view against which I argued in the last chapter), and if you were to place, as I, but not he, do, any such ringing$_t$ in 2018, Canute would be a long-dead ringer when he rings$_t$.

More on Actions and Times

As we saw above, an agent, P, bends his finger, turns the valve, closes the sluice on a dam, stops the flood, and thereby improves the lives of the inhabitants living downstream. P did each action on the list by doing its predecessor (if it has one). These are different actions. Actions take time, although they can be completed at a time. So, in this section, I return to consider, briefly, actions-in-progress rather than actions-as-completed. I intend to cover, in these remarks, only telic verbs that can take a meaningful imperfective aspect form in the sentence being considered (remember the problem with Vendler's example of 'find' in Chap. 3, if used in a sentence such as 'P finds a ten-euro note').

Suppose P stops$_t$ the flood at t4, say, but stopping$_t$ the flood takes time. How much time? How long did it take P to stop$_t$ the flood? A good way to measure the time the stopping$_t$ takes is the time from when he first bends his finger at t1 (because that is when he started the stopping$_t$ of it) until he stops$_t$ the flood at t4. (He didn't improve the lives of the inhabitants until t5, so it took him even longer to improve the lives of those downstream.) But he also turned the valve at, say, t3. How long did that take? The turning$_t$ can be completed at t3, but the turning$_t$ may have taken from t1, when he started the turning$_t$ of the valve, to t3, when his turning$_t$ was completed. How best to theorise these facts?

Helen Steward has done interesting work on processes, work that offers one way in which to do so.[9] If processes can have parts, if they can 'nest' one inside another, one could say that the process of his turning$_t$ of the valve is a part of the whole process of his stopping$_t$ of the flood, which itself is part of the even larger process of his improving$_t$ of the lives of those people. I don't have strong views about this way in which to theorise these temporal facts; perhaps it is correct. Such processes would overlap, so they would not be distinct. But I think we can also offer a way of understanding these facts that does not involve the idea of a process, and so does not involve any mereological considerations about processes. All we need is the idea of distinct actions (they are not identical and they don't overlap) and stretches of time, whose parts do overlap.

What was P doing between t2 and t3? Well, I've just said that he was turning$_t$ the valve during that time. But since t2−t3 is within the longer temporal expanse of t1−t5, he was also stopping$_t$ the flood, and improving$_t$ the lives of the people downstream, during t2−t3. These actions were running parallel, as it were, some of the time. If he was turning$_t$ the valve at t2, at t3 his turning$_t$ was over and done, completed, so from t3−t5, he will be doing one less thing. If he stopped$_t$ the flood at t4, that was over and done by t5, at which time he was only still improving$_t$ the lives of the people. So instead of thinking of processes and parts, we can theorise these facts in terms of a temporal expanse and its parts, as ways of dating different actions that take different amounts of time, and whose temporal expanses overlap. Since the actions have different temporal expanses, they can't be identical. But they can share periods of temporal extent.[10]

It's easiest to see this in the cases in which a perfect or derived nominal can be formed from the verb: 'the betrayal of Norway', 'the closure of the window', and 'the destruction of Rotterdam' (all in the product sense). P's closure of the window was at t4, but his closing$_t$ of the widow extended from t1−t4, and during that same stretch of time, from t1 to t4, P may have been doing lots of other things too, all leading to that betrayal, closure, or destruction.

So agents are very busy bees. They do lots of things in the same temporal expanse; the shorter the expanse, the more they might be doing. Think of an action chain as running from left to right, with the basic or grounding action on the left and the action goal somewhere to the right of that (but not necessarily the end point, as the case of improving$_t$ the lives of the people downstream demonstrates, since he may not have aimed at doing that.) Other things being equal, as one moves to the left on the action chain, the temporal expanses become shorter, fitting into the longer temporal expanse occupied by the time it takes to complete the actions on its right. P's improving$_t$ of the lives of those downstream took the longest amount of time, his stopping$_t$ of the flood took less, all within that longest amount, his closing$_t$ of the sluice took even less, all within the time it took to stop$_t$ the flood, and so on. Once the accordion effect deflates and goes to the left even of the basic action, say, inside the agent, temporal assignment becomes much more complicated, but I shan't pursue those complications here.

Austere Theory and Intrinsic Events

Recall the earlier action chain I described and consider the action, P's bending$_t$ of his finger. Its intrinsic event is the bending$_i$ of P's finger. On that action chain, P also closed$_t$ the sluice, stopped$_t$ the flood, and improved$_t$ the lives of those living downstream. Their intrinsic events are the closing$_i$ of the sluice the stopping$_i$ of the flood, and the improvement$_i$ of those lives, respectively. Is 'event e is the intrinsic event of action a' a transparent locution?

The first theories to consider are prolific theories and austere theories of act individuation. First, consider a prolific theory. Each action has a different intrinsic event; no two actions have the same one. For prolific theorists, on the action chain now under consideration, the actions are not identical. Moreover, the intrinsic events are not identical. The bending$_t$ has only the one of the three events intrinsic to it, and of course similarly for the closing$_t$ and the stopping$_t$. So one might believe that identities are substitutable salva veritate in 'event e is the intrinsic event of action a', because no absurdity is generated, such as 'the event of the flood's stopping$_i$ is intrinsic to P's bending$_t$ of his finger'.

So one might think, but another consideration shows that 'event e is the intrinsic event of action a' cannot be transparent, for either austere or prolific theories, if one-particularism is true. If 'event e is the intrinsic event of action a' were transparent, it would also be true that 'event e is the intrinsic event of event e' and 'action a is the intrinsic event of action a'. To avoid that absurdity, '_is the intrinsic event of_' cannot be transparent. It matters how the items between which the relation holds are described, on every theory.

On austere theory, '_is the intrinsic event of_' cannot be transparent for a second reason. For austere theorists, on the action chain under consideration, the bending$_t$=the closing$_t$=the stopping$_t$. If 'event e is the intrinsic event of action a' were transparent, the bending$_t$ would have all three events intrinsic to it, and of course similarly for the closing$_t$ and the stopping$_t$, since they are all names for the same action. On austere theory, events are intrinsic to actions only as described, or qua being described in one way rather than another. I offer this not as a criticism but merely in order to draw out an implication. If austere theory claims that these are different descriptions for the same action, it is hardly surprising that there will be a different intrinsic event description for each description of the action. No surprises there. Note that this is not the claim that a single intrinsic event can be differently described, depending on how the single action is described. After all, the three intrinsic events are distinct events, not one event that can be described in three different ways. Rather, it is that the single action will have many intrinsic events, depending on how it, viz., the action, is described.

What about the standard theory of action? In what follows, I take P's bending$_t$ of his finger to be an example of a basic or (as Davidson calls it) a primitive action. The standard theory of action, it will be recalled, holds that (at least) a primitive or basic action, like P's bending$_t$ of his finger, is identical to an event, when that event is caused nondeviantly by the mental states that rationalise it. That event is (in this case) the bending$_i$ of P's finger. The addition of 'when that event is caused nondeviantly by the mental states that rationalise it' should not mislead. The identity is between a token action and a token event: a=e. In the case of a true identity of this sort, the token event *is* one that will have met the causal requirements set by the theory. Identities are not qualified by phrases such as 'when that event is caused nondeviantly by the mental states that rationalise it' in order to be true. In the case at hand, that event will be the event intrinsic to the action (on the assumption that the action being considered is nominated by an ergative verb). P's bending$_t$ of his finger=the bending$_i$ of P's finger.

But exactly how does one combine standard theory with an austere theory of act individuation, which is its most common form? Call the conjunction of austere theory and standard theory 'the conjunction'. The conjunction identifies a token basic action like P's bending$_t$ of his finger with the token event of P's finger's bending$_i$ (standard theory). It also identifies a basic action like P's bending$_t$ of his finger with P's stopping$_t$ of the flood (austere theory), and similarly for the other actions on the action chain. This means that the conjunction holds that P's stopping$_t$ of the flood=the bending$_i$ of P's finger, which is a trifle odd but acceptable.

The conjunction cannot in addition identify the stopping$_t$ of the flood or the closing$_t$ of the sluice with their intrinsic events, as a prolific theory can. If P's stopping$_t$ of the flood, for example, were identical both to the flood's stopping$_i$ (the event intrinsic to the stopping$_t$) and to P's bending$_t$ of his finger, and since P's bending$_t$ of his finger=the token event of P's finger's bending$_i$, it would follow that the bending$_i$ of P's finger=the flood's stopping$_i$. But on any plausible account of event identity, that is absurd. It may be true on the conjunction of austere theory and standard theory that the flood's stopping$_i$ *is* the event intrinsic to P's stopping$_t$ of the flood *as so described*, but P's stopping$_t$ of the flood, and similarly for actions on the action chain other than the basic action(s), must, for the conjunction, be given some account other than identifying them with their intrinsic events, for example, accounting for P's stopping$_t$ of the flood as P's bending$_t$ of his finger causing the flood to stop$_i$. The identity of an action and its intrinsic event works, on the conjunction, only for the case of basic actions.

It may be acceptable even if odd that P's stopping$_t$ of the flood=the bending$_i$ of P's finger on the conjunction of theories. But it is not acceptable that P's bending$_t$ of his finger=the stopping$_i$ of the flood. Suppose P's bending$_t$ of his finger=the stopping$_i$ of the flood. Since his bending$_t$ of his finger=his stopping$_t$ of the flood, his stopping$_t$ of the flood would be identical to the flood's stopping$_i$, which we have just seen that it cannot be.

These last few paragraphs suggest a different way in which the conjunction of austere and standard theory could address the applicability of the idea of an intrinsic event. Proponents of the conjunction don't often use the language of intrinsic events in their theories. The conjunction might simply dispense with the idea of intrinsic events for non-basic actions altogether. Even though it is undeniable that 'P stops$_t$ the flood' entails 'The flood stopped$_i$', the (CA), and even though there is an event, the flood's stopping$_i$, that makes the RHS of that inference true, they might hold that there is no sense in which that event is intrinsic to any action. Perhaps the idea of an intrinsic event has only a limited applicability to basic action, at least for the conjunction. To say that P stops$_t$ the flood iff P causes the flood to stop$_i$ is perhaps an *alternative* to thinking that the stopping$_i$ of the flood is intrinsic to P's stopping$_t$ of it. It does seem to me that the conjunction has some difficulty in really taking the idea of an intrinsic event seriously.

Assuming that we continue with the idea that the conjunction of austere and standard theory remains committed to the idea that all (or almost all, as we have seen in the case of 'sell' and 'pass' for example) actions named by ergative verbs have an event intrinsic to them, we can summarise then, the theses they must hold for the example I have been using: (1) P's bending$_t$ of his finger=the bending$_i$ of P's finger; (2) P's stopping$_t$ of the flood=P's bending$_t$ of his finger; (3) the flood's stopping$_i \neq$ P's stopping$_t$ of the flood, (4) the stopping$_i$ of the flood is the event intrinsic to P's stopping$_t$ of the flood, but only as so described, (5) P's bending$_t$ of his finger$\neq$the stopping$_i$ of the flood, but (6) P's stopping$_t$ of the flood=the bending$_i$ of P's finger (odd but acceptable). (1) follows from the standard theory; (2) follows on an austere theory of act individuation.

I leave it to proponents of the conjunction of these two theories to explain why all of these assertions and denials of identity are well motivated. Whenever I describe the standard theory as identifying an action like P's bending$_t$ of his finger with its intrinsic event, the bending$_i$ of P's finger, I intend to claim that this sort of identity is true (on standard theory plus austere theory) only for the case of basic or primitive action.

I now want to deal with two arguments against one-particularism that I can anticipate: (1) the action causation argument and (2) the time argument (which takes up the challenge presented by (b)). I am sure there are others but these are the ones that strike me as the most urgent.

The First Argument: The Action Causation Argument

(1) First, I address what I call 'the action causation argument'. In what follows, as before, I mean by 'an action chain', a chain of actions such that each action is done by doing its predecessor on the chain, if it has one. On the other hand, a causal chain is a chain of particulars (of whatever metaphysical sort whose instances can be a cause or an effect) such that each is the effect of its predecessor cause, if it has one. It will be no part of my argument to explicate the idea of an action chain, so I do not really rise to Bratman's challenge below. I do think that action chains and causal chains are different. The first is a teleological idea; the second is (obviously) a causal one. In general, I'm no fan of the compatibilist idea that teleology can be explicated by causality. But I do not wish to take on that debate. My question is far more limited: can two adjacent actions on an action chain also appear as an immediate cause and effect on a causal chain?

Before I begin my argument, I want to make some remarks about the sense in which an action chain is a teleological idea. The example I gave of an action chain is probably best understood as embodying the agent's plan for his eventual stopping$_t$ of the flood. If so, one action on it is the result at which the agent is aiming: his stopping$_t$ of the flood. It's in virtue of that fact that one can say that the idea of an action chain is a teleological idea. Moreover, many of the actions on the chain leading up to that stopping$_t$ will be deliberate, intentional actions that the agent will take because he thinks that they are actions by which he can achieve that goal. But not all of the actions on the chain need to be deliberate or even intentional. In the example I gave, the agent improved$_t$ the lives of those downstream by stopping$_t$ the flood. But he may not have intended to do so, and indeed may not even be aware that he has done so. Another example is this. On the action chain as I described it, there were five actions: the finger bending$_t$, the valve turning$_t$, the sluice closing$_t$, the flood stopping$_t$, and the improving$_t$ of the lives. The middle three actions were surely part of the agent's deliberate plan; he may or may not have thought much about his finger bending$_t$. But there are or can be many actions on the action chain between each of the ones I explicitly mentioned, and, assuming that the accordion effect goes inwards as well as outwards, there may be ones even before the bending$_t$ and even after the improving$_t$. For example, after the agent, P, turned$_t$ the valve, some mechanism of which he may have been unaware, say the rotating$_i$ of some flywheels, occurred. Being mechanically challenged, he did not even know that there were any flywheels involved in what he was doing. But it would still be true that he stopped$_t$ the flood by rotating$_t$ those flywheels, and that he rotated$_t$ those flywheels by turning$_t$ the valve. In order to be an action chain that embodies an agent's plan, not all the actions on that chain must be part of his plan.

One could, if it were helpful to do so, distinguish between two senses of an action chain. In the first, and stronger, sense, only those actions are on the chain that are part of the agent's deliberate plan and are done intentionally. In the second, and weaker, sense, the action chain contains many of the agent's actions that are not intentional and are no part of his explicit plan, like the rotating$_t$ of the flywheels or the improving$_t$ of the lives of those who live downstream, as long as it's an action he takes by which as a matter of fact he does further his goal or is an action that results from his achieving of that goal. My preference is for the weaker sense, on the grounds of the difficulty of deciding what should count as part of the agent's plan in the stronger sense. Is his bending$_t$ of his finger part of his plan in the stronger sense? He surely bent$_t$ his finger intentionally. But if asked about his plan in advance, he wouldn't mention that action as part of his plan. It's not that the agent has to be explicit about all the actions his plan includes, but it is difficult to see how to impose a rational cut-off that includes some actions, like his bending$_t$ of his finger, but excludes any others of which it is also true that he achieves his goal by doing them.

Now for the argument addressing action chains and causality. It is an unquestioned view held by almost every action theorist that I have read, that in an action chain that includes, for example, an agent's bending$_t$ of his finger and his stopping$_t$ of the flood (so that the agent stops$_t$ the flood by bending$_t$ his finger), that his bending$_t$ of his finger cannot not also cause his stopping$_t$ of the flood. The standard view is that the agent stops$_t$ the flood by his bending$_t$ of his finger, that the agent's bending$_t$ of his finger causes the flood to stop$_i$, but that his bending$_t$ of his finger does not stand in a causal relation to his stopping$_t$ of the flood. This view asserts that actions on an action chain cause the events intrinsic to the action subsequent to them on that chain, but do not cause the actions themselves. The view is widespread but often unargued. For example, Kim (1973, 3) simply asserts that an action like 'my turning [of] the knob does not cause my opening [of] the window'. Again, in his (1974): 'The relation between the actions, however, is not causal-my turning the knob does not cause my opening of the window', with no further argument (45). Michael Bratman (1978) just announces that 'one intuition about these events [like the ones we are discussing] which is shared by many philosophers (among them Davidson, Goldman and Kim) is this: Though my raising [of] my hand causes my nose's rising, it does not cause my raising [of] my nose' (367–368). Bratman leaves the view as an 'intuition'.

Alvin Goldman's *A Theory of Human Action* (1970) develops the view at some length. For example, in one of the four paradigms of an action chain that Goldman describes ('the four species of level generation'), the idea is that if two actions are related by causal generation (one is done by doing the other), it follows that they are *not* related by causation. Causal generation is not a causal relation, but is somewhat confusingly so named because an action can *cause* the event intrinsic to its successor action on the action chain (Goldman, 22–23). Thus, 'Two acts can never be related both by causal generalisation and by causation' (Goldman, 23).

Why should acts related by causal generation (the by-relation) not also be related by causation? It is not as if two actions can never be related by causation. Actions can appear on causal chains too. Goldman accepts the obvious point that actions can sometimes be both the relata of the causal relation: 'Suppose that S locks himself out of his car, and this deed of his forces him to break the window in order to get back in. S's act of locking himself out of the car causes his act of breaking the window; but it does not causally generate the latter act' (Goldman, 23). The ban on causation between actions only comes into force for Goldman, and others, if the actions are related by causal generation, or by one of the other species of level generation other than augmentation.

Since on my view actions are identical to their intrinsic events, and since it is generally agreed that an action on an action chain cause a successor action's intrinsic event (after all, that is how Goldman's causal generation relation between two actions is partially defined), and since the causal relation is extensional, it follows on one-particularism that many actions can cause their successor actions. (In fact, in teaching philosophy of action, I find it hard to convince students otherwise.) It also follows that, in such cases, each intrinsic event causes its successor intrinsic event too. Nor is there any reason to discount mixed stories, on which actions cause intrinsic events, which in turn cause actions. All these causal claims will be true if one-particularism is true and if the causal relation is extensional. Some actions can be caused by the same action by which it is done. (I don't think action chains are extensional in the same way in which causal chains with actions on them are. If P stops$_t$ the flood by turning$_t$ the valve, he does not stop$_t$ the flood by the valve's turning$_i$. Action chains connect particulars only as described as actions, not as described as events intrinsic to actions.)

So I am denying Goldman's claim by holding that *some* action pairs can be related both by the by-relation and by causation. I think there are also some clear cases of action chains on which the relata of the by-relation do not stand in a causal relation: '...S checkmates his opponent by moving his queen to king-knight-seven...' (Goldman, 21). This is a bona fide case of two actions, S's checkmating$_t$ and S's queen-moving$_t$, which the by-relation relates but which can't stand in any causal relation. Goldman and I agree about this case.

But there will be many other cases about which we do not agree. To be more precise, my claim is this: consider a pair of actions, a1 and a2, such that: (1) P does a2 by doing a1; (2) action a2 has an event e2 intrinsic to it; a1 causes e2. If (1), (2), and (3), then a1 causes a2. In the chess example he gives about which we agree, 'checkmate' means 'to place one's opponent in check'. 'Place' is not an ergative verb and so has no event intrinsic to it. (Levin 1993, 49–51, lists 'place' as an example of locative alternation, not causative alternation.) So Goldman's chess example falls outside the range of my claim.[11] As Hornsby's remarks on pushing, remarks that I will quote almost immediately below (I am just substituting the example of 'place' for the one she will give for 'push'), P's opponent's being placed in checkmate isn't an event that P is causing, since the opponent's being placed in checkmate (by P) IS just P's placing of his opponent in checkmate.

Why does Goldman think that no action on a causal chain can cause its successor(s)? 'Level-generation is precluded between these acts [that are related causally] because [in the case of causation] one of them is subsequent to the other.' Goldman's thought is this: a cause must occur temporally before its effect and not simultaneously with it. But the two actions related by causal generation always occur at the same time, on his view, so it follows that they cannot be causally related. I will deal with the time issue more fully in (2) below, since I reject his way of ascribing times to actions. I do not know of any other compelling reason to deny that actions on an action chain like the one with the hand-moving$_t$ and the flood-stopping$_t$ on it can also be causally related. Meanwhile, I think I can make a few useful observations.

Bratman's paper (1978), cited above, advances an interesting argument and is worth more careful consideration than I will give it here. The gist is this: a prolific theorist, like Kim or Goldman, who wishes to deny that actions on an action chain are causally related, needs to specify a relation, Bratman calls it 'an action-transmitting relation', that differs from causation (it's the relation that Goldman called 'causal generation'). Bratman's argument is that they fail in the task of distinguishing between the relation of causation and the relation of non-causal action-transmission. Both for example are said to be asymmetric, transitive, and irreflexive. Consider just one such attempt to distinguish the two relations. Suppose you think that, in order for there to be causation, there must be a causal generalisation lurking, perhaps only a rough-and-ready one (Goldman 1970, 72–76).

Bratman argues like this: what might be the lurking causal generalisation in the case of an action (his moving$_t$ of his hand) causing the non-action event (the door's opening$_i$), which is meant to be a permissible singular causal claim on the Goldman-Kim theory? The only plausible guess would be something like this: Whenever anyone moves$_t$ his hand in circumstances c, a door opens$_i$. Circumstances c will have to include a great deal of contextual information. But if one thinks that in principle a causal generalisation can be found, there is no reason to think that the following causal generalisation cannot also be found: 'whenever any one moves$_t$ his hand in circumstances c, he opens$_t$ a door', which is meant to be impermissible on the Goldman-Kim theory. Bratman uses this, and other arguments he puts forward, as arguments against any such prolific theory of action. Suppose that the generalisation in question is only a heteronomic one, in Davidson's sense.[12] Even so, if there is an underlying homonomic generalisation in a different vocabulary in the case of the action causing an intrinsic event, Bratman could argue that there is as much or little reason to think that there is also one in the case of an action causing another action as well.

I would read Bratman's argument differently, not as an argument against prolific theory as he intends it to be, but as an argument against assuming that there is no causal relation between at least some pairs of actions on an action chain. If, unlike Bratman, one accepts a prolific theory, then Bratman's argument shows that at least some pairs of actions on an action chain can be 'covered' by a causal generalisation in the same way in which an action and an event intrinsic to its successor action can be covered by a causal generalisation, and hence that the former pair can be causally related if the latter pair can be. One-particularism accepts that consequence.

The Second Argument: The Time of an Action Argument

(2) I have already mentioned the time argument above. The thought must be that if, as Goldman says, the actions on an action chain all happen at the same time, then the relation between them can't be causal, since cause and effect cannot be simultaneous. One might dispute the non-simultaneity requirement for causation, but I will argue that many of the actions on an action chain do *not* happen simultaneously, and so can be causally related, even assuming that cause and effect cannot be simultaneous. One may also concede that some examples of pairs of actions on an action chain are simultaneous: the example earlier is such a case: '…S checkmates his opponent by moving his queen to king-knight-seven…'. I am not going to try and produce a theory of why some action pairs on an action chain are simultaneous and some not, but I think that cases of conventional or linguistic upshots (what Goldman calls conventional generation, Goldman, 25–26) will provide some very plausible examples of simultaneity. In addition to the chess example, performative utterances also seem to provide likely cases. If P promises P* to F, by P's

saying to P*, 'I hereby promise to F', then P's promising P* and P's saying to P* what he said, occur simultaneously. These cases of simultaneous actions are not plausible candidates for being related as cause and effect.

But other examples cannot be conceded to Goldman in the same way. Goldman says that if S turns off the lights by flipping the switch, the turning off$_t$ of the light is not subsequent to his switch flipping$_t$. S does not flip the switch and then, later, turn off the light. So on his view, we have another pair of actions done at the same time. And since they are done at the same time, the relation between them can't be causal.

However, since one-particularism identifies the turning$_t$ off of the light with the light's turning$_i$ off, it follows that if S flips$_t$ the switch at t and the lights turn$_i$ off at t*, then S turns$_t$ off the light at t*, which is subsequent to his switch flipping$_t$ at t. One-particularism does envisage two actions at two different times, even when one is done by doing the other. So I reject the view that all of the actions on a single action chain are simultaneous, even if there are some examples that are. Goldman's argument for this conclusion is that 'it would be incorrect to say', and 'it would be inappropriate to say' in this sort of case (where 'by doing' is relevant), that the one action was subsequent to the other (21).

There are many cases in which it is inappropriate to say something even if it is strictly and literally true. There may be pragmatic reasons for not saying something; for instance it may suggest something false to the hearer in spite of not entailing the falsity. For example, the use of 'subsequently' might suggest that more effort is required to do the second action than was required to do the first, and although that is true in action plans like the one about building a ship that I used as an example in Chap. 2, it is not true in the case of action chains of the sort we are now considering. It is in those former kinds of action plans in which 'later' and 'subsequently' are appropriate (Goldman agrees that this is so in the case of the locking oneself out of a car and the breaking of the window to enter, cited earlier), but not appropriate, perhaps, in chains like the ones we are discussing now, ones in which, if it is cooperative, nature just rolls on after the agent has finished expending any effort. But the inappropriateness might arise from the false suggestion that the second kind of chain is like the first kind in requiring more effort, and not because of any literal falsity in the temporal claim.

Even so, the longer the time interval between the two actions, the less inappropriate it sounds to say that one occurred subsequently to the other. The agent moved$_t$ his hand in London at t, and stopped$_t$ the flood much later, six hours later. It seems perfectly appropriate to me to say that he stopped$_t$ the flood long after he moved$_t$ his hand. On what is perhaps the most plausible view of this, the only requirement is that he remains alive and conscious in the interim.

However inappropriate it might sound to say that one such action was 'subsequent' to another, Goldman's view has a matching 'inappropriateness' with 'at the same time'. On his view, the agent stopped$_t$ the flood in Edinburgh *at the same time as* he turned$_t$ the handle in London. But that does not seem true at all, and not just inappropriate. Not for nothing did I say that there were bullets to bite on all the options. The temporal choice for the two actions (and he and I agree that there are two actions), between one occurring subsequently to the other and the two happening at the same time, mirrors the original choice of bullets to bite with which we began. The important point as far as I am concerned is to point out that Goldman's view does not 'win' on points about 'inappropriate' consequences for the timing of actions, since his view has problems of its own that in a sense are parallel to the ones that might be brought against one-particularism.

Goldman does not say anything as far as I am aware about the spatial location of action. If his view accepted that actions have a location (I think he is in fact mute on this point), it would seem that a natural consequence of his view would be to say that not only do all the actions on an action chain occur at the same time but also that they occur in the same place. This would allow very many actions to occupy the same smallest zone that contains all of them. That is a somewhat odd consequence, in my view. Hardly a defeater, just a bit odd.

A Note on Non-ergative Action Verbs

I offer a distinctive theory of one-particularism as an attempt to understand the nature of those actions that are nominated by perfect nominals or nominal gerunds formed from ergative verbs. But this theory could therefore only be a part of a complete view about the metaphysics of action, for there are very many actions whose descriptions do not use ergative verbs: push, pull, clap, fold, and many others. I have not tried to offer any account of them.

Ergative verbs offer the best opportunity for two-particularism. In my view, two-particularism doesn't even get off to a plausible start with non-ergative verbs. If two-particularism fails in the case of actions nominated by ergative verbs, it is certainly going to fail for cases of action nominated by non-ergative verbs.

Recall Hyman's and Alvrez' unsuccessful attempts, described in the last chapter, to extend the account given in cases of actions nominated using ergative verbs to cases of actions nominated using non-ergative verbs. There seem to be at least two kinds of cases of non-ergative verbs. First, in 'P ran$_i$,' (P may not even have run a race, he may just have been running), 'to run$_i$' is intransitive. Since it is itself intransitive, the only event on offer is P's running$_i$. There just aren't two particulars to consider. Second, in 'P pushed$_t$ the cart', 'to push' is transitive. If P pushed$_t$ the cart, P's pushing$_t$ of the cart is one particular. What might the other particular be? It is hard to see what proposal could be offered that would lend any plausibility to a two-particulars view for this case either. 'The cart's being pushed$_t$ by P' uses the passive of the transitive verb, 'to push$_t$'. And so the cart's being pushed$_t$ by P IS P's pushing$_t$ of the cart. There is in this case too only one particular on offer.

One of the few places of which I know that raises this problem for actions nominated by non-ergative verbs, lacking an intransitive alternate form, is in Hornsby (2011, 105–127). I have lifted the cart-pushing example from her discussion: 'there seems to be no candidate for an event that her action is causing' (107). 'a cart's being pushed' isn't an event that P is causing, since the cart's being pushed (by P) IS just P's pushing of the cart.

Hornsby rightly restricts a version of (PT) for non-ergative verbs only to an entailment from LHS to RHS (using my terms and with some change in letters): for such verbs: 'P is F_t-ing b…only if P is causing something characteristic of b's being F_i-ed.' I think this is right. It embodies in essence the criticism I made in Chap. 5 of Hyman's and Alvarez' attempt to extend (PT) to non-ergative cases. She says: P is pushing the cart only if P is causing something characteristic of a cart being pushed. But P's causing something characteristic of a cart being pushed does not entail that P is pushing a cart, because P can certainly be causing something characteristic of a cart being pushed (cf the discussion in Chap. 5: something characteristic of swimming or a running) without pushing a cart (cf: without swimming or running). On the other hand, Hornsby also says that P's 'causing the suitcase to be somewhere else than it was is itself an event'. I explain in Chap. 7 why I don't think that that is the case.

For reasons that will became apparent later, it is important to note that 'to cause' is not an ergative verb. It has no intransitive form. 'is or was caused' is merely the passive form of the transitive verb. More on that in the next chapter.

Notes

1. Notice that (PT) isn't the same as the view that an action *is* the causing of an event. (PT) just says that an agent acts iff he causes an event intrinsic to his action. On its own, that does not yet commit to what an action *is*. Nor does it commit to their being such things as causings.
2. Some of the ideas in this section are also expressed by Hornsby (2012, 234).
3. Compare (CA) to this entailment:
    (CB): FROM 'surface s is red' TO: 'surface s is coloured'. (CB) does not of course speak of two distinct kinds of colouring for s. The conclusion of (CB) is merely less informative than the premise, which is why the premise entails the conclusion but the conclusion does not entail the premise. COLOURED is the determinable; Red is a determinate of that determinable. If a surface is red, it does not have two colours: red and coloured. Saying that a surface is coloured is just to say less about its colour status than to say that it is red, or any other determinate colour. So even if 'coloured' is a red-free description of a surface, it does not follow that the surface itself is red-free. 'The colour of the surface' refers to its redness, without that being obvious from the description itself.
4. Davidson, Donald 1967 (1980), 'The Logical Form of Action Sentences'.

5. But not always: sometimes both of the relata really change. If you and I wrestle, the wrestling is a real change in us both.
6. For Cambridge changes in numbers, see Dummett 1973: Chapter 14, 'Abstract Objects.'
7. I have been influenced by Larry Lombard's reply to my earlier account of 'Cambridge events' (Lombard 2003). I trust that I have addressed the second 'main problem' he had about my earlier account.
8. For completeness, it may be worth mentioning that I do think that there is another kind of Cambridge change in which there really are two changes, one real and the other Cambridge. For example, when Socrates drank hemlock and died, Xantippe became a widow. These are two changes, not one, but they pair with one another in an obvious, non-contingent way. The first change is a change in Socrates; the other, a change in Xantippe. The two changes did happen at the same time, but they need not have done so. There could have been a legal convention that a woman only becomes a widow a short time after her husband's death. And the two descriptions certainly involve different constituent properties: being a widow and drinking-hemlock-and-dying. And they occur to different subjects. It seems to me to be important not to conflate these two different kinds of Cambridge changes. There may even be other kinds. But I stress the only kind I am discussing in this chapter is the first kind, in which there is only one change, not two, and such that typically (in the case in which P does not cause the change in himself) one of the relata really changes and the other only Cambridge changes.
9. Helen Steward 2013, 'Processes, Continuants and Individuals'; 2015, 'What is a Continuant?'; 2012, 'Actions as Processes'.
10. My own opinion is that the idea of a process in action theory is often an illegitimate extension from its core application; that core application is well described by Munsat (1969).
11. In the example I gave of an action chain earlier in the chapter, I claimed that the multiplicity was in the actions and not the descriptions. So I believe in that case. Goldman says that the causal generalisation relation (the 'by-relation') is 'asymmetric, irreflexive and transitive' (23). But I am even not committed to thinking that there can be *no* example of an action chain pair in which the same action figures twice, under a different description each time. I remain neutral on this further claim.
12. Donald Davidson, 'Mental Events', reprinted in his *Essays on Actions and Events*, 1970 (1980).

Bibliography

Alvarez, Maria. 1999. Actions and Events: Some Semantical Considerations. *Ratio*, new series XII (3): 213–239.
Bennett, Jonathan. 1973. Shooting, Killing, and Dying. *Canadian Journal of Philosophy* 2: 315–323.
Bratman, M. 1978. Individuation and Action. *Philosophical Studies* 33: 367–375.
Clarke, Randolph. 1995. *Agents, Causes, Events*. Edited by Timothy O'Connor, 201–215. New York: Oxford University Press.
———. 2010. Skilled Activity and the Causal Theory of Action. *Philosophy and Phenomenological Research* 80 (3): 523–550.
Davidson, Donald. 1967 (1980). The Logical Form of Action Sentences, reprinted in his *Essays on Actions and Events*. Oxford: Clarendon Press, 105–118.
———. 1970 (1980). Mental Events, reprinted in his *Essays on Actions and Events*. Oxford: Clarendon Press, 207–225.
Davis, L. 1979. *Theory of Action*. Englewood Cliffs, NJ: Prentice-Hall.
Dummett, Michael. 1973. *Frege: Philosophy of Language*. London: Duckworth.
Geach, Peter. 1969. *God and the Soul*. London: Routledge & Kegan Paul.
———. 1981. *Logic Matters*. Oxford: Basil Blackwell.
Ginet, Carl. 1990. *On Action*. Cambridge: Cambridge University Press.
Goldman, Alvin. 1970. *A Theory of Human Action*. Englewood Cliffs, NJ: Prentice-Hall.
Haack, Susan. 1978. *Philosophy of Logic*. Cambridge: Cambridge University Press.
Hornsby, Jennifer. 1980. *Actions*. London: Routledge & Kegan Paul.
———. 2011. Actions in their Circumstances. In *Essays on Anscombe's Intention*, ed. Anton Ford, Jennifer Hornsby, and Frederick Stoutland, 105–127. Cambridge, MA: Harvard University Press.
———. 2012. Actions and Activities. *Philosophical Issues* 22: 233–245.
Kenny, Anthony. 1963. *Action, Emotion and Will*. London: Routledge & Kegan Paul.
Kim, J. 1973. Causes and Counterfactuals. *Journal of Philosophy* 70 (17): 570–572.
———. 1974. Noncausal Connections. *Nous* 8: 41–52.
———. 1976. "Events as Property Exemplifications". In *Action Theory*, ed. M. Brand and D. Walton, 159–177. Dordrecht: Reidel. Reprinted in *Supervenience and Mind: Selected Philosophical Essays*, Cambridge: Cambridge University Press, 1993, pp. 33–52.

Levin, Beth. 1993. *English Verb Classes and Alternation*. Chicago: University of Chicago Press.

Lombard, Lawrence. 2003. The Cambridge Solution to the Time of a Killing. *Philosophia* 31 (1–2): 93–106.

Mackie, David. 1997. The Individuation of Action. *The Philosophical Quarterly* 47 (186): 38–54.

Munsat, Stanley. 1969. What is a Process? *American Philosophical Quarterly* 6 (1): 79–83.

Parsons, Terence. 1994. *Events in the Semantics of English*. Boston: MIT Press.

Ruben, David-Hillel. 1990 (1992). *Explaining Explanation*. London: Routledge. Second edition (2012), Paradigm Publishers, Boulder, CO.

———. 1995. Mental Overpopulation and the Problem of Action. *Journal of Philosophical Research* 20: 511–524.

———. 2003. *Action & Its Explanation*. Oxford: Oxford University Press.

Steward, Helen. 2012. Actions as Processes. *Philosophical Perspectives* 26 (1): 373–388.

———. 2013. Processes, Continuants, and Individuals. *Mind* 122 (487): 781–812.

———. 2015. What is a Continuant? *Proceedings of the Aristotelian Society, Supplementary Volume* LXXXIX: 109–123.

Wittgenstein, Ludwig. 1953. *Philosophical Investigations*. Translated by G.E.M. Anscombe. New York: Macmillan Company.

7

Causing in Some Way

What's in the Chapter

This chapter will attempt to show that there are no particulars that are causings, no acts or events of causing. Agents cause things to happen (and the imperfective forms: agents are/were causing things to happen), but that does not license inference to causing particulars. (There are of course causes of things, but that is irrelevant. Causings were never thought to be the same as causes. I will elaborate on this in what follows.) Part of the argument in this chapter bears some resemblance to my argument in Chaps. 2, 3 and 4 against alleged trying-particulars.

After some brief remarks about the verb 'to cause', I turn and focus only on its gerund 'causing'. I describe the importance that alleged causings have had in recent action theory. As in the chapters on trying, it is important to show (a) some of the negative consequences of introducing causing-particulars; (b) that there is no need to reify causings in that way; and (c) that there is an alternative to their introduction. Unlike in Chaps. 2, 3 and 4, these three points are more interrelated in this chapter and many of its arguments speak to more than just one of (a)–(c).

The discussion of Descartes is meant to lend credence to (a). Introducing causings as particulars also introduces unwanted and unnecessary problems about their time and location. Some of the linguistic evidence for (b) is non-conclusive but suggestive, especially when I look at alleged uses of 'the causing of e' as a nominal gerund. But I also defang a Davidsonian argument that would show, if sound, that in order to understand cause-sentences with adverbial modifications, we would need particular events or acts of causing. The argument is very similar to the one I constructed about trying-sentences in Chap. 3. I show why these adverbial modifications in such cause-sentences should not be attributed adjectively to any alleged causing particulars.

It is a bit rich of me to call the argument from adverbial qualification of the verb 'to cause' to the reification of causings as particulars a 'Davidsonian argument'. Davidson explicitly rejects the idea of there being any causings: 'It seems clear that it must in general be a mistake to suppose that whenever an event is caused there must be something called a causing ... to say someone made his arm go up (or caused his arm to go up) does not necessarily introduce an event in addition to the arm going up' (Donald Davidson 2004, 102–103). But others have worried about the implications of adverbial qualification of 'to cause', so, without meaning to attribute the argument to Davidson, for the sake of consistency with the terminology of Chap. 3, I will continue to think of such an argument as 'Davidsonian', with apologies to the philosopher himself. One does need to explain why his argument, assuming that it works for the verbs he discusses, like 'to butter', fails for the case of 'to cause'. The 'Davidsonian' argument works no better in the case of cause-sentences than it does in the case of trying-sentences.

As for (c), the argument is that there is no work that causing-particulars could do that isn't done either by the verbal gerund of 'to cause', or by 'the/a cause' as a noun, both of which survive intact after the excision of both alleged causing particulars and the nominal gerund of 'to cause'. My claim, then, is that, sentences that purport to speak of causings as particulars are equivalent to sentences which eliminate that occurrence and use only the verb, 'to cause', or 'causing' as a verbal gerund. Further, those latter sentences with the verb or verbal gerund do not themselves require quantifying over any causing particulars in turn.

There is however one adverbial modification that needs special examination: 'with instrument i'. Consider a sentence like: 'P caused the door to open$_i$ with a crowbar.' It's true that the sentence is somewhat stilted as a sentence of English, but the problem I address only arises if there are such causing sentences that use instrumentals in this way. If you do not think there are any such sentences, the problem I am confronting vanishes. But how could there fail to be such a meaningful sentence, however stilted? The left-to-right inference in (PT) is committed to there being such a sentence as, 'P caused the door to open$_i$' on the RHS. Adding the phrase, 'with a crowbar' surely can't deprive an otherwise perfectly good sentence of any sense.

I have already said in the Appendix to Chap. 5 that (PT) is formulated in such a way that does not address the general question of how to recapture on RHS the adverbial information embedded on the LHS of (PT). But we now need to address the question of the adverbially qualified inference for the specific case of instrumental qualification: does (1) 'P opened$_t$ the door with a crowbar' imply (2) 'P caused the door to open$_i$ with a crowbar'? If so, it seems that (2) attributes 'with a crowbar' either to an opening$_i$ or to *a* causing. What other options might there be? The second option would give us causing particulars.

According to a rule of Terence Parsons', the first option is ruled out. Instrumentals must be attributed to actions, not events, and so, extrapolating this to the case of causing something, one seems to need an act of causing to which the instrumental could be attributed. I look at an 'ingenious' solution due to Maria Alvarez that accepts that rule, but would still not require any quantification over causings. I then consider a reply to her by Erasmus Mayr that shows that her solution will not work. I end by showing how one-particularism solves the problem, but at the cost of denying Parsons' rule. But I undercut the plausibility of that rule by examining the relation between instrumentality and agency.

Is 'Cause' an Action Verb?

This chapter is about causing. It is not about action, unless you think that 'to cause' (as in 'P caused e' or 'P caused the fact that e') is itself an action verb. There are at least two ways in which 'cause' might count as an action verb. (a) First, the verb 'cause' might represent a general concept, such that verbs like 'close', 'open' 'cut', 'bend', 'pull', 'ring', and so on represent specific instances of it. So, for example, on this first option, 'cause', in 'P's causing$_t$ b to V_i' (P causing the door to open), might be a general action verb, and 'open', in 'P's V_t-ing b' (P's opening$_t$ the door), might be a more specific action verb, applicable in one specific case of someone's causing something.

It might be thought that the relation between 'to cause' and specific action verbs could be understood as the determinable-determinate relation. One might think that just as something is coloured insofar as it is either red, or blue, or ... etc., so too the verb 'to cause' is an action verb just insofar as the causing is a case of someone opening or closing or pushing or pulling, etc., something.

I want to express a doubt about whether that latter relation could be an appropriate way in which to understand the relation between a generic verb 'to cause' and specific action verbs, on proposal (a). There are many differences between the general-specific and the determinable-determinate relations, but here is one that applies specifically to our case: colour is a determinable; specific colours are its determinates and they collectively exhaust what it is to be coloured. But as we have seen in Chap. 5, actions don't exhaust cases of causing something; there are instances in which an agent causes some outcome but has not acted, because the event he causes is not an event intrinsic to any action he does, for one reason or another. So, to revert to the picture at the end of Chap. 5, the large circle in the Venn diagram includes all cases of someone's causing something, so it contains his actions but also instances of that agent's causing something but in which he does not act. No determinable can be like that. There is no conjunctive determinable, for example, of sounds & colours, such that specific colours are amongst its determinates. Similarly, there can't be a determinable, someone causing something, some of whose determinates are actions and some not.

But, if we dismiss the idea that the determinable-determinate relation might help us understand in what way 'to cause' is also an action verb, a more promising line of thought is that 'cause' nominates a general action type and specific action verbs nominate specific action types that are instances of the more general type. Anscombe, in a difficult but very suggestive passage, says that 'the word "cause" is highly general' (Anscombe 1981, 137). The suggestion is that in learning a language, 'we learned the linguistic representation and application of a host of causal concepts… Very many of them were represented by transitive and other verbs of action.' That is 'how we come to our primary knowledge of causality'. Perhaps it was something like (a) that she had in mind.

(b) Second, 'cause' might just be an action verb like others, alongside them as it were. 'Cause' might be an action verb on its own, on a par as it were with other action verbs and not a more general category of action verb to which they all belong as specific instances. That is perhaps less plausible, insofar as it suggests that when P opens$_t$ the door, for instance, he *also* causes the door to open$_i$, so that he does thereby two actions, an opening$_t$ and a causing. That would be pretty extravagant.

'Cause' might not, of course, be an action verb at all. If you think that sentences about agent causation are elliptical and when expanded are sentences about event causation, and since in general in sentences with the form 'event e caused event f', 'cause' is not an action verb (that assertion depends also on whether or not all causal sentences require an agent, and I have already said something about that and will say much more in what follows), then 'cause' is not an action verb in sentences like 'P caused e' either. In 'P opened$_t$ the door', 'open$_t$' is an action verb. Even if 'P opened$_t$ the door' implies 'P caused the door to open$_i$', it does not follow that 'to cause' is an action verb just because 'to open$_t$' is.

Even those who think that such agent causal sentences are not elliptical for event causal sentences typically stress the univocality of 'cause' in both event and agent contexts. So if 'cause' is not an action verb in one sort of context, it shouldn't be an action verb in the other either, or anyway so one might think. A plausible view is that 'cause' should be an action verb in all its uses, or never be an action verb in any of its uses. I can see no reason for thinking that 'cause' bears somewhat different senses in event causation and in agent causation contexts. On the other hand, if you think that all it means to say that the verb 'to cause' is an action verb in contexts such as 'P caused…' is that the verb takes an agent in subject position in those contexts, and does not do so in event causation contexts, then the view that 'cause' is an action verb in such contexts is trivially true.

Even if 'to cause' is an action verb, it is not an ergative verb so has no intransitive form ('was caused' is merely the passive voice). This is important, because if it were ergative and the LHS-to-RHS inference in (PT) applied to it, threat of a regress might loom, an issue that I will discuss in Chap. 8.

Whether or not you think that 'cause' is an action verb, the goal of this chapter is to look at its *gerunds*: I want to know if there are any causings.

Some Remarks on the Verb 'To Cause'

I want to make another brief detour before I begin the discussion of my topic. I think it will be helpful to get clear on the way in which the verb, 'to cause', is and is not subject to the imperfectivity paradox, and is or is not telic, because the gerund of 'to cause' will inherit some of those features from the verb, and the gerund will be a main focus in what follows. I have already said that it is not an ergative verb.

Is 'to cause' a telic verb and is it subject to the imperfective paradox? The same answer should work whether the subject of 'to cause' is an agent or an event. I won't consider cases in which an agent causes a fact, but I don't think that that alternative formulation will make any difference to my conclusions. To recap again the imperfective paradox:

(1) P was pushing the cart $\Rightarrow$ P pushed the cart.
(2) P was opening the door $\Rightarrow$/P opened the door.

The first sentence is not subject to the paradox; the second is. I won't adjust the sentences for various tenses.

Is 'to cause' subject to the paradox? Consider these two sentences, which I will assume are representative if but only if the object of 'cause' is a nominal gerund of a second verb (I agree that these sentences are rather far from ordinary usage, but they seem to me to be perfectly intelligible):

(3) P was causing the pushing of the cart⇒Pcaused the pushing of the cart.

It is perhaps unsurprising that (3) is true, since 'push' is not subject to the paradox. P caused the pushing for as long as he was causing it. If it is true that he was causing the pushing from t to t*, he caused its pushing between those times too. 'Cause', when followed by a verb not subject to the paradox, is not subject to the paradox either.

But consider a verb that is subject to the paradox: 'open'.

(4) P was causing the opening of the door⇒P caused the opening of the door.

(4) is also true, even though 'open' is subject to the paradox. P caused the opening of the door even if the door never finally opened; he caused it for as long as the door was opening. In both these instances, (3) and (4), 'cause' is not subject to the paradox. Even in (4), like in (3), P caused the opening of the door for as long as he was causing it.

One might say: 'It seems fine to say that someone can be causing something that he never caused, so it doesn't follow that he caused it from the fact that he was causing it'. But that thought treads on an ambiguity in 'something he never caused'. It's one thing to cause the opening of the door, but quite another to cause the door to open (which I have not been considering).

Contrast (4) with (5):

(5) P was causing the opening of the door⇒/P caused the door to open.

In that formulation, 'cause' does seem subject to the paradox, because 'caused the door to open' ('noun-to-verb') assumes that the door did open, whereas 'was causing the opening of the door' does not. P could have been causing the opening of the door (and hence could have caused the opening of the door) without ever having finally caused the door to open. An open door may have never come to be.

Finally consider cases in which the object of 'cause' is the perfect or derived nominal of a second verb rather than a nominal gerund of a second verb: 'explode' or 'close' ('open' has no perfect nominal):

(6) P was causing the dynamite's explosion? P caused the dynamite's explosion.
(6*) P was causing the door's closure? P caused the door's closure.

The meaning of the antecedent of (6) and (6*) is somewhat strained, but suppose they are true. Recalling the distinction between a process and product reading for a perfect or derived nominal from Chaps. 3 and 6, and assuming that the derived nominal gets the *same* reading in both antecedent and consequent, then I think that neither (6) nor (6*) is subject to the paradox. If 'explosion' and 'closure' are taken in the product sense, then both antecedent and consequent assume that the door was closed and the explosion occurred, so the entailment holds. If P was causing the product, he caused the product. If 'explosion' and 'closure' are taken in the process sense, the entailment also holds, because if P was causing the process, he caused the process, even if no final result occurred.

(3), (4), (6) and (6*) demonstrate that 'to cause' is not subject to the paradox, whether or not the verb buried in the nominal gerund following 'was/is causing' is subject to it and whether or not the derived nominal following 'was/is causing' receives a process or product reading (assuming only that the reading is consistent in antecedent and consequent). However, 'cause' is subject to the paradox, when 'was/is causing' is followed by the 'b to V_i' (the 'noun-to-verb') form.

Is 'cause' telic? Like 'try', I think it is telic when followed by a gerund made from a telic verb, and atelic when it is followed by a gerund made from an atelic verb. Just use the 'keep on' test. Just as P can keep on pushing the cart *sine die*, he can keep on causing the pushing of it *sine die*, throughout the period of time in which he is pushing it. But if P is opening the door, he can't keep on causing its opening once it is opened. When opened, the opening of the door has to have stopped, and so too does P's causing the opening of it.

Causing and Action Theory

Talk of causing seems to have become something of a fashion in some quarters of action theory. We saw this already in Chaps. 5 and 6. Causation more generally in action theory is of course itself hardly new. On the standard theory, an action is an event caused in the right way by the right things. On agent causalist theory, an agent acts when that agent causes an event. But what is perhaps newer is the idea of a causing (the gerund formed from the verb in imperfective aspect): that if an agent causes, or is/was causing, an event, there is a causing of that event by the agent. We need to think about what must be true in order for agents to cause an event. Must there be causings of events, particular causings, when (or if) agents cause events?

Traditionally, it was agreed that causation was a relation, although there was disagreement about what the relata of that relation were: events, agents, tropes, and facts have all been candidates.[1] (I have taken the view that both facts and events can figure as the second relatum of the causal relation.) Relations have instances, but instances of relations are not particulars. For example, an instance of the relation, x loves y, might be Othello loving Desdemona, which is a state of affairs (or a trope, but clarifying the metaphysics of instances is not my topic here).

However, a survey of the agent causalist literature puts 'a causing' (or a close cognate, like 'a producing' or 'a making', and their plurals) in the mouths of many. Since the indefinite or definite article precedes 'causing', presumably it purports to be a particular of some sort. Whatever a causing is meant to be, it certainly does not sound like a relation or an instance of a relation. Chisholm, Taylor, and von Wright, all used 'a causing' as a central idea in their philosophy of action some time ago. Recent examples include (in no significant order): Steward, Mayr, Pietroski, O'Connor, Hyman, and Alvarez. How are we meant to get from the thought that cause is a relation to causings as particulars, if that is what they are?

As we saw above, it is beyond doubt that the verb 'to cause' can occur in imperfective aspect, as in 'P is (or was) causing event e'. 'Paul was causing a lot of trouble. So he was expelled.' It is similarly beyond doubt that there are many examples of sentences which use 'causing' as a verbal gerund: 'Paul's causing trouble was the reason for his expulsion'. But there is no derived nominal for the verb 'cause' that works like 'a betrayal' for 'betraying'. 'Betrayal' (as a derived nominal: 'he witnessed Quisling's betrayal') can refer either to the product or upshot of an act of betraying or to the process of betraying; a cause is neither the same as a process of causing nor the product or upshot of causing, so 'a cause' is not a derived nominal, and is not related to 'to cause' in the way in which 'a betrayal' is related to 'to betray'.

Bennett's and Alexiadou's distinction between the perfect (or derived) nominal, the nominal gerund, and the verbal gerund in Chap. 3, concluded that only the perfect nominals and nominal gerunds can give us particulars. The verbal gerund does not. If there can be facts that use the verbal gerund and if facts are particulars, then there is an indirect sense in which one might say that verbal gerunds have a connection with particulars. But verbal gerunds themselves do not refer, and a fortiori do not refer to particulars.

Are there uses of 'causing' as a nominal gerund? The use of 'causing' as a verbal gerund (which we saw in the case of naughty Paul, above) and its alleged use as a nominal gerund are not always kept distinct. As one example from many, in discussing Richard Taylor, Tim O'Connor says: '… there are factors producing precisely the event that is my causing e…' (O'Connor, P&C, 52:); 'My directly causing events internal to myself is my activity par excellence' (72, fn. 11) (n.b., there is no 'of' in either of these two quotations). At other times he says that 'Causal relations are the producings of events…' (77). These are mere slips and, as far as I can tell, they have no untoward substantive consequences for O'Connor's views, but they are an indication of a certain widespread looseness in dealing with this important distinction between nominal and verbal gerunds, especially in application to 'cause'.

I have some doubts whether there is any genuine use of 'causing' or its close cognates as a nominal gerund. (Sure, we can say that his new clothes were the making of Henry, in his ongoing attempt to impress Henrietta, but 'making' in that use does not mean just 'causing'. His new clothes did not bring him into existence or create *him*.) Kent Bach (1980, 119) noticed 'that expressions of the form 'A's bringing about e', as well as [verbal] gerundive forms of action verbs generally, do not refer', but his observation seems to have gone unnoticed. Indeed, Bach's argument that actions are not events rests on saying that 'an action is performed if and only if someone has brought about an event' (Bach 1980, 119), and on construing 'someone's bringing about an event' as a verbal gerund which does not function as a referring term.[2] Causings are instances of a relation and 'instances are not individuals and not subject to quantification' (Bach, 119).[3]

Ralf Stoecker suggested the same idea too: 'actions are causings...' (Stoecker 1993, 285), '... the action is not the event but the causing [?] of the event. And from an ontological point of view that is not enough to survive' (286). (My question mark is meant to query how anything could both be THE causing of an event and there is no such thing.) However, '... causings are not events... and, moreover, since causings are not entities at all, neither are... actions-there are no killings, destroyings, insultings, etc.' (282). Stoecker is more explicit than Bach in accepting the consequence that there are no actions. Davidson, in his reply to Stoecker, says that 'This thesis [that there are no actions] seems to me very hard to defend...' (Stoecker 1993, 288). Stoecker might have strengthened his case if he had noticed that the 'causing' he needs is only in the form of the verbal gerund and that he need not have inserted 'the' or 'of' in a claim that says what he wants to say: perhaps, 'for a person to act is for him to cause an event'. Davidson goes on to say that 'defending [the thesis] would require, among other things, rethinking the semantics of a large number of sentences', and this is exactly what Maria Alvarez does, whose views I will explain later in the chapter. With Stoecker and Bach, we have two examples of philosophers who deny that there are any causing particulars. I agree. But unlike these authors, I would not let the scepticism spread from causings to actions. I agree with Bach and Stoecker about no-causing-particulars, I don't agree with them about no-action-particulars, and so I will want to break the link they (and Alvarez) make between no-causing-particulars and (hence) no-action-particulars.

I suppose that the question is this: is there anything that is said by '... causing of ...' as a supposed nominal gerund that cannot be captured equally well by 'causing...' as a verbal gerund, or by the noun, 'cause...'? The question is not meant to be rhetorical; it is a challenge to find bona fide cases of 'causing' as a nominal gerund that supposedly make reference to a particular, and that can't be explained less awkwardly by the verbal gerund or by 'cause' as a noun. If there were a nominal gerund of 'causing', we should be able to pluralise and count causings. We would need to quantify over them and find criteria for their numerical and qualitative identity. In brief, we would need to take their status as particulars seriously. In that case, 'How many causings of death were there?' would make sense. To my ear, that is just to ask how many ways there were in which to die. If there are causing particulars, a host of further questions arise about them: Do they have physical location; do they occur at a time? The same time and location as that of what they are the causings of, or of what or whom they are causings by? Are they mereological simples or do they have parts? If they have parts, what parts do they have? The literature addressing these issues is extensive, but I think fundamentally misguided. My view makes the answering of these questions unnecessary.

In natural science and in ordinary speech, we can talk of electrical storms causing fires, radioactive activity causing Geiger counters to click, and so on. All of these employ 'causing' as a verbal gerund. No one in general philosophy, or in the philosophy of science, in discussing any issue that involves event causation, as far as I am aware, has ever felt the need to use a nominal gerund and hence to speak of *causings* as particulars. The use of an allegedly nominal gerund deriving from 'to cause' seems quite alien to the discourse of the philosophy of science, as it reflects on the metaphysics implied by scientific discourse. Importing causings as particulars from the use of the alleged nominal gerund, the causing of, seems to have been reserved for agent causalists and perhaps for others writing in action theory. If there were such a legitimate use of the nominal gerund, one might have expected it to appear not just in action theory but in explications of event causation too, or even in the philosophy of natural science. Why only in the philosophy of action, especially since it is typically alleged that the fundamental idea of a cause is the same for both event causation and agent causation uses? If there were causing particulars assumed by agent causal sentences, why aren't causing particulars assumed by all event causal sentences?

Indeed, a case can be made for saying that an unspoken and untheorised use of causing of, as a nominal gerund, might be what lay behind Descartes' mistake about the pineal gland. To put it simply, Descartes, as a dualist interactionist, thought that there are mental occurrences and physical occurrences, and tokens of each can cause tokens of the other. Mental occurrences can be dated but are not spatial; physical occurrences can be placed both in time and physical space. But then Descartes was asked where their causal interaction takes place. He gave an answer: the pineal gland. Even assuming for a moment the truth of Cartesian substance dualism, did he just give the wrong place for where their interaction occurs? I think he just should have replied that the question was ill formed, given his interactionism.

It may be that Descartes was thinking, quite unconsciously, that the causing of the physical token by the mental token was a particular, additional to the mental and physical token occurrences that are the causes and effects, and, as such, must itself have a spatial and temporal location of its own. But if this was the thought that propelled his reply, it is surely based on an error. Once one has given the time at which the mental occurrence happens, and the temporal and spatial location of the physical token, there just are no more timings or placings of a further particular to be given. Think of the various theories of causation: the covering law theory, the property determination theory, a probabilistic account, and the counterfactual dependence theory. None of these leaves any room for an additional place and time for a causing, in addition to whatever places and times are given to the relata of the causation relation. None assumes causing particulars, although they might use 'causing' as a verbal gerund.

An Argument for Causings?

My discussion thus far is not meant to be conclusive, only suggestive. I have shared my doubts about the existence of an alleged nominal gerund of 'cause', and therefore about causings as particulars, and I have found a few allies, but I do not take it that I have demonstrated conclusively that there is no legitimate nominal gerund for 'cause'. Linguistic intuitions vary; perhaps some readers will think of some legitimate use for 'the causing of the tides', etc. that isn't just the same as 'causing the tides' or 'the cause of the tides'.[4]

Perhaps we could strengthen the case for causing particulars in the following way. Is there a Davidsonian style argument (remember: however, an argument certainly not to be attributed to him) for the existence of causing particulars? We saw in Chap. 3 that there are no valid grounds for thinking that there were adverbial modifications of 'try to' that require acts of trying modified by the corresponding adjective. How do matters stand with 'Person P caused… G-ly'? Do we need particular causings that have some property, G, to explain any sentences about causing in some way, causing G-ly? Does 'P caused e G-ly' entail that there was a causing, of e, and it was G?

'Cause' is often followed by a perfect nominal when there is one ('P caused the explosion of the dynamite') or a nominal gerund ('P caused the dynamite's exploding'), or with the 'object-to-verb' form ('P caused the dynamite to explode'). As with 'try', so too with 'cause', we have a second verb or gerund or a derived nominal, all of which are available for modification rather than 'cause', and the question is whether any adverbial modifications in the cause-sentence ('G-ly') must be attributed to the verb, 'to cause', rather than either attach to the second verb that follows 'cause', in whatever form it takes, or perhaps attach sometimes to the agent.

Some adverbial qualifications in cause-sentences are by phrase or sentence adverbs. 'P cleverly caused the window to open' is 'It was clever of P to cause the window to open.' 'P probably caused the opening of the door' is 'It is probable that P caused the door to open.' But what can we make of the genuine cases of mode adverbs in cause-sentences? Just as we saw in the case of 'trying', in many cases it is obvious that the adverbial modification attaches, not to 'cause' or 'causing', but to that second verb or gerund: 'P caused the flood to stop abruptly' is most naturally construed as attributing the abruptness to the flood's stopping. But there is another possible reading of 'P caused the flood to stop abruptly'. Let me start by repeating and slightly amending a paragraph from Chap. 3 (after all, it was so long ago that you read it), by substituting in it 'cause' for 'try':

> Sometimes it does not seem appropriate to allow the adverbial qualification to be of the explicit verb inside the context governed by 'cause'. Consider for example 'P caused the flood to stop abruptly'. (And assume that it was

not P himself who was abrupt.) The stopping might not have been abrupt at all. The stopping itself might have been quite gradual. Many mode adverbial qualifications in cause-sentences, 'in a G-ish manner', really attribute a property to some implicit event on the causal chain of events, or to some action on the action chain by which the agent accomplished what he aimed to do, prior to the explicit effect, and not to the effect itself, let alone to some alleged act or event of causing. For example, suppose P caused the flood to stop abruptly. If as a matter of fact, he caused the flood to stop by turning the tap, it was certainly not an alleged causing and might not have been the stopping that was abrupt but rather the turning. And if neither his stopping nor his turning was abrupt, nor any other event on the causal chain nor any other action on the action chain, leading from the agent to the effect, nor the agent himself, it is hard to see what saying that some alleged act of causing was abrupt could mean. It is here that our metaphysical intuitions about the bearers of properties kick in: how could an act of causing, if there were such a thing, have the property of being abrupt? What could it mean to attribute a property to such an alleged act, if neither what the agent finally caused, nor any of the intermediate links in the causal chain leading to that effect, nor the agent himself, had that property?

We saw in the case of trying that there were three sorts of cases that were recalcitrant to the treatment above: (1) adverbs of speed, (2) temporal, and (3) spatial location. How do they fare with causing? (1) I think that a prima facie candidate for adverbial modification of '… causes…', rather than any other of the options I have mentioned, are adverbs of speed. In Chap. 3, I gave a story about Henry and Henrietta, so that the door's opening was slow but Henry's causing was quick. (Henry, it will be remembered, was a slowcoach as well, so 'quick' cannot be construed as a phrase adverb either.) So I do think there can be occasions when it *seems* that we want to attribute some degree of speed to the causing, and not to the event caused, nor to an event by which that event was caused, nor to any intermediate event on the causal chain, nor to the agent. So what to do?

At the level of grammatical acceptability, 'Slow-off-the-mark Henry quickly caused the door to open slowly' is fine, albeit a bit of a mouthful. But the question is whether we are really attributing a property to a causing in such a sentence. I will argue that we never do attribute speed to something called a causing, in the same way in which we might attribute speed to a dance for example (recall the example from before: jitterbugs are fast dances; foxtrots are slow dances). In case you think you have heard this before, you have. My argument here closely parallels the one I gave for speed adverbs in trying-sentences.

John Morreall is adamant that 'Causing is not an action ...causing is not quick or slow, because it is not an action' (Morreall, 516); '...causing is not an action ... Saying that X caused Y or that X was the cause of Y is not the description of an action, but the description of the connection between one action, event, or state of affairs and another ... because cause points to the connection between actions and events, and is not a description of a single action, John cannot cause slowly...Causal relations do not have speed' (Morreall 1976, 517).

I agree with Morreall's basic intuition, but we do need to account for sentences like 'Slow-off-the-mark Henry quickly caused the door to open slowly', which might sometimes be true. Morreall's diagnosis is correct: '...[Causation is] the description of the connection between one action, event, or state of affairs and another...', and so to say that someone caused something slowly or quickly is to say something about that 'connection'.

According to my account of adverbs of speed in Chap. 3, they have two senses or uses: (a) an intrinsic use and (b) a temporal relational use. To say that P quickly caused the slow opening of the door (where the 'quickly' tells us something about the speed at which he caused it to open slowly, which is the temporal relational rather than the intrinsic use of 'quickly') is to say that there was a relatively short period of time between some unspecified event which will be understood in the context (it's the event that occurred, say at t, that triggered him into starting the door opening process), and the commencement of the slow process of the door's opening (say at t*).

On my account, 'a quick causing' is in reality an adjective of a pair of events, {c,e}, 'c caused e and c and e are close in time'. Adverbs of speed in their temporal relational use don't attribute properties to particulars (unless you count time as a particular). They mark the relative temporal distance between the times of two or more events or actions. There will be obvious adjustments for the imperfective of 'to cause', as well as when 'door-to-open' is substituted for 'the opening of the door'.

(2) and (3): What of adverbs of place and time? 'P caused b to V_i in place p at time t' assigns a place and time either to where P was, or to where b's V_i-ing occurred, or to some event in the causal or action chain that P initiated in order for b to V_i, or to the spatial or temporal extension occupied by some or all of the events on one of those chains up to and including the time and place at which b V_i-ed, if b finally does V_i.

Instrumentals

The strategy so far is to attach the adverbial qualification, 'G-ly', in sentences of the form, 'P caused b to V_i G-ly' to the event, b's V_i-ing, as an adjective, 'G'. Or if not to that event, to some other event or action in the chain of actions that P did or chain of events that P brought about, in order to bring about b's V_i-ing, or perhaps even as a phrase adverb attributable to P himself, or to the time between two events on the causal chain leading to b's starting to V_i or to b's completed V-ing$_i$. In this way, we hoped to avoid attaching 'G-ly' to 'cause', and thereby obviating the need for causing particulars that are G. Maria Alvarez and John Hyman (but I focus mainly on her views in what follows, as her 1999 paper is the more comprehensive treatment of the issue) think that (1) all actions *are* causings of events, the last of which are not themselves actions but the results (intrinsic events) of actions (this is meant, I think, to be an analysis in the traditional sense), (2) that actions or causings are not themselves events; (3) and that no quantification is required over actions (and hence not over causings) but only over the events caused by the agent (this is part of Alvarez' proposal on logical form).

As for (1) and (2): 'to act is to cause or bring about an event; but an action, a causing of an event, is not itself an event'. The view isn't just that if P acts, it follows that P causes a certain event (that is the left-to-right inference of (PT), which I accept). (1) is the view that if P acts, P's action is *a* causing, a causing that is identical to P's action. As she says, 'an action, a causing of an event by one or more agents…' (238); 'actions are the causings of these events' (217); 'an action is a causing of an event'

(217, 218). Neither actions, nor the causings which those actions are, are events; 'an action, a causing of an event, is not itself an event' (218).

As for (3): 'quantification over the actions is redundant in logical paraphrases of action sentence' (Alvarez 1999, 218). '... quantification over actions...[is] redundant' (218). Or, in the Alvarez and Hyman joint article (1998): they require 'quantification over events, but not over actions themselves' (234, fn. 34). So she (indeed, they) believe that only event results require quantification; neither actions nor causings are subjects of quantification.

I agree with Alvarez that no quantification is required over causings. I don't of course agree with her about actions not requiring quantification. I think that there are actions but no causings, which is consistent since I don't think that actions *are* causings. But what we agree about is this: no quantification over causings is required. And it is that which will be the sole question on which I focus in the remainder of the chapter.

Unlike Stoecker for example, Alvarez does not actually say that there are no actions and no causings, because she does not thinking that quantification is the test for ontological commitment. I do think that it is (or anyway, I don't have a better suggestion to make) and so I will express her view in this way, not relying on her own way of expressing her ontological views. If we take the criterion of ontological commitment to something's being a particular to be the willingness to make it the subject of quantification (plus other considerations, like pluralisation, being countable, and criteria of identity),[5] there are, strictly speaking, neither actions nor causings to which she is ontologically committed.

Unlike her, I accept that 'a theory is committed to those and only those entities to which bound variables of the theory must be of referring in order that the affirmations made in the theory are true.... We look to bound variables in connection with an ontology not in order to know what there is, but in order to know what a given remark or doctrine... says there is' (Quine 1961, 13–15). Alvarez' positive account of causing, at least in this article, is this: '... to act is to exercise a causal power... that the exercise of a causal power is not itself an event; and that an action is, therefore, a causing of an event ... but it is not an event' (1999, 238). It seems to me that it could be true that to act is to exercise a causal power, without believing that there is something called '*an* exercise of a causal power'. This is just what I have been arguing with regard to trying-sentence and causing-sentences. Alvarez accepts the legitimacy of 'causings', 'actions', 'exercises' (all pluralisations), and of 'the causing', 'the action', 'the exercise' (with the definite and indefinite article), and makes identity claims about actions and causings, and I find it hard to understand any of this without some sort of ontic commitment to some sort of particulars being involved. But once we have particulars, what point is there to denying quantification over them?

However, whatever agreement or disagreement there is between us aside, I don't think that she succeeds in showing that quantification is not required over causings. I will offer my own alternative account that supports that view. Since I do not accept (1) above, I will often change her (and Erasmus Mayr's) examples to ones that are about cause-sentences rather than action sentences. I want to stress once again at the outset that I am not interested in this chapter in her account of action sentences more generally, given that I do not accept (1). But I am very interested in what she might say about cause-sentences, since I agree with her (and Bach and Stoecker) about that. No causings. It isn't always easy to separate out what Alvarez wants to say about causing from her view about action, because she presents them as a package. But let's see if I can do so.

If one is trying to show that there are no causing particulars, instrumental adverbs offer a crucial difficulty. As Alvarez says, '… according to [Terence] Parsons, instrumental modifiers cannot be treated in this way [that all adverbial modifiers are predicates of events which are the results of action] [for me, the effects of causings], and none are predicates of actions [for me, causings]…Parsons views implied that (at least) one kind of modifier requires quantification over actions [for me, causings] because it tells us with what instrument an action [for me, a causing] is performed' (Alvarez 1999, 230, 232). If Parsons is right, instrumental adverbial qualification cannot be dealt with as I was trying to do above. On Parson's view, the instrumental adverbs do not qualify the results of action [for me, the results of causings] but qualify the actions themselves [for me, the causings]. If Parson's view is right, it would follow that there must be actions [for me, causing particulars] that are instrumentality qualified. I have, in the above sentences, including the quotation from Alvarez, replaced 'action' by 'causing' in line with the issues I want to address in what follows. So let's call this 'Parson's Rule':

> (PR) Instrumental modifiers are predicates of actions [causings], and not predicates of the events that are the results of those actions [the results of those causings].

'With-instrument i' would thus be construed as a dyadic relation, with one of the relata specified; it attributes the with-relation to the ordered pair, some particular (to be determined) and some instrument i. So, now switching from 'action' to 'causing', the thought is that one must attribute the relational predicate, '_with-instrument_' to a causing and an instrument, rather than to the event result of the causing and an instrument, and so there must be a causing that stands in that relation to some instrument.

I have chosen to represent the instrumental relation as the with-instrument relation: x with-instrument y, where the 'y'-slot is filled by the name of a particular instrument, say 'i'. (What fills the 'x'-slot? That is the subject matter of what follows.) Another candidate might be: 'by', but since the 'by' in an instrumental use could easily be conflated with the 'by' in the idea that one action can be done by doing another, I have selected 'with-instrument' as the choice with the least baggage for the discussion of instrumentality. Obviously, 'with' itself does not always signify instrumentality. 'He opened the door with a heavy heart' does not mean that his heavy heart was any type of instrument. 'Henry did it with Henrietta' certainly does not always mean, one hopes, that Henry used Henrietta as an instrument. It is sometimes an indicator of joint agency (more on that later). That is why I have called the relation, the with-instrument relation, and not just the with-relation.

It will be best to deal with cases in which the second verb is an ergative verb, which I think makes intuitions clearer. I start from the assumption, defended above, that there are some sentences about causing an event that contain instrumentals: (a) 'P caused the opening$_i$ of the door with his crowbar.' Given that there are some sentences of that sort (whatever view we might take about the relation between action and causing), we want to understand how those sentences work and whether we can avoid quantifying over causings: (b) 'There was a causing of the opening$_i$ of the door by P, and it (the causing) was with his crowbar.' (b) quantifies over a causing. Must we accept (b) as providing the correct logical form of (a)? (PR) says that (b), or something in the same spirit, provides the correct logical form for (a), and in particular (b) shows that the instrumental qualification amounts to the attribution of a dyadic relation, applying to a causing and to an instrument, and not to an event (say, the opening$_i$) that is the result of the causing and to an instrument. So, on (b), there are causings.

What is the reason that event results cannot take instrumental qualification, and that only actions (or causings) can? On (PR), P's opening$_t$ of the door can stand in the dyadic with-instrument relation to the crowbar (or less promisingly, the monadic property of being with-a-crowbar can be a property of P's opening$_t$ of the door), but (2) the opening$_i$ of the door cannot stand in such a relation (or have such a property). As a matter of linguistic awkwardness, the sentence, 'P's opening$_t$ of the door stands in the with-instrument relation to the crowbar' is already pretty awkward; I'm not sure that the sentence, 'the opening$_i$ of the door stands in the with-instrument relation to the crowbar' is any worse on the score of awkwardness.

Alvarez' Ingenious Solution

Maria Alvarez, not wishing to import causings into her ontology, has argued for an ingenious solution to the problem posed by (PR) in her proposals for the logical form of action sentences.

'I propose that we use "Cause" as an operator to form predicates of the results of action from modifiers; hence modifiers will be formalized by means of an n-place predicate "Cause+preposition/adverb", depending on the kind of modifier' (231). Her idea is to accept (PR), that instrumental adverbs would only be attributable to actions (or causings), but to argue that we don't need such instrumental adverbs at all, in giving the logical form of sentences like 'he caused e with instrument i.'[6]

On her view, as I understand it, by using the 'cause'-operator, what can be done is to create non-instrumental predicates from instrumental adverbs, predicates that *can* be attributed to the results of actions (or the results of causings), consistently with (PR). Parson's predicate, 'was (done) with y' is a predicate applicable to actions (or for me, causings). Her predicate, 'was caused with y', is a predicate applicable to the results of actions. (She illustrates her proposal with adverbs of place and speed, but I will use instrumental adverbs, since they provide, according to Parsons, the recalcitrant cases for avoiding causings).

As I have said, I will only deal with her treatment of causing an event and not of action more generally. Nor will I deal with her examples such as 'I unlocked my car with my key-ring by pressing the button' because any additional problem with this sort of sentence only arise on the assumption that P's unlocking his car=P's pressing the button, so that 'by' cannot be construed as a relation that relates two distinct actions. I have disputed this austere theory of act individuation in Chap. 6, so the problem can't be raised in that form for me. (Alvarez does not say that she holds this austere theory either. But she means, I think, only to point out, with this example, what Davidsonians might have to give up in order to respond to some of the issues she raises).

On her account, the logical form[7] of 'P opened$_t$ the door with a crowbar' would be: 'There was an event, x, such that x was an opening$_i$, and such that the door was the patient and P was the agent, and the relational property of being-caused-with was true of the ordered pair, the event x and the crowbar.' Causation, via the 'Cause'-operator, becomes part of the relational predicate, which is applied to the event, the opening$_i$ of the door and the instrument, in this case, the crowbar. Her thought is this: accepting as she does (PR), the with-relation cannot be attributed to the opening$_i$, because instrumentals cannot be attributed to events, only to actions and causings. We don't want quantification over causings (or actions). However, the relational predicate, 'caused-with', which is not itself an instrumental, at least not in the same sense as 'with a crowbar' is, although formed from one, *can* be attributed to events. Attributing the non-instrumental caused-with relation to an opening$_i$ of a door and an instrument does not make the opening into an opening$_t$. It remains an opening$_i$. (I'm deliberately not yet 'translating' her view, or Mayr's subsequent critique, into its one-particularist counterpart version.)

What then would the logical form of that cause-sentence look like? On her account, the logical form of the cause-sentence would look exactly as it does for the corresponding action sentence, which must be right since she thinks that (1) is true, that the cause-sentence provides the analysis of the action sentence. So I suggest that this is what she would say about a cause-sentence if she had addressed this issue explicitly: P caused the door to open$_i$ with a crowbar iff there was an event, x, such that x was an opening$_i$, and such that the door was the patient and P was the agent and the [non-instrumental] relational property of being-caused-with was true of the ordered pair, x and the crowbar. The sentence on the RHS uses 'caused with' in revealing the logical form of 'P caused…'. But as this is not an analysis (in an analysis, one would not want the term being analysed on the LHS to reappear on the RHS: see footnote 7), but a logical form proposal, that does not matter.

Problems for the Solution

In unpublished comments, Erasmus Mayr makes two points about Alvarez' claim (these are his arguments, not mine, so I make no claim to originality.[8] But I will change his example for my own). Mayr's argument is tailored to Alvarez' account of action sentences, but I can extrapolate it to the remarks about cause-sentences that I am making.[9] Both in Alvarez' and Mayr's discussions, 'Caused' must be read as 'was caused' (transitive verb in the passive voice).

(a) 'First, I take it that we would want to have an entailment from '[was] Caused with a crowbar (x)' to [both] (a) 'x was caused' and (b) 'There was something that caused x', which we don't get.'

It is clear that there are some cause-sentences that fail to have any adverbial qualification, instrumental or otherwise: e.g., 'P caused the door to open'. The 'cause' operator introduced by Alvarez takes adverbs or adverbial phrases and produces predicates, but sometimes there are no adverbs or adverbial phrases in the cause-sentence. What Mayr is saying, I think, is that both of the predicate forms, 'was caused with', and 'was caused by' must entail 'was caused' as a (passive) verb form, so that we can sometimes assert that some event was caused, full stop. 'Caused…' on its own (the operator with no operands) is syncategorematic on her account. 'Caused' cannot just be buried into a predicate in the way she wants, since we sometimes do want to say just that something was caused. How do we account for such sentences? How does her proposal for logical form allow us to say that, and not just that the event was caused in some way? How do we get from 'caused with' to 'caused'? Further, Mayr wants an account of logical form that shows not only how we can understand 'x is caused', but also an account that shows that 'x is caused' *follows* from 'x is caused in some way'. Alvarez spends some time showing generally how detachment inferences can be validated on her account of logical form (Alvarez 1999, 219–225), but Mayr is asking about a specific detachment inference: from 'x was caused G-ly' to 'x was caused', and her general remarks don't address that question.

Alvarez is bound not to be able to meet that requirement. There simply is no way, on her account, to derive 'x was caused' from 'x was caused with instrument i'. No relation of the form 'xRy' entails a non-relational form, 'Rx'. If 'R' is being used univocally in the two sentences, 'Rx' is ungrammatical.

One of the clauses in Alvarez' proposals for the logical form of action sentences is this: 'Agent (x, P)': i.e., P is the agent of x. She says that this is equivalent to: 'P is the causer of x' (232), or '…'is the author of', 'makes happen', 'Produces', 'Brings about', etc., since in my view, to be the agent of an event is to cause it to happen' (219). So surely if we have 'P is the causer of e', we have 'P caused x'. And that, by grammatical transformation, is 'x was caused by P'. But yet again, we cannot get 'x was caused' from 'x was caused by P', because 'was caused by' would have to be a dyadic predicate (remember we don't want: 'there was *a* causing by P…'), and 'caused' is a non-relational, monadic predicate. The entailment from 'x was (is) caused by P' to 'x was (is) caused' is surely valid, but nothing in Alvarez' logical form proposals captures it.

Is there really such a complete predicate as 'was caused'? 'x was caused' does not use an intransitive verb. It uses the passive form of the transitive verb. But perhaps you think that the passive transitive 'was (or, is) caused' is not complete; it is elliptical for 'x was caused by someone', and the latter does follow from 'P caused x'. So problem solved.

I think that 'x was caused' is a complete thought; it is not elliptical for 'x was caused by something'. Kenny's discussion of completeness in action sentences is relevant: '"Caesar was killed" is a complete sentence, exhibiting no "unsaturatedness"; and it is not a relational sentence... It might be said, for instance, that a sentence such as "Caesar was killed" is elliptical; it really means "Caesar was killed by something or other"... If we are to call "Caesar was killed" elliptical, we must compare it with a relational sentence where one term is not omitted but unspecified' (Kenny 1963, 155–162). Kenny gives two arguments for the completeness of 'Caesar was killed', in addition to the 'no-unsaturatedness' claim: (1) we can learn something from 'Caesar was killed' in the way in which we can learn nothing from 'Caesar preceded something or other'; (2) if 'Caesar was killed' is elliptical for 'Caesar was killed by someone', the latter-with just as much justification-could be regarded as merely elliptical for 'Caesar was killed by someone, somewhere, in some manner, etc.'. 'If we cast our net widely enough, we can make... ["Caesar was killed"] into a sentence which describes, with a certain lack of specification, the whole history of the world.' So I conclude that Alvarez' problem is not solved: 'x was caused' is not elliptical and therefore cannot be shown, on her logical form proposal, to follow from 'x was caused by P' on the grounds that it is merely elliptical for the latter. Similarly to my treatment of 'broke' in Chap. 5, 'x was caused' is entailed by 'something caused x', but that does not make 'x was caused' elliptical. Nor is that entailment due to logical form. Alvarez still needs to explain how we get from the one to the other.

(b) Mayr's second point is this: 'Two persons can, either jointly or separately, kill the king...cause the downfall of an Empire, sink a ship, etc.' Mayr's remarks could cover both the possibilities of overdetermined action and joint action. Given doubts about the very possibility of overdetermination, let me be clear that the case that I now offer is meant to be one of joint action, of either of the two kinds I have delineated. In cases of joint action, each agent is a part cause of the event, so we need to read 'cause' in her 'Agent (e,P)' as 'is a part cause of'. I will change various features of Mayr's example. In particular, I will bring the example against a cause-sentence, not an action-sentence, I substitute 'part-cause' for 'cause', and I will use an ergative verb.

Suppose it takes two people working together to cause the door to open. Each, let us say, is a part-cause of the result. James opens the door, using a crowbar; John opens the door, using a battering ram. Now consider the sentence: (a) 'James part-causes the door to open with a crowbar, and John part-causes the door to open too.' Mayr says that Alvarez would offer this as (a)'s logical form: (b) '($\exists$x) (Opening$_i$ (x) & Part-Agent (James, x) & Part-Agent (John, x) & Patient (door, x) & Part-caused-with (the crowbar, x)).' Mayr says that this entails, wrongly, that John part-caused the door to open$_i$ with a crowbar (by deletion of 'Part-Agent (James, x')). 'For the fact that an effect was brought about in a certain way and that it was brought about by X does not entail that it was brought about by X in that way'. To put the same point differently, attribution of this logical form would involve information loss, and thereby entail misinformation. The LHS tells us which agent was using the crowbar and which was using the battering ram; the RHS does not tell us which agent it was who used either one but then entails, by deletion, that the wrong agent used one of the instruments (and also that both agents used it).

What we would have to add is some clause tying, say, the instrument with James or John. No addition of additional, independent clauses, which don't 'cross-reference' which agent uses which instrument, etc. will solve this problem, because whatever additional clauses we add, by deletion, they can give us wrong result. What wouldn't be acceptable would be just to introduce a new triadic predicate, 'x is caused by agent y with instrument z' (which in effect ties the right agent of the opening with the right instrument, i.e., with the one he used), in addition to the two dyadic predicates, 'x is caused by agent y' and 'x is caused with instrument z'. That will immediately give rise to the problem of variable polyadicity. We would not be able to recover the inferences we want.[10] Perhaps one could say that the opening had two unbreakable properties, it was an opening-with-a-crowbar-for-James, and an opening-with-a battering-ram-for-John. (I discussed the issue of attributives in Chap. 3.) These all appear as desperate measures.

So far, so bad. Alvarez' proposal to avoid quantifying over causings seems not to have worked, since Mayr's criticisms stick. Would that her proposal had worked. Are we stuck now with causings, which neither she nor I want? What can I say in support of my view that persists in rejecting causings?

The One-Particular View and the Rejection of (PR)

On my view, which rejects (PR), if P causes the opening$_i$ with instrument i, what he causes is a with-i sort of opening$_i$. It's an opening$_i$-with-a-crowbar, rather than an opening$_r$-with-a-crowbar. On a view that accepts (PR), in Mayr's example, the two instrumentals would attach to two different part-causings: with-a-crowbar to James' part causing and with-a-battering ram to John's part causing. But on my view, both instrumentals are attached to the same opening$_i$. Won't it follow then that the same door opened$_i$ both with a battering ram and with a crowbar? One opening$_i$ has two instrumentals attached to it. That does indeed follow, and it is true. As I understand Alvarez' solution, it would have a similar implication: the same opening$_i$ is both caused-by-a battering-ram and caused-by-a-crowbar.

Let's look again at Parson's Rule:

> (PR) Instrumental modifiers are predicates of actions [causings], and not predicates of the events that are the results of those actions [the results of those causings].

Attentive readers will surely have noticed that (PR) as formulated assumes a two-particulars view of (CA). If a modifier such as 'with a crowbar' can be predicated of P's V_t-ing of b, but cannot be predicated of b's V_i-ing, it follows that P's V_t-ing of b $\neq$ b's V_i-ing. If a and b are discernible, a$\neq$b. The conjunction of (PR) as it has been understood so far and the one-particular view are inconsistent. On one-particularism, instrumental modifiers can be attributed both to actions and to their intrinsic events, since they are the same. If one-particularism is true, and if the expression, 'x-with-instrument-i', is extensional, then if he opened$_t$ the door with a crowbar, then the door opened$_i$ with a crowbar. If there was an opening$_t$ by him of the door with a crowbar, then there was an opening$_i$ with a crowbar. However, the distinction that must be preserved, even on one-particularism, is that between agent-directed descriptions and descriptions that contain no agent-directed information. Does that give my view a problem? Let's see.

The RHS of (CA) can't entail its LHS, so what I need to hold is that the addition of 'with instrument i' to an event description on the RHS of (CA) does not change that description from one that has no agent-directed information in it to a description that does carry such information. Remember from Chap. 5: the crucial difference between the *descriptions*, 'he opened$_t$ the door' and 'the door opened$_i$', is that the first contains agent-directed information and the second does not. If an attribution of an instrumental to a particular under its non-agent-directed description compromised the status of that description and made it an agent-directed description, then the inference in (CA) would run from right-to-left as well as from left-to-right. And that would be a decisive reason for not making such attributions to events as so described.

I claim that no agent-directedness is *entailed* by 'the door opened$_i$ with instrument i'. The description of an event as an event to which an instrumental is ascribed does not entail that any action has occurred: 'there was an opening$_i$ of the door with a crowbar' entails no agency, and does not entail that any agent opened$_t$ the door. That this is so allows me to attach the instrumental to the event caused rather than to a causing, and hence deny the need for a causing particular of which the instrumental is true.

You might think that (a) 'there was an opening$_i$ of the door with a crowbar' is either equivalent to or entails (b) 'the crowbar opened$_t$ the door', or is somehow elliptical for (c) 'some agent opened$_t$ the door with a crowbar'. If so, that would be a reason for accepting (PR) after all, rather than my alternative proposal. However, I think that the answer to the question of what relation, if any, (a) has to (b) or (c) depends—to return to a question first raised in Chap. 5—on just how broad we should take agency to be. If you think that all substances are agents, and since a crowbar is certainly a substance, then the crowbar opened$_t$ the door.

If (a) were equivalent to (b), in 'P opened$_t$ the door with a crowbar', we have two agents rather than one: both P and the crowbar. On that option, the crowbar was a joint agent with P and it also co-opened$_t$ the door along with P. There would be two agents of the opening$_t$. It seems to me that any plausible theory of action needs to find room for a distinction between descriptions codifying information about agency and ones only codifying information about instrumentality. Henry's doing something with a crowbar needs to be distinguished from joint action, when Henry does something with Henrietta. The first is the 'with' of instrumentality; only the second is the 'with' of joint agency.

Recall Hyman's claim that even nerve cells and muscle fibres were agents. But suppose we plump for a more restricted view of agency, say one that includes only persons or, more widely, all animals, or even more widely still, all animate things (but not necessarily their proper parts). I don't think that doing something with a crowbar ever assumes agency on the part of the crowbar, even though a crowbar is a substance. The with-instrument relation would turn out to be with the with-relation of joint agency after all. So although the distinction between what it is reasonable to count as an agent and what not is vague, there are some pretty clear cases and crowbars are, I submit, clear cases of particulars that are not agents, at least not when agents use them to open things.

You might reply: 'But I am an agent and someone could open the door using me as a battering ram!' Indeed they could. But there is the contrast between my moving$_t$ of my body when I open the door and my body's merely being moved$_i$ by someone when they use me as a battering ram. In the latter case, I am his instrument for his opening$_t$ of the door. I think it would be absurd to count this latter case as joint agency-both he and I opening$_t$ the door. This constitutes a paradigm case of my passivity. But if he wisely substitutes the real battering ram for me, I can't see why that would make the instrument he is now using any more of an agent than I was when I was the instrument.

What about (c): (a) 'there was an opening$_i$ of the door with a crowbar' is somehow elliptical for (c) 'some agent opened$_t$ the door with a crowbar'. If you ask me to say something more about what (a) mean, I would say that (a) means (c*) rather than (c): (c*): 'some crowbar-involving event opened$_t$ the door'. It is true that (c*) uses the transitive of 'to open', whereas (a) used the intransitive of 'to open', but even so, no agency is implied by (c*), since there is none in (a). (CA) is true: 'the door opened$_i$ with a crowbar' does not entail 'the crowbar opened$_t$ the door'; at most, it entails something about a crowbar-involving event standing in the *event causal relation* to an opening$_i$. Suppose the crowbar fell off of a shelf and its falling against the door caused the door to open$_i$. Such a case is certainly possible and it follows that (c) can't be what (a) means when unpacked. There is no agency in such a case. The crowbar's fall might be a mere event. What is true in such a case is the transitive but agent-free sentence, 'the crowbar's falling against the door opened$_t$ the door (or '… caused it to open$_i$')'.

I remarked before about the equal oddness of 'P's opening$_t$ of the door was with a crowbar' and 'the opening$_i$ of the door$_i$ was with a crowbar'. Yet, if the instrumental adverb becomes an adjective attaching to a particular, the choice must be between those two options. If the first is acceptable, I cannot see why it is wrong in saying the second.

If that is right, then information about instruments can be added to a description like 'an opening$_i$', without thereby converting that description into a description that carries any agent-directed information. Instruments don't do things. But the point I am primarily interested in making here relates to causing and not to acting. One can attribute the instrument to 'the opening$_i$', or to whatever other nominal gerund or perfect nominal follows 'cause', and not to an agent causing.

On one-particularism, if the opening$_t$ was with instrument i, so too the opening$_i$ was with instrument i. If they are identical, then that must be so. Which description we use, the agent-directed description or the description that omits that information, should not matter. To repeat: only the descriptions themselves remain distinctive, in order to disallow the inference from right to left in (CA), and attribution of the instrumental description to an event (suppose for instance that the event is a mere event) does not entail that there was any action, or agent causing.

So let's sum up where we are. Instrumental adverbs were meant to be the main problem forcing us to quantify over agent causings, because of sentences like, 'P caused e with instrument i.' It might appear that that commits us to there being an agent causing that is a causing with-i. Maria Alvarez wanted to avoid that, and I agree with that goal. She accepted

Parson's Rule that such adverbial modification could only be adjectives of actions (causings), not of event results (results of the causing). Her solution was to introduce new predicates, which 'absorbed' the instrumentality, yielding 'caused with instrument i', and which thereby converted instrumental adverbs into non-instrumental predicates that could be predicated of events, consistently with retaining (PR). I looked at some criticisms by Mayr, both of which I agreed presented her proposal for logical form with an insuperable difficulty. (I still think that her attempted solution was pretty ingenious, even if it finally fails.)

My own solution was to reject (PR), a solution that follows from the one-particular view I defended in the last chapter. The question of the plausibility of (PR) in the end comes down to the question of how widely we allow the phenomenon of agency to be. I can see that the widest, and I think implausible, view of agency, would provide an argument in favour of (PR), since it would prevent us from formulating any agency-free description that contained an instrumental. (I'm assuming that instruments generally are substances.) The description that appeared to have no agency-directed information in it would turn out to be an agency-directed description after all. But on a more circumscribed view of agency, (PR) seems to me to have little in its defence. Whether the event is extrinsic or intrinsic to an action, we don't need agent causings as particulars in order to account for causing-sentences with instrumentals in them.

Notes

1. See for example Zeno Vender (1962).
2. Bach also thinks that to act is to cause something to happen, and obviously I do not agree.
3. Once again, I avoid discussion of trope theory at this point, which might be one way in which to understand Bach's 'instances', because trope theorists are themselves divide as to whether or not tropes are particulars.
4. My scepticism about causings as particulars most definitely does not extend in general to the particular events referred to by the nominal gerunds of other verbs, since I did not dispute the general form of the Davidsonian argument outlined in Chap. 3 for events. Alvarez (private

communication) tells me that she thinks that causings and meltings, stoppings, closings, etc. have the same ontological status, and wonders why I distinguish between them on ontological grounds. I don't think they do have the same ontological status, because I, unlike her, accept, at least pro tem, the Davidsonian argument from adverbial modification for the last three but I see no hope of such a sound argument for the first. That is what the section following this footnote aims to show.

5. The Quinean criterion for existence claims is something that Hyman at least would also reject (private communication).
6. Another way to word her view is this: she replaces an instrumental like 'with a crowbar' by a new type of instrumental, 'caused with a crowbar', but as far as I can see, that is merely a way to restate the same thesis I am attributing to her. It's just a dispute about what to call 'an instrumental'. I'm going to call expressions such as 'with a crowbar' names of an instrumental relations, and expressions such as 'caused with a crowbar' as names of non-instrumental relations, but it would be easy enough just to substitute here the terminology of two different kinds of instrumental relations. She would still have to hold that one kind of instrumental is exclusively predicable of actions and the other kind, exclusively of events and results of actions.
7. Here is another thorny issue I don't want to deal with: the relation between analysis and logical form (I intimated the distinction above in comparing the status of (1) and (2)). That's a big issue. Certainly, proposals about logical form and about analysis constrain one another in various ways. Alvarez is clear: she is offering proposals for the logical form of a sentence, in the same tradition as Davidson, Parsons, and others. But her view that actions are causings of events must be intended as an analysis.

I take it that one difference between an analysis and a logical form proposal is this: where 'r' and 'q' are sentences, if one proposes that 'r' is the analysis of 'q', 'r' cannot entail or presuppose 'q' or any concept used essentially in 'q', on pain of circularity. On one view of logical form (there are many), the logical form of a sentence is its translation into a 'perfect language' in which both inference and ontology are perspicuous. On such a conception, one would expect many of the concepts used on the LHS to reappear on the RHS. It cannot be any criticism of the account that Alvarez offers on logical form that there is 'circularity' in this sense.

8. As I mentioned in the Preface, discussing these issues with Alvarez was helpful, and I can no longer separate what she said to me and what I have added myself.
9. Alvarez does consider the logical form of cause-sentences very briefly:

    '(18) 'John caused an explosion' can be paraphrased thus:

    (19) $(\exists x)(\text{Explosion}(x) \ \& \ \text{Agent}(x, \text{John}))$; that is, 'There is an event x such that x was an explosion of which John was the agent'

    Sentences of this kind are closest in surface structure to the logical form I am suggesting action sentences have.' (1999, 225)
10. Compare: Bennet has explored the idea of what I call 'cross-referencing' in his 1988, 203–206, in a way which he hoped would avoid events altogether.

Bibliography

Alvarez, Maria. 1999. Actions and Events: Some Semantical Considerations. *Ratio*, new series XII (3): 213–239.
Alvarez, Maria, and John Hyman. 1998. Agents and Their Actions. *Philosophy* 73: 219–245.
Anscombe, G.E.M. 1981. *Metaphysics and the Philosophy of Mind*. Oxford: Basil Blackwell Publisher.
Bach, Kent. 1980. Actions are Not Events. *Mind* 89 (353): 114–120.
Bennett, Jonathan. 1988. Adverb-Dropping Inferences and the Lemmon Criterion. In *Actions and Events: Perspectives on the Philosophy of Donald Davidson*, ed. Ernest LePore and Brian McLaughlin, 193–206. Oxford: Blackwell.
Davidson, Donald. 2004. Problems in the Explanation of Action. In *Problems of Rationality*. Oxford: Oxford University Press.
Kenny, Anthony. 1963. *Action, Emotion and Will*. London: Routledge & Kegan Paul.
Morreall, John. 1976. The Nonsynonymy of Kill and Cause to Die. *Linguistic Inquiry* 7 (3): 516–518.
Quine, W.V.O. 1961. On What There Is. In *From A Logical Point of View*. New York: Harper and Row.
Stoecker, Ralf. 1993. Reasons, Actions, and their Relationship. In *Reflecting Davidson*, ed. Ralf Stoecker, 265–286. Berlin: De Gruyter. Reprinted, 2011.
Vendler, Zeno. 1962. Effects, Results and Consequences. In *Analytical Philosophy*, ed. R.J. Butler, 1–15. Oxford: Blackwell.

8

Regress Issues and Action Scepticism

> 'Expressions which are in no way composite signify ... action and affection.... 'to lance', 'to cauterize', action; 'to be lanced', 'to be cauterized', [are terms indicating] affection'
> (Aristotle, 'De Categoriae', 4).

What's in the Chapter

This chapter has two sections, both of which develop some of the consequences of one-particularism. The two sections are unconnected to one another. The first section is about the possibility that some regress, vicious or otherwise, arises on the conjunction of one-particularism and the left-to-right inference of (PT). I shall show why this is not so. My argument on this topic relies on my argument in Chap. 7, which explains why I deal with this question only in this final chapter of the book rather than earlier, in Chap. 6, where it would more naturally belong.

The second question is a sceptical question. Perhaps a person has some special knowledge about what it is that he is doing when he intentionally acts, as many have claimed. Of course, even that claim would have to be hedged with all sorts of bells and whistles. I make no claims about whether, or in what sense, that might be so. But what can we say about a person's knowledge of the actions of others (independently of the question of knowledge in general about the external world and other minds)? Could there be a possible world in which no other agents, minded like ourselves, ever act, either intentionally or unintentionally, although, for all the events that would have been intrinsic or extrinsic to their actions had they acted, there are intrinsically qualitatively identical mere events that occur anyway? That of course is a metaphysical question. If there were such a possible world, how would a person know whether the world that he is in is that world or some other world in which other agents really do act? How could we, as observers, know which world it is, in which we are? I attempt to answer the epistemological question by returning to the experiments described by William James, 'the pathological cases', that I have discussed in Chaps. 2 and 3. That is a possible entry point for a form of scepticism.

The question I am asking has close parallels with the question of knowledge of other minds; call it 'the question of knowledge of other actions'. In order to insure that the other actions question is independent from the other minds question, I pretend that we somehow have knowledge of the minds of others, and raise the question of the actions of others with that pretence in place. Do I solve the sceptical question about knowledge of the actions of others that I introduce? No. If I could, I'd be King of the Philosophy World. Or near enough. I tentatively outline (but do not commit myself to) a 'disjunctivist' suggestion for addressing the sceptical question. The discussion on scepticism also allows me to apply (CTT) from Chap. 4 and to demonstrate how it works in thinking about this question about others' actions. It also allows me to make some points of (I believe) some interest about the epistemology of action.

Regress?

The reader may have wondered whether the conjunction of one-particularism and the left-to-right inference in (PT), both of which I accept, generates a vicious regress. I did not deal with this issue in Chap. 6, which would have been the more natural location for such a discussion, because part of my answer to the question of regress requires some of my conclusions on causing from Chap. 7. I propose to deal with this question now: does the conjunction of one-particularism and the left-to-right inference of (PT) entail a regress of some kind?

According one-particularism, if one accepts the left-to-right entailment of (PT), exactly what sort of event is it that the agent is meant to cause? It can't be a mere event, by definition, since a mere event has no agency in its causal ancestry. The relation between extrinsic events and actions is contingent (assuming no necessity of causal origin). So for every token event that is in fact an extrinsic event of some token action, that very event could have occurred even if the action had not occurred. The law of universal causation, that every event has a cause, is not a metaphysically necessary truth, if it is a truth at all. Similarly, the law of universal effectiveness, that every event (and so every action) has an effect, is not a metaphysically necessary truth either, if it is a truth at all. It is metaphysically possible for an event and so for an action to have no contingent effects at all, no contingent consequences whatever. (That claim does not of course include an action's intrinsic event.)

If we yet again restrict our sights to cases of ergative verbs, the event mentioned in the RHS of (PT) must be, of course, an intrinsic event, and that is the obvious assumption made by the philosophers and linguists we quoted in Chap. 5, at least insofar as they were dealing with ergative action verbs, and perhaps explains the frequent conflation between (CA) and (PT). So, what (PT) says (left-to-right) is this: if P V_t-ed b, then P caused b's V_i-ing, where b's V_i-ing is the event intrinsic to P's V_t-ing of b.

In what follows, I stress once again that I am not interested in providing an overview in any sense of agent causalism. I am only interested in what (PT) claims that agents do in fact cause, assuming (PT) is restricted to ergative verbs. Whatever agent causalism is, many agent causalists, and perhaps others too, assert that the fact that agents cause something or other follows from their having acted, and I want to get clear on what that 'something' is. It is that issue alone at which I want to look. Recall also that, as far as I am concerned, that 'agent P caused e' is consistent both with the view that agent causation is sui generis and that it is merely elliptical for some agent-involving event or action having caused e.

One-particularism, conjoined with the left-to-right entailment of (PT) and the extensionality of 'cause' in 'Agent P caused…', has some surprising consequences. I underline places in the sentences below into which identities are substitutable salva veritate: Here is one surprising result:

(1) If P melted$_t$ the ice, then P caused <u>the melting$_i$ of the ice</u>. (left-to-right inference of (PT))
(2) <u>P's melting$_t$ of the ice</u>=<u>the melting$_i$ of the ice</u> (one-particularism)
(3) Therefore, if P melted$_t$ the ice, P caused <u>P's melting$_t$ of the ice</u>.

On the one-particular view, can the distinction between an agent causing his action and an agent causing the event intrinsic to his action be maintained? No, it can't. Consider again (CA). On the one-particular view, whatever makes 'PV$_t$b' true also makes 'bV$_i$' true. Return to (PT). Given the extensionality of the causal relation, at least when events or actions are the second relata of the relation (I deal with fact causation later), 'P's V$_t$-ing (of) b' must be substitutable for 'b's V$_i$-ing' in (PT), salva veritate. So if the left-to-right inference of (PT) were true, so too would be (PT*): 'P V$_t$-ed b only if P caused P's [that is, his very own] V$_t$-ing (of) b'.

One caveat: 'P V$_t$-ed b' is made true by P's V$_t$-ing of b, but 'P V$_t$-ed b' speaks of a successful telic action, whereas the nominal gerund, 'P's V$_t$-ing of b', does not require for its truth that P successfully V$_t$-ed. I pointed out this discrepancy in my discussion of (CA) in Chap. 5.

So if the sentence on the LHS is in perfective aspect: 'P opened$_t$ the door', the door opened$_i$. But 'the opening$_i$ of the door', the nominal gerund, on the RHS can be true without the door ever having been finally opened$_i$. The same can be said for 'P's opening$_t$ of the door'. Both the opening$_i$ of the door and P's opening$_t$ of it may never have been brought to completion, so I need to add a further condition to the RHS. I also need this statement of (PT) to contain places for event and action names, unlike the earlier formulation in Chap. 5 that did not, so I slightly reword (PT) to make the place for names of actions and events salient:

(1) P V$_t$-ed b only if P caused <u>b's (successful) V$_i$-ing</u>. (inference from LHS to RHS of PA)
(2) <u>P's (successful) V$_t$-ing of b</u>=<u>b's (successful) V$_i$-ing</u>. (the one-particular view)

(3) P V$_t$-ed b only if P caused P's (successful) V$_t$-ing of b. (substitution of identities salva veritate)

The argument is valid. So the assumptions that (1) agents, when they act, cause the events intrinsic to their actions, if there is one, (2) the one-particular view, and (3) the assumption that the context that follows 'agent P caused…' is extensional, conjointly entail the claim that agents do cause their actions.

Some early contemporary versions of agent causalism, for example by Richard Taylor (Taylor 1980), claimed that agents caused their actions. As Taylor put it: '…I am the cause of my own actions…' (Taylor, 112). Randolph Clarke says something similar to Taylor: 'What is directly caused [by the agent] is her acting for a particular ordering of reasons' (Clarke 1993) but for Clarke this provides an account of free action, not of action. It says that if P's act is free, P is the cause of that action ('for a particular ordering of reasons'). Roderick Chisholm offered a similar but somewhat more complicated version, built around the idea of an undertaking, which he took to be the same concept as trying. On his view, an agent undertakes 'a certain activity', which is explicated as the agent causally contributing to his own activity (Chisholm 1980, 201–203).

That version of agent causalism was subjected to attack by Davidson, and partly as a consequence of that attack, fell out of favour (Davidson 1971, in Davidson 1980, 52–53). Davidson considered, and dismissed, agent causation in the formulation of an agent causing his action, not in the formulation of the agent causing an event. More recent versions of agent causation stress that they do not assert that agents cause their actions: '…an action may be defined in terms of an agent's causing certain events (typically bodily movements)…' (a view described by Bishop 1983, 61); 'Nor do I think that agents cause their actions. They cause the results of their actions…' (Alvarez 1999, 217); '…we will not say … that there is an irreducible causal relation between the agent and his… action. My directly causing events internal to myself is my activity par excellence' (O'Connor 2000, 72, fn. 11).[1] So, it is an event and not an action that the agent is supposed to cause when he acts, on these more modern versions of agent causalism. My account is a departure from these modern versions, and reverts to Taylor's and Chisholm's original idea.

Since I accept (1), the left-to-right entailment of (PT), and, since I believe both that one-particularism is true, and that the agent causal relation is extensional, I accept the conclusion above, (3). I assume that there is nothing false or nonsensical about (3), without a further compelling argument to the contrary. Thalberg queried the intelligibility of these assertions: 'Is it even intelligible to report that a person caused himself to walk, that he brought about his own locomotion?' (Thalberg 1967, 198). In reply to Thalberg, a user-friendlier version of the same assertion might go like this: 'P made himself walk' or 'P brought it about that he walked' or 'P got himself to walk', and those claims certainly seem intelligible to me.

Return to the 'causing an event' formulation. Even though there is an entailment from (a) to (b), I think it is obvious why (b), 'P caused the V_i-ing of b', cannot count as even a part of a philosophical analysis of (a), 'P V_t-ed b'. Analyses are meant to be illuminating, to explicate the less clear in terms of the clearer. My remarks are similar to Davidson's well-known dismissal of agent causation ('Agency', 52–53, in Davidson 1980), except that I do not trace the problem just to the use of 'causing' as the name of a particular in the way in which he did. Since (3) is entailed by (1) & (2), to say that, when P V_t-ed b, it follows that P caused the V_i-ing of b, is equivalent to saying, that when P V_t-ed b, it follows that P caused P's V_t-ing of b. Davidson remarked: 'For then what more have we said when we say the agent caused the action than when we say he was the agent of the action? The concept of cause seems to play no role.' But that isn't quite right. When we say that the agent caused the action, we do say something *more* than he was the agent of the action. We *repeat* that he was the agent of the action (i.e., he acted, P V_t-ed b), without illuminating that in any way, and then add an additional commitment to causation (i.e., P caused it), which increases rather than helps to resolve our original perplexity.

The above discussion assumes that (PT) should be interpreted using the idea of causation of events and actions (by agents). That is certainly its standard formulation. But suppose we decided to substitute causation of facts by agents for causation of events and actions by agents. I have already committed myself to the need for fact causation in Chap. 3 for some cases of trying, so how would fact causation affect this discussion?

(4) P V_t-ed b only if P caused the fact that b V_i-ed.

Let's assume that the agent causal relation is extensional, even when facts are the second relatum. So any description of the fact that b V_i-ed, can be substituted in (4) salve veritate. But what descriptions denote the same fact? On one-particularism, do 'the fact that P V_t-ed b' and 'the fact that b V_i-ed' denote the same fact? Regardless of any views about the degree to which facts are fine-grained or course-grained, it is obvious that these can't denote the same fact, simply because P is a constituent of one fact but not of the other (there may be other reasons too, but this one will suffice). And since they do not denote the same fact, 'P V_t-ed b' cannot be substituted for 'b V_i-ed' in (4) salva veritate, to give:

(4*) P V_t-ed b only if P caused the fact that P V_t-ed b.

In what follows, I will assume event causation, not fact causation. Fact causation, since it does not allow the substitutability salva veritate that generates this odd result, would simplify my task. So by using event causation, I am making my life harder than it would be with fact causation.

Standard Theory and Causing Actions

In case the reader might think that the problem that is raised by the conjunction of one-particularism, the extensionality of the causal relation, and the left-to-right inference of (PT) is somehow peculiar to one-particularism, let me show how the standard theory of action (that an action is an event caused in the right way by the appropriate mental states) faces the same sort of question that one-particularism faces, at least for the case of primitive action. Consider standard theory in its austere form regarding act individuation (it is even more of a problem in its prolific form). In what follows, I won't complicate the discussion with the qualifications described in the section, Austere Theory and Intrinsic Events, in Chap. 6.

Standard theory must accept (CA), since it is an indisputable truth: 'P moves$_t$ his arm' entails 'P's arm moves$_i$'. Moreover, standard theory identifies P's moving$_t$ of his arm and the moving$_i$ of P's arm, because on that theory a basic action like P's moving$_t$ of his arm is identical to P's arm moving$_i$ when the latter is caused nondeviantly by the mental states that rationalise it. (I assume that this is a case in which a person moves$_t$ his arm and not by doing something else. In Davidson's lingo, it is a 'primitive' action.)

As I explained in Chap. 6, it does not alter matters by adding, 'but only when the latter is caused… etc.'. The identity is between the token basic action and the token event intrinsic to that action, and that token event just is so caused. Identity is identity is identity. Furthermore, assume also that standard theory accepts at least the left-to-right inference of (PT): if P moves$_t$ his arm, P causes <u>the moving$_i$ of his arm</u>. But then, substituting identities salva veritate, if P causes <u>the moving$_i$ of his arm</u>, it follows that P causes <u>P's moving$_t$ of his arm</u>. So standard theory conjoined with an austere theory of act individuation produces the same regress as does one-particularism, for basic or primitive actions. Standard theory conjoined with a prolific theory of act individuation will generate the same regress for all actions nominated by an ergative verb.

Explanation of Actions and Explanation of Intrinsic Events

Since, on my view, a token action=its token intrinsic event, by the indiscernibility of identicals, whatever is true of the one must be true of the other. Therefore, whatever causes and effects the event has, so must the action have as well. We saw this in the discussion of action chains and causality in Chap. 6. In Chap. 5, we understood 'P causes e' (where 'e' uses the intransitive form of an ergative verb) as 'P is one of the causes of e', since there can also be providers, encouragers, enablers, commanders, and so on for e. So too, in 'P causes his V_t-ing of b', in addition to P, the agent, there can also be providers, encouragers, enablers, commanders, and so on for P's V_t-ing of b, indeed the very same ones that there were for b's V_i-ing.

But it is a commonplace view that explanation, including causal explanation, is not extensional in the way in which causation is. So an explanation of some thing as described in one way may be acceptable, but as described in another way, merely puzzling or, if not puzzling, just plain different. Let me use as an example of a single act, described in two non-synonymous ways, one that even a most-prolific theorist would agree are two descriptions of the same act: same property, same agent, same time (I am slightly altering Goldman's example 1970, 12). Suppose John is the town executioner, whose task it is to execute Smith. John's executing Smith at t=the executioner's executing Smith at t. If I were asked to explain why John executed Smith, a correct reply would be that it is because he is the executioner. On the other hand, if I were asked why the executioner executed Smith, a correct reply would surely recount some of Smith's peccadillos that were among the reasons for his execution. The non-extensionality of explanation insures that the explanations of the same thing under different descriptions will often diverge. (On austere theory, the divergence will be even more dramatic.) How things are described matters to explanation and one and the same thing can give or be given different explanations depending on how it is described.

Let's assume we are being asked why-questions (the answer might go differently for how-questions). Why did the flood stop$_i$? One answer is that P stopped$_t$ the flood, that's why. That is explanation by re-description. The inquirer did not know whether the stopping was a mere event or an intrinsic event or an extrinsic event, and telling the inquirer that P stopped$_t$ the flood tells him that it is an intrinsic event. But now suppose someone asks why P stopped$_t$ the flood (he is asking about the same token particular, but differently described). He can't be asking whether it is an intrinsic or a mere event or an extrinsic event that has occurred, since by using the description, 'P's stopping$_t$ of the flood', it is clear that he (believes that he) knows the answer to that question. He knows it is an intrinsic event because he knows it is an action. The answer one gave in the first case would be otiose, redundant. The inquirer in the second case is probably asking a question about P's reasons for stopping$_t$ the flood: to improve the lives of the townspeople downstream. (Suppose P did what he did for that reason.) Notice that this too, like the executioner example, is a case in which under one description we give the agent's reasons and under another description, we do not.

What about the two different versions of the RHS of (PT) given in the argument above: P's causing event e; P's causing his own action a (where e is the event intrinsic to a)? In the first case, someone might be asked to explain why P caused the flood to stop$_i$; in the second case, one might be asked to explain why P caused himself to stop$_t$ the flood. In the first case, to explain why P caused the flood to stop$_i$ may well also be answered in terms of P's reasons: to improve the lives, etc. The two explananda: P stopped$_t$ the flood (from above), and P caused the flood to stop$_i$, may have the same explanans in terms of reasons. But what of my oddball: why did P cause himself to stop$_t$ the flood? Put in the vernacular, it is perhaps not quite so oddball: why did P get himself, or bring himself, to stop$_t$ the flood? Although the answer in terms of reasons would not count as wrong, but since there is an easier way to elicit the same explanans, probably the question is asking for something different from P's reasons. A different answer might be: 'Look, there was no one else around to do it, P was otherwise reluctant to get involved, but if P hadn't done it, the town would have been submerged.' In truth, that might even be an acceptable explanans for why P caused the flood to stop$_i$, if one places the emphasis correctly: why was it that it was P [rather than someone else] who caused the flood to stop$_i$? Why was it P [emphasis on 'P'] who caused the flood to stop$_i$?

The upshot is that the identity of P's (successful) V_t-ing of b and b's (successful) V_i-ing is consistent with offering different explanations for P's (successful) V_t-ing of b and b's (successful) V_i-ing, and is consistent with offering different explanations for why P caused event e and why P caused his own action a (where e is the event intrinsic to a).

A Vicious Regress?

So far, perhaps just about so acceptable. But is there worse to come? Here is what purports to be a valid argument:

(1) P's melting$_t$ of the ice=the ice's melting$_i$. (One-particularism)
(2) If P melts$_t$ the ice, P causes the melting$_i$ of the ice. (The left-to-right entailment of (PT))
(3) If P causes the melting$_i$ of the ice, P causes P's melting$_t$ of the ice. (from 1 & 2, which I accept)

(4) If P causes <u>P's melting$_t$ of the ice</u>, then P causes <u>P's causing of the melting$_i$ of the ice</u>.

The accusation that an agent causing his own actions, rather than an event, engenders a regress is hardly new. The accusation was famously made by Davidson (1980, 52) and is often repeated-for example by Helen Steward (2012, 38). Any such claim of regress requires some additional premisses to be valid. I won't look at the arguments for a regress using the additional premisses provided by Davidson or Steward, to name just those two philosophers. But I shall ask a specific question: does my account in particular generate such a regress, when the claim that an agent causes his own actions is coupled with the premisses about the extensionality of the causal relation and the left-to-right entailment of (PT)?

How might (4) be thought to follow from (1)–(3), since it is not obvious that it does? In 'P causes <u>P's melting$_t$ of the ice</u>' (the consequent of (3) and the antecedent of (4)), if one substitutes '<u>P's causing of the melting$_i$ of the ice</u>' for '<u>P's melting$_t$ of the ice</u>', then one obtains (4). If so, with further similar substitutions, the regress will be ad infinitum.

But I have not committed myself to any such identity as: P's melting$_t$ of the ice=P's causing of the melting$_i$ of the ice. In Chap. 7, I argued that 'P's causing the melting$_i$ of the ice' (no 'of' following 'causing') is a verbal gerund that does not refer, and so cannot take a position flanking either side of an identity sign. 'P's melting$_t$ of the ice=P's causing the melting$_i$ of the ice' is not grammatically well formed on my view. 'P's melting$_t$ of the ice=P's causing of the melting$_i$ of the ice' would be well formed, but I deny that there is such as a nominal gerund as 'P's causing of the melting$_i$ of the ice' and a fortiori I deny that there is any particular to which it refers.

A different thought is this: if 'cause' is an action verb, then presumably 'P causes P's melting$_t$ of the ice' is also about an action in addition to the melting$_t$. If one then subjects 'P causes P's melting$_t$ of the ice' to the same treatment that 'P melts$_t$ the ice' was given in (2), then one might think that a regress ensues. Suppose one argues like this: (2), the left-to-right inference of (PT), says that if P acts, P causes the event intrinsic to that action. So, by (2), but now using 'P causes P's melting$_t$ of the ice' on the

LHS rather than on the RHS, it would appear to follow on the RHS that P causes whatever event it is that is intrinsic to the action on the LHS. What event is it that is intrinsic to that action on the LHS, P's causing of P's melting$_t$ of the ice?

It won't be just P's melting$_i$ of the ice or P's melting$_t$ of the ice. So, when P caused P's melting$_t$ of the ice, suppose the intrinsic event to that action were P's causing of P's melting$_t$ of the ice. So, by (2), on the RHS, P caused that intrinsic event, namely the intrinsic event, P's causing of P's melting$_t$ of the ice. Since that would now be the intrinsic event that P caused on the RHS (on this supposition), it follows that P caused P's causing of P's melting$_t$ of the ice, and hence (4) would follow. Only by making that action the intrinsic event of the action on the LHS would one generate the regress in (4). If 'P caused P's causing P's melting$_t$ of the ice' is again about an action, the same analysis would reapply to it and a regress would be generated.

But none of this follows from anything I have said. Quite the contrary. Are you having trouble following this argument above? No wonder. The discussion is somewhat absurd (I am sure the reader will have already noticed this. It's just that I have had to reply to just this charge on several occasions.) Suppose that 'to cause' is an action verb. (I am unsure about this, as I explained.) But 'to cause' is not an ergative verb even if it is an action verb, and therefore it has *no* event intrinsic to it. The entire attempt to generate a regress on this basis is based on a misconception about 'to cause'. Further, I have repeatedly explained why 'to cause' has no nominal gerund. The expression that follows 'P caused…', namely 'P's causing of P's melting$_t$ of the ice' is illicit because ungrammatical, so the substitutions would be illegitimate. (1)–(3) do not generate any regress for either of the two alleged reasons I have considered and dismissed.

Finally, in spite of everything I have just argued, suppose my account was regressive. After all, it depends crucially on my view that there are no causing particulars, and some will no doubt still not be convinced. But not all regresses are vicious. If one-particularism were regressive, it would be saddled with the view that when an agent acted, there were in fact an infinite number of causings, and causings of causings, and so on, that the agent did. Such a view is unintuitive and would be a cost to the theory that entailed such a regress. But the cost wouldn't be by itself prohibitive and thereby bankrupt the theory. A vicious regress would take the form that there were an infinite number of things that had to be done first before one could do anything at all. The tortoise-and-the-hare purports to be a vicious regress of that kind, since it alleges that the hare must cover an infinite number of increasingly small distances before he can catch up to the tortoise (Sainsbury 1988, 17–24). But the regress that says that, when an agent acts, he also does an infinite number of other actions is not a vicious regress. Indeed, for anyone, unlike me, who accepts that right-to-left entailment of (PT), and thinks that an agent acts whenever he causes or part-causes an event, with no restriction placed on temporal distance from the agent or the partial nature of the agent's role in generating the consequence, then on the assumption that there are an infinite number of consequences that an action causes when a person acts, it would follow that the person does an infinite number of actions.

What of the alleged regress on the standard theory? Select an example of a basic or primitive action. (I'm not thinking of standard theory necessarily in its most austere form.) Although standard theory does not identify P's melting$_t$ of the ice and the ice's melting$_i$, as in my earlier example, it does, as we have seen, identify a basic action, like P's moving$_t$ of his arm, with its intrinsic event, P's arm's moving$_i$. If it accepts the left-to-right inference of (PT), then it also holds that if P moves$_t$ his arm, P causes the moving$_i$ of his arm. But then P causes P's moving$_t$ of his arm. We have already seen this much above.

Suppose standard theory also were to accept that there are causing particulars, so that, when P moves$_t$ his arm, there is a causing of the moving$_i$ of P's arm by P. P's token moving$_t$ of his arm=P's token causing of the moving$_i$ of his arm. If standard theory also were to accept that one can substitute 'P's token causing of the moving$_i$ of his arm' for 'P's moving$_t$ of his arm', then one would again obtain the dreaded: if P causes P's moving$_t$ of his arm, then P causes P's causing of the moving$_i$ of his arm. And the regress would repeat, ad infinitum. Since standard theory is defined as the theory that identifies a basic action with the event non-deviantly caused by the mental states that rationalise it, in order to avoid the regress, it would either have to reject the extensionality of the causal relation, the left-to-right inference of (PT), or the positing of causing particulars. Or it could accept the regress as non-vicious. So tu quoque.

Our Knowledge of the Actions of Others

There is a much-discussed problem, and a vast literature, about how, or even whether, an agent knows with some special sort of certainty what it is that he is doing, assuming that he is acting, and whether this can be based on observation.[2] But what is not discussed as far as I am aware is the question of how a person can know that someone else has physically acted, and what evidence a person might have to come to such a conclusion. The problem of the knowledge of the physical actions of others parallels the problem of the knowledge of other minds. In what follows, although I start with a reconsideration of the pathological cases of action discussed in Chaps. 2 and 3, which are about what an agent knows in his own case, I take a third-person point of view for the rest of the discussion. I consider the position of the external observer observing others, and not mainly that of the agent or wannabe agent observing (if that is the right word) himself. I start by showing that there is a metaphysically possible world in which no one ever acts, but look-alike things happen, both to the bodies of its inhabitants and in the world external to them, things that mimic what would happen if they had acted. I then conclude with some thoughts about how we might rise to the epistemological challenge of knowing whether we are observing that strange world or the world in which others really do act. I am not proposing any definitive ways in which to meet that challenge; I only intend to suggest a possible response. So the chapter ends on a somewhat inconclusive, perhaps disappointing, note. Sorry.

So, start with the actual world, w. It will be helpful to the thought experiment to assume that I somehow have access to the minds of others. We know that these others have minds and that we can know somehow what mental states they are in. This will make no difference to the outcome of the thought experiment, since the same assumption is made across the various worldly scenarios we will compare. If the others mentally act, we can know that too. I am going to be dealing only with a form of physical action scepticism, neither with causal scepticism as a general problem (although I have done this in Ruben 1982), nor with scepticism about our knowledge of other minds, nor with knowledge of mental action.

In w, in addition to having minds, agents do things, they physically act: they open$_t$ windows, they break$_t$ vases, they move$_t$ their hands, they bend$_t$ their fingers, they rotate$_t$ discs, they ring$_t$ bells, and they stop$_t$ floods. (Read all of these with subscript 't'.) In w, they have intentions, make decisions, choose, and try to do those things, they have supporting beliefs and desires, wants, and wishes, that cause them to have those intentions or to make those decisions and choices, and eventually they act in the ways they intended, decided, or chose. They believe that they act, and they usually believe that truly. Their actions also cause events that are sometimes only extrinsic to their actions. w is our world (one assumes), the actual world.

Now consider a possible world w*: in w*, agents are in the same mental states as they are in in w. They decide, choose, intend, believe, and desire just as they do in w. They believe that they act, just as they do in w. They have the same sensations of proprioception, of expenditure of effort, the same kinaesthetic sense, and so on as those in w. But the wannabe agents in w* *never* act, although their bodies move$_i$ (quite coincidentally) in characteristic ways exactly similar to the ways in which agents moved$_t$ their bodies in w when its inhabitants did act. Since it is metaphysically possible for an event to be wholly inefficacious, let the agents, or their mental states and events, or their mental actions, have no effects at all. Alternatively, let those mental items have some effects, but only effects other than the events that would be intrinsic to their actions if they had acted.

Further, mere events beyond those that pertain only to the bodies of the inhabitants of w* also occur in w*, and which perfectly intrinsically replicate (look exactly like) what happened in w. It is an amazing coincidence in w* that their bodies and external objects both move$_i$ just as if they had moved$_t$ them. Why do these mere events in w* happen in that way? Who knows? Certainly not as a consequence of anything to do with the wannabe agents of w*. Perhaps that old Malevolent Demon is at it again, having grown tired of tricking the Brain-In-The-Vat on Alpha Centauri.

In w*, P wants to stop$_t$ the flood by opening$_t$ the sluice of the dam, and he wants to open$_t$ the sluice by turning$_t$ his hand, but his wants go nowhere. The want is a dead loss, at least from the point of view of action.

But the external causal order, which includes mere events, rolls on. Lo and behold, his hand moves$_i$, its moving$_i$ causes the sluice to open$_i$, and the sluice's opening$_i$ causes the flood to stop$_i$. These are three mere events; they are events that are neither intrinsic nor extrinsic to actions (because there are none in w*), nor do they have any causal connection with P or with anything about him qua agent (obviously when P's hand moves$_i$, that moving is a moving$_i$ of *his* hand, but that does not involve P qua an agent). There is obviously causality a-plenty in w*, and we are privy to such causal knowledge, namely the causal relations between the mere events and also the causal connections between the items within P's mind (his belief and desire may cause his intention or his decision). But there are no causal connections between what goes on in the mind of P, or with P qua an agent, on the one hand, and on the other hand what happens to his body or what happens elsewhere in the physical world, although P is unaware of this lack of connection.

Malebranche held that it is God who brings it about that our volitions are correlated with the motions of our body. In w*, there are these correlations, but no God to explain them, because nothing does. They are accidental correlations. (A good question: if God were responsible for the correlation of the volitions and the motions$_i$ of the bodies of the inhabitants of w*, would that suffice to make the motions of their bodies into their actions? Wouldn't they be acting through Him, as it were; would He not be just an external version of whatever mechanism in w internal to an agent connects the agent's mental states with the agent's movements?) Lets call inhabitants of such a world as w*, 'Malebranchers'. Malebranchers don't ever act. The Malebranchers of w* are forever thwarted in doing what they want to do or to accomplish, but because of the appearance of parallel mere events anyway, that replicate whatever it was that they wanted to do or to accomplish, they might never feel thwarted. So maybe forever thwarted, but always rewarded in spite of it all. They are rewarded because what they wanted happens anyway. But *they* can never bring off what they wanted to do, because what they wanted to do happens anyway, in spite of their action failures.

In w*, windows still open$_i$, vases still break$_i$, floods still stop$_i$, hands still move$_i$, bells still ring$_i$, and fingers still bend$_i$ (read these all with subscript 'i'), just when and where agents had wanted to open$_t$ windows, break$_t$ vases, stop$_t$ floods, ring$_t$ bells, move$_t$ hands, and bend$_t$ fingers, but these are mere events, neither the intrinsic results of any actions nor the extrinsic events caused by actions. w and w* are 'experientially equivalent' to the external observer. We might think of Malebranchers as semi-zombies of a sort. Zombies have no mental states and hence their bodies merely move in ways that perfectly imitate actions. Malebranchers have the mental states required for action, but the movements$_i$ of their bodies, and what those movements$_i$ in turn cause, replicate a zombie's bodily movements$_i$.

We know from the cases reported by William James (the cases of Dr. Landry's and Professor Strümpell's patients in Chap. 2) that a person can falsely believe that he has acted when he has not: 'He [Professor Strümpell's wonderful anaesthetic boy] thought constantly that he opened$_t$ and shut$_t$ his hand, whereas it was really fixed' (James, 490; subscripts in this quote and the next are of course my additions). Dr. Landry's patient 'supposes his limb to have taken the position he intended to give it' (i.e., he believes he has moved$_t$ his limb) although it remained unmoved. So both patients falsely believed that they have acted, opened$_t$ a hand or moved$_t$ a limb, when they had not done so.

The reported cases would have made the same point if, for example, Professor Strümpell's wonderful anaesthetic boy's hand had been opened$_i$ and shut$_i$ after all, not by him, but rather by some impersonal force made invisible to him. When his blindfold would have been removed, the wonderful anaesthetic boy might still have falsely believed that he had acted, a belief now based on the fact that, unseen by him, some mere physical force had moved$_i$ his hand, and so a movement$_i$ of his hand had occurred, timed just when he would have moved$_t$ his hand, and which he would then misidentify as his action. So the examples reported by William James do not have to concern beliefs about action, rendered false by total lack of movement, as in the cases James actually reports. As in the example above, they could be rendered false by the occurrence of some event that is not an action, but is only a mere event. If the blindfold had been removed for the experiment, but the impersonal force that moved his hand remained hidden, the boy might have seen the opening$_i$ of his hand, or that his hand had opened$_i$, and this would seem to him to confirm that he has acted, that he has opened$_t$ his hand. But he would have believed falsely. In such a case, he would misidentify a mere event as his action. He can't tell the difference. In these cases, as amended by me, the wonderful anaesthetic boy and Dr. Landry's patient don't know whether they are in effect in w or w*. They think they are in w, whereas they are in a localised version of w*.

What exactly is it that P doesn't know? What P doesn't know is whether he has caused the event that he can observe. On the standard theory and on agent causalism, if only he could know that he (or his relevant mental states) had caused that event, he would know it was his action; if he could know that he had not caused it, he would know that he had not acted. Since Dr. Landry's patient and Professor Strümpell's wonderful anaesthetic boy do not know that they have *not* acted (because they believe that they have), they don't know that they have not caused the events they observe (the opening$_i$ of the hand, the moving$_i$ of the limb). They believe that they have caused the events even though they have not. They believe that they are in w when they are in w* (or local versions thereof).

The cases that James reports are about basic actions. What about failures to know that one has not non-basically acted? Of course, P can try and fail to stop$_t$ the flood (just as he tried and failed to open$_t$ and shut$_t$ his hand), but continue to believe falsely that he has stopped$_t$ it in spite of that failure (just as he can continue to believe falsely that he had opened$_t$ and shut$_t$ his hand in spite of his failure to open$_t$ and shut$_t$ it). But this common-and-garden failure to know about one's non-basic action failures is a result of the world's causal order not working to plan. What *is* interesting is the consequence of these failures to know in cases of basic action for failure to know in cases of non-basic action. Those later failures to know have a different source than in the common-and-garden case. Once it can be shown that P can fail to know whether or not he has basically acted, it will follow that he can fail to know whether or not he has non-basically acted either. He will falsely believe that he has done the non-basic actions by doing the basic one, so the failure to know whether he has acted basically will carry through to his not knowing whether he has acted non-basically.

Could this really be? An extensive literature has grown up about self-knowledge in action, inspired in the first instance by the enigmatic writings of Professor Anscombe (Anscombe 1963, and for a flavour of the discussion: Falvey 2000; Moran 2001; Setiya 2004; Velleman 2000).

There are several claims, all in the vicinity of the idea of an agent's special knowledge about his action, but here is one such claim: '...if an agent is acting intentionally, he will know without observation *what* [my italics] he is doing, under the description(s) on which the action is intentional' (Paul 2009, 2). The Anscombian claim is, roughly, that if an agent is intentionally acting, then he has some sort of knowledge about that action. The Anscombian claim assumes that the agent is intentionally acting, and then asks about the epistemological consequences of that for the agent. It does not address the doubt one might have about whether the agent can know whether he is acting or not at all. The Anscombian claim does not assert that he will know without observation whether or not he is acting. It does not address the problem of hyperbolic doubt that I have raised.

Comparing W and W*

Is there anything missing in w* compared to w (other than the obvious: action)? Consider cases in which P (P is in w) does act intentionally. Does P try to act in w? Yes. I have already supposed that the inhabitants of w, including P, do intentionally act. P tries in w iff in the closest possible world to w in which (a) P has the narrow ability to act, (b) P is in the same mental states that he was in in w (e.g., he believes that he is able to act), (c) he has the opportunity to act, (d) he knows how to act, and (e) there are no preventers or blockers, (plus some other bells and whistles not relevant here), P acts intentionally (the RHS of the conditional is true). No world is closer to w than w itself. If all those conditions are satisfied and he acts in w, it follows that he tries in w (the LHS is true).

But what about w*, the world in which the Malebranchers do *not* act? Do they try to act? If they don't even try to act, that would be a difference between the Malebranchers and us, when their and our worlds were meant to be the same except for the presence/absence of action. If the Malebranchers don't even try, no sceptical conclusion follows. The inhabitants in w don't act either when they don't try. If they in w* don't even try, it would hardly be surprising that they don't act. For our thought experiment to be of any value, shouldn't the Malebranchers try, just as we do? But how do we decide whether the Malebranchers in w* try to act?

Since the Malebranchers never act, I think that the first issue is to decide whether all the antecedent conditions in the subjunctive conditional are satisfied in their world, w*. I think that a case might be made for saying that they do not know how to act in the strange world of w*, or even that they do not have the ability to act in w*. Something in the antecedent conditions listed in the RHS of (CTT) must surely be missing in w*. But on balance, I do not think that lack of ability or absence of know-how is the right diagnosis of what is missing. On the narrow idea of ability I used in Chap. 4, Malebranchers seem to have the same abilities in w* and that agents have in w. And as far as know-how is concerned, there seems to be no practical knowledge that agents lacks in w* that the agents in w possess.

It seems to me that in the thought experiment, the Malebranchers have been deprived of the opportunity to act in w*. When I first introduced the idea of opportunity, no doubt we did not have anything quite like this in mind. The idea of lack of opportunity was introduced to cover such cases as the person who can't write if he has no access to paper, who can't play football if he has no access to a football pitch, who can't play the violin if he has no access to one. The metaphysical supposition of w* deprives an agent from having an opportunity for any action, at a fell swoop. We might think of this as a super-duper lack of opportunity. In general, failure to act does not entail lack of opportunity. There are so many other reasons why someone might not act. But the thought experiment is set up so that they have no opportunity for action. I don't think there are preventers or blockers to acting in w*; to say so would stretch the meaning of 'preventer' and 'blocker' beyond acceptable limits. Nor are they missing ability in the narrow sense or any practical knowledge. But it seems reasonable to say that they have no opportunity to act.

If the Malebranchers do not have the opportunity to act, the next question is: do the Malebranchers try to act, say to F? If they never try to act, as I said above, we should hardly be surprised that they never act. In that case, w* wouldn't really be a 'sceptical' world at all. The lack of action in w* would be what it would be in our world too. So do they try? I think they do. Here is why. The Malebranchers try in w* iff in the closest possible world to w* (call it w**) in which they have the ability to act, have the opportunity to act, have the same mental states as they have in w* (e.g., believe they have the ability to act), know how to act, and there are no preventers and blockers, etc., they do act. Even though those antecedents were not fulfilled in w* (lack of opportunity in w*), those antecedent conditions *are* fulfilled in w** by assumption, and they do act in w**. But that means that the trying-conditional is true for w*: in the closest possible world to w* in which the conditions are fulfilled (and that is w**), they act. So the Malebranchers do try in w*.

There is a trade off between trying in w* and having the opportunity to act in w*. If the Malebranchers had had the opportunity to act in w* (and all the other antecedent conditions were satisfied) but they never acted, then the world closest to w* in which all the antecedents of the trying conditional were satisfied would be w* itself. Since they do not act in w*, it would then follow that they did not try in w* (the trying conditional would have a true antecedent but a false consequent). But granted that they do *not* have the opportunity to act in w*, the world closest to w* in which all the antecedent conditions are fulfilled is no longer w* itself, but is now w**, in which they do have the opportunity to act, and in w** they do act. In that case, the trying conditional is true in w* (because in w** it has a true antecedent and a true consequent), so they do try in w*. Worlds w and w* do not differ over whether their inhabitants try to act.

In Which World Are We?

Let's suppose we have successfully imagined a metaphysically possible world in which the Malebranchers never act. But now comes the epistemological problem. I am observing some inhabitants, but I'm not sure whether they inhabit w or w*. (It will be obvious why I have focussed on knowledge of the action of others. If observation or perceptual experience provides the method by which we know whether others are acting, it does not seem to provide the method by which each agent knows whether he is acting.) How would I know whether I am observing inhabitants of w or inhabitants of w*, normal agents or Malebranchers? My sensory evidence would be identical whichever of the two worlds I was in. In the end, we are interested not in what agents or wannabe agents, like Professor Strümpell's wonderful anaesthetic boy or Dr. Landry's patient, believe about themselves, but about what third parties believe or know about what others do or fail to do.

It seems even easier to imagine that we as onlookers could get it wrong. If, like Dr. Landry's patient or the wonderful anaesthetic boy in the actual world, the Malebranchers in w* could get it wrong about themselves, all the more so could the rest of us, since we don't have any evidence that they don't have. No perceptual evidence available to the onlooker, or the inhabitants, in w or w*, can discriminate between w and w*. We don't have any evidence that they lack about causation (by agents or by their mental events) of the relevant physical events. Since, on our thought experiment, the contents of the minds of the inhabitants of w and w* are revealed to us, we would know whether or not someone, P, believes that he has acted or not acted. But, as we have seen, his belief might be false even when he thinks it to be true. Evidence about their beliefs about their own action failures is just more evidence that is consistent with them being real agents and with them being mere Malebranchers, because there is nothing in the story so far that would justify our (or their) assuming that their beliefs that they had acted or failed to act were true rather than false.

Is there any way in which to reply to this sceptical challenge: how do we know whether we are observing w or observing the strange, actionless world of w*? Because the failure of knowledge about others' actions focuses on failure to hold true beliefs about causation (or lack thereof) between (a) physical events and (b) agents or their metal states, neither the standard theory nor agent causalism (both the reductive and non-reductive kinds) has the resources to respond to the sceptical question. If you hold that actions are causings of events by agents, or that actions are identical to events with a specific causal history, then scepticism about knowledge of the causal connection between (a) and (b) will entail some sort of scepticism about knowledge of action. For these theories, scepticism about knowledge of the actions of others is a special case of causal scepticism, causal scepticism restricted to the case of the constant conjunctions between the agents or their mental lives on the one hand and the events that occur to their bodies or in the world on the other.

Notice that one-particularism would describe this situation somewhat differently from other theories of action, although it is not clear exactly what difference this will make in answering the question. On standard theory and agent causalism (of both the reductive and non-reductive kinds), the particular that someone observes in either of the two worlds, w or w*, call it 'e', can be the very same particular (or its counterpart). What will be different about e in the two worlds will be its causal history. In w, e will be caused either by the agent or non-deviantly by the agent's mental states that rationalise it. In w*, e will not have that causal history. (As before, I assume no necessity of causal origin.) For one-particularism on the other hand, the particulars observed in w and w* can be neither numerically the same nor of the same type: in w, one observes e1, which is an event intrinsic to an action (e1=a); in w*, one observes a mere event, e2 (e2≠a). It follows that e1≠e2. Mere events and actions are two exclusive types of particular. Since there is no single particular that metaphysically could be an action in one world and a mere event in another, the event in w and the event in w* can't be the same particular, or even two particulars of the same type. Does one-particularism have the resources that the other theories lack, in order to respond to the sceptical question? I'm not sure. I want, however, to sketch two possible responses, but without fully committing to either.

First, causation relates to action for one-particularism differently than it does for the other two theories. There is no identity between P's moving$_t$ of his body and either his body's moving$_i$ or his causing of his body's moving$_i$. For one-particularism, what is true is only that if (for instance) P moved$_t$ his body, it follows that P caused his body to move$_i$. That is the left-to-right inference of (PT), which the three theories, standard theory, agent causalism, and one-particularism, all accept. And the contrapositive is therefore true: if it is false that P caused his body to move$_i$, then it is false that P moved$_t$ his body. Now suppose you cannot know whether or not P caused his body to move$_i$, as our sceptical hypothesis asserts. Does it follow that you cannot know, by modus tollens, whether or not P moved$_t$ his body?

The story so far assumes that causality is not directly observable, that you cannot observe whether or not P caused his body to move$_i$. That assumption has been denied. Examples include C. J. Ducasse's classic paper on the topic, 'On the Nature and the Observability of the Causal

Relation' (Ducasse 1926). A view in the same neighbourhood is Susan Siegel's (2009), 'The Visual Experience of Causation'. Her thesis is that visual experience can 'represent causal relations' (which isn't quite the same thing). I mark the possibility of this alternative way in which to reply to the sceptic but do not pursue it. In its strongest form, it would assert that we could know whether the inhabitants who are the objects of our observation are in w or w*. I take it as established in what follows that one cannot know this by observation, cannot know by observation whether or not P caused his body to move$_i$.

Does it follow from the fact that one cannot know whether or not P caused his body to move$_i$ that one cannot know that P moved$_t$ his body? The question has a strong similarity to Nozick's reply to the sceptic (Nozick 1984, 197–211). If knowledge is not closed under known logical implication, then one can know that P has acted, and can know that if P has acted, then P has caused some event, and yet not know whether or not P has caused that event.

Nozick's tracking theory, however, is not without problems of its own. For instance, it has been pointed out that in assigning truth-values to the antecedent conditions of the tracking conditionals that he uses to explicate knowledge, Nozick needs to beg the question by assuming that he is in a non-sceptical world; that is, he needs to make assumptions about which world is actual in order to assess what is true in the closest possible worlds to the actual world.

In terms of the case of an observer's knowledge that P had moved$_t$ his left hand, one would need to show that in the closest possible world to the actual world in which P had *not* moved$_t$ his left hand, the observer would not believe that P had moved$_t$ his left hand, perhaps because P would have moved$_t$ some other part of his body, say, his right hand. That is true if the actual world is w. Suppose, on the other hand, that we are observing the inhabitants of w*. In that case, if P had not moved$_t$ his left hand (because no one can act in w*), the observer may still believe that P has moved$_t$ his left hand. In that case, this tacking conditional would be false (there are of course two tracking conditional associated with each knowledge claim on Nozick's theory). So these judgements of relative comparative similarity required by the subjunctive-tracking conditional that a Nozick-style reply would require assume that the observer is observing an actual world in which people really do act.[3]

The second possible response is this. It might be suggested that there are very close affinities between the epistemology of others' action on the one-particular view of action and the epistemology appropriate for perception on disjunctive theories of perception. So in w, I observe one type of particular, an action; in w*, I observe a different type of particular, a mere event. There are those who think that there is a compelling disjunctivist reply to scepticism about perceptual experience: the reply that divides experiences into two kinds, veridical experiences of objects and non-veridical look-alike experiences of illusions and so on.[4] These two kinds of experience have no 'lowest common denominator'. Someone who finds that line of argument compelling might try to export it to the case of action scepticism; that reply would also divide the observations that we have been considering into two kinds: observations of actions and observations of look-alike mere events, which, it would be claimed, also have no 'lowest common denominator'. As Adrian Haddock says (in private communication): 'perceptual experiences of perceptually indistinguishable things can differ in epistemic significance. In the jargon: they come in good and bad sorts. Having an experience of the good sort puts the subject in a position to know things about the environment. And not only that: it equally puts the subject in a position to know that he is having an experience of the good sort. Having an experience of the bad sort, by contrast, does not put the subject in a position to know things about the environment. And not only that: it equally does not put the subject in a position to know that he is having an experience of the bad sort. As it might be put: if the subject is having an experience of the good sort (i.e., if he is not being fooled) then this puts him in a position to know that he is not being fooled. Whereas if the subject is having an experience of the bad sort (i.e., if he is being fooled), then this does not put him a position to know that he is being fooled.'

To be sure, even on one-particularism, the difference between e1 and e2 in the two worlds is marked by a difference in their causal history. In w, in which e1=a, it follows from the fact that P F-ed, that P caused the event intrinsic to his action, f. (That's just (PT), left-to-right.) So causality and action are essentially tied; and indeed e2 in w* is necessarily not so caused. But on the disjunctivist-style reply to the sceptical question about knowledge of action, those causal facts could not be what are salient when a person observes the difference between an intrinsic event (=an action) and a mere event, if that difference is indeed observable in some sense that disjunctivism would require. Being caused and not being caused are not observable properties of a particular on anyone's theory.

Perhaps there is still an analogy here with perceptual disjunctivism. Although there are no 'appearances' common to both veridical and non-veridical perception, and disjunctivism is intended to be an *alternative* to a causal theory of perception, no one denies that there is some sort of causal story that has some place in perception. So causality could still have a place, even a necessary place, in the distinction between actions and mere events on a disjunctivist-type response to scepticism, even if causality is not the ground for the discriminatory difference between the two.

I wish that I did have the confidence required to use this disjunctive idea in answering our epistemological question. I don't. First, there is the question of the aptness of the analogy between the case of action and the case of perception. Second, I don't know how having a good experience (an observation of an action) can put you in the position to know that you are having an experience of the good sort (an observation of an action). Moreover, if the observer is having an experience of a bad sort (an observation of a mere event), it is admitted that he is not in a position to know that he is. So if the person I am observing is in w*, I am in no position to know whether I am observing his actions or mere events. And if he is in w, it is supposed to be the case that I can know I am observing his actions (at least in non-pathological cases). But it still remains to be explained how we can know whether the observer is observing someone in w or w*.

Epilogue

There is a wise Jewish custom of never concluding a reading of Scriptures in the Synagogue with words of threat or doom. Although the comparison of my book on the metaphysics of action to Scriptures is something of an exaggeration, to say the least (the word 'chutzpah' pops to mind), I will follow that same custom. I don't want to end the book with the section on the sceptical problem that I can't solve (but I think I have done something to advance the discussion). I'd rather conclude on a positive note by reminding you of what I believe I have achieved in the book as a whole.

Chapters 2, 3 and 4 advance what I believe is a novel approach to understanding what it is for an agent to try to do something. Spatial location of, timing of, and causal and mereological questions about, trying particulars have appeared to many philosophers as raising difficult problems; my approach releases one from those metaphysical questions. Along the way, I have been able to say quite a bit about intentions, proximate intentions, and the role they play in action, as well as on the mereology of actions, multiple realisability, naked trying, the opacity of 'to try', imperfectivity, the existential independence of particulars, explanation, finks and reverse cycle finks, supervenience, and much more.

Chapter 5 disputes the alleged inference from an agent causing some event to the agent acting (with that event as an intrinsic event to his action). Also along the way, I think I have given an account of an intrinsic event that is more detailed and extensive than any other of which I am aware. I have offered an account of action that (1) allows for many causers but only one doer, unless it is a case of genuine joint action, and hence allows for causers who are not doers, and (2) also allows for the case of a remote causer or causers, none of whom are doers. I explain the role of commanders, enablers, encouragers, and providers. Causal participation in action is so much richer than merely the doing of that action. In the Appendix to Chap. 5, I have tried to separate an empirical thesis about the relation between a transitive and an intransitive form of verb use from a genuinely philosophical thesis.

Chapter 6 introduces a novel account of action: one-particularism. It shows why Causative Alternation is true but also shows why the idea of an agent acting cannot be given an illuminating analysis in terms of an agent causing the event intrinsic to the action. It develops and defends the idea of an intermediate theory of action individuation, focussing as it does on the idea that information loss (and hence some difference in constituting properties) is not inconsistent with identity. It also argues for a novel approach to the questions of dating and locating actions, and relies on the idea of Cambridge change (and actions).

Chapter 7 does for causing what Chaps. 2, 3 and 4 did for trying. Using the same set of distinctions from the discussion of trying, it distinguishes between verbal and nominal gerunds of the verb. It deals, as did Chap. 3, with adverbial modifications of the verb, 'to cause', but it discusses modification in depth with the case of instrumental modification. It examines a proposal for dealing with this and argues against it. The preferred solution is to assert that an instrumental can figure in the description of a particular without thereby adding any agent-directed information into that description. The overall point of the chapter is to deny any need for causing particulars.

Finally, Chap. 8. First, I trace out the implications of holding simultaneously the one-particular reading for (CA) and the left-to-right inference of (PT). One might think that some regress is brought about by my commitment both to one-particularism and to the left-to-right inference of (PT). I show why that is not so, in light of my argument in Chap. 7. I argue that the standard theory of action faces a similar question for basic action.

And that leads us to the last part to this chapter. Actions are particulars that are directly observable. But there is a sceptical challenge: how might a person ever know whether he is observing an action or extrinsic event on the one hand, or a mere event on the other? In sketching out the sceptical scenario, I defend the idea that even in the world in which no one ever acts, the inhabitants of that world still try to act. I sketched out two possible responses to the sceptical question about our knowledge of the actions of others, but perhaps unsurprisingly, given the staying power of all forms of scepticism, I am not yet convinced by either of them. I bet you are not either. But I also think that both are of sufficient interest and promise to warrant a further, more extended investigation.

Notes

1. Examples of this view include: Bishop, John 1983, 'Agent-causation', *Mind*, Vol. XCII, 61–79; Hornsby, Jennifer 1980, *Action*, Routledge & Kegan Paul, London; Alvarez, Maria 1999, 'Actions and Events: Some Semantical Considerations', *Ratio* n.s. XII, September, 213–239; O'Connor, Timothy 2000, *Persons & Causes*, Oxford University Press, Oxford.

2. G.E.M. Anscombe, *Intention*, is perhaps the best-known example of this genre.
3. I'm sure this criticism is not original to me, and that I have read it somewhere, but I cannot now find where I first came across it. Apologies to the original but unattributed source.
4. Perhaps the fullest statement of that view is by McDowell (2013). Hats off to Adrian Haddock for trying to convince me that perceptual disjunctivism succeeds in dealing with skepticism. He thinks it does and I'm unsure. For me, the jury is still out.

Bibliography

Alvarez, Maria. 1999. Actions and Events: Some Semantical Considerations. *Ratio*, new series XII (3): 213–239.
Anscombe, G.E.M. 1963. *Intention*. Oxford: Oxford University Press.
Bishop, J. 1983. Agent-Causation. *Mind* 92: 61–79.
Chisholm, Roderick. 1980. The Agent as Cause. In *Action Theory*, ed. M. Brand and D. Walton, 199–211. Dordrecht: D. Reidel Publishing Company.
Clarke, Randolph. 1993. Toward a Credible Agent-Causal Account of Free Will. *Nous* 27 (2): 191–203.
Davidson, Donald. 1971. Agency, reprinted in his *Essays on Actions and Events*. Oxford: Oxford University Press, 1980 and 2001.
Ducasse, C.J. 1926. On the Nature and Observability of the Causal Relation. *Journal of Philosophy* 23 (3): 57–68.
Falvey, Kevin. 2000. Knowledge in Intention. *Philosophical Studies* 99 (1): 21–44.
Goldman, Alvin. 1970. *A Theory of Human Action*. Englewood Cliffs, NJ: Prentice-Hall.
Hornsby, Jennifer. 1980. *Actions*. London: Routledge & Kegan Paul.
McDowell, John. 2013. Perceptual Experience: Both Relational and Contentful. *European Journal of Philosophy* 21 (1): 144–157.
Moran, Richard. 2001. *Authority and Estrangement: An Essay on Self-Knowledge*. Princeton: Princeton University Press.
Nozick, Robert. 1984. *Philosophical Explanations*. Oxford: Oxford University Press.
O'Connor, Timothy. 2000. *Persons and Causes*. Oxford: Oxford University Press.

Paul, Sarah. 2009. How We Know What We are Doing. *Philosophers' Imprint* 9 (11): 1–24.
Ruben, David-Hillel. 1982. Causal Scepticism. *Ratio* XXIV (2, Dec.): 161–172.
Sainsbury, R.M. 1988. *Paradoxes*. Cambridge: Cambridge University Press.
Setiya, Kieran. 2004. Explaining Action. *The Philosophical Review* 112 (3): 339–393.
Siegel, Susanna. 2009. The Visual Experience of Causation. *The Philosophical Quarterly* 59 (236, July): 519–540.
Steward, Helen. 2012. *A Metaphysics of Freedom*. Oxford: Oxford University Press.
Taylor, Richard. 1980. *Action and Purpose*. Harvester Press.
Thalberg, Irving. 1967. Do We Cause Our Own Actions? *Analysis* 27 (6): 196–201.
Velleman, J. David. 2000. *The Possibility of Practical Reason*. Oxford: Oxford University Press.

Bibliography

Adams, F. 1986. Intention and Intentional Action: The Simple View. *Mind and Language* 1 (4): 281–301.

Adams, F., and A. Mele. 1992. The Intention/Volition Debate. *Canadian Journal of Philosophy* 22 (3): 323–337.

Alexiadou, Artemis. 2013. Nominal vs. Verbal–ing Constructions and the Development of the English Progressive. *English Linguistics Research* 2 (2): 126–140.

Allen, Robert L. 1966. *The Verb System of Present-Day American English*. The Hague and Paris: Mouton & Co.

Alvarez, Maria. 1999. Actions and Events: Some Semantical Considerations. *Ratio*, new series XII (3): 213–239.

Alvarez, Maria, and John Hyman. 1998. Agents and Their Actions. *Philosophy* 73: 219–245.

Annas, Julia. 1977–78. How Basic are Basic Actions? *Proceedings of the Aristotelian Society* LXXVIII: 195–213.

Anscombe, G.E.M. 1963. *Intention*. Oxford: Oxford University Press.

———. 1965. The Intentionality of Sensation: A Grammatical Feature. In *Analytic Philosophy*, second series, ed. R.J. Butler, 158–180. Oxford: Blackwell.

———. 1981. *Metaphysics and the Philosophy of Mind*. Oxford: Basil Blackwell Publisher.

Aristotle, De Categoriae. 1966. In *The Basic Works of Aristotle*, ed. Richard McKeon. New York: Random House.

Armstrong, D.M. 1978. *Universals and Scientific Realism, Vol. II: A Theory of Universals*. Cambridge: Cambridge University Press.

———. 1981. Acting and Trying. In *Nature of Mind and Other Essays*, ed. D. Armstrong. Brighton: Harvester Press.

Armstrong, David. 1997. *A World of States of Affairs*. Cambridge: Cambridge University Press.

Atwell, John E. 1969. The Accordion Effect Thesis. *Philosophical Quarterly* 19 (77): 337–342.

Austin, J.L. 1956. A Plea for Excuses. *Proceedings of the Aristotelian Society* 57: 1–30. Reprinted in *Philosophical Papers*, 1970, second edition, Oxford, Oxford University Press, 175–204. Page references in text to the reprint.

———. 1970. *Philosophical Papers*. Oxford: Oxford University Press.

———. 1979. Ifs and Cans. In *Philosophical Papers*. New York: OUP.

Austin, John. 1998. *The Province of Jurisprudence Determined*. Indianapolis: Hackett Publishing.

Bach, Kent. 1980. Actions are Not Events. *Mind* 89 (353): 114–120.

Barnes, Jonathan, trans. 1975. *Aristotle, Posterior Analytics*. Oxford: Oxford University Press.

Bayne, Tim, and Michelle Montague. 2011. *Cognitive Phenomenology*. Oxford: Oxford University Press.

Beebee, Helen, Christopher Hitchcock, and Peter Menzies. 2012. *The Oxford Handbook of Causation*. Oxford: Oxford University Press.

Bennett, Jonathan. 1973. Shooting, Killing, and Dying. *Canadian Journal of Philosophy* 2: 315–323.

———. 1988a. Adverb-Dropping Inferences and the Lemmon Criterion. In *Actions and Events: Perspectives on the Philosophy of Donald Davidson*, ed. Ernest LePore and Brian McLaughlin, 193–206. Oxford: Blackwell.

———. 1988b. *Events and Their Names*. Oxford: Oxford University Press.

———. 1998. *The Act Itself*. Oxford: Oxford University Press.

Bishop, J. 1983. Agent-Causation. *Mind* 92: 61–79.

———. 1989. *Natural Agency*, 117–120. Cambridge: Cambridge University Press.

Bratman, M. 1978. Individuation and Action. *Philosophical Studies* 33: 367–375.

———. 1987. *Intentions, Plans and Practical Reason*. Cambridge: Harvard University Press.

Bratman, Michael. 2006. What is the Accordion Effect? *Journal of Ethics* 10 (1): 5–19.

Buckareff, A. 2007. Mental Overpopulation and Mental Action: Protecting Intentions from Mental Birth Control. *Canadian Journal of Philosophy* 37 (1): 49–65.

Butler, R.J., ed. 1962. *Analytic Philosophy*. Oxford: Blackwell.

———., ed. 1965. *Analytic Philosophy*, second series. Oxford: Blackwell.

Chisholm, Roderick. 1964. The Descriptive Element in the Concept of Action. *Journal of Philosophy* 61: 613–624.

———. 1966. *Perceiving: A Philosophical Study*. Cornell: Cornell University Press. Originally published 1957.

———. 1980. The Agent as Cause. In *Action Theory*, ed. M. Brand and D. Walton, 199–211. Dordrecht: D. Reidel Publishing Company.

Choi, S. 2005. Do Categorical Ascriptions Entail Counterfactual Conditionals? *Philosophical Quarterly* 55 (220): 495–503.

———. 2009. The Conditional Analysis of Dispositions and the Intrinsic Dispositions Thesis. *Philosophy and Phenomenological Research* LXXVIII: 568–590.

———. 2012. Intrinsic Finks and the Dispositional/Categorical Distinction. *Nous* 46 (2): 289–325.

Clark, Romane. 1970. Concerning the Logic of Predicate Modifiers. *Nous* 4 (4): 311–335.

Clark, Romane, and Paul Welsh. 1962. *Introduction to Logic*. Princeton, NJ: Van D. Nostrand and Company Inc.

Clarke, Randolph. 1993. Toward a Credible Agent-Causal Account of Free Will. *Nous* 27 (2): 191–203.

———. 1995. *Agents, Causes, Events*. Edited by Timothy O'Connor, 201–215. New York: Oxford University Press.

———. 2010. Skilled Activity and the Causal Theory of Action. *Philosophy and Phenomenological Research* 80 (3): 523–550.

———. 2015. Abilities to Act. *Philosophy Compass* 10: 893–904.

Cleveland, Timothy. 1997. *Trying Without Willing*. Aldershot: Ashgate Publishing Company.

Correia, Fabrice. 2008. Ontological Independence. *Philosophy Compass* 3 (5): 1013–1032.

Cross, T. 2012. Recent Work on Dispositions. *Analysis* 72: 115–124.

Cruse, D.A. 1972. A Note on English Causatives. *Linguistic Inquiry* 3 (4): 520–528.

Davidson, Donald. 1963 (1980). Actions, Reasons, and Causes, reprinted in his *Essays on Actions and Events*. Oxford: Clarendon Press, 3–19.

———. 1967 (1980). The Logical Form of Action Sentences, reprinted in his *Essays on Actions and Events*. Oxford: Clarendon Press, 105–118.

———. 1970 (1980). Mental Events, reprinted in his *Essays on Actions and Events*. Oxford: Clarendon Press, 207–225.

———. 1971. Agency, reprinted in his *Essays on Actions and Events*. Oxford: Oxford University Press, 1980 and 2001.

———. 2001. Aristotle's Actions. In *Truth, Language, and History*, ed. Donald Davidson. 2005. Oxford: Oxford University Press.

———. 2004. Problems in the Explanation of Action. In *Problems of Rationality*. Oxford: Oxford University Press.

Davis, L. 1979. *Theory of Action*. Englewood Cliffs, NJ: Prentice-Hall.

Dorr, C. 2008. There are No Abstract Objects. In *Contemporary Debates in Metaphysics*, ed. T. Sider, J. Hawthorne, and D. Zimmerman, 32–63. Oxford: Basil Blackwell.

Dowe, P. 2001. A Counterfactual Theory of Prevention and 'Causation' by Omission. *Australasian Journal of Philosophy* 79: 216–226.

Ducasse, C.J. 1926. On the Nature and Observability of the Causal Relation. *Journal of Philosophy* 23 (3): 57–68.

Duff, R.A. 1996. *Criminal Attempts*. Oxford: Oxford University Press.

Dummett, Michael. 1973. *Frege: Philosophy of Language*. London: Duckworth.

Ehring, Douglas. 1997. *Causation & Persistence*. New York: Oxford University Press.

Enoch, D. 2012. Comment on Yaffe's Attempts. *Jerusalem Review of Legal Studies* 6: 20–35.

Evnine, Simon. 2011. Constitution and Composition: Three Approaches to Their Relation. *ProtoSociology* 27: 212–235.

———. 2016. *Making Object and Events*. Oxford: Oxford University Press.

Falvey, Kevin. 2000. Knowledge in Intention. *Philosophical Studies* 99 (1): 21–44.

Feinberg, Joel. 1970. *Doing and Deserving*. Princeton: Princeton University Press.

Fine, Kit. 1999. Things and Their Parts. In *Midwest Studies in Philosophy*, ed. Peter A. French and Howard K. Wettstein, vol. XXIII, 61–74. Boston: Blackwell.

Fockner, Sven. 2013. What is the Accordion Effect: Harmonizing Bratman's Principles F and D. *Springer Plus* 2: 279.

Fodor, J.A. 1970. Three Reasons for Not deriving 'Kill' from 'Cause to Die'. *Linguistic Inquiry* I: 429–438.

———. 1975. *The Language of Thought*. Cambridge, MA: Harvard University Press.
Ford, Anton. 2011. Action and Generality. In *Essays on Anscombe's Intention*, ed. Anton Ford, Jennifer Hornsby, and Frederick Stoutland. Cambridge, MA: Harvard University Press.
———. 2014. Action and Passion. *Philosophical Topics* 42 (1): 13–42.
Ford, Anton, Jennifer Hornsby, and Frederick Stoutland, eds. 2011. *Essays on Anscombe's Intention*. Cambridge, MA: Harvard University Press.
Frankfurt, Harry. 1988. Alternate Possibilities and Moral Responsibility. In *The Importance of What We Care About*. Cambridge: Cambridge University Press.
Gandevia, S.C. 1982. The Perception of Motor Commands or Effort During Muscular Paralysis. *Brain* 105: 151–159.
Geach, Peter. 1969. *God and the Soul*. London: Routledge & Kegan Paul.
———. 1981. *Logic Matters*. Oxford: Basil Blackwell.
Gettier, Edmund. 1963. Is Justified True Belief Knowledge? *Analysis* 23 (6): 121–123.
Ginet, Carl. 1990. *On Action*. Cambridge: Cambridge University Press.
Goldman, Alvin. 1970. *A Theory of Human Action*. Englewood Cliffs, NJ: Prentice-Hall.
Gorovitz, Samuel. 1965. Causal Judgments and Causal Explanations. *Journal of Philosophy* LXII (23): 695–711.
Gozanno, Simone, and Christopher Hill, eds. 2012. *New Perspectives on Type Identity*. Cambridge: Cambridge University Press.
Grünbaum, Thor. 2008. Trying and the Argument from Total Failure. *Philosophia* 36 (1): 67–86.
Haack, Susan. 1978. *Philosophy of Logic*. Cambridge: Cambridge University Press.
Haddock, Adrian. 2005. At One with Our Actions, but at Two with Our Bodies. *Philosophical Explorations* 8 (2): 157–172.
Hare, R.M. 1964. *The Language of Morals*. Oxford: Oxford University Press.
Hart, H.L.A., and Tony Honoré. 1985. *Causation in the Law*. 2nd ed. Oxford: Oxford University Press.
Heath, P.L. 1971. Trying and Attempting. *Proceedings of the Aristotelian Society, Supplementary Volume* 45: 193–208.
Hobbes, Thomas. 1946. *The Leviathan*. Oxford: Basil Blackwell.
Honoré, A.M. 1964. Can and Can't. *Mind* 2 (292): 463–479.
Horgan, Terence. 1978. The Case against Events. *The Philosophical Review* 87 (1): 28–47.

———. 1993. From Supervenience to Superdupervenience: Meeting the Demands of a Material World. *Mind* 102 (408): 555–586.
Hornsby, Jennifer. 1995. Reasons for Trying. *Journal of Philosophical Research* XX: 525–539.
———. 1997. *Simple Mindedness*. Cambridge: Harvard University Press.
———. 1980. *Actions*. London: Routledge & Kegan Paul.
———. 2011. Actions in their Circumstances. In *Essays on Anscombe's Intention*, ed. Anton Ford, Jennifer Hornsby, and Frederick Stoutland, 105–127. Cambridge, MA: Harvard University Press.
———. 2012. Actions and Activities. *Philosophical Issues* 22: 233–245.
Hovav, Malka Rappaport, and Beth Levin. 2012. Lexical Uniformity and the Causative Alternation. In *The Theta System*, ed. Martin Everaert, Marijana Marelj, and Tal Siloni. Oxford: Oxford University Press.
Hyman, John. 2015. *Action, Knowledge, & Will*. Oxford: Oxford University Press.
James, William. 1950. *Principles of Psychology*. Vol. 2. New York: Dover Publications.
Jeannerod, M. 1995. Mental Imagery in the Motor Context. *Neuropsychologica* 33 (11): 419–432.
Jones, O.R. 1983. Trying. *Mind* XCII (367): 368–385.
Johnston, M. 1993. Objectivity Refigured: Pragmatism Without Verificationism. In *Reality, Representation, and Projection*, ed. J. Haldane and C. Right. New York and Oxford: OUP.
Katz, Jerrold. 1970. Interpretative Semantics vs. Generative Semantics. *Foundations of Language* 6 (2): 220–259.
Kenny, Anthony. 1963. *Action, Emotion and Will*. London: Routledge & Kegan Paul.
Kim, J. 1973. Causes and Counterfactuals. *Journal of Philosophy* 70 (17): 570–572.
———. 1974. Noncausal Connections. *Nous* 8: 41–52.
———. 1976. "Events as Property Exemplifications". In *Action Theory*, ed. M. Brand and D. Walton, 159–177. Dordrecht: Reidel. Reprinted in *Supervenience and Mind: Selected Philosophical Essays*, Cambridge: Cambridge University Press, 1993, pp. 33–52.
Koslicki, Kathrin. 2012. Varieties of Ontological Independence, Chapter 7 in Correia, Fabrice, and Benjamin Schnieder.
Lakoff, G. 1965. *On the Nature of Syntactic Irregularity*. Mathematical Linguistics and Automatic Translation, Report No. NSF-16, Computational Laboratory of Harvard, Cambridge, MA.

Lakoff, G., and John Ross. 1972. A Note on Anaphoric Islands and Causatives. *Linguistic Inquiry* 3 (1): 121–125.
Levin, Beth. 1993. *English Verb Classes and Alternation.* Chicago: University of Chicago Press.
Lewis, D. 1986. *Philosophical Papers.* Vol. II. Oxford: Oxford University Press.
———. 1997. Finkish Dispositions. *The Philosophical Quarterly* 47 (187): 143–158.
Lombard, Lawrence. 1986. *Events: A Metaphysical Study.* London: Routledge & Kegan Paul.
———. 1990. Causes, Enablers, and the Counterfactual Analysis. *Philosophical Studies* 59: 195–211.
———. 2003. The Cambridge Solution to the Time of a Killing. *Philosophia* 31 (1–2): 93–106.
Lowe, E.J. 2010. *Personal Agency: The Metaphysics of Mind and Action.* Oxford: Oxford University Press.
Ludwig, Kirk. 1992. Impossible Doings. *Philosophical Studies* 65: 257–281.
———. 2010. Adverbs of Action and Logical Form. In *A Companion to the Philosophy of Action*, ed. Timothy O'Connor and Constantine Sandis, 40–49. Chichester: Wiley Blackwell.
MacBride, Fraser. 2005. The Particular-Universal Distinction: A Dogma of Metaphysics? *Mind,* new series 114 (4555): 565–614.
Mackie, David. 1997. The Individuation of Action. *The Philosophical Quarterly* 47 (186): 38–54.
Mackie, John. 1965 (1993). Causes and Conditions. *American Philosophical Quarterly* 2 (4): 245–264. Reprint in Sosa and Tooley (eds.), Causation (Oxford 1993). 33–55.
———. 1974. *The Cement of the Universe.* Oxford: Oxford University Press.
Mackie, Penelope. 2009. *How Things Might Have Been.* Oxford: Oxford University Press.
Maier, John. 2014. Abilities. *Stanford Encyclopedia of Philosophy.*
———. 2015. The Agentive Modalities. *Philosophy and Phenomenological Research* XC (1): 113–134.
Mandelbaum, Maurice. 1955. Societal Facts. In *Modes of Individualism and Collectivism*, ed. John O'Neill, 221–234. London: Heinemann Educational Books.
Marcus, Eric. 2009. Why There are No States. *Journal of Philosophical Research* 34: 215–241.
———. 2012. *Rational Causation.* Cambridge, MA: Harvard University Press.

Martin, Fabienne, and Florian Schäfer. 2014. Causation at the Syntax-Semantics Interface. In *Causation in Grammatical Structures*, ed. Bridget Copley and Fabienne Martin. Oxford: Oxford University Press. Part II, chapter 9, 209–244.

Massin, Olivier. 2013. L'Explication de l'action. *Analyses contemporaines, Recherches sur la philosophie et le langage*, no. 30, Vrin, Paris.

Mayr, Erasmus. 2011. *Understanding Human Agency*. Oxford: Oxford University Press.

McCann, Hugh. 1975. Trying, Paralysis, and Volition. *The Review of Metaphysics* 28 (3): 423–442. Reprinted in McCann (1998), 94–109.

———. 1998. *The Works of Agency*. Ithaca: Cornell University Press.

McDaniel, Kris. 2007. Extended Simples. *Philosophical Studies* 133: 131–141.

McDowell, John. 2013. Perceptual Experience: Both Relational and Contentful. *European Journal of Philosophy* 21 (1): 144–157.

Melden, A.I. 1961. *Free Action*. London: Routledge & Kegan Paul.

Mele, A. 1992. *Springs of Action*. Vol. 72, 167. New York: Oxford University Press.

———. 2003. Agents' Abilities. *Nous* 37 (3): 447–470.

Menzies, Peter. 2012. Platitudes and Counterexamples. In *The Oxford Handbook of Causation*, ed. Helen Beebee et al., 341–367. Oxford: Oxford University Press.

Mill, John Stuart. 1970. *A System of Logic*. London: Longman Group.

Moore, G.E. 1966. *Principia Ethica*. Cambridge: Cambridge University Press.

Moran, Richard. 2001. *Authority and Estrangement: An Essay on Self-Knowledge*. Princeton: Princeton University Press.

Morreall, John. 1976. The Nonsynonymy of Kill and Cause to Die. *Linguistic Inquiry* 7 (3): 516–518.

Mourelatos, Alexander P.D. 1978. Events, Processes, and States. *Linguistics and Philosophy* 2 (3): 415–434.

Munsat, Stanley. 1969. What is a Process? *American Philosophical Quarterly* 6 (1): 79–83.

Neeleman, Ad, and Hans van de Koot. 2012. The Linguistic Expression of Causation. In *The Theta System*, ed. Martin Everaert, Marijana Marelj, and Tal Siloni, 78–100. Oxford: Oxford University Press.

Nolan, D. 1997. Impossible Worlds: A Modest Approach. *Notre Dame Journal of Formal Logic* 38: 535–572.

Nozick, Robert. 1984. *Philosophical Explanations*. Oxford: Oxford University Press.

O'Connor, Timothy. 1995. *Agents, Causes, Events*. New York: Oxford University Press.

———. 2000. *Persons and Causes*. Oxford: Oxford University Press.
———. 2011. Agent-Causal Theories of Freedom. In *The Oxford Handbook of Free Will*, ed. Robert Kane, 2nd ed., 309–328. Oxford: Oxford University Press.
O'Neill, John, ed. 1973. *Modes of Individualism and Collectivism*. London: Heinemann Educational Books.
O'Shaughnessy, Brian. 1973. Trying as the Mental Pineal Gland. *The Journal of Philosophy* 70 (13): 365–386.
———. 1980. *The Will*. Vol. 1 and 2. Cambridge: Cambridge University Press.
Parsons, Terence. 1972. Some Problems Concerning the Logic of Grammatical Modifiers. In *The Semantics of Natural Language*, ed. Donald Davidson and Gilbert Harman, 2nd ed., 127–141. Dordrecht: Springer.
———. 1994. *Events in the Semantics of English*. Boston: MIT Press.
Pattaro, Enrico. 2005. *A Treatise of Legal Philosophy and General Jurisprudence*. Vol. 1. Dordrect, Netherlands: Springer.
Paul, Sarah. 2009. How We Know What We are Doing. *Philosophers' Imprint* 9 (11): 1–24.
Pietroski, Paul. 2000. *Causing Actions*. Oxford: Oxford University Press.
Pitt, David. 2011. Introspection, Phenomenality. And the Availability of Intentional Content. In *Cognitive Phenomenology*, ed. Tim Bayne and Michelle Montague, 141–173. Oxford: Oxford University Press.
Preston, Jesse, and Daniel Wegner. 2008. Elbow Grease: When Action Feels Like Work. In *Oxford Handbook of Human Action*, ed. E. Morsella, John Bargh, and Peter Gollwitzer, 569–586. Oxford: Oxford University Press.
Quine, W.V.O. 1960. *Word and Object*. Cambridge, MA: MIT Press.
———. 1961. On What There Is. In *From A Logical Point of View*. New York: Harper and Row.
Richard, Mark. 2001. "Seeking A Centaur, Adoring Adonis: Intensional Transitives and Empty Terms". *Midwest Studies In Philosophy* 25 (1): 103–127.
Richardson, Louise. 2015. Perceptual Activity and Bodily Awareness. *Proceedings of the Aristotelian Society* 115: 147–165.
Ruben, David-Hillel. 1977, second edition 1979. *Marxism and Materialism*. Hassocks, Sussex: Harvester Press.
———. 1982. Causal Scepticism. *Ratio* XXIV (2, Dec.): 161–172.
———. 1985. *The Metaphysics of the Social World*. London: Routledge & Kegan Paul.
———. 1988. A Puzzle about Posthumous Predication. *The Philosophical Review* 97 (2): 211–236.
———. 1990 (1992). *Explaining Explanation*. London: Routledge. Second edition (2012), Paradigm Publishers, Boulder, CO.

———. 1991. Review of John Bishop, Natural Agency. *Mind*, new series 100 (2, Apr.): 287–290.

———. 1995. Mental Overpopulation and the Problem of Action. *Journal of Philosophical Research* 20: 511–524.

———. 1999. Actions and Their Parts. Proceedings of the 20th World Congress of Philosophy, vol. 2, Boston, 73–80.

———. 2003. *Action & Its Explanation*. Oxford: Oxford University Press.

———. 2010. The Causal and Deliberative Strength of Reasons for Action. In *Causing Human Action: New Perspectives on the Causal Theory of Action*, ed. Jesus H. Aguilar and Andrei A. Buckareff. Cambridge, MA: Bradford Books/ The MIT Press.

———. 2013. Trying in Some Way. *Australasian Journal of Philosophy* 91 (4): 719–733.

———. 2015. Beyond Supervenience and Construction. *Journal of Social Ontology* 1 (1): 121–141.

Sainsbury, R.M. 1988. *Paradoxes*. Cambridge: Cambridge University Press.

Savellos, Elias, and Ümit Yalçin. 1995. *Supervenience: New Essays*. Cambridge: Cambridge University Press.

Schäfer, Florian. 2009. The Causative Alternation. *Language and Linguistics, Compass* 3 (2): 641–681.

Searle, John. 2001. *Rationality in Action*. Cambridge: The MIT Press.

Setiya, Kieran. 2004. Explaining Action. *The Philosophical Review* 112 (3): 339–393.

Shoemaker, Sydney. 1980. Causality and Properties. In *Time and Cause*, ed. P. van Inwagen. Dordrecht: D. Reidel Publishing Company.

Siegel, Susanna. 2009. The Visual Experience of Causation. *The Philosophical Quarterly* 59 (236, July): 519–540.

Silverstein, Harry. 1980. The Evil of Death. *Journal of Philosophy* 77 (7): 401–424.

Simons, Peter. 2000. *Parts: A Study in Ontology*. Oxford: OUP.

Smith, Carlota. 1970. Jespersen's "Move and Change" Class and Causative Verbs in English. In *Linguistic and Literary Studies*, ed. Mohammad Ali Jazayery, Edgar C. Polomé, and Werner Winter, 101–108. The Hague: Mouton Publishers.

———. 1972. On Causative Verbs and Derived Nominals in English. *Linguistic Inquiry* 3: 136–138.

Sosa, Ernest. 2015. *Judgment and Agency*. Oxford: Oxford University Press.

Steward, Helen. 1997. *The Ontology of Mind*. Oxford: Oxford University Press.

———. 2012a. Actions as Processes. *Philosophical Perspectives* 26 (1): 373–388.

———. 2012b. *A Metaphysics of Freedom*. Oxford: Oxford University Press.
———. 2013. Processes, Continuants, and Individuals. *Mind* 122 (487): 781–812.
———. 2015. What is a Continuant? *Proceedings of the Aristotelian Society, Supplementary Volume* LXXXIX: 109–123.
Stoecker, Ralf. 1993. Reasons, Actions, and their Relationship. In *Reflecting Davidson*, ed. Ralf Stoecker, 265–286. Berlin: De Gruyter. Reprinted, 2011.
Taylor, Barry. 1985. *Modes of Occurrence*. Aristotelian Society Series, vol. 2. Oxford: Basil Blackwell.
Taylor, Richard. 1973. *Action and Purpose*. Atlantic Highlands, NJ: Humanities Press.
———. 1980. *Action and Purpose*. Harvester Press.
Thalberg, Irving. 1967. Do We Cause Our Own Actions? *Analysis* 27 (6): 196–201.
———. 1983. *Misconceptions of Mind and Freedom*. Lanham, MD: University Press of America.
Velleman, J. David. 2000. *The Possibility of Practical Reason*. Oxford: Oxford University Press.
Vendler, Zeno. 1962. Effects, Results and Consequences. In *Analytical Philosophy*, ed. R.J. Butler, 1–15. Oxford: Blackwell.
———. 1972. *Res Cogitans*, 210–216. Ithaca: Cornell University Press. Appendix II.
Vesey, G. 1961. Volition. *Philosophy* 36: 325–365.
Vihvelin, Kadri. 2013. *Causes, Laws, & Free Will*. Oxford: Oxford University Press.
Von Wright, G.H. 1971. *Explanation and Understanding*. London: Routledge & Kegan Paul.
———. 1977. *Norm and Action*. London: Routledge & Kegan Paul.
Wiggins, David. 1980. *Sameness and Substance*. Oxford: Basil Blackwell.
Wilson, George. 1989. *The Intentionality of Human Action*. Stanford: Stanford University Press.
Wilson, Jessica. 2010. What is Hume's Dictum, and Why Believe It? *Philosophy and Phenomenological Research* XXX (3): 595–637.
Wittgenstein, Ludwig. 1953. *Philosophical Investigations*. Translated by G.E.M. Anscombe. New York: Macmillan Company.
———. 1984. *Notebooks 1914–16*. 2nd ed. Chicago: University of Chicago Press.
Yaffe, Gideon. 2010. *Attempts*, 72–105. Oxford: Oxford University Press.

———. 2012. Reply to Enoch, Dahan-Katz, and Berman. *Jerusalem Review of Legal Studies* 6: 51–78.

Zhu, Jing. 2004. Intention and Volition. *Canadian Journal of Philosophy* 34 (2): 175–194.

Zimmermann, Thomas Ede. 2006. Monotonicity in Opaque Verbs. *Linguistics and Philosophy* 29 (6): 715–761.

Index[1]

A

Ability, 24, 93, 104, 111, 122, 125–132, 134, 138–144, 146, 148, 152–154, 156, 157, 159n5, 161n12, 207, 247, 321–323

Accordion effect, 44, 45, 189, 190, 218n9, 219n10, 245, 251, 256

Action
  agents of *vs.* participants in, 186, 187
  basic *vs.* non-basic, 10, 18, 21, 84, 138, 231, 238, 320
  metaphysically impossible, 104, 138, 139, 142, 230
  plans, 20, 21, 23, 261
  times of, 284

Adams, F., 136, 137, 161n14

Agent causalism, 169, 305, 307, 320, 324, 325

Alexiadou, Artemis, 60, 62, 85–87, 278

Allen, Robert, 58

Alvarez, Maria, 8, 9, 84, 167–169, 173, 174, 177, 178, 217n5, 232, 263, 271, 277, 279, 285–287, 289–295, 298, 299n4, 300n7, 301n8, 301n9, 307

Analysis, philosophical analysis, 3, 4, 7, 9, 121–123, 125, 126, 131, 135, 137–140, 142–145, 152, 153, 155, 160n10, 165, 166, 169, 175–178, 183, 209, 210, 285, 291, 300n7, 308, 314, 329

---

[1] Note: Page numbers followed by 'n' refer to notes.

Index

Annas, Julia, 38
Anscombe, G.E.M., 21, 70, 272, 273, 320, 331n2
Anscombian, 321
Antidotes (maskers) and Mimickers, 160n10
Aristotle, 65, 69
Armstrong, David, 54, 105
Attributivity
  attributive adjectives, 65
  attributive adverbs, 66
Atwell, John, 218n9

B

Bach, Kent, 216n4, 278, 279, 287, 299n2, 299n3
Bennett, Jonathan, 32, 60, 66, 84–87, 90, 92, 246, 278
Bishop, John, 147, 149–151, 167, 168, 216n4, 307
Blockers and preventers, 104, 116, 122, 125, 127, 128, 131, 132, 138, 141, 142, 144–146, 148, 149, 152, 154, 160n10, 321–323
Bratman, Michael, 98n7, 118, 146, 147, 152, 159n8, 161n14, 255, 257, 259, 260
Buckareff, A., 16

C

Cambridge events, Cambridge actions, 224, 239, 243–248, 265n7
Cartesian hyperbolic doubt, 9
Causative alternation (CA), transitivity alternation, 5, 165, 169–175, 215n2, 216n3, 216–217n5, 258, 329
Cause
  agent vs. event, 9, 168, 169, 183, 188, 195, 225, 228, 229, 232, 273, 277, 280, 285, 292, 293, 298, 305–308, 324, 329
  causal field, 194–197, 199
  causal proximity, 203
  causes vs. (background) conditions, 197, 200
  a cause vs. the cause, 175, 194–204, 270
  causing, 2–6, 9, 14, 16, 26, 62, 115, 157, 165–215, 223–264, 269–299, 305–311, 313–315, 324, 325, 329, 330
  extensionality, 224–225, 306, 309, 313
  fact vs. event, 92, 188, 224, 274, 308, 327
  observability vs. unobservability, 7
  remoteness vs. partiality, 166, 188, 191
Chisholm, Roderick, 3, 121, 216n4, 277, 307
Choi, S., 140
Clark, Romane, 86, 98n4
Clarke, Randolph, 127, 128, 225, 241, 307
Cleveland, Timothy, 15, 38, 41, 42, 44–46
Composition, 29
Constitution, 29–30, 107
Context of enquiry (inquiry), 196, 200

Index

Context of occurrence, 196
Continuants, 23, 24, 84
Correia, Fabrice, 106, 107
Cross, Tony, 160n10
Cruse, D. A., 176, 214

D

Davidson, Donald, 7, 21, 56, 60–65, 67, 70–72, 114, 170, 177, 178, 232, 233, 252, 257, 260, 270, 279, 300n7, 307, 308, 310, 313
Davidsonian arguments, 65, 67, 270, 299–300n4
Davis, Lawrence, 38, 167, 233
Derivation thesis (DT), 9, 166, 209–215
Derived (or perfect) nominal, 57, 58, 64, 85–89, 95, 96, 170, 238, 250, 262, 276, 278, 282, 298
Descartes, Rene, 36, 270, 280, 281
Disjunctive theories, 327
Dispositional vs. non-dispositional, 121, 143
Dorr, Cian, 161n13
Dowe, P., 144, 145
Dr. Landry's patient, 34, 36, 38, 82, 83, 145, 152, 319, 320, 324
Ducasse, C. J., 325, 326
Duff, Anthony, 40, 56, 96, 97, 98n2
Dummett, Michael, 112, 113

E

Endurance theory, 83, 85
Enoch, David, 139, 140, 160n12

Ergative verbs, non-ergative verbs, 166, 170, 173–175, 178–189, 192, 204, 215, 218n9, 223, 226, 252, 254, 258, 262–264, 274, 288, 294, 305, 310, 314
Evnine, Simon, 26, 29, 89
Explanation, 6, 37, 68, 90, 93, 94, 104, 110, 111, 116, 118, 155–158, 196, 197, 200, 218n10, 225, 233, 310–312, 329

F

Falvey, Kevin, 320
Feinberg, Joel, 44, 189, 190, 218n9
Finks and reverse-cycle finks, 104, 116, 139–141, 160n10, 329
Fluky failure, 130–132
Fluky success, 104, 130, 134
Fockner, Sven, 219n10
Fodor, Jerry, 210, 213
Ford, Anton, 12n1

G

Gandevia, S.C., 49n10
Geach, Peter, 239, 241, 242
Gettier, Edmund, 4
Ginet, Carl, 47n1, 66, 234
Goldman, Alvin, 28, 66, 224, 231, 233, 235–237, 257–262, 265n11, 311
Gorovitz, Samuel, 196
Grünbaum, Thor, 38–40, 117

H

Haack, Susan, 224
Haddock, Adrian, 327, 331n4
Hare, R. M., 110
Hart, H. L. A., 218n10, 219n11
Hobbes, Thomas, 15, 58, 137, 187
Honoré, Tony, 219n11
Horgan, Terence, 98n4, 109, 110
Hornsby, Jennifer, 6, 18, 36, 38, 47n1, 56, 87, 93, 98n2, 105, 129, 134–137, 170, 171, 173, 175, 181, 183, 184, 202, 208, 226, 258, 263, 264, 264n2
Hovav, Malka Rappaport, 216n2
Hume, David, 105–107
Hyman, John, 167–169, 173, 174, 178, 181–184, 186, 201, 202, 208, 217n5, 263, 277, 285, 286, 297, 300n5

I

Idle wishes, 40
Imperfective and perfective aspect, 5, 58, 59, 63, 89, 123, 170, 249, 277, 306
Indeterminism, 134
Intention, 5, 16, 17, 19, 33–36, 41–44, 46, 48n2, 49n11, 60, 67, 93, 95, 96, 104, 105, 118, 119, 141, 142, 145, 148–154, 159n7, 169, 180, 228, 317, 318, 329
  intentional action, 45, 46, 126, 130, 145–155, 255
Intrinsic event, 10, 165–172, 183, 190, 223, 228–233, 235, 237–240, 243, 248, 251–254, 257, 258, 260, 285, 295, 305, 309–312, 314, 315, 328, 329

J

James, William, 32–34, 38, 39, 48n8, 82, 119, 150, 151, 154, 155, 294, 295, 304, 319, 320
Jeannerod, M., 49n10
Johnston, M., 160n11
Jones, O.R., 56, 61, 71, 74

K

Katz, Jerrold, 184, 186, 211, 218n10
Kenny, Anthony, 71, 98n3, 124, 233, 293
Kim, Jaegwon, 66, 231, 257, 259
Know-how, 35, 111, 116, 117, 127, 131, 132, 134, 143, 144, 152, 153, 156, 157, 322, 323, 328

L

Lakoff, George, 210
Leviathan, 187
Lavin, Doug, 11
Levin, Beth, 173, 176, 184, 215–216n2, 216n5, 258
Lewis, David, 26, 89, 138, 143, 166, 190, 191, 194, 195, 198, 200, 204–209, 248, 249
Logical form, 3, 61, 62, 67, 68, 71, 84, 170, 232, 233, 285, 289–294, 299, 300n7, 301n9

Lombard, Larry, 265n7
Lowe, E.J., 12n1
Ludwig, Kirk, 67, 159n8

M

MacBride, Fraser, 98n6
McCann, Hugh, 38, 47n1, 56, 105, 167
McDaniel, Kris, 113
McDowell, John, 11, 331n4
Mackie, John, 194–196, 198, 199
Mackie, P., 112, 113
Maier, John, 127–130
Malebranche, Nicolas, 318, 324
  Malebranchers, 318, 319, 321–324
Mandelbaum, Maurice, 3
Marcus, Eric, 11, 108
Martin, Fabienne, 176, 215n1, 216n5, 218n7
Massin, Oliver, 16, 48n2, 94, 95
Mayr, Erasmus, 9, 173, 271, 277, 287, 290–295, 299
Mele, Alfred, 148, 149, 152, 161n14
Menzies, Peter, 196, 199, 200
Mereological sums, the mereological view, 2, 23–30, 46
Mill, John Stuart, 194, 198
  Mode adverbs, 76, 77
  of degrees, 79–81
  of effort and frequency, 79
  instrumental adverbs, 73
  of manner, 67, 73–76, 81
  of place and time, 78–79
  of speed, 67, 76–78
    temporal relational reading *vs.* intrinsic reading, 76, 77

Moore, G.E., 7, 176
Moran, Richard, 320
Morreall, John, 284
Mourelatos, Alexander, 98n9, 124
Multiple-realisabilty, 7, 13, 17–20, 329

N

Necessary (existential) connection, 106
Necessity of origin, 108, 112
Neeleman, Ad, 218n10
Nolan, D., 160n9
Nominal gerund, 62, 63, 85–89, 238, 262, 270, 274, 276, 278–282, 298, 299n4, 306, 313, 314, 330
Nozick, Robert, 326

O

Occurrents, 84
O'Connor, Timothy, 307
One-particularism, 9, 224, 231–235, 237–241, 243, 244, 251, 254, 258, 260–262, 271, 295, 296, 298, 303–306, 308–310, 314, 325, 327, 329, 330
Opacity, 69–73, 329
Opportunity, 116, 117, 122, 125–129, 131, 132, 134, 138, 141–144, 146, 152–154, 156, 157, 219n10, 263, 321–323
O'Shaughnessy, Brian, 47n1, 56, 105

P

Paradox of Imperfectivity, 124, 170
Paraphrase thesis (PT), 165, 166, 169, 170, 174–183, 185, 190, 193, 194, 208–211, 214, 215, 216n3, 216n4, 216–217n5, 223, 224, 263, 264n1, 271, 274, 285, 303–306, 308–311, 313, 315, 325, 327, 330
Parsons, Terence, 98n4, 171, 173, 176, 226, 271, 287
Particularist theories vs. non-particularist theories, 118
Particulars, 7, 85–90, 104–121, 229–241, 277–285
Pattaro, Enrico, 29
Paul, Sarah, 35, 49n11, 104, 149, 321
Perdurance theory, 83, 85
Phrase adverbs, 64, 65, 67, 73, 74, 76, 77, 81, 91, 212, 283, 285
Pietroski, Paul, 47n1, 277
Pitt, David, 49n13
Preston, Jesse, 48n10
Process, 41, 77, 78, 86, 87, 105, 139, 144, 145, 171, 195, 203, 211, 247–250, 265n10, 276, 278, 284
Professor Strümpell patient, 31, 33, 48n8, 82, 116, 118, 319

Q

Quine, W.V.O., 7, 286
Quinean, 300n5

R

Regress, 9, 274, 303–330
Richard, Mark, 70
Rigid existential dependence, generic existential dependence, 107
Roedl, Sebastian, 11
Rosen, Gavriel, 219n12

S

Sainsbury, R. M., 72, 98n8, 315
Scepticism, 39, 109, 279, 299n4, 303–330
Schäfer, Florian, 176, 215n1, 216n5, 218n7
Searle, John, 104, 105
Segal, Gabriel, 90
Sentence adverbs, 64, 65, 84, 282
Setiya, Kieran, 321
Shoemaker, Sydney, 158n3
Siegel, Susanna, 326
Simons, Peter, 48n6
Smith, Carlotta, 44, 45, 213, 214, 215n2, 216n3
Standard theory, 233, 252–254, 277, 309–310, 315, 320, 324, 325, 330
Steward, Helen, 201, 249, 265n9, 277, 313
Stoecker, Ralf, 279, 286, 287
Stout, Rowland, 11
Subjunctive conditional, 6, 116, 121, 122, 126, 128, 129, 133, 134, 152, 161n13, 322
Supervenience, 7, 108–111, 158n1, 158n2, 329

T

Taylor, Barry, 64
Taylor, Richard, 15, 49n12, 56, 278, 307
Telic and atelic verbs, 60
Temporal parts, 23–31, 46, 48n5, 83, 84
Tensed view of semantics, 83
Thalberg, Irving, 49n12, 308
Theories of act individuation
　austere, 66, 251
　intermediate, 66
　prolific, 66, 251
Thompson, Michael, 11
Trying
　attempts and attempting, 48n10, 57, 79, 96, 97
　conditional theory of trying (CTT), 8, 96, 103–158, 304, 322
　endeavours and endeavouring, 57, 118
　naked trying, 8, 13–15, 32, 33, 36, 38–47, 49n12, 79, 81–85, 103–104, 117, 119, 123, 187, 329
　physical action theory of trying, 8, 13–47, 137
　ubiquity of trying thesis (TUT), 37, 39, 114, 118, 129, 130, 136, 155–157, 159n6
　volitions, 6, 7, 105

V

van de Koot, Hans, 218n10
Velleman, J. David, 321
Vendler, Zeno, 88, 89, 98n9, 216–217n5, 249
Verbal gerund, 55, 62, 63, 85–88, 90, 270, 277–281, 313
Vesey, G., 49n12, 123
Vihvelin, Kadri, 92, 93, 116, 128
Von Wright, G.H., 147, 148, 167, 168, 170, 216n4, 231, 277

W

Wegner, Daniel, 48n10
Welsh, Paul, 86
Wiggins, David, 112
Williams, Jessica, 106
Wilson, George, 15, 38, 41–46, 49n12
Wittgenstein, Ludwig, 38

Y

Yaffe, Gideon, 38, 97, 118–120, 126, 129, 131, 139, 159n7, 160n11, 160n12

Z

Zhu, Jing, 105
Zimmermann, Thomas Ede, 70
Zombies, 319

The manufacturer's authorised representative in the EU is Springer Nature Customer Service Centre GmbH, Europaplatz 3, 69115 Heidelberg, Germany. If you have any concerns regarding our products, please contact ProductSafety@springernature.com

Printed and bound by CPI Group (UK) Ltd, Croydon, CR0 4YY

23/03/2026

02076672-0014